THEORIZING BLACK FEMINISMS

Theorizing Black Feminisms outlines some of the crucial debates going on within contemporary Black feminist activity. In doing so it brings together a collection of some of the most exciting work by Black women scholars around, it encompasses a wide range of diverse subjects, and it refuses to be limited by notions of disciplinary boundaries or divisions between theory and practice. *Theorizing Black Feminisms* combines essays on literature, sociology, history, political science, anthropology, and art, amongst others. As such it will be vital reading for anyone – activist, student, artist or scholar – interested in exploring the multidisciplinary possibilities of Black feminisms.

Most importantly, each essay in the volume begins from the premise that Black women are not simply victims of various oppressions. They are also, say the authors, visionary and pragmatic agents of change.

Stanlie M. James is currently Assistant Professor of Afro-American Studies and Women's Studies at the University of Wisconsin-Madison. **Abena P. A. Busia** is Associate Professor of English and Women's Studies at Rutgers University.

THEORIZING BLACK FEMINISMS

The Visionary Pragmatism of Black Women

Edited by
Stanlie M. James and
Abena P. A. Busia

London and New York

First published 1993
by Routledge
11 New Fetter Lane, London EC4P 4EE

Simultaneously published in the USA and Canada
by Routledge
29 West 35th Street, New York, NY 10001

Typeset in 10/12pt Baskerville by Florencetype Ltd, Kewstoke, Avon
Printed and bound in Great Britain by T J Press Ltd, Padstow, Cornwall

British Library Cataloguing in Publication Data

Theorizing Black Feminisms:
The visionary pragmatism of Black women
I. James, Stanlie M.
II. Busia, Abena P. A.
305.48

Library of Congress Cataloging in Publication Data

Theorizing Black Feminisms:
The visionary pragmatism of Black women
[edited by] Stanlie M. James and Abena P. A. Busia.
p.   cm.
Includes bibliographical references and index.
1. Feminist theory.   2. Feminism.   3. Afro-American women.
4. Women, Black.   I. James, Stanlie M. (Stanlie Myrise)   II. Busia,
Abena P.A.
HQ1190.T47 1993
305.42′08996073–dc20   92-47346

ISBN 0-415-07336-7 (hbk)
ISBN 0-415-07337-5 (pbk)

CONTENTS

Part III On controlling our bodies

Part IV On the language of identities

FOREWORD

Johnnetta Betsch Cole

It seemed almost inevitable that Spelman College would be one of the sites where this long-overdue anthology, *Theorizing Black Feminisms*, would be nurtured. We were happy to provide a haven for the sisters who gathered in September 1991 for the second Black Feminism Seminar. Such a gathering was a reflection of the vision I had for Spelman when I became the first African-American woman to head what was then a 107-year-old institution for educating African-American women.

In 1987, I expressed the hope that Spelman would become a renowned center for scholarship on women of African descent. I saw Spelman as a nurturing place, a second home, if you will, for scholars, teachers, artists, policy analysts and community leaders committed to the empowerment of Black women. Expanding on the work of the Women's Research and Resource Center, work which is expressed, for example, by the publication of the highly respected journal *SAGE: A Scholarly Journal on Black Women*, I imagined that Spelman would blossom as an intellectual center of Black Women's Studies. I hoped that my own scholarship in the area of Women's Studies would make a modest contribution to the growth of such an intellectual center. Supporting the institutionalization of Black Women's Studies at Spelman would enhance, I believed, the fundamental mission of the college to educate Black women leaders since 1881.

The book *Theorizing Black Feminisms* captures so much of the discourse that I hoped would take place at Spelman, a special womanist college for African-American sisters. Clearly, then, we treasure the association of Spelman with this powerful and provocative work. The book is edited by Spelman alumna Stanlie James, and includes a chapter on the development of Women's Studies at the college written by Spelman alumna Beverly Guy-Sheftall, the Anna Julia Cooper Professor of Women's Studies. The Black feminist content and diasporan framework of the book are also central themes in many intellectual discussions at Spelman

College and reflect the everyday ways in which many of us view ourselves and our world.

The issues of race and gender, crucial to the development of a Black feminist consciousness, are carefully dissected here and then reassembled into formations that are more understandable to us. As few other volumes have managed to do, this quality work puts women right in the middle of Black Studies and Black folks are made central to Women's Studies.

Theorizing Black Feminisms will become a major text in Black Studies and Women's Studies. Surely it will be adopted for classroom use in diverse liberal arts classrooms throughout the academy. Certainly, it will become required reading in African-American and Women's Studies courses here at Spelman. Perhaps more important is the possibility that Black feminist perspectives on the serious problems we face throughout the world will be embraced as a result of the particular insights we gain from my sisters here.

ILLUSTRATIONS

NOTES ON CONTRIBUTORS

Evelyn L. Barbee is a Black feminist nurse anthropologist who was educated at Teachers College, Columbia University and the University of Washington. Her writings are published in anthropology and nursing journals. Her current research interests are cultural strategies used by women of color to deal with dysphoria, and violence against women of color.

Rose M. Brewer is chair and Associate Professor of Afro-American and African Studies at the University of Minnesota. She is the editor of *Bridges of Power: Women's Multicultural Alliances* (with Lisa Albrecht) and has published widely on feminist issues. She is currently working on a book entitled *Race, Gender and Political Economy: The African-American Since the New Deal.*

Abena P. A. Busia is an Associate Professor of English, Comparative Literature and Women's Studies at Rutgers, the State University of New Jersey, New Brunswick. She has published numerous articles on Black women's literature and colonial discourse, and her poetry has been anthologized in journals and anthologies in Africa, Europe and North America. Her first volume of poems, *Testimonies of Exile*, was published in 1990. She is currently completing *Song in a Strange Land: Narratives and Rituals of Remembrance in the Novels of Black Women of Africa and the African Diaspora.*

Cheryl Clarke is a Black lesbian poet who has written three books of poetry: *Narratives* (1983), *Living as a Lesbian* (1986) and *Humid Pitch* (1989). She has been published widely in lesbian, gay, feminist and Black publications and is currently completing her fourth book, entitled *experimental love*. She has been an administrator at Rutgers University, New Brunswick, since 1969.

Cindy Courville is an Assistant Professor of Political Science at Occidental College, Los Angeles. Her research interests include a comparative study of revolutions in Africa, a comparative study of the

African state in southern Africa, southern African women in revolution, and resistance movements.

Beverly Guy-Sheftall is the Founding Director of the Women's Research and Resource Center and Anna Julia Cooper Professor of English and Women's Studies at Spelman College. She is founding co-editor of *SAGE: A Scholarly Journal on Black Women*, the editor or co-editor of various publications including *Sturdy Black Bridges* and *Double Stitch*, and the author of *Daughters of Sorrow: Attitudes Toward Black Women, 1880–1920* (1991).

Stanlie M. James is Assistant Professor of Afro-American Studies and Women's Studies at the University of Wisconsin-Madison. She has published in *Africa Today, Women and Politics* and *Feminist Collections*. She is currently working on a book entitled *The Construction of a Black Feminist Generation of International Human Rights*.

Marilyn Little, PhD University of Minnesota, is an Assistant Professor in Geography at the University of Wisconsin-Madison. A medical geographer by specialization, her research is primarily concerned with the political ecology of malnutrition. Her most recent publication is "Charity Versus Justice: The New World Order and the Old Problem of World Hunger" in *Eliminating Hunger in Africa* (eds Newman and Griffith).

Nellie Y. McKay is a Professor of American and Afro-American Literature at the University of Wisconsin-Madison. McKay is the author of *Jean Toomer, Artist: A Study of Literary Life and Work* and editor of *Critical Essays on Toni Morrison*. She publishes widely on feminist issues in Afro-American women's literature and is working on a book that explores identity in Black women's autobiography.

Christine Obbo is a Ugandan anthropologist who has conducted research in rural, urban and low income areas in Africa and the United States. She is widely published on issues of social change and women. She is the author of *African Women: Their Struggle for Economic Independence* (with Nici Nelson).

'Molara Ogundipe-Leslie is a Nigerian professor, literary critic, poet and social activist who has published numerous articles, books and popular essays. Her most recent works are *African Women and Critical Transformations* (Africa World Press, 1993) and (with Carol Boyce-Davies) *Moving Beyond All Boundaries: A Critical Anthology* (Pluto Press, 1993). She served in 1992–3 as the sixth occupant of the Laurie New Jersey Chair in Women's Studies at Rutgers University.

Loretta J. Ross is the national program director for the Center for Democratic Renewal in Atlanta, a national non-profit clearinghouse for information on hate groups and bigoted violence, including the Ku-Klux-Klan. A lifelong women's rights activist, Loretta Ross has been program director for the National Black Women's Health Project director of Women of Color Programs for the National Organization of Women, and she organized the first national conference on Violence and Third World Women in 1980, and the first national conference on Women of Color and Reproductive Rights in 1987.

Andrea Benton Rushing is Professor of English at Amherst College, Mass., and the co-editor of *Women in Africa and the African Diaspora* (1989).

Filomina Chioma Steady is the Director of Women's Studies at California State University, Sacramento, and the editor of *The Black Woman Cross-Culturally* (1981).

Freida High W. Tesfagiorgis is Professor of African-American and Contemporary African Art in the Department of Afro-American Studies at the University of Wisconsin-Madison. She has been Chair of the Department from 1990 to 1993. She has published numerous exhibition catalogue essays, and other essays, articles and reviews that have appeared in, among other journals, *Faith Ringgold: Twenty Year Retrospective*; *Pattern and Narrative* (An Exhibition of Contemporary African Art); *The Wisconsin Connection: Black Artists Past and Present*; *SAGE: A Scholarly Journal on Black Women*; and *African Arts*. Her work has been exhibited at many galleries and museums in the USA, Senegal and Italy. She is currently curating an exhibition of contemporary African art that focuses on academic artists.

Patricia J. Williams is Professor of Law at Columbia Law School and the author of *The Alchemy of Race and Rights* (Harvard University Press, 1991).

Melvina Johnson Young is currently a graduate student in the United States Women's History PhD program at the University of Wisconsin-Madison. Her area of interest is nineteenth- and twentieth-century Afro-American Women's history. After completing her degree, she plans to teach US, African-American and Women's History in a university setting.

INTRODUCTION

Stanlie M. James

The 1990s mark the era when issues of multiple oppression were finally being addressed in conferences held by various academic disciplines. However, as a newly minted PhD recently admitted to the ranks of assistant professorship, I was having difficulty finding interdisciplinary conferences which specifically addressed issues of Black feminisms. Although familiar with the works of many sociologists, historians, political scientists, literary critics, essayists, poets and visual artists, etc. who either identified themselves as Black feminists or, as bell hooks has argued, "advocated" feminism (hooks, 1984: 30), I was finding it difficult to establish the kind of mutually supportive interdisciplinary intellectual network in which my work would flourish. Troubled by this sense of isolation, and feeling that perhaps other Black feminists, particularly those within the academy, might be struggling with this or similar problems, I sought support from my department, Afro-American Studies at the University of Wisconsin-Madison, to deal with the problem.

In response, the department agreed to sponsor a small three-day multidisciplinary Black Feminist Seminar, May 10–12, 1990. Participants from my home university included Nellie Y. McKay, Freida High W. Tesfagiorgis, Patricia J. Williams, Vanessa Northington Gamble, Marilyn Little, Evelyn L. Barbee, Sandra Adell, Josephine Beoku and Deborah Johnson. Abena P. A. Busia from Rutgers University, Beverly Guy-Sheftall from Spelman College, Rose M. Brewer from the University of Minnesota, Cindy Courville from Occidental College, Bessie House Midamba from Kent State, and 'Molara Ogundipe-Leslie, a visiting scholar from Nigeria, also participated in the seminar.

Seminar participants shared their favorite or sometimes their most provocative work in a supportive atmosphere which included intense discussions about Black feminisms today and in the future. We also explored some of our mutual problems as Black women scholars in the often hostile environment of the white academy. The seminar provided an important opportunity for these scholars to get to know each other personally and intellectually, as many of us were familiar with each other

1

only through our written work; it proved critical to the development of a nurturing network of junior and established scholars in our multi-dimensional roles as Black women scholars, and included the careful and helpful critiquing of each other's work.

One outcome of this first seminar was our decision to work together on an anthology that would represent an interdisciplinary approach to Black feminist theorizing. The Black Feminist Seminar convened for a second meeting in the supportive environment of Spelman, a Black women's college in Atlanta, Georgia, September 20–22, 1991 to discuss the development of the anthology. Much of that time was spent critiquing each other's contributions to the anthology, a process that continued the nurturance of our emergent network.

As an institution, the Black Feminist Seminar provides an alternative to the sense of isolation individuals often experience in the competitive environment of the academy. It envisions a vigorous model of simultaneous multifaceted collaboration at the level of the intellectual and the visceral, the individual and the community. In short it provides a haven for theorizing by Black feminists engaged in articulating through their writings oppositional/marginalized values.

Theorizing by Black feminists develops out of Black women's experiences of multiple interrelated oppressions including (but not limited to) racism/ethnocentrism, sexism/homophobia and classism. While reflecting the diversity of its many adherents it also struggles to embrace contradictions. Thus Black feminists' theorizing reflects a proactive/reactive stance of pragmatic activism which addresses those issues deemed deleterious to the well-being of Black women. Although Black women are often characterized as victims, theorizing is a form of agency that provides them with opportunities to "learn, think, imagine, judge, listen, speak, write and act" (Stimson, 1989) – which transforms not only the individual (from victim to activist, for example) but the community, and the society as well.

Black feminism's theorizing is rooted in Black communities and nourished by them even as it challenges those very communities to address issues of internal oppression. African-American Women in Defense of Ourselves, a self-described grassroots initiative of 1,603 women from the academy, the arts and the community, serves as an example of Black women challenging external/internal oppressions. In a spontaneous response to the Anita Hill/Clarence Thomas debacle, this group of women from around the nation expressed their outrage in a *New York Times* advertisement in November of 1991. The ad defined the issues of racist and sexist oppression surrounding the sinister nomination of Thomas by the Bush administration, supported Anita Hill's right to make public allegations of sexual harassment, solicited the support of the Black community and critiqued the circus of the senate judiciary hearings.

Black feminists are simultaneously envisioning incremental changes and radical transformations not only within Black communities but throughout the broader society as well. Ultimately, the humanistic visionary pragmatism of theorizing by Black feminists seeks the establishment of just societies where human rights are implemented with respect and dignity even as the world's resources are equitably distributed in ways that encourage individual autonomy and development.

The tradition of Black feminist theorizing spans our African and American heritage and includes the work of such African-American women as Maria Stewart, Linda Brent, Harriet Tubman, Sojourner Truth, Mary Church Terrell, Ida B. Wells, Anna Julia Cooper, Mary McLeod Bethune, Rosa Parks, Daisy Bates, Septima Clark and Ella Baker, etc. However, the theorizing of contemporary Black feminists is a product not only of our historical tradition of activism but of the social change movements for civil rights and Black Power of the 1960s. These movements gave rise to some 300–500 Afro-American Studies programs in white universities around the USA. Their mission, according to Manning Marable, was to "endeavor to articulate . . . [an] understanding of the collective experiences of the people of the African diaspora" (Marable, 1991). They were in turn instrumental in the rise of Women's Studies programs in the 1970s which, by 1985, numbered nearly 500 in universities and colleges across the USA, along with some 50 research centers for women. The Black social movements of the 1960s fostered the development of others including the gay and lesbian, the Chicano/Chicana, the welfare rights and the farm workers' movements, for example.

Both oppositional discourses of Afro-American Studies and Women's Studies programs sought first to expand knowledge through the addition of Blacks or women to such traditional disciplines as English, history and sociology. Unfortunately these disciplines were not seriously engaged in the task of revisioning in ways that inclusively incorporated Blacks and/or women. Additionally, to paraphrase the title of a well-received anthology of the period, the assumption was often that "all the women are white [and] all the Blacks are men" (Hull *et al.*, 1982), thus virtually ignoring the issues and concerns of Black women. As a response to this dual marginalization occurring within both traditional disciplines and these multidisciplinary "studies programs," a Black feminist critique began to emerge in the 1970s.

Compelled to address these shortcomings in their writings (and speaking and activism), contemporary Black women's voices began to be heard again in the 1970s and 1980s through such important collections as *The Black Woman* edited by Toni Cade and *Home Girls: A Black Feminist Anthology* edited by Barbara Smith. Authors such as bell hooks (1981), Angela Davis (1983) and Paula Giddings (1984) deepened this discussion by retrieving the history of African-American women from obscurity, exploring the parameters of a Black feminist perspective and addressing issues of multiple oppression.

Literary criticism has been in the vanguard of this area of inquiry[1] although social scientists are now also making significant contributions to the theorizing of Black feminists, as indicated by the recently released anthology *Black Women in America: Social Science Perspectives* edited by Micheline R. Malson, Elisabeth Mudimbe-Boyi, Jean F. O'Barr and Mary Wyer.[2] Additionally, attempts to bring together the writings of Black feminists from Africa and around the Black diaspora can be found in the pioneering work of Filomina Chioma Steady, editor of *The Black Woman Cross-Culturally*, and in the more recent *Women in Africa and the African Diaspora*, edited by Rosalyn Terborg-Penn, Sharon Harley and Andrea Benton Rushing.[3]

Theorizing Black Feminisms: The Visionary Pragmatism of Black Women contributes to these ongoing oppositional discourses in which boundaries of nationality and academic disciplines are tested and transgressed, and as such is critical to the continuous interdisciplinary, international process of revisioning, sometimes referred to as shifting paradigms. Critical problems and issues are illuminated through the prism of multi-faceted Black feminist visions which, like the African-American experience described by Loretta Ross elsewhere in this volume, "is the deliberate combination of the personal and the objective that creates [its] authority, authenticity and uniqueness." Together the wide-ranging essays in this anthology respond to the summons of Patricia Hill Collins to engage in "theoretical interpretations of Black women's reality by those who live it" (Collins, 1990: 22).

Through participating in struggles to retrieve the reality of Black women's lives from the periphery of the margin of African and African-American experiences, *Theorizing Black Feminisms* simultaneously challenges these limited experiential theoretical visions, and traditional western ways of theory-building. At the same time the emphasis on making *this* theorizing easily accessible is reflected in its language which is that of the activist and the academic.

Theorizing Black Feminisms consists of four sections. Part I, "On revisioning paradigms," contributes to the theoretical process of gendering African-American and African experiences in ways which articulate the realities of multiple oppression and exploitation. In "Theorizing race, class and gender: The new scholarship of Black feminist intellectuals and Black women's labor," sociologist Rose M. Brewer sets the tone for the rest of the anthology by insisting that any discussion of Black women must be holistic and historical, and placed firmly within the theoretical frame of gender, race, class dynamics. Her examination of Black women's labor in North Carolina is informed by the comprehensiveness of the "polyvocality of [their] multiple social locations." This gendering of African-American labor scholarship is crucial to the process of shifting paradigms.

Political scientist Cindy Courville's concern with the issue of African women's oppression and exploitation is apparent in her chapter "Re-examining patriarchy as a mode of production: The case of Zimbabwe." She critiques Marxist feminist notions of patriarchy as mode of production and argues that it is the transhistorical nature of patriarchy as an ideology that shape(s) "the construction of African women's oppression."

In "Mothering: A possible Black feminist link to social transformation?" political scientist Stanlie M. James re-examines the concept of "mothering" and argues that Eurocentric conceptualizations fail to capture the interdependent communal nature of African and African-American understandings of its complex roles. She goes on to suggest that reconceptualizations of othermothering and community othermothering may be useful in creative discussions of empowerment and social transformation.

Melvina Johnson Young combines her personal experiences of growing up poor, Black and female in the South with the tools of a historian to develop an important critique of the oral accounts of formerly enslaved African-Americans. In "Exploring the WPA narratives: Finding the voices of Black women and men," Young argues that while scholars of the institution of slavery in the USA have utilized the narrative data, they have omitted analyses that incorporate an understanding of the impact of racism, sexism and classism on the interview processes themselves. This essay explores the nature of that oppression as a means of revisioning the lives of African women.

Part II, "On theory and action," demonstrates the symbiotic relationship of theory and action in Black feminists' theorizing. In "A Black feminist perspective on transforming the academy: The case of Spelman College," Beverly Guy-Sheftall, director of the Women's Studies Research Center at Spelman, describes her careful efforts to develop a viable Black Women's Studies program in a historically Black women's college – an environment not necessarily receptive to feminism. The piece is enhanced by the incorporation of her own recollections of her personal intellectual development as a Black feminist.

Anthropologist Filomina Chioma Steady pays tribute to her mentor as she presents a cross-cultural perspective on female models and argues their usefulness as transformational models. In an article which is in some ways similar to that by James, Steady also argues that changes in decision-making and power relations (rather than duplication of existing models) between women and men, and among women, can lead to major societal change.

In "African women, culture and another development" literary critic 'Molara Ogundipe-Leslie examines development literature and practice, and argues that the dominant approaches to development are man-centered, as indeed is its very language. This in turn has led to a critical failure in developing an understanding of the forms of oppression faced by African women. This essay identifies six common forms of oppression and argues that they must be incorporated into more efficacious conceptualizations of development.

In "Disorder in the house: The new world order and the socio-economic status of women" law professor Patricia J. Williams examines contemporary global socioeconomic upheavals, including the relationships of multinationals to labor problems that were mentioned in the Brewer article. She compares the rise of sophisticated forms of discrimination and the attendant deterioration of race and gender relations in the USA to the developments of deleterious definitions of "minorities" in the wake of collapsing Eastern European systems.

Part III, "On controlling our bodies," examines ways in which Black women are confronting issues of control – or the lack of control – of their bodies at personal and institutional levels. Writer Andrea Benton Rushing shares with the reader the violence of rape and the trauma of recovery. This devastating piece in one sense racializes rape as she struggles with the inherent contradictions of violation by a "brother" and help from the institutional support network established by the white community.

Loretta J. Ross shares the personal experiences that led to her activism in the reproductive freedoms movement in "African-American women and abortion: 1800–1970." Ross's holistic historicized approach and along with it her personal recollections illustrate the proactive/reactive stance of Black feminist pragmatic activism and the manner in which it informs the political struggle to redefine the movement.

In "HIV transmission: Men are the solution" anthropologist Christine Obbo presents the stunning results of her fieldwork on the AIDS epidemic in Uganda. She presents critical information on sexual activity and sexuality in Ugandan society in a manner that explains the rapid spread of this killer disease.

Utilizing the interlocking model of gender, race, class oppression Evelyn L. Barbee and Marilyn Little have collaborated on "Health, social class and African-American women." Their examination of census documents reveals some shocking statistics on the incidence of such diseases as hypertension and diabetes among Black women. This piece enhances the personal nature of the previous papers by providing additional information on Black women and violence – including rape, AIDS and reproductive freedom.

Part IV, "On the language of identities," interrogates the existence,

6

meaning and impact upon their work of Black women's multiple and interrelated identities. In "Performance, transcription and the languages of the self: Interrogating identity as a 'post-colonial' poet" Abena P. A. Busia speaks of her many identities including those of American, British colonial subject, Ghanaian, exile and poet. In this piece, Busia elaborates on the polyvocality of identities as they relate to her work as an academic, more specifically as a poet and in particular in regards to the poem "Mawu/Mawo." She brings together the diverse issues of her creative process, parentage, ethnicity, her language(s) and her mode of dress in a manner that is concerned not with resolving contradictions but rather with providing coherence.

Cheryl Clarke reflects upon the development of her multifaceted identities as a Black, lesbian poet within the context of the civil rights/ Black Power movement of the 1960s and beyond. She interrogates the dialectic of Blackness and homosexuality, questions gender role expectations and male domination in the Black community, and briefly contemplates socialist feminism as she finally arrives at an anti-sexist/heterosexist, anti-racist, feminist stance.

"In search of a discourse and critique/s that center the art of Black women artists" by Freida High W. Tesfagiorgis argues that Black women's art has been excluded from European-American art history, included in African-American history in a "complementary" manner, and marginalized in the western feminist tradition. Therefore there is a critical need to develop a Black feminist discourse wherein our works will be inscribed into history and critiqued in ways that illuminate their meanings and their intervention into society. Black feminist historicized critiques reject conventional art-historical critiques that establish hierarchies in artists, styles and materials. Rather they embrace a multifaceted polyvocality of styles, materials and meanings that cohere to the multiple realities of existence and identity for Black women artists.

English professor Nellie Y. McKay's concluding piece "Acknowledging differences: Can women find unity through diversity?" was written in the aftermath of the Anita Hill/Clarence Thomas debacle. Using that case, reflections on how her father would have responded to the situation, and a literary text, McKay illuminates the traditional formidable racial barriers to sisterhood and the deep schism between African-American women and men. In the tradition of theorizing Black feminists, McKay expresses her dismay and sorrow at the situation and then moves beyond that as she charges academic women from all groups with the necessity of developing a humanistic praxis out of the richness of diversity in sisterhood that will result in social transformation.

June 1992

NOTES

1 See, for example, Bell, Parker and Guy-Sheftall, 1979; Christian, 1985; Pryse and Spillers, 1985; Davies and Graves, 1986.
2 Certainly the work of Patricia Hill Collins is an exciting contribution to Black feminism from a social sciences perspective. See especially Collins, 1990. See also Simms and Malveaux, 1986.
3 Other works of this nature include, for example, Rodgers-Rose, 1980; Lindsay, 1983; Moraga and Anzaldua, 1981; Davies and Fido, 1990; DuBois and Ruiz, 1990; and Mohanty, Russo and Torres, 1991.

BIBLIOGRAPHY

African-American Women in Defense of Ourselves (1991) *New York Times*, November 17.

Bell, Roseann P., Parker, Bettye J. and Guy-Sheftall, Beverly (eds) (1979) *Sturdy Black Bridges: Visions of Black Women in Literature*, New York: Anchor Books.

Braxton, Joanne M. and McLaughlin, Andrée Nicola (eds) (1990) *Wild Women in the Whirlwind: Afra-American Culture and the Contemporary Literary Renaissance*, New Brunswick, NJ: Rutgers University Press.

Cade, Toni (ed.) (1970) *The Black Woman: An Anthology*, New York: New American Library.

Christian, Barbara (1985) *Black Feminist Criticism: Perspectives on Black Women Writers*, New York: Pergamon Press.

Cole, Johnnetta B. (ed.) (1986) *All American Women: Lines that Divide, Ties that Bind*, New York: Free Press.

Collins, Patricia Hill (1990) *Black Feminist Thought: Knowledge, Consciousness, and the Politics of Empowerment*, Boston, Mass.: Unwin Hyman.

Davies, Carole Boyce and Fido, Elaine Savory (eds) (1990) *Out of the Kumbla: Caribbean Women and Literature*, Trenton, NJ: Africa World Press.

Davies, Carole Boyce and Graves, Anne Adams (eds) (1986) *Ngambika: Studies of Women in African Literature*, Trenton, NJ: Africa World Press.

Davis, Angela (1983) *Women, Race and Class*, New York: Vintage Books.

—— (1989) *Women, Culture and Politics*, New York: Random House.

DuBois, Ellen Carol and Ruiz, Vicki L. (eds) (1990) *Unequal Sisters: A Multi-cultural Reader in U.S. Women's History*, New York: Routledge.

Giddings, Paula (1984) *When and Where I Enter . . .: The Impact of Black Women on Race and Sex in America*, New York: William Morrow.

hooks, bell (1981) *Ain't I a Woman: Black Women and Feminism*, Boston, Mass.: South End Press.

—— (1984) *Feminist Theory: From Margin to Center*, Boston, Mass.: South End Press.

—— (1989) *Talking Back: Thinking Feminist, Thinking Black*, Boston, Mass.: South End Press.

—— (1990) *Yearning: Race, Gender and Cultural Politics*, Boston, Mass.: South End Press.

Hull, Gloria T., Bell-Scott, Patricia and Smith, Barbara (1982) *All the Women are White, All the Blacks are Men, But Some of Us are Brave*, Old Westbury, NY: Feminist Press.

Joseph, Gloria I. and Lewis, Jill (1981) *Common Differences: Conflicts in Black and White Feminist Perspectives*, Boston, Mass.: South End Press.

Lindsay, Beverly (ed.) (1983) *Comparative Perspectives of Third World Women: The*

Impact of Race, Sex and Class, New York: Praeger.

Malson, Micheline R., Mudimbe-Boyi, Elisabeth, O'Barr, Jean F. and Wyer, Mary (eds) (1990) *Black Women in America: Social Science Perspectives*, Chicago: University of Chicago Press.

Marable, Manning (1991) "Blueprint for Black Studies and Multiculturalism," paper presented at the Wisconsin Conference on Afro-American Studies in the Twenty-First Century, April 18–20.

Mohanty, Chandra Talpade, Russo, Ann and Torres, Lourdes (eds) (1991) *Third World Women and the Politics of Feminism*, Bloomington, IN: Indiana University Press.

Moraga, Cherrie and Anzaldua, Gloria (eds) (1981) *This Bridge Called My Back: Writings by Radical Women of Color*, Watertown, Mass.: Persephone Press.

Pryse, Marjorie and Spillers, Hortense J. (eds) (1985) *Conjuring Black Women, Fiction and Literary Tradition*, Bloomington, IN: Indiana University Press.

Rodgers-Rose, LaFrances (ed.) (1980) *The Black Woman*, Newbury Park, Ca.: Sage Publications.

Simms, Margaret C. and Malveaux, Julianne M. (eds) (1986) *Slipping through the Cracks: The Status of Black Women*, New Brunswick, NJ: Transaction Publishers.

Smith, Barbara (ed.) (1983) *Home Girls: A Black Feminist Anthology*, New York: Kitchen Table, Women of Color Press.

Steady, Filomina Chioma (ed.) (1981) *The Black Woman Cross-Culturally*, Cambridge, Mass.: Schenkman.

Stimson, Catharine R. (1989) "Setting Agendas, Defining Challenges," *The Women's Review of Books* VI (5) (February): 14.

Terborg-Penn, Rosalyn, Harley, Sharon and Rushing, Andrea Benton (eds) (1989) *Women in Africa and the African Diaspora*, Washington, DC: Howard University Press.

Wallace, Michelle (1978) *Black Macho and the Myth of the SuperWoman*, New York: Dial Press.

White, Evelyn C. (ed.) (1990) *The Black Women's Health Book: Speaking for Ourselves*, Seattle, WA: Seal Press.

Williams, Patricia J. (1991) *The Alchemy of Race and Rights: Diary of a Law Professor*, Cambridge, Mass.: Harvard University Press.

Part I

ON REVISIONING PARADIGMS

1

THEORIZING RACE, CLASS AND GENDER

The new scholarship of Black feminist intellectuals and Black women's labor

Rose M. Brewer

At the centre of the theorizing about race, class and gender in the USA is a group of Black feminist intellectuals. These are academics, independent scholars and activists who are writing and rethinking the African-American experience from a feminist perspective. In this chapter, I am most concerned with the ideas of those women involved in knowledge production who are situated in the academy: colleges and universities throughout the USA. Their insights are essential to the rethinking which must occur in conceptualizing the African-American experience. Although they are few in number, their recent placement in Women's Studies, Ethnic Studies and traditional disciplines such as sociology, political science, history, English, anthropology, comparative literature and so on, is strategic to the current upsurge in Black feminist scholarship.

What is most important conceptually and analytically in this work is the articulation of multiple oppressions. This polyvocality of multiple social locations is historically missing from analyses of oppression and exploitation in traditional feminism, Black Studies and mainstream academic disciplines. Black feminist thinking is essential to possible paradigm shifts in these fields; for example, in Black Studies to begin explaining the African-American experience through the multiple articulations of race, class and *gender* changes the whole terrain of academic discourse in that area. Black feminist social scientists deconstruct existing frameworks in sociology, history and a range of other disciplines.

In the ensuing discussion I look more carefully at how Black feminist theorizing is central to our rethinking the African-American experience. I examine Black women's labor and African-American class formation to illustrate how race, class and gender in intersection contribute to our understanding of African-American life. I organize the chapter around the following three themes: (1) an examination of the context of recent

Black feminist theorizing in the social sciences; (2) a closer analysis of a major proposition of Black feminist thought, "the simultaneity of oppression," given race, class and gender as categories of analyses in the social sciences; and (3) sketching out a reconstructed analysis of Black women's labor and African-American class formation through the lenses of race and gender.

THE SOCIAL CONTEXT OF RECENT BLACK FEMINIST THEORIZING

The theory and practice of Black feminism predates the current period. Even during the first wave of feminism, according to Terborg-Penn (1990), prominent Black feminists combined the fight against sexism with the fight against racism by continuously calling the public's attention to these issues. Turn-of-the-century Black activist Anna Julia Cooper conceived the African-American woman's position thus:

> She is confronted by a woman question and a race problem, and is as yet an unknown or unacknowledged factor in both.
> (*A Voice from the South by a Black Woman of the South*, 1892)

Although early-twentieth-century Black suffragettes saw women's rights as essential to relieving social ills, they repeatedly called attention to issues of race. Nonetheless, within the vise of race, African-American women forged a feminist consciousness in the USA. Such women might be called the original Black feminists. Again, the life and work of Anna Julia Cooper is a case in point. Guy-Sheftall and Bell-Scott (1989: 206) point out that Cooper's work, *A Voice from the South by a Black Woman of the South* (1892), "has the distinction of being the first scholarly publication in the area of Black women's studies, though the concept had certainly not emerged during the period."

Yet the gateway to the new Black feminist scholarship of the past twenty years is the civil rights movement and the mainstream feminist movement of the late 1960s and early 1970s. E. Frances White, an activist in the civil rights movement, captures the recent historical context in which contemporary Black feminists are located. She says:

> I remember refusing to leave the discussion at a regional black student society meeting to go help out in the kitchen. The process of alienation from those militant and articulate men had begun for me.
>
> (1984: 9)

White goes on to point out that:

> many of today's most articulate spokeswomen, too, participated in the black student, civil rights, and black nationalist movements.

Like their white counterparts, these women felt frustrated by restraints imposed on them by the men with whom they shared the political arena.

(1984: 9)

For Cynthia Washington, an activist in the Student Nonviolent Coordinating Committee (SNCC), this incipient Black feminism is given a different slant. She points out that although Black women's abilities and skills were recognized in the movement, the men categorized the women as something other than female (Echols, 1989). Both these positions reflect the historic path of Black feminist development in the second wave of US feminism. White and Washington's interpretations of the movement point to the multiple consciousness which informs Black feminist thinking and struggles. Black feminism is defined as a multiple level engagement (King, 1988).

This is strikingly exemplified by the Combahee River Collective. The organization was formed by a group of Black lesbian feminists in the mid-1970s. In the context of murder in Boston, Barbara Smith and a group of other Black women founded the collective. Smith was insistent that the murder of Black women was not only a racial issue. The fact that thirteen Black women were killed cruelly exhibited how sexism and racism intersected in the lives of African-American women. Given this, the collective argued:

> The most general statement of our politics at the present time would be that we are actively committed to struggling against racial, sexual, heterosexual, and class oppression, and see as our particular task the development of an integrated analysis and practice based upon the fact that major systems of oppression create the conditions of our lives. As Black women we see Black feminism as the logical political movement to combat the manifold and simultaneous oppressions that all women of color face.
>
> (Smith, 1983: 272)

Importantly, Black feminist theorizing places African-American women at the center of the analyses (Hull *et al.*, 1982; Collins, 1986, 1990; King, 1988; Dill, 1979). By theorizing from the cultural experiences of African-American women, social scientists such as Collins argue epistemologically that experience is crucial to Black women's ways of knowing and being in the world. Thus capturing that cultural experience is essential to a grounded analysis of African-American women's lives. This means analysis predicated on the everyday lives of African-American women. More difficult has been linking the everyday to the structural constraints of institutions and political economy (Brewer, 1983, 1989). Indeed, a challenge to Black feminist theory is explicating the interplay between agency and social structure. However, nearly all the recent writing has been about everyday lived experiences. Less successful and visible is the explication of the interrelationship between lives and social structure.

Finally, running through Black feminist analyses is the principle of "the simultaneity of oppression" (Hull *et al.*, 1982). This is the conceptual underpinning of much of recent Black feminist reconceptualization of African-American life. In the following discussion, "the simultaneity of oppression" is examined more carefully and is central to our understanding of Black women's labor and African-American class formation. Furthermore rethinking the social structure of inequality in the context of race, class and gender intersections is crucial to this discussion, using Black women's textile industry work in North Carolina as a case in point.

RACE, CLASS AND GENDER: "THE SIMULTANEITY OF OPPRESSION"

The conceptual anchor of recent Black feminist theorizing is the understanding of race, class and gender as simultaneous forces. The major propositions of such a stance include:

1 critiquing dichotomous oppositional thinking by employing both/and rather than either/or categorizations
2 allowing for the simultaneity of oppression and struggle, thus
3 eschewing additive analyses: race + class + gender
4 which leads to an understanding of the embeddedness and relationality of race, class and gender and the multiplicative nature of these relationships: race × class × gender
5 reconstructing the lived experiences, historical positioning, cultural perceptions and social construction of Black women who are enmeshed in and whose ideas emerge out of that experience, and
6 developing a feminism rooted in class, culture, gender and race in interaction as its organizing principle.

Importantly, the theorizing about race, class and gender is historicized and contextualized.

RACE, CLASS AND GENDER: AS CATEGORIES OF ANALYSIS

Race has been defined in a number of ways, yet a few powerful conceptualizations are useful to our discussion of Black feminist theory. Recently feminist historian Higginbotham notes:

Like gender and class, then, race must be seen as a social construction predicated upon the recognition of difference and signifying the simultaneous distinguishing and positioning of groups vis-à-vis one another. More than this, race is a highly contested representation of relations of power between social categories by which individuals are identified and identify themselves.

(1992: 253)

The embeddedness of gender within the context of race is further captured by Higginbotham. She notes that:

in societies where racial demarcation is endemic to their socio-cultural fabric and heritage – to their laws and economy, to their institutionalized structures and discourses, and to their epistemologies and everyday customs – gender identity is inextricably linked to and even determined by racial identity. We are talking about the racialization of gender and class.

(1992: 254)

Omi and Winant point out:

The effort must be made to understand race as an unstable and decentered complex of social meanings constantly being transformed by political struggle.

(1987: 68)

And finally, Barbara Fields conceptualizes race ideologically:

If race lives on today, it does not live on because we have inherited it from our forebears of the seventeenth century or the eighteenth or nineteenth, but because we continue to create it today.

(1970: 117)

Relatedly, gender as a category of analysis cannot be understood decontextualized from race and class in Black feminist theorizing. Social constructions of Black womanhood and manhood are inextricably linked to racial hierarchy, meaning systems and institutionalization. Indeed, gender takes on meaning and is embedded institutionally in the context of the racial and class order: productive and social reproductive relations of the economy.

Accordingly, class as an economic relationship expressing productive and reproductive relations is a major category of analysis in the notion of the simultaneity of oppression. Yet recent Black feminist writers (hooks, 1984; Collins, 1990; King, 1988) point out the tendency of theorists writing in the class traditions to reduce race and gender to class. Similarly Black feminist economist Rhonda Williams (1985) places changes in the labor market squarely in a race, gender and class framework that cannot be explained through traditional labor/capital analyses.

Yet we can fall into the trap of overdetermination, especially in the case of race as a category of analysis. In fact, Higginbotham (1992) draws our attention to the metalanguage of race in which internal issues of gender and class are subsumed to a unitarian position of African-Americans. Here, class is hidden or misspecified and gender is rendered invisible in this conceptualization of African-American inequality. Indeed, race in the context of the globalization of capitalism makes gender the center of the new working class. Thus the following discussion draws upon recent Black feminist theorizing to place Black women at the center of an analysis of labor and African-American class formation emphasizing the relational and interactive nature of these social forces.

BLACK WOMEN'S LABOR AND AFRICAN-AMERICAN CLASS FORMATION THROUGH THE PRISM OF RACE, GENDER AND CLASS

The contestation among scholars on race and class reflects conceptual, political interests and careerist concerns. Yet, the debate on the relative importance of race and class has been fought largely on a nongendered terrain. The writings of Black feminist intellectuals give us some new insight into how the race and class might be viewed in the context of gender. Indeed, as theorists explicate the intersection of race, gender and class, our conceptualizations of racial inequality will change. The complexity of race, gender and class interactions suggests that scholarly work must accomplish a number of difficult theoretical tasks especially around interrelationships. Thus, in the context of explaining Black women's labor and class formation, at least one question is key: How does explicating African-American's women poorly paid productive or unwaged social reproductive labor recenter our understanding of African-American inequality and class formation? I can begin to answer this question by examining more closely the changes in Black women's labor, drawing upon the insights of Black feminist theorizing.

Striking is the research on race and labor. Baron (1971), in a classic essay titled "The Demand for Black Labor," essentially discusses Black men's labor. This tendency is pervasive in a good deal of the work on the Black experience (Collins, 1986, 1990). Consequently, the inequality of African-American life is conflated with Black men's inequality. Indeed, much of the discussion of inequality in the USA has been centered on the dynamics of either race or gender which translates into discussions of white women or Black men. Dismissing intersections of race and gender in such autonomous analyses conceptually erases African-American women. Recent Black feminist thinking strongly emphasizes the error in this kind of analysis.

Accordingly, a critical defining element of the current time is the regionalization and internationalization of women's work. Indeed, a crucial determinant of Black life today is not simply Black men's marginalization from work but the social transformation of Black women's labor. Furthermore, the transformation of Black women's labor is tied to structural changes in the state and economy as well as to shifts in the racial/gender division of labor.

Three major labor transformations in Black women's waged labor are key: (1) movement from domestic to industrial and clerical work, a process still incomplete and particularized by region and class (Simms and Malveaux, 1986); (2) integration into the international division of labor in low-paid service work which is largely incapable of providing a family wage (Brewer, 1983); and (3) the increasing impoverishment and fragmentation of Black women, children and families (Sidel, 1986). An analysis of the North Carolina textile industry is a good case in point of the above processes. These changes are matched by the pervasive peripherization of Black men from manufacturing work and the labor force (Beverly and Stanback, 1986). Theorizing race, class and gender in the context of these broad-based structural changes in Black women's labor exemplifies a division of waged labor built on racial norms and values, as well as material arrangements embedded in a gendered division of labor. More recently, uneven economic growth and internationalization have involved Black women in the complex circuitry of labor exchange of women nationally and globally. In short, capitalist firms do not have to depend upon Black labor, either male or female. Low-wage, low-cost labor can be found all over the world. The world labor force is a cheap substitution for Black labor in the USA. Yet this is further complicated by the feminization of much of labor (low-paid women within the USA and outside). Furthermore, women's work in the USA is gender/race divided. Disproportionate numbers of Black women are at the bottom of this division of labor, rooted in social meanings systems which get remade in the material context of social practices as well as the calculus of profit. Structually such processes anchor a disproportionate number of African-American women at the bottom of the service sector with some regional variation and some convergence of women's status across race in gender-segregated jobs. Thus African-American women represent a significant component of the new working classes. What more can be said about the social forces integral to African-American labor changes and class formation? To answer this, I will look carefully at the structural shifts of the last thirty years.

The concrete manifestation of regional political economy is uneven capitalist development (Clavell *et al.*, 1980). Today, US workers compete in an international market for labor power. There is a worldwide latent reserve labor force which competes with unskilled and semi-skilled labor in both the USA and Europe. White women, men and women of color, and increasingly white male workers in the USA either directly compete with or are bypassed in favor of cheaper labor in Malaysia, Mexico, Singapore, the Philippines and the Dominican Republic among others (Williams, 1985).

Thus, a regional and international approach to political economy is central to this analysis. However, this must be matched by a concern with racial/cultural formation, gender inequality and concrete political struggles. White workers have historically been in competition with Black workers (Bonancich, 1976).They have been able historically to close rank against Black labor for the best jobs. Black women and men have often been left with the least desirable work, but some work. Today, this is not so for many African-Americans. During the era of advanced capitalism, competition moves beyond the confines of single industries and nations and becomes internationalized (Williams, 1985).

Economic changes are not abstractions from the activities of agents. Choices are made: who will be used, who will not. These choices are not wholly separated from cultural/racial/gender practices which get remade under conditions of internationalization of the economy. This means that much of the explanation of African-American marginalization from the economy is explained as cultural deficit. The economic locking-out of the Black poor and working poor is defined as a reflection of a culture of poverty rather than the remaking of racism, sexism and economic oppression under conditions of advanced capitalism. The white power elite makes decisions based on profit as well as the ideology of race and gender.

Given this, uneven economic development encompasses more than a labor/capital struggle. It is shaped by cultural processes reflecting long-standing definitions, perceptions of what is natural and given around hierarchies of race and gender. It is the issue of who loses. And, increasingly, the answer is young Black women and men of American inner cities. Moreover, the concern with the changing division of labor through economic restructuring is matched in this discussion by a concern with racial and gender divisions of labor. Pivotal here is the intersection of race/gender hierarchies and the way contemporary economic restructuring is shaped by existing arrangements of race/gender divisions. Furthermore, class fractioning within the racial/gender divisions of labor intersects with racial constraints within the gender/class division of labor. These processes take on an urban, regional and international form. Consequently, although at issue is the tranformation of Black women's labor, it should be viewed as a transformation in three moments: race, gender and class simultaneously.

Finally, historically and currently, politics and the state appear to mediate the process of class, race and gender struggle. Hence, uneven economic development and economic restructuring are a political process, too. The state and its political relations are part of the calculus of change and restructuring engaged in by capital. For example, Perry and Watkins (1977) explain the political and economic nature of sunbelt growth and development: a state/business coalition created desirable conditions in the sunbelt. So, moving defense money to sunbelt-based industries, providing tax breaks and R & D subsidies, was essential to early sunbelt growth. It was as much a political as an economic process.

Thus, economic restructuring, uneven economic growth and internalization of the labor force embody cultural, gender, political and economic moments. The consequence of this now in the USA is that about two-thirds of all working persons are engaged in services (Williams, 1985). A good number of these are African-American women performing public reproductive work in the form of nurses' aides and old-age assistants, and in fast food outlets and cafeterias. Indeed, nearly all new job growth during the 1970s and 1980s was in the service category. Externally and internally women are filling these new service jobs. They are the new working class. Under conditions of economic restructuring, highly skilled labor is largely technical labor and unskilled labor is largely manual and clerical labor. Thus, Black women's work today in the USA reflects the high demand for clerical labor emerging out of restructuring. Moreover, Black women's clerical work reflects the *partial* collapsing of a racial/gender division of labor. Both Black and white women do the same work in most places in the USA. Even so, Black women are more likely to be supervised and white women are more likely to supervise (Simms and Malveaux, 1986). Nonetheless, structural changes in the American economy and globally are changing cities and regions. This restructuring is changing Black women's work and all women's relation to work.

The second transformation in Black women's labor reflects a changing relationship to the new international division of labor. There is a diasporic connection with African women in the Americas, the USA, the Caribbean and South America. In sub-Saharan Africa, in the wake of colonialism and imperialism, there has been a profound reconstitution of Africa's women's productive and reproductive labor (Amadiume, 1988). What is not well understood in this process is what further changes African women globally will undergo. Within the USA, shifts will be costly in human terms under conditions of uneven economic development, restructuring, regional and international labor change. Job loss is occurring for many Black women or they are in part-time rather than full-time jobs (Woody and Malson, 1984). Their unemployment rate is among the highest in the USA (Simms and Malveaux, 1986). And paradoxically, just as some Black women are being more firmly tied to white-collar/clerical work, others are being excluded from the economy altogether. This job loss is linked to the replacement of the most vulnerable women of color with women workers outside the country and new immigrant women within the society.

This labor exchange process is increasingly being studied by scholars in research on labor transformation and Third World women globally (Nash and Safa, 1976; Fernandez-Kelley, 1983; Leacock and Safa, 1986). These writers discuss the impact of the new international division of labor on women of color globally. It is arguable that Third World women internationally are an essential part of the search for cheap labor (Safa, 1983). Fuentes and Ehrenreich concur (1983). Women generally, and Third World women specifically, have become essential to cheap labor in the global capitalist economy.

Hence given the international division of labor, some Black women within the USA are losing work just as they are making a niche for themselves in regional industries such as textiles. The racial/gender division of labor historically in the USA has opened from the bottom for Black women. This continues to be the case. For example, as southern white women in textiles moved to more desirable industrial jobs in the past two and half decades, Black women in North Carolina, South Carolina and across the textile South have filled the unskilled and semi-skilled jobs. Black women now hold over 50 per cent of the operative positions in many southern plants (Woody and Malson, 1984). Yet, with plant closedown and internationalization, many of these women are being fired. Textile workers peaked at over 1 million in the 1950s; in 1978 there were 754,296 (Sawars and Tabb, 1984). As usual Black women were again the last hired, the first fired.

Given the regional evolution of Black women's work within the USA, North Carolina serves as a good case study of the racial/sexual division of labor for African-American women. Some work has already been done on this process in the state through the 1930s (Janiewski, 1985). Clearly, Black women's work has been carefully crafted by economic and cultural forces. Well into the 1960s, economically and politically the state of North Carolina was completely dominated by whites. Jim Crow was only officially coming to an end, and the vestiges of the civil rights struggle lingered. White males dominated the state politically and socially. Nonetheless, all whites shared in a cultural heritage of white supremacy dating back to the days of slavery, accepting the notion of their special-ness vis-à-vis Black women, whether they themselves were economically privileged or not. This meant that poor white women were committed to the premises of white supremacy as well as wealthier women.

Despite a shared heritage around white supremacy, a racial order built on the belief and ideology of white supremacy alone would have top-pled. It was solidified and maintained through the domination of politi-cal institutions and the economic control by white male elites. Economics, politics and culture meshed to form a special kind of racial order in North Carolina, but the linchpin of the system was white male domination and control of key political and economic institutions.

Certainly by the time of the incorporation of Black women into the textile mills of the region, usually in the dirtiest and most distasteful jobs, the racial and gender distinctions were strong enough to generate four separate groups of labor: white men, white women, Black men, Black women. The gender distinctions generated a different kind of labor hierarchy: white men, Black men, white women, Black women.

Black women in North Carolina have been overwhelmingly concentrated in the secondary sector of the state. Secondary jobs are dirtier, harder and lower-waged than primary sector jobs. Job turnover is greater and job benefits are fewer in the secondary sector. Indeed jobs are different in the secondary and primary sectors. US census data for 1980 show that Black and white women held different types of jobs in North Carolina. A typical job for a white woman was white-collar. A large number of white women were clerical workers, and others were involved in teaching, health allied professions and retail sales work. Black women in the state were in blue-collar occupations. These include nondurable goods, operatives, private household workers, service workers. And unlike the nearly complete shift of Black women out of domestic work nationally, a somewhat greater percentage of the Black women in the state were involved in domestic work. Overall, there had not been major penetration into white-collar clerical work for these women. They were nearly all in the lower reaches of the occupational structure.

Thus, when Black women moved into industrial work in North Carolina textile mills, they did so without parity with white women. The gender division of labor was overlaid with the particularities of race. Only in the 1980s did Black and white women begin to share a common occupational trajectory. Currently, there is some convergence similar to the national convergence of all racial ethnic women. Some Black women in the state are moving into clerical work. Moreover, there is a racially mixed workplace for women in North Carolina textile mills today. Even still, Black women occupy a disproportionate percentage of low income work in this industry in the South (Woody and Malson, 1984). They bear the brunt of lay-offs and the industry has been devastated by plant mobility and closedowns.

More broadly, as noted earlier, uneven economic growth and internationalization have involved these women in a complex circuitry of female labor exchange nationally and globally. Racial segmentation of labor persists, rooted in cultural assumptions and social practices, as well as the calculus of profit. Consequently, although occupational segregation separates all women from men in the labor process, there is noise around race.

23

Race in the context of gender and class means African-Americans are quite vulnerable. For example, Black women are still more likely than white women to be paid less, to be unemployed, to be supervised rather than to supervise (Simms and Malveaux, 1986). Given these differences (Wallace, 1980), their relationship to capital is different from that of white women. Even still, a small group of Black women are moving into the white-collar occupations. Their numbers are indicative of the growing significance of class relative to race in national labor markets.

Nonetheless, it is the service sector in which a disproportionate number of African-American women work. This job slot for Black women cannot provide a family wage for high school educated and/or less skilled urban Blacks. This is highly problematic in the midst of extremely high Black male unemployment rates. In the case of African-American adolescents, the nearly complete erasure of their labor force participation has occurred. Phyllis Wallace (1974) is one of the few early scholars who place this reality in context. She points out that:

> Black teenage females constitute one of the most disadvantaged groups in the labor markets of large metropolitan areas.
>
> (1974: 8)

Woody and Malson (1984) elaborate this point:

> Current employment patterns indicate substantial underrepresentation in hiring black women in all income levels in key U.S. industry and a strong possibility of discrimination based on race.
>
> (1984: 3)

Indeed the working poor as a significant segment of the working class must be understood in a gendered context. Black male joblessness alone does not account for the tremendous disadvantage of the Black poor. Race/gender segmentation and low wages as reflected in the positioning of African-American women are conceptually central to African-American class inequality today.

SOCIAL REPRODUCTION: GENDER INEQUALITY AT HOME AND WORK IN THE CONTEXT OF BLACK WOMEN'S LABOUR TRANSFORMATION

Labor is not simply about waged work at the site of production. Within households, Black women perform a significant portion of the social reproductive labor. The socialization of children and the cleaning, cooking and nurturing functions are all disproportionately Black women's work. Indeed, poor Black women are often expected to do everything. Their work within the home is devalued, even though housework is accomplished under trying circumstances: substandard housing, no household washers and dryers, or few appliances. Yet these women are increasingly expected to work in low-paid jobs to qualify for Aid to Families with Dependent Children (AFDC). Indeed "workfare" is the key to recent public "welfare reform" legislation. Here again, race and gender intersect to anchor African-American women in a different stratum from white women or Black men.

Furthermore, the public service work referred to earlier is increasingly public social reproductive work: care for aged, sick and children. It falls disproportionately on Black women and other women of color. Yet, wages are very low and the average service salary is less than $12,000 per year (Williams, 1985). There simply is not enough money to support a family. Given this, some form of state support should make up a portion of the social wage for young Black people. Realistically, with severe cutbacks in the social wage, increasing immiseration for poor African-Americans is likely. Thus, Black male marginalization from work, and a particular type of work and welfare for the poorest African-American women, point to extremely difficult times ahead for the Black population in the USA. The increasing impoverishment of the Black family must be viewed in this context: Black women's placement in poorly paid jobs, Black men's increasing marginalization from work altogether and little state social support for men, women or children. Out of these processes emerges the lowest sector of the Black class structure.

For this reason, although there has been an assault on the Black working class, there is still a working class. It is conflated with the working poor. It is highly exploited and has experienced heavy assaults on its wage. It is a class which is often poor and female. Sidel (1986) points out that many poor families are headed by women who work all year long. For those households, the problem is not lack of work, it is low wages. The problem is also, as noted in the North Carolina example, sex segregation demarked by a racial/gender division of labor. The labor force participation of Black men has dropped precipitously and now about 55 per cent of them are in the labor force. Such realities have profound implications for African-American life. Understanding Black men's placement in the economy provides only a partial analysis of what is happening. Explicating Black women's labor transformation in the context of race, class and gender gives us a fuller understanding of the African-American experience in the 1990s.

SUMMARY

My purpose in this chapter has been to explicate some of the recent theorizing on race, class and gender by Black feminist thinkers in the academy. This theorizing is further explored in an analysis of Black women's labor and African-American class formation. The labor transformation of Black women has been explicated in terms of economic restructuring and capital mobility, racial formation and gender inequality. It is a process linking Black women in the northeast and midwest to the south and southwest, Asia, Africa and the Caribbean. It is not the tie of poverty to prosperity, but the tie of subordinate status to subordinate status cross-cut by internal class differences in all these regions. Because of class, which intersects with race and gender, a sector of Black women is in the upwardly mobile integrated sector of a servicized economy. These are women who are moving out of the fast-growing female service sector made up of clericals into the somewhat slower-growing high technology fields which are male dominated. Even still, the rate of change into high-paying fields has been slow for Black women. In 1970, 1 per cent of African-American women were engineers and by 1980 only 7 per cent were (Amott and Matthaei, 1991). More often Black women professionals are ghettoized in the lowest-paying professional fields. They are poorly represented in engineering, computer science, and other highly skilled fields with high pay. Currie and Skolnick (1984) aptly note that "short of an unprecedented shift in the sex composition of these occupations, their growth (highly paid professionals) seems unlikely to have a very strong effect on the overall distribution of (Black) women in the job hierarchy."

Finally, a discernible number of Black women are subemployed (desire full-time rather than the part-time work they have) or have been marginalized from work altogether (Woody and Malson, 1984). This occurs across regions; it is especially evident in northern and southern inner cities and rural areas. About half of all poor female-headed Black families are in the South. Additionally, the bifurcation of Black women's labor plays out a certain logic. Somewhat higher levels of clerical and white-collar service work are being performed by skilled Black women in the northeast, midwest and west while capital mobility has devastated the Black male semi-skilled and unskilled working class in older industrial areas. What is left is a service sector of racial minority women working for low wages. Simultaneously, there is a marginalization of some Black women from work altogether. They depend upon transfer payments, the informal economy of bartering, hustling, exchange, and kinship support.

Even now, the largest category of Black women workers in the USA is clerical and service workers (Simms and Malveaux, 1986). The latter is a category encompassing household workers, cleaners, janitors and public service workers, jobs which are extensions of the private household service role. Internationally, there is a broad base of women doing semi-skilled labor in the electronics, computer and other "sunrise" industries which have gone abroad. This is the work, primarily, of the white and Asian working-class female in the internal national women's economy.

Finally, the intersection of race, class and gender, in interplay with economic restructuring, accounts for the internal fractioning and separation of women from one another. Yet, this is not the entire story. Cultural practice, beliefs and ideology also structure female labor. The ideology of what is appropriately Black women's work is played out in the arena of the public social reproduction of labor. Kitchen and cafeteria workers, nurses' aides: these are defined as appropriate jobs for Black women, very much as the domestic labor of a generation ago was defined as "Black women's work." It is only when all these processes are better understood that perspectives on African-American inequality will be more accurate.

Crucially, the Black class structure is made in the context of economic, state restructuring and political struggle, and the recreation of race, and a gender/racial division of labor. These are not unrelated phenomena. The result is a highly complicated positioning of the Black population with some sectors clearly worse off than in the past, and other sectors more securely tied to mainstream institutions. African-American women are at the center of this reconstitution of Black labor and class formation. Most importantly, only in theorizing the complexity of the intersections of race, class and gender can we adequately prepare to struggle for social change in the African-American community.

CONCLUSIONS

In theorizing the construction of race, class and gender in intersection, three key themes are apparent. First, gender alone cannot explain the African-American woman's or man's experience. Feminism must reflect in its theory and practice the race and class terrain upon which hierarchy and inequality are built globally and within the USA. Secondly, the simultaneity of these social forces is key. In turn, practice and struggle must be anti-sexist, anti-classist, anti-racist and anti-homophobic.

Finally, the "gender, race, class" dynamic is the major theoretical frame through which gender is incorporated into discussions of the position of Black women. Alone, they are rather sterile categories infused with meaning developed out of many decades of social thought on class and race. In interplay with the concept gender, the paradigm becomes fairly rich (Brewer, 1989). It is the simultaneity of these forces which has been identified and theorized by Black feminist thinkers. Preliminary thinking in this direction suggests that any such analyses must be historically based and holistic.

Given the writings of Black feminist thinkers in the social sciences, social scientific analyses embodying race, class and gender are growing. Simms and Malveaux (1986), Dill (1979), Collins (1986), King (1988) and Higginbotham (1992) are among a growing number of Black feminist social scientists. These writers critique parallelist tendencies and oppositional dualistic thinking. The old additive models miss an essential reality, the qualitative difference in the lives of African-American women through the simultaneity of oppression and resistance. Thus we must rethink many of the extant analyses on African-Americans through the lenses of gender, race and class. This is just the beginning phase of the kind of work which must be done for a robust and holistic understanding of African-American life.

BIBLIOGRAPHY

Amadiume, Ifi (1988) *Male Daughters, Female Husbands*, London: Zed Books.

Amott, Theresa and Matthaei, Judith (1991) *Race, Gender and Work*, Boston, Mass.: South End Press.

Baron, Harold (1971) "The Demand for Black Labor: Historical Notes on the Political Economy of Racism," *Radical America* (March–April).

Beverly, Creigs C. and Stanback, Howard J. (1986) "The Black Underclass: Theory and Reality," *The Black Scholar* 17: 24–32.

Bluestone, Barry and Harrison, Bennett (1982) *The Deindustrialization of America*, New York: Basic Books.

Bonancich, Edna (1976) "Advanced Capitalism and Black/White Relations," *American Sociological Review* 41: 34–51.

Braverman, Harry (1974) *Labor and Monopoly Capital: The Degradation of Labor in the Twentieth Century*, New York and London: Monthly Review Press.

Brewer, Rose M. (1983) "Black Workers and Corporate Flight," *Third World Socialists* 1: 9–13.

—— (1989) "Black Women and Feminist Sociology: The Emerging Perspective," *American Sociologist* 20 (1): 57–70.

Clavell, Pierre, Forester, John and Goldsmith, William (eds) (1980) *Urban and Regional Planning in an Age of Austerity*, New York: Pergamon Press.

Collins, Patricia Hill (1986) "Learning from the Outsider Within: The Sociological Significance of Black Feminist Thought," *Social Problems* 33 (6) (December): 14–32.

—— (1989) "Toward a New Vision: Race, Class and Gender as Categories of Analysis and Connection," keynote address, delivered at Integrating Race and Gender into the College Curriculum: A Workshop Sponsored by the Center for Research on Women, Memphis State University, Memphis, TN, May 24, 1989.

—— (1990) *Black Feminist Thought: Knowledge, Consciousness, and the Politics of Empowerment*, Boston, Mass.: Unwin Hyman.

Combahee River Collective (1982) "A Black Feminist Statement," in Hull, Bell-Scott and Smith (1982): 13.

Cooper, Anna Julia (1892) *A Voice from the South by a Black Woman of the South*, Ohio: Aldine.

Currie, Elliott and Skolnick, Jerome H. (1984) *America's Problems*, Boston, Mass.: Little, Brown.

Davis, Angela (1981) *Women, Race and Class*, New York: Random House.

Dill, Bonnie (1979) "The Dialectics of Black Womanhood," *Signs: Journal of Women in Culture and Society* 3: 543–55.

Echols, Alice (1989) *Daring to Be Bad*, Minneapolis, MN: University of Minnesota Press.

Fernandez-Kelly, Maria Patricia (1983) *For We Are Sold*, Albany, NY: State University of New York Press.

Fields, Barbara (1990) "Slavery, Race and the Ideology in the United States of America," *New Left Review*: 181.

Fuentes, Ann and Ehrenreich, Barbara (1983) *Women in the Global Factory*, Boston, Mass.: South End Press.

Glenn, Evelyn Nakano (1985) "Racial Ethnic Women's Labor: The Intersection of Race, Gender and Class Oppression," *Review of Radical Political Economics* 17 (3): 86–108.

Gordon, David, Edwards, Richard and Reich, Michael (1982) *Segmented Work, Divided Workers*, Cambridge: Cambridge University Press.

Gough, Ian (1981) *The Political Economy of the Welfare State*, New York: Macmillan.

Guy-Sheftall, Beverly and Bell-Scott, Patricia (1989), "Black Women's Studies: A View from the Margin," in C. Pearson, J. S. Touchton and D. C. Shavlik (eds) *Educating the Majority: Women Challenge Tradition in Higher Education* New York: Macmillan

Higginbotham, Evelyn Brooks (1992) "African-American Women's History and the Metalanguage of Race," *Signs: Journal of Women in Culture and Society* 17 (2): 253–4.

hooks, bell (1984) *Feminist Theory: From Margin to Center*, Boston, Mass.: South End Press.

Hull, Gloria T., Bell-Scott, Patricia and Smith, Barbara (1982) *All the Women are White, All the Blacks are Men, But Some of Us are Brave*, Old Westbury, NY: Feminist Press.

Janiewski, Dolores E. (1985) *Sisterhood Denied*, Philadelphia, PA: Temple University Press.

Jones, Jacqueline (1985) *Labor of Love, Labor of Sorrow*, New York: Basic Books.

King, Deborah K. (1988) "Multiple Jeopardy, Multiple Consciousness: The Context of a Black Feminist Ideology," *Signs: Journal of Women in Culture and Society* 14 (1) (August): 42–72.

Leacock, Eleanor and Safa, Helen I. (1986) *Women's Work: Development and the Division of Work by Gender*, South Hadley, Mass.: Bergin & Garvey.

Lorde, Audre (1983) "Age, Race, Class, and Sex: Women Redefining Difference," in *Sister Outsider, Essays and Speeches*, New York: Crossing Press: 114–23.

Mohanty, Chandra (1991) "Introduction: Cartographies of Struggle. Third World Women and the Politics of Feminism," in Chandra Talpade Mohanty, Ann Russo and Lourdes Torres (eds) *Third World Women and the Politics of Feminism*, Bloomington, IN: Indiana University Press.

Nash, June and Fernandez-Kelly, Maria Patricia (1983) *Women, Men and the International Division of Labor*, Albany, NY: State University of New York Press.

Nash, June and Safa, Helen I. (1976) *Sex and Class in Latin America*, New York: Praeger.

Noyelle, Thierry and Stanback, Thomas M. Jr (1983) *The Economic Transformation of American Cities*, Totowa, NY: Rowman & Littlefield.

Omi, Michael and Winant, Howard (1987) *Racial Formation in the United States*, New York: Routledge & Kegan Paul.

Perry, David and Watkins, Alfred (1977) *The Rise of Sunbelt Cities*, Beverly Hills, CA: Sage.

Sacks, Karen (1989) "Toward a Unified Theory of Class, Race, and Gender," *American Ethnologist* 16 (3).

Safa, Helen I. (1983) "Women, Production and Reproduction in Industrial Capitalism," in Nash and Fernandez-Kelly (eds).

Sawers, Larry and Tabb, William K. (1984) *Sunbelt/Snowbelt*, New York: Oxford University Press.

Sidel, Ruth (1986) *Women and Children Last*, New York: Viking Press.

Simms, Margaret C. and Malveaux, Julianne M. (eds) (1986) *Slipping Through the Cracks: The Status of Black Women*, New Brunswick, NJ: Transaction Publishers.

Smith, Barbara (ed.) (1983) *Home Girls: A Black Feminist Anthology*, New York: Kitchen Table, Women of Color Press.

Staples, Robert (1991) "The Political Economy of Black Family life," in *The Black Family*, Belmont, CA: Wadsworth.

Terborg-Penn, Rosalyn (1990) "Historical Treatment of Black Women in the Women's Movement," in Darlene Clark Hine (ed.) *Black Women in United States History*, Brooklyn: Carolson Publishing Co.

Vogel, Lise (1983) *Marxism and the Oppression of Women*, New Brunswick, NJ: Rutgers University Press.

Wallace, Phyllis (1974) *Pathways to Work*, Cambridge, Mass.: MIT Press.

—— (1980) *Black Women in the Labor Force*, Cambridge; Mass.: MIT Press.

White, E. Frances (1984) "Listening to the Voices of Black Feminism," *Radical America*: 7–25.

Williams, Rhonda (1985) "Competition, Class Location and Discrimination: Black Workers and the New Growth Dynamic," unpublished paper presented at the Current Economic Revolution in Black America Conference, University of Texas, Austin, Tex.

Wilson, William J. (1980) *The Declining Significance of Race*, Chicago: University of Chicago Press.

—— (1987) *The Truly Disadvantaged*, Chicago: University of Chicago Press.

Woody, Bette and Malson, Michelene (1984) "In Crisis: Low Income Black Employed Women in the U. S. Workplace," Working Paper no. 131, Wesley College, Center for Research on Women, Wellesley, Mass.

Wright, Eric Olin (1985) *Classes*, London: Verso.

2

RE-EXAMINING PATRIARCHY AS A MODE OF PRODUCTION

The case of Zimbabwe

Cindy Courville

Constant evaluation of our theoretical framework is essential and should not be seen as an act of "disloyalty" to the cause, because failure to do so is likely to increase the risk of the feminist movement withering under the weight of fossilized theories.

(Ramphele, 1990: 8)

It was not until the influence of both radical feminist and Marxist feminist studies that we began to focus on the implications of the relations between the mode of production and patriarchy in the emerging class divisions for African women. In the 1970s theoretical foundations of radical feminism were forged in Kate Millett's book *Sexual Politics*, published in 1971, and Shulamith Firestone's book *Dialectics of Sex*, published in 1972. Firestone and Millett argued that women's oppression is a direct result of gender exploitation and not class exploitation, making women's oppression the most fundamental form of oppression. In contrast the 1980s Marxist feminist writings of Heidi Hartmann, Michele Barrett and Karen Sacks have analyzed women's oppression in terms of "gender relations as and where they may be distinct from, or connected with the processes of production and reproduction understood by historical materialism" (Barrett 1988:9). Prior to these studies, class was conceptualized as gender-free, with the relationship of women to the system left unaddressed.

Much of the work done on women in Africa reflects the difficulty of understanding "patriarchy," "reproduction" and "ideology" within the historical material context of the culturally diverse condition of the continent. The studies of precapitalist and colonial capitalist modes of production, patriarchal relations and class relations by contemporary feminists Jane Parpart, Jeanne Koopman Henn, Sharon Stichter, Christine Obbo, Elizabeth Schmidt, Mamphela Ramphele, Penelope Roberts, Claire Robertson and Nancy Folbre have contributed much to our understanding of African women's oppression from a materialist mode of production analysis. There is a marked tendency to explain women's oppression in terms of autonomous patriarchal structures; and/or in terms of autonomous reproductive structures; and/or in terms of autonomous ideological structures. While "sexual and gender relations" are critical to our understanding of African women's oppression, these relations do not explain the historical limits, changes and differences for the society as a whole (Ramphele, 1990: 9).

The development of a theory to explain African women's oppression is being shaped by the contributions of both feminist and Marxist schools of thought. The "patriarchal mode of production" framework focuses on the "material basis of sexism." This perspective constructs a gender-relations-based class society in which the "class of patriarchs" owns and controls the means of production and a "dependent class" of workers, comprised of wives, unmarried daughters and younger sons, provides the labor. The primary motivation of the patriarchal class is the accumulation of social dependants. Accordingly the structural relations in Africa would be based on a sexual division of labor; production based on women's farming systems; and land ownership based on acceptance of sexual roles and patrilineal and matrilineal inheritance patterns.

While feminist analyses have made great strides in furthering our comprehension of African women's exploitation and oppression, the "patriarchy as a mode of production" framework is plagued by problems of inadequate conceptualization and operationalization of the terms: mode of production, reproduction, social reproduction, relations of production, social formation, division of labor, cultural production of gender, and ideology (Ramphele, 1990: 7). An understanding of these concepts within the context of a Marxist feminist framework requires an examination of "the relations between the organization of sexuality, domestic production, the household and so on, and historical changes in the mode of production" (Barrett, 1988: 9). In a precapitalist mode of production, exploitation "occurs when one section of the population produces a surplus whose use is controlled by another section" (Bottomore, 1983: 157). However, in a capitalist mode of production,

> exploitation takes the form of the extraction of surplus value by the class of industrial capitalists from the working class, but the other exploiting classes or class fractions share in the distribution of surplus value . . . access depends upon the ownership of property . . . capitalist production generates a surplus because capitalists buy workers' labor-power at a wage equal to its value but, being in control of production, extract labor greater than the equivalent of that wage.
>
> (Bottomore, 1983: 157–8)

Oppression is defined as the unjust or excessive exercise of power or

32

authority. The study of African women's exploitation and oppression requires an understanding of the transhistorical nature of patriarchy as an ideology, and how patriarchy as an ideology and *not* as a mode of production shaped the construction and reproduction of African women's oppression.

A re-examination of the framework "patriarchy as a mode of production" is the focus of this chapter in terms of the following questions: (1) What is the precise relationship of patriarchy to the particular mode of production in which it exists? and (2) Is patriarchy trans-historical?

PATRIARCHAL RELATIONS IN PRECAPITALIST ZIMBABWE

In African precapitalist societies ancient slavery and feudalism were the dominant modes of production that featured simple commodity production. While simple commodity production was a method of production, it did not constitute a distinct historical stage of production (Ake, 1981: 61). According to Claude Ake, the main features of precapitalist modes of production were as follows:

(1) The family, immediate or extended, is the basic unit for the organization of production. (2) Land is the essential means of production. (3) Land tends to be communally owned but usually privately "exploited" subject to certain obligations. (4) Commodity exchange among relatively equal petty producers who produce predominantly use-values. (5) Limited production of exchange-values and intermittent contact of some petty producers with wage labor.

(Ake, 1981: 62)

Although Ake has identified the economic determinants of a mode of production, he has failed to explain or even address the role of gender.

Unlike many other world areas, *labor* not *land* was the scarce factor of production in Africa. The extended family was the fundamental production and consumption unit, with women and children forming the economic sub-unit. The sex-gender roles and sexual division of labor identified in the familial structure reflect the patriarchal ideological determinants of the social formation of the family and the state. Women's productive and reproductive capacity made them a social and economic resource which provided men with political leverage. African women were primarily responsible for the economic, social and political reproduction of the household; the bearing of and caring for children; the production, storage and preparation of food. As well, women had exchange-value within the context of marriage, forming alliances between households, clans and nations. The precolonial state recognized

33

the exchange-value of women: they were given as rewards for warriors; they were used to form political alliances; they provided immunity from future wars; and they were given as tribute to elders (Schmidt, 1987: 60–1). The exploitation and oppression of African women were shaped within the context of patriarchy and simple commodity production (Gaidzanwa, 1985: 11).

Within precapitalist Shona and Ndebele economies the dominant classes used patriarchal ideology to control the productive and repro- ductive labor of women across class lines. Women are not always exploited or oppressed, nor have all women experienced the same level of exploitation and/or oppression. But in this case if we are to explain under what conditions and when the exploitation and oppression of women occur, it must be in terms of how "gender" shapes the reciprocal relations of family, society, production and reproduction (Gaidzanwa, 1985: 98–9). By analyzing how precapitalist modes of production shape patriarchal relations, I hope to shed light on how women's exploitation and oppression were structured in terms of the political, economic and social relations of the Shona and Ndebele societies.

Political power in the Shona and Ndebele feudal states rested in the hands of the chief and the elders who were bonded by the structure of social relations of the patriarchal extended family. Under the feudal/ tributary mode of production, land ownership was solely in the hands of the king. As the result of their class and gender position, Shona and Ndebele women of royal lineage possessed formal political power. The power of the aristocracy was based on their control and ownership of the usufruct. African peasant males were granted only a "usufruct," that is, use of and control over the land. The master and serf class structure of feudal Shona and Ndebele societies was based on who owned the land usufruct and not on the sexual division of labor, resulting in the exploitation of peasant labor in general. But while men and women both engaged in simple commodity subsistence agricultural production, peasant women with no controlling rights over the land or the pro- duction and distribution of its products were primarily responsible for its cultivation (Beach, 1984).

The precapitalist Shona society revealed power stratifications and class affiliations shaped by tributary and feudal-based economies. The Shona society was engaged primarily in simple commodity agricultural pro- duction; and secondarily in the herding of livestock, hunting, mining, manufacturing and trade (Schmidt, 1970: 70). The feudal structure of the Shona state codified and legitimized the social reality of the patri- archal familial relations; in particular, the political position of women. The daughters, sisters and paternal aunts of the Shona Mutapa king and the daughters of subordinate kings and lords who owed allegiance to the king were sometimes appointed as rulers over subject territories because of their gender, class and familial position. The king was able to entrust noble women with substantial authority because they were not considered rivals as male counterparts would be (Schmidt, 1987: 52–4).

In contrast, the precapitalist Ndebele society was marked by an intricate class structure based on feudal, military and pastoral economies. The Ndebele were primarily engaged in livestock herding, especially cattle. Agricultural production was limited and men as raiders of grain provided an alternative source of agricultural accumulation. According to Tendai Mutunhu, "[Ndebele] queens maintained small courts in regimental towns to which the king would go on national visits. These courts became an important source of political information about what was happening in the different parts of the domain" (Mutunhu, 1976: 181).

Shona and Ndebele peasant women, because of their class and gender position, lacked formal political power, but they exercised informal means of control, influence and authority within the familial household (Schmidt, 1987: 30). Peasant women exercised influence based on their marital status, their age and their reproductive ability. For instance, a Shona woman who experienced difficulties within her marriage might name her child Takawira, which meant "We have fallen"; or one whose husband was forced from his home might name her child Mutizwa, meaning "the outcast." Through songs, barbed lyrics and the naming of their children Shona women publicly voiced their grievances experienced within the familial household (Schmidt, 1987: 31–4). These methods of influence were culturally recognized forms of customary law that allowed women to voice criticism and grievances. In both Shona and Ndebele societies the practice of brideprice or *lobola* signified the validity of the marriage. It was regarded as compensation to a father for the loss of the daughter and as a means of stabilizing the marriage. Marriage for Ndebele women in the precolonial period was not allowed across class lines (Child, 1968: 57). Ndebele peasant women engaged in limited agricultural production: "because of their lesser contribution to production, their labor power was less needed and hence bridewealth paid for them was smaller than paid for Shona women" (Weinrich, 1979: 15).

With age a woman's status in a patriarchal society increased as she amassed control over her children, her daughters-in-law and her grandchildren. Elder women controlled and supervised the familial household labor, were responsible for the formal education of young children and practiced as midwives, healers and visionaries. They were able to accumulate wealth for their midwife services and received the "cow of motherhood" upon the marriage of a daughter. In the precolonial Shona community elderly and post-menopausal women were endowed with wisdom, long experience, respect, self-esteem and influence in the community. Older women formed groups for the brewing of ritual beer to offer to the spirits and performed singing and dancing to honor the ancestors (Schmidt, 1987: 41–2). Through *ngano* (folktales and historic accounts) they instructed the young as to their appropriate roles and behavior in the community (Schmidt, 1987: 35–7). At the onset of menstruation young Ndebele girls were ceremonially instructed by older women, perhaps their grandmothers, about their role as women (Child, 1968: 53). These elder women possessed spiritual powers. For instance, only female mediums possessed the spirit of Nehanda, a female *mhondoro* (royal ancestor); according to Elizabeth Schmidt Nehanda's spirit is said to "possess both the power of making rain and the power of war." The status and authority of older women and men was elevated in society because they were able to communicate directly with their ancestors.

Strong familial ties existed between mothers and daughters. When a young Shona woman entered into marriage she was considered an outsider among her husband's family. A wife retained her clan identity, with her familial household responsibilities and ceremonial rituals becoming the source for female bonding (Fry, 1976: 22). Women formed work parties to prepare the fields, to plant and to weed while harvesting involved the labor both of men and of women (Lan, 1985: 72). The collective action engaged in by Shona and Ndebele women was a source of their empowerment.

The patriarchal structured nature of Shona and Ndebele societies, in which hierarchical power and authority were based on gender identity, and the precapitalist mode of production, in which class positions were determined by the control of surplus labor, resulted in both oppression and exploitation of peasant women. But despite the oppressive and exploitative nature of precolonial patriarchal societies African women were not powerless victims. They challenged the repressive structures of their societies and contributed to the well-being and preservation of their cultures. Women's responsibilities in the familial household were not only the site of their oppression and exploitation, but also the source of their social standing and their limited protection within the society, and the site and foundation for collective action to express their dissatisfaction and bring about change.

PATRIARCHAL RELATIONS IN COLONIAL CAPITALIST ZIMBABWE

As a result of the forced introduction of colonial capitalism, African precolonial societies experienced a radical transition from simple commodity production to foreign monopoly capitalist commodity production. It is necessary to contextualize the colonial capitalist transformation in Africa. Colonialism was the process of the forced and violent integration of the African continent into the world capitalist system. This process of integration was accomplished through military intervention, monetization of African economies, penetration and domination of imperialist colonial trade, foreign metropolitan investment and foreign infrastructural development (Ake, 1981: 32). The economic relations were characterized by an aggregation of disparate modes of production, dependence on external trade and technology, disarticulation of resources, development of export commodities, market imperfections, and limited indigenous capital to mobilize for investment and development. The social relations of the colonial society were based on disparate aggregations of African and European patriarchies accompanied by racially structured domination and subordination (Ake, 1981: 43–65).

Capitalist commodity production is based on the monopoly of the means of production by the capitalists who are able to exploit the labor of others by forcing them to produce commodities of greater value than the laborers are paid in wages (Ake, 1981: 15–16). In Europe, capitalism as a mode of production reshaped the class and gender structure of the societies. European political relations featured a centralization of bourgeois power, liberty, equality, fraternity and popular rule based on universal suffrage. Economic relations were revolutionized by industrial production and the development of a wage-based working class. Social relations were shaped by the ideology of patriarchy which institutionalized the power of the male in the nuclear family.

But in Africa colonial capitalism did not create the same political, economic and social divisions. Based on the policy of indirect rule, the colonial state controlled and supervised the separate political and economic development of the colonizer and the underdevelopment of the colonized (Palley, 1966: 216). Under the dominance of colonial capitalism, the social relations of the African extended family were thrown into a state of flux and the dominance of kinship and lineage within precolonial African societies was distorted by: the individualization of land holdings; the growth of large-scale capital farms; the alienation of land from peasants to capitalist farms; and the growth of agricultural wage labor. The value of traditional African women's labor was changed as the result of colonial capitalism's separation of the workplace from the family. The state and industrial enterprises restricted the majority of urban wage jobs to African men.

The colonial state sanctioned and institutionalized the political and legal status of African women as minors and/or dependants subject to male control (Obbo, 1980: 21–3). In section 14 of the charter granted to the British South African Company the legal status of African women was first set forth. Hence:

[in] the administration of justice to the said peoples or inhabitants, careful regard shall always be had to customs and laws of the class or tribe or nation to which parties belong, especially with regard to the holding, possession, transfer and disposition of land and goods, testate and intestate succession thereto and marriage, divorce, legitimacy and other rights of property and personal rights, but subject to British law.

(Kazembe, 1986: 381)

Women's oppression was further institutionalized with the Native Marriage Ordinance which reaffirmed customary law by relegating a woman to the status of minor under the control of her father, guardians, or husband. By 1916 African women's sexuality was legally subjected to legislative control under the Native Adultery Punishment Ordinance making adultery a criminal offense in which women were the principal offenders (Schmidt, 1987: 742–3).

Some social aspects of African patriarchy were repugnant to European culture. European missionaries and colonial administrators intervened against what they considered excessive African patriarchal oppression: the killing of widows, the use of women and children as collateral for debt, and child marriage. The Marriage Ordinance of 1901 outlawed the custom of contracting prearranged marriage of children (CNC s138/47, "Pledging of Children: Native Marriage Ordinance"). Missionaries provided safe havens for young African women and girls who rejected parental opposition to their entering a religious order or choosing a husband. These actions were the part of the positive consequences of the colonization process of African women.

However, when conflicts arose between the need to keep women working both on the farms and export crops and the desire of the state or church to challenge what was considered repugnant in terms of African patriarchal rule, African patriarchal power over women was upheld in the interest of colonial profit (Weinrich, 1979: 120). Both the state and the church regarded African females as a threat to the recruitment of African labor. Colonial authorities recognized the significance of patriarchal power in mobilizing the labor of women and children and the state maintained the right of African patriarchs to mobilize "family labor" and control land and crop production. The state and church's recognition of only monogamous Christian marriages and the condemnation of polygynous African marriages was important, not for the protection of the well-being of women, but for the reproduction of the labor force and the reproduction of European cultural norms and values.

The economic infrastructure of the colonial economy was divided along the lines of rural and urban production. This resulted in the geographical separation of the family, with wage-earning males concentrated in the urban areas, a minority of women engaged in wage earning in the urban areas, and the majority of females engaged in subsistence production relegated to the rural sectors. African women's access to wage labor primarily in the urban areas was limited to domestic work, beer brewing, hawking, prostitution and childminding. Because they were engaged in wage labor in the informal sector or the second economy, women in the urban sectors challenged their husbands' control over the familial household (Weinrich, 1979: 55).

The forced implementation of the colonial capitalist structure of production had far-reaching effects on the labor time of both men and women and on the social relations of production between them. The production of export crops altered the sexual division of labor and significantly increased the total labor of the majority of women as members of the rural household. Women not only took up the slack in food production, but also helped with the harvesting and processing of new colonial crops (Ramphele, 1990: 13). Rural women's access to wage labor jobs was limited to seasonal work: crop processing, bagging or shelling (Weinrich, 1979: 55). In the rural areas many women felt that they had no option but to accept their husbands' control, because under both traditional law and colonial law, they were denied ownership and control of the land and the goods they produced. It was the unpaid labor of African rural women and children which subsidized the colonial wage. The colonial state utilized both household structure and familial ideology to structure women's oppression (Barrett, 1988: 158).

While African women escaped from some of the harsher elements of African patriarchal oppression, they were still subjected to the class, gender and racial exploitation and oppression of the colonial capitalist patriarchal society (Weinrich, 1979: 120–2). The racist and sexist attitudes of colonial administrators and missionaries added another level of exploitation and oppression to their colonial experience. African women were stereotyped as lazy, immoral, indolent, savage, uncivilized, flighty, moody, feather-headed and depraved (NAZ, CNC S 138/150). African women's traditional roles of influence as healers, spirit mediums, midwives and brewers of ritual beer were undermined by both state and church. African women were either denied access or given very limited access to education both by African and European patriarchs.

Under colonialism many African women were raped into submission, were exploited as laborers, and endured subhuman status as slaves as a result of colonial European and African patriarchal oppression and capitalist exploitation. As women, they were exploited and oppressed because of their racial identity by both European males and females. African women were afforded no formal legal protection from being raped by white males. The Purity League was formed in 1911 by whites to prevent illicit intercourse between white males and African females (MacDonald, 1970: 170–1). In the 1930s European women lobbied for the legislation that would prevent African women from being employed as domestic servants because they feared the "yellow peril" – intercourse between European males and African females. These actions undertaken by white women were designed only to protect white society. There was no recognition of the power or influence of African women based on their class or gender identity. Neither the state nor the church was concerned with the protection of African women from exploitation and oppression. Instead, both were engaged in the restructuring of exploitation and oppression under the colonial capitalist state.

African women were constantly challenging the dual exploitation and oppression they experienced under both African and colonial patriarchal systems. As the level of exploitation and oppression increased in the rural sector, some women engaged in profitable production and sale of beer, vegetables and grain to supplement the low wages of males. Many women were unable to support themselves and their families solely on the basis of agricultural production because of the lack of fertile or well-watered land. In an effort to survive many women sought refuge in the towns, mining centers and commercial farms. This exodus of women from the villages meant the loss of productive labor power for African elders. For the colonial authorities an influx of African women into these urban and industrial areas meant a loss of subsistence production which subsidized low male wages. These actions undertaken by African women threatened the stability of African patriarchal authority and power as well as economic stability of the colonial state.

The exploitation and oppression experienced by African women were shaped by the coexistence of dual political systems, dual patriarchal systems and dual modes of production. The nature of patriarchal oppression of African women changed with the forced incorporation of African precapitalist societies into the colonial capitalist mode of production.

THE TRANSHISTORICAL NATURE OF PATRIARCHY IN ZIMBABWE

The transhistorical nature of patriarchy is based on the conceptualization of patriarchy as an ideology, and the materiality of patriarchal relations as determined by the mode of production. Patriarchy as an ideology is "the site for the construction and reproduction of women's oppression" in the political, economic and social structures of society (Barrett, 1988: 253). According to Zillah Eisenstein:

A patriarchal culture is carried over from one historical period to

40

another to protect the sexual hierarchy of society; the sexual division of society is based on real differences that have accrued from years of ideological pressure. Material conditions define necessary ideologies, and ideologies in their turn have impact on reality and alter reality

(Eisenstein, 1979: 24–5)

It is critical not to define or situate women's exploitation and oppression only at the level of ideology, because it does not explain how it is constructed historically in relation to production, and culturally bound. Patriarchal ideology constructs the image women are supposed to conform to within society. Ideology cannot be disassociated from the economic relations if we are to explain the patriarchal exploitation and oppression of African women (Althusser, 1971: 164).

The construction of the social reality of precapitalist Shona and Ndebele women in society took place in a plurality of institutions: the family apparatus, the cultural apparatus and the political apparatus. The extended family was the site for the reproduction of the social construction of reality; it was also the primary unit for the reproduction of production (Barrett, 1988: 205). Familial ideology limited women's access to control of land and reinforced the inferiority and inequality of women.

Within the precapitalist gender-based familial household, women were designated as producers and reproducers in the family. The institutionalization of gender differences was achieved through the historical maintenance of Shona and Ndebele precapitalist cultural practices such as *lobola* (brideprice), virginity, polygynous marriage, and patrilineal and matrilineal inheritance. These culturally bound practices reinforced the division of labor on the basis of family, sex and age.

The construction of gender identity does not take place exclusively within familial relations. The state was the site for the reproduction of the material reality of familial and cultural relations (Althusser, 1971: 150). The African precapitalist state institutionalized the social relations of patriarchy to control of labor power and production, legitimizing the cultural and familial exploitation and oppression of men and women (Barrett, 1988: 229).

The introduction of the colonial capitalist mode of production did not necessitate the dismantlement of Shona and Ndebele patriarchal relations, but "the oppression of women, although not a functional prerequisite of capitalism . . . acquired a material basis in the relations of production and reproduction of capitalism" (Barrett, 1988: 249). Patriarchal relations do not determine the material basis of the relations of production and reproduction. What is revealed here is that an examination of only the patriarchal relations of both precapitalist and colonial capitalist societies will not explain how women's exploitation and oppression were shaped by the historical limits, changes and differences of these societies. The cultural, familial and political reality of African women was restructured with the introduction of commodity production based on monopoly of the means of production, racist ideology, and a policy of separate political and economic development. Under colonial capitalism African women experienced three forms of exploitation based on African women's position in production, African women's position in the family and African women's racial position in colonial society.

There is still much work to be done in terms of the problems of contextualization, conceptualization and operationalization of feminist and Marxist frameworks in terms of understanding the similarities and differences in the historical construction and reproduction of post-colonial African women's exploitation and oppression. The study of this must be grounded in the historical analysis of the relations of economic organization of the household, familial ideology, the educational system, the operations of the state, the cultural processes, the division of labor and the relations of production in society.

BIBLIOGRAPHY

Ake, Claude (1981) *A Political Economy of Africa*, New York: Longman.

Althusser, Louis (1971) *Lenin and Philosophy and Other Essays*, New York: Monthly Review Press.

Barrett, Michele (1988) *Women's Oppression Today*, London: Verso.

Beach, D. N. (1984) *Zimbabwe Before 1900*, Gweru: Mambo Press.

Bottomore, Tom (ed.) (1983) *A Dictionary of Marxist Thought*, Cambridge, Mass.: Harvard University Press.

Child, Harold (1968) *The History of the amaNdebele*, Ministry of Internal Affairs, Government of Rhodesia.

Eisenstein, Zillah (ed.) (1979) *Capitalist Patriarchy and the Case for Socialist Feminism*, New York: Monthly Review Press.

Fry, Peter (1976) *Spirits of Protest: Spirit Mediums and the Articulation of Consensus Among the Zezuru of Southern Rhodesia (Zimbabwe)*, Cambridge: Cambridge University Press.

Gaidzanwa, Rudo B. (1985) *Images of Women in Zimbabwean Literature*, Harare: College Press.

Kazembe, Joyce L. (1986) "The Women's Issue," in Ibbo Mandaza (ed.) *Zimbabwe: The Political Economy of Transition*, Daker: CODESRIA.

Lan, David (1985) *Guns and Rain: Guerrillas and Spirit Mediums in Zimbabwe*, Harare: Zimbabwe Publishing House.

MacDonald, Sheila (1970) *Sally in Rhodesia*, London/Bulawayo: Books of Rhodesia.

Mutunhu, Tendai (1976) "The Matabele Nation: The Dynamic Sociopolitical and Military Development of an African State, 1840–1893," *Journal of African Studies* 3: 165–82.

Obbo, Christine (1980) *African Women: Their Struggle r Economic Independence*, London: Zed Press.

Palley, Claire (1966) *The Constitutional History and Law of Southern Rhodesia 1888–1965*, London: Oxford University Press.

Ramphele, Mamphela (1990) "Do Women Help Perpetuate Sexism? A Bird's Eye View from South Africa," *Africa Today* 37 (1): 7–17.

Schmidt, Elizabeth Suzann (1987) "Ideology, Economics, and the Role of Shona Women in Southern Rhodesia, 1850–1939," PhD dissertation, University of Wisconsin–Madison.

Weinrich, A. K. H. (1979) *Women and Racial Discrimination in Rhodesia*, Paris: UNESCO.

Zimbabwe Women's Bureau (n.d. [*c.* 1980]) *Black Women in Zimbabwe*, Zimbabwe: Zimbabwe Women's Bureau.

Government Documents

CNC s138/47, Acting Chief Commissioner, Salisbury to Department, "Pledging of Children: Native Marriage Ordinance."

NAZ, CNC S 138/150 February 23, 1954.

3

MOTHERING
A possible Black feminist link to social transformation?

Stanlie M. James

The death of my grandmother in 1988 served to reunite physically and emotionally all her living children, grandchildren, some of her great-grandchildren, and a host of other biological and fictive kin. My 9-year-old daughter who was trying to adjust to our recent move from Colorado to Wisconsin was nearly overwhelmed by the trauma of her great-grandmother's death. Since she seemed to be unable to "hear" what I was trying to say to her about these critical moments in her young life, it became apparent that a need existed for someone else to step in to provide a listening ear as well as the wisdom so necessary for her support as she attempted (successfully) to navigate through these crises.

The woman who so graciously accepted the role of "othermother" for my child had been a "neglected child" – although neither term was used in those days. "Othermothered" by my grandmother, she had become an informally adopted member of our network of fictive kin.[1] It had been my grandmother's simple belief that all children must be fed, clothed and sent to school. If for some reason their biological parents were unable or unwilling to discharge these obligations, then it was incumbent upon some other member of the community to accept that responsibility. This fictive kin who stepped in to counsel my daughter was upholding a family tradition that had been modeled by my grandmother some fifty years before.

The acceptance of responsibility for the welfare of non-blood related children in their community shown by my grandmother and her fictive daughter is hardly unique to the African-American[2] community. While western conceptualizations of mothering have often been limited to the activities of females with their biological offsprings,[3] mothering within the Afro-American community and throughout the Black diaspora can be viewed as a form of cultural work or what Bernice Johnson Reagon calls "the entire way a community organizes to nurture itself and future generations" (Reagon, 1989: 167–80). Thus my grandmother and her

44

fictive daughter were upholding a tradition which enlarges upon limited conceptualizations of mothering.

This chapter will examine Afro-American and West African concepts of othermothering and its importance to the survival of the Black community. My thesis is that these forms of mothering, which have their roots in a traditional African world-view, may serve as an important Black feminist link to the development of new models for social transformation in the twenty-first century.

Othermothers can be defined as those who assist blood mothers in the responsibilities of child care for short- to long-term periods, in informal or formal arrangements. They can be, but are not confined to, such blood relatives as grandmothers, sisters, aunts, cousins or supportive fictive kin. They not only serve to relieve some of the stress that can develop in the intimate daily relationships of mothers and daughters but they can also provide multiple role models for children (Troester, 1984; Collins, 1987). This concept of othermothering which has its roots in the traditional African world-view and can be traced through the institution of slavery, developed in response to an evergrowing need to share the responsibility for child nurturance.

In the traditional African world-view as in the world-views of indigenous peoples around the globe, a very high value is placed on reproduction. As John Mbiti has argued, reproduction is perceived as a means of strengthening the human group and ensuring the survival of life. It is, in fact, equated with the life force itself. The status of women – whose activities are centered around reproduction, the physical and emotional nurturance of children, and household maintenance – is enhanced by the supreme symbolic link attached to them and their crucial role in reproduction. Thus within the indigenous African context, mothering is highly regarded. It incorporates the symbolism of creativity and continuity, and as such forms an integral aspect of women's identity (Mbiti, 1969).

While mothering does indeed incorporate a nurturing component for one's biological offspring, it is also not uncommon for African women to undertake nurturing responsibilities for children other than their immediate offspring (Oppong, 1973). For example, women in traditionally polygynous relationships, who were compatible with each other, often shared the care of all children within the household so that they could more easily and efficiently discharge their household maintenance responsibilities. This was especially true in many traditional West African societies where the nurturing aspect of the mothering role also incorporated economic productivity (Henn in Hay and Stichter, 1984; Cutrufelli, 1983; Njoku, 1980; Smock in Giele and Chapman, 1977).

The role of women in the former Gold Coast or what is now called Ghana is instructive in this regard. At the time of colonization, the Gold

Coast was comprised of some 200 separate political units of which the most important were the Akan, Ewe, Ga and the "Northern." Throughout the region women were expected to marry and produce children for the survival of the lineage. As wives and mothers, they were responsible for the physical and emotional nurturance of children. They were also responsible for maintaining the household. In order to discharge these responsibilities, including providing a share of the economic basis for household maintenance, women in the Gold Coast were economically active in their own right – not merely as auxiliaries to their husbands. Those who were farmers, cultivated their own plots of land and although men were responsible for clearing all the land, women were not reciprocally obligated to cultivate the crops on men's plots. Women planted, weeded and harvested nonstaple foodstuffs such as vegetables. They fed their families, sold any remaining surplus and used the profits in ways they deemed necessary. Other women who lived on the coast and were married to fishermen undertook the preservation of fish through smoking and then bartered or sold the catch. Still others produced handicrafts and many engaged in trading. Regardless of their vocations or class positions, women were expected to provide a share of the household and children's expenses out of their financial profits (Smock, 1977; Callaway, 1976; Pellow and Chazan, 1986).[4]

In addition to patterns of shared child care in polygynous households, childcare responsibilities were also diffused through the common African practice of fostering children. African communal societies were characterized by high degrees of interdependence and the belief that individual self-development and personal fulfillment were dependent upon the well-being of all members of the community. Fostering children was one means of promoting these communal values and ensuring the likelihood of co-operative interaction. Unlike contemporary American fostered children, African fostered children were usually not orphans nor were their parents unwilling or unable to care for them. Fostering was a means of minimizing what was often viewed as a dysfunctional emphasis on individualism within a communal setting. It was a means of diffusing children's primary relationships to larger numbers of people within the extended family and the community. It was also a means of relieving individual women of some of the responsibilities involved with nurturing and child care.

Although enslaved West Africans were obviously unable to replicate traditional family and communal patterns and values in the new world, some traditions, including the emphasis on the interconnectedness and interdependence of communities, appear to have been adapted within the enslaved communities as a means of coping with slavery's highly destructive system of exploitation and oppression (Gutman, 1976).

Defined and treated as chattels, enslaved African-Americans were not entitled to the right to establish families in either the westernized or African sense. The public/private dichotomy of gendered activities so often characteristic of western societies was neither encouraged nor supported within enslaved African-American families. While enslaved women were largely responsible for child care and such household maintenance chores as cooking and cleaning in the cabins of the slave quarters, both enslaved males and females were expected to be economically productive for their "owners"[5] (Davis, 1981, 1983) with women being constrained to toil alongside men in cruel parodies of equal opportunity employment.

Marriage between enslaved African-Americans usually existed at the whim of the master and could be severely damaged, if not effectively destroyed, through the sale of a partner. Women were also subjected to sadistic forms of sexual harassment and appropriation, such as rape by white males. In the meantime, African-American males were not allowed to protect or provide for their families in the ways in which white males were expected to. Thus enslaved families were often characterized by high degrees of instability. Whatever stability did exist often developed out of a mother's relationship to her children rather than from her relationship to her husband. In other words, the nurturance provided for enslaved children was primarily provided by already over-burdened enslaved women (White, 1985; Jones, 1986).

If enslaved children were orphaned through the death or sale of their parents, other women within the quarters often assumed the additional responsibility for their care. Thus the African tradition of fostering was adapted to meet the needs of the enslaved community in the USA (Gutman, 1976; Sudarkasa, 1988) and has since become known as other-mothering. This practice of othermothering continues to this day to play a critical role in the African-American community.

African-American patterns of mothering and othermothering have in turn stimulated what Patricia Hill Collins refers to as "a more generalized ethic of care where Black women feel accountable to all the Black community's children . . . [and treat them] as if they were members of their own families" (Collins, 1987: 5). Sometimes it is recognized that many people within a community are experiencing the same or similar problems which may only be responsive to collective action. At that point, women who may have informally "apprenticed" as othermothers might deem it necessary to assume the role of "community other-mother"[6] to remedy the situation.

The status of community othermother is bestowed upon women who are often over 40 years of age, not only because over time they have exhibited the ethic of care so critical to the survival and well-being of their communities, but also because they have lived long enough to have a sense of the community's tradition and culture.[7] Typically, the woman's behavior as a mother and/or othermother has been exemplary and she is considered to be wise. Commanding a powerful position of respect as a result of these characteristics, the community othermother was/is able successfully to critique the behavior of individual members of the community and to provide them with directions on appropriate behavior(s). Based upon her knowledge and her respected position, a community othermother is also in a position to provide analyses and/or critiques of conditions or situations that may affect the well-being of her community. Whenever necessary, she serves as a catalyst in the development and implementation of strategies designed to remedy these harmful conditions.

It should be noted that othermothering does have the potential for controversy because community othermothers do occupy political space within a community. If for some reason the community is not in agreement about the role, possibilities and privileges of othermothers, tension may arise as that space is contested, and negotiations may be necessary to accommodate both sides. These kinds of activities call into question popular notions of African-American women as profoundly powerless victims – for a number of reasons a troubling characterization which will be examined below.

African-American mothers, othermothers and community othermothers have frequently labored in obscurity, although some, including Ida B. Wells, Mary McLeod Bethune, Septima Clark and Fannie Lou Hamer, have achieved a certain degree of national recognition. Among those community othermothers who have not received the attention they deserve are Daisy Bates, who led the struggle to integrate the public schools of Little Rock, Arkansas in the mid-1950s, and Ella Baker, a community organizer who was active in several major civil rights organizations for over thirty years. The lives of each of these women illustrate how one's resources can be utilized to intervene in situations in a manner that fosters change.

Daisy Bates and her husband L. C. Bates were owners and publishers of the weekly newspaper the *State Press*. They were also prominent and active members of the National Association for the Advancement of Colored People (NAACP). The leadership role assumed by Daisy Bates especially resonates with a strong mothering or nurturing theme. The Bates home became the daily meeting place for the Little Rock Nine – the Black teenagers chosen to integrate Little Rock's Central High School. In the morning parents brought their children to the Bates home so that they could prepare to face the mobs that surrounded Central High School during the early part of the school year and the dangerous hostile environment that existed within the school throughout the year. Afterwards, the children would return to her home to discuss the day's events, develop coping strategies, do their homework and eat a snack. Thus the Bates home became a haven in which the psychological and emotional nurturance of the children, so critical to their survival and to the success of the struggle, could occur in safety. Later the children's parents would retrieve them from the Bates home only to return them the next day to repeat the process.

As a result of these activities, both Daisy and L. C. Bates were subjected to a variety of terroristic harassment. Daisy Bates regularly received threatening phone calls; rocks and bombs were hurled through their windows; shots were fired at their home; and the Ku-Klux-Klan burned crosses in their yard. Daisy Bates was arrested three times, and she and her husband witnessed the demise of their newspaper as a result of a financial boycott by their advertisers (Bates, 1962).

Despite these efforts to silence her, Bates never lost her belief in the legitimacy of the struggle. In *The Long Shadow of Little Rock* Bates writes:

> L. C. and I have committed our lives to this crusade [for equality]. Together we continue to take an active part in the fight for the emancipation of the Negro in the South. . . . Together we look to the time when the citizens of this land will erase the shame of Little Rock, when the Constitution of the United State will embrace every man regardless of his color, when brotherhood will be more than a mere topic for an annual church sermon.
>
> (Bates, 1962: 225)

Ella Baker serves as the second example of a person who assumed the roles of othermother and community othermother. Baker's activism, like that of many othermothers and community othermothers, developed out of her childhood socialization to accept responsibility for the "uplift of the race" through care of other less fortunate individuals within the family and the community. Thus as an adult she was prepared to assume the role of othermother when the need arose for her to adopt and raise a niece – although she had no biological children of her own.

Baker's role as a community othermother began in 1938 when she joined the NAACP and began traveling throughout the South to recruit membership – an extremely dangerous undertaking at the time. Later she served as a kind of political midwife at the births of the Southern Christian Leadership Conference (SCLC) and the Student Nonviolent Coordinating Committee (SNCC) in the 1950s and 1960s. It was Baker who insisted that the spirit and momentum of the Montgomery Bus Boycott could not be allowed to dissipate. She along with others including Bayard Rustin and Stanley Levison encouraged Martin Luther King to establish SCLC. Baker went on to serve (reluctantly) as its first acting director while its board searched for a male minister to become the organization's administrator. She later agreed to return to that position

– with a cut in pay – when the male who was eventually hired was unable to discharge his duties in a satisfactory manner.

Baker's willingness to return to this position illustrates the kind of gender-based tension that could arise between community othermothers and their community. Although she recognized the inherent patriarchy of the SCLC as exemplified by the pay cut, she was willing to accommodate them so long as she was able to "keep her eyes on the prize" (to paraphrase an old Negro spiritual).

Galvanized by the spread of the sit-in movement across the South in the early 1960s, Baker encouraged students in a number of ways that included getting SCLC to support a conference for student activists which eventually led to the establishment of SNCC. As she had done for SCLC, Baker went to work with SNCC to help them establish their organization. She was also one of the guiding forces behind the emergence of the Mississippi Freedom Democratic Party (MFDP) – an organization which would later challenge Lyndon Johnson and the Democratic Party. That challenge wrought fundamental changes in Democratic party rules on such critical issues as the delegate selection process. These efforts to foster inclusion of diverse voices would eventually result in the capacity of Jesse Jackson to mount a viable campaign for the Democratic nomination for the presidency.

It is only recently that Baker's story has been retrieved from history, and from that retrieval process a picture of Baker is emerging as "a wise woman, an elder, a calming force who could bring clarity to issues and [who] was respected"[8] (Payne, 1989; Cantarow, 1980).

Baker was especially cognizant of the necessity to develop effective models for social change with the available resources. Suspicious of dependency on individual forms of charismatic leadership, Baker envisioned the development of alternative forms of leadership that were group centered. Thus her energies were focused on devising strategies that would enhance people's self-sufficiency while at the same time developing the kind of leaders who were skillful in dealing "nondestructively with their own need for recognition" (Payne, 1989). Long years of experience in these various social change organizations as a community organizer convinced Baker that social change resulted from tedious, painstaking work and was best accomplished from within the community by members of the community. Thus her leadership/teaching style, which she characterized as facilitative, was designed to nurture individual growth and empower community people to assume responsibility for the mundane tasks that would foster social change (Payne, 1989; Cantarow, 1980).

African-American history has been most often characterized by two major themes – the struggle to survive at the margin of society under hostile conditions, and the related struggle to change society into a more hospitable and inclusive environment. These struggles have been waged with minimal access to the usual resources generally associated with traditional concepts of power such as control of the distribution of society's resources, and command of its wealth, armed forces and mass media. At the same time, as previously mentioned, African-American women have often been characterized as profoundly powerless victims of the multiple oppression of gender, race and class. However, as Mamphela Ramphele has noted, the victim image is "ultimately disempowering . . . because it denies human agency in history which is inherent in the very essence of our humanity." She goes on to warn that "Projecting people as hapless victims patronizes and paralyses them [and it] promotes the image of the oppressor as 'invincible' in relation to their own 'powerlessness'" (Ramphele, 1990: 14).

Power has frequently been described vaguely as something very real, possessed by an individual or group, who may or may not choose to use it (Barnes, 1988: 59). It has also been assumed that the possession of power by one actor or agent either diminishes or precludes its possession by another (Ramphele, 1990: 14). Ramphele challenges this position and argues that power should be perceived as the "use of resources of whatever kind to secure outcomes, power then becomes an element of action, and refers to a range of interventions of which an agent is capable" (ibid.).

Because of their lack of access to traditional sources of power, especially those mentioned above, African-Americans have had to rely on their abilities to develop power out of nontraditional resources and forms of intervention. Historically othermothering and community othermothering have been critical to the survival of Black communities. Not only have forms of othermothering nurtured and sustained African-American communities, but they were also powerful nontraditional resources utilized to intervene creatively in situations or conditions that threatened the survival of the community. Thus they exemplify Ramphele's conceptualization of power as a range of interventions that achieve outcome and should be viewed as potentially effective agencies for social transformation.

Contemporary African-American communities must continue to struggle around the dual themes of survival and social change while also confronting such critical problems as drug addiction, gang-related violence, the AIDS epidemic, rising numbers of hate crimes, depression and unemployment, and concerted attacks on hard-won civil rights legislation and affirmative action policies. These and other problems not only threaten the survival of the African-American community in the twenty-first century, but may also foster disempowering feelings of impotence.

The development of an understanding of othermothering and community othermothering is useful in a number of ways. First it is helpful

51

in dispelling feelings of impotence through illustrating historical non-traditional patterns of empowerment for Black women. Second through examining the activism of such women as Daisy Bates and Ella Baker emphasis is placed on the conceptualization of power as a verb as opposed to a noun. Finally the abilities to analyze, critique and strategize around issues developed through community othermothering are critical resources that can and should be creatively utilized to address contemporary needs. This in turn becomes what R. J. B. Walker refers to as a "transformative assault . . . that carr[ies] the possibility of reconstructing the conditions for a decent life from the bottom up" (Walker, 1988: 8).

NOTES

1 Carol B. Stack describes fictive kin as friends who assume the responsibilities of kinsmen and are given a fictive kin term. See Stack, 1974: 60.
2 The terms African-American, Afro-American and Black American will be used interchangeably throughout this chapter.
3 For example, Nancy Chodorow has defined mothering as tasks performed primarily by biological mothers within a nuclear family setting, which include the bearing, nurturing and socializing of children. She argues that the mothering role bears a major burden for the production and reproduction of dichotomous gender differences, and also serves to perpetuate and reinforce the relative powerlessness of women within society. See Chodorow, 1978: 31.
4 It is interesting to note that after a woman had discharged her responsibilities for the maintenance of her family any remaining profits belonged to her, to do with as she pleased – without accounting to her husband.
5 In "Reflections on the Black Women's Role in the Community of Slaves" Angela Davis has pointed out that enslaved women were expected to be not only economically productive but reproductive as well. See Davis, 1981: 2–15.
6 For a discussion of these various forms of mothering see, for example, the articles by Rosalie Riegle Troester (1984) and Gloria Joseph (1984) in *SAGE: A Scholarly Journal of Black Women*. See also Patricia Hill Collins, 1987 and 1990.
7 For an important discussion on a parallel conceptualization to community othermothering see Bernice Johnson Reagon, 1989: 167–80.
8 Telephone interview by the author with Zoharah Simmons (formerly Gwen Robinson), a Mississippi Project Director in SNCC during the 1960s, May 22, 1988, Philadelphia, PA.

BIBLIOGRAPHY

Barnes, B. (1988) *The Nature of Power*, Cambridge, UK: Polity Press.
Bates, D. (1962) *The Long Shadow of Little Rock: A Memoir*, New York: David McKay.
Callaway, B. J. (1976) "Women in Ghana," in L. B. Iglitzin and R. Ross (eds) *Women in the World: A Comparative Study*, Santa Barbara, CA: Clio Press.
Cantarow, E. with O'Malley, S. G. and Strom, S. H. (1980) *Moving the Mountain: Women Working for Social Change*, Old Westbury, NY: Feminist Press.
Chodorow, N. (1978) *The Reproduction of Mothering: Psychoanalysis and the Sociology*

of Gender, Berkeley, CA: University of California Press.

Collins, P. H. (1986) "Learning from the Outsider Within: The Sociological Significance of Black Feminist Thought," *Social Problems* 33 (6) (December): 14–32.

―――― (1987) "The Meaning of Motherhood in Black Culture and Black Mother/Daughter Relationships," *SAGE: A Scholarly Journal on Black Women* IV (2): 2–10.

―――― (1990) *Black Feminist Thought: Knowledge, Consciousness, and the Politics of Empowerment*, Boston, Mass.: Unwin Hyman.

Cutrufelli, M. R. (1983) *Women of Africa: Roots of Oppression*, London: Zed Press.

Davis, A. (1981) "Reflections on the Black Women's Role in the Community of Slaves," *The Black Scholar* 12 (6) (November–December): 2–15.

―――― (1983) *Women, Race and Class*, New York: Vintage Books.

Gutman, H. G. (1976) *The Black Family in Slavery and Freedom: 1750–1925*, New York: Vintage Books.

Henn, J. K. (1984) "Women in Rural Economy: Past, Present and Future," in M. J. Hay and S. K. Stichter (eds) *African Women South of the Sahara*, London: Longman.

Jones, J. (1986) *Labor of Love, Labor of Sorrow: Black Women, Work and the Family, from Slavery to the Present*, New York: Vintage Books.

Joseph, G. I. (1984) "Mothers and Daughters: Traditional and New Perspectives," *SAGE: A Scholarly Journal on Black Women* I (2) (Fall): 17–21.

Joseph, G. I. and Lewis, J. (1981) *Common Differences: Conflicts in Black and White Feminist Perspectives*, Boston, Mass.: South End Press.

Mbiti, J. (1969) *African Religions and Philosophies*, New York: Anchor Press.

Njoku, J. E. E. (1980) *The World of the African Woman*, Metuchen, NJ: Scarecrow Press.

Oppong, C. (1973) *Growing Up in Dagbon*, Tema, Ghana: Ghana Publishing Corporation.

Payne, C. (1989) "Ella Baker and Models of Social Change," *Signs: Journal of Women in Culture and Society* 14 (Summer): 885–99.

Pellow, D. and Chazan, N. (1986) *Ghana, Coping with Uncertainty*, Boulder, CO: Westview Press.

Ramphele, M. (1990) "Are Women Not Part of the Problem Perpetuating Sexism? – A Bird's Eye View from South Africa," *Africa Today* 37 (Spring): 7–17.

Reagon, B. J. (1989) "African Diaspora: The Making of Cultural Workers," in R. Terborg-Penn, S. Harley and A. B. Rushing (eds) *Women in Africa and the African Diaspora*, Washington, DC: Howard University Press: 167–80.

Smock, A. C. (1977) "Ghana: From Autonomy to Subordination", in J. Z. Giele, and Chapman (eds) *Women: Roles and Status in Eight Countries*, New York: John Wiley: 175–216.

Stack, C. B. (1974) *All Our Kin: Strategies for Survival in a Black Community*, New York: Harper & Row.

Sudarkasa, N. (1988) "Interpreting the African Heritage in Afro-American Family Organization," in H. P. MacAdoo (ed.) *Black Families*, 2nd edn, Newbury Park, CA: Sage: 27–43.

―――― (1989) "The Status of Women in Indigenous African Societies," in R. Terborg-Penn, S. Harley and A. B. Rushing (eds) *Women in Africa and the African Diaspora*, Washington, DC: Howard University Press: 25–41.

Troester, R. R. (1984) "Turbulence and Tenderness: Mothers, Daughters, and 'Othermothers' in Paule Marshall's *Brown Girl, Brownstones*," in *SAGE: A*

Scholarly Journal on Black Women I (2) (Fall): 13–17.

Walker, R. B. J. (1988) *One World, Many Worlds: Struggles for a Just World Peace*, Boulder, CO: Lynne Rienner.

White, D. G. (1985) *Ar'n't I a Woman? Female Slaves in the Plantation South*, New York: W. W. Norton.

4

EXPLORING THE WPA NARRATIVES

Finding the voices of Black women and men

Melvina Johnson Young

PREFACE

I was born in 1963 and raised in the segregated South. The first words that I learned to read were "colored" and "whites only." But, long after these words disappeared from over doorways of restaurants, movie houses, restrooms, etc., I, even as a small Black child, knew that I was still not to step inside those doors. The attitudes of the white people of my small rural hometown were more than enough to keep us out even if the Federal government said that we were equal and free to do as we pleased.

Life in the small cotton-farming community was pleasant enough as long as we stayed in our part of town and didn't get "out of our places" as Negroes. We did not. I grew up watching young white children, younger than myself, ordering my grandparents about and calling them by their first names. This last was the epitome of disrespect in Black culture. But my grandparents simply laughed it off behind the white folks' backs, explaining that white children were quite ill-bred. They told us not to worry about it. They also warned us to never try it or we would live to regret it. It was simply axiomatic of Black life, especially in the South, that you did not reveal your true self to white people because if they did not like what they saw, they had a very real power to harm you.

Therefore, when I began to read the Work Progress Administration (WPA) ex-slave interviews, I realized that many of them sounded the way my grandparents had sounded when they talked to white people – polite, guarded and evasive. Further, the interviews did not sound very much like the things that my elders had told me about slavery. None of my foremothers had ever told me that, to them, slavery represented "the good old days" or that field work was "fun." Since I had spent every summer since I was 8 years old chopping cotton, I knew better anyway.

So then it became important to me to find out who the interviewers of the ex-slaves were. Why *were* Black women and men saying the things that they were saying in the WPA interviews? Luckily, I found two books that lent great insight to my project. One was the volume of interviews with ex-slaves taken by a Black woman, Ophelia Settle Egypt, from Fisk University, fully eight years before the WPA interviews were taken (Rawick, 1974). The other work was *Weevils in the Wheat*, interviews with ex-slaves in Virginia (Barden *et al.*, 1976). The Fisk interviews read much more like the tales of slavery that I had heard when I was growing up. *Weevils in the Wheat* allowed me the luxury of trying to guess from reading the interviews, if the interviewer was Black or white – I was usually right. *Weevils in the Wheat* also had the list of questions asked of the ex-slaves. The questions were alarmingly personal; some were down-right disrespectful, insulting, even outright racist. The ex-slaves were asked things like, "Did slaves have sex relations without being 'mar-ried'?" or "Were newborn slave babies good-looking?" or even worse, "Did Blacks mind being called nigger?" I have never met a Black person who did not mind. At any rate, because of the personal and sexual nature of many of the questions it seemed that doing a racial analysis was not enough; a gender analysis seemed necessary. Then I started to wonder at the dynamics of same-race interviews – how gender as well as the class and educational level of the interviewer affected the inter-viewee. Once I took the race, gender, class and educational level of the interviewer into account, the interviews made much more sense to me.

I would like to thank my mother Sadie L. Young for helping me to learn to read a language that we both had only heard and spoken all of our lives, a language which my formal education had almost pressured me to forget, as it was "incorrect," largely because it is primarily a spoken/oral means of communication.

I would also like to thank Jeanne Boydston for her helpful suggestions and most especially Linda Gordon for her encouragement and the direction that she lent this project.

THE WPA NARRATIVES

In light of the growing scholarship on the history of African-American[1] women and men, the 1937 WPA Federal Writers Project, interviews with ex-slaves,[2] has taken on an even greater significance as primary source material. However, there are many factors to be considered when trying to find the real voices of Black women and men in the WPA interviews. Historically, racism, gender oppression of Black women and classism, all of which often worked to block channels to formal education, as well as the dominant culture's ignorance about African-American and slave culture, have all been major factors in rendering Black women and men unseen and unheard in historical literature. All of these factors must be considered when trying to determine why Black women and men responded as they did in the WPA interviews. The dynamics of the relationship between the interviewer and the person who had been enslaved made honest discourse impossible on the basis of the racism, sexism and/or classism of the interviewer. It would seem, then, that when these factors are eliminated, we get truer impressions of what Black women and men felt their experiences in bondage to have been. What will follow will be an examination of how each of the factors above may have hindered if not completely silenced the voices of Black people within the WPA interviews.

The WPA interviews can only be fully explored within the context of the era and areas from which they were collected. The Federal Writers Project was a result of Franklin D. Roosevelt's Depression era New Deal and was implemented primarily to hire out-of-work white-collar workers to prepare a "comprehensive and panoramic American guide" to all US culture (Yetman, 1970: 346). The interviews were taken for the most part in the southern states between 1937 and 1938. The interviewing positions went almost entirely to native-born white men and women as a result of discriminatory hiring practices (Davis and Gates, 1985: 90).

Some ten to fifteen years before the interviews took place the Harlem Renaissance revived interest in Negro literature, culture, art and folklore. The population of Black people who had endured enslavement proved to be a valuable resource for gathering the latter, but many of the ex-slaves were aged or dying. Historians, sociologists and folklorists began to feel the urgency of questioning them about other aspects of life in bondage before it was too late. Consequently, between 1937 and 1938 the WPA workers visited the homes of women and men who had experienced bondage to interview them.

In 1937, in the South, Black people lived separately from white people under Jim Crow. Black people could not live, eat, learn, or even use the restroom, in the same spaces as white people. Moreover, there were time-honored, albeit unspoken, codes of behavior that reinforced ideals of white supremacy and stipulated how Black people should act and react to white people. It would seem that even though legal slavery had ended, the attitudes and mores that had allowed the successful existence of the "peculiar institution" had not. In fact, since the end of the reconstruction era southern states had taken many petitions to Congress calling for the re-enslavement of Black people (Doyle, 1937: 117).

These sentiments, held by the majority of southern whites, could hardly have gone unnoticed by the southern Black population. Bertram W. Doyle in his book *The Etiquette of Race Relations in the South* (published in 1937) stated:

Instances appear in which persons who felt a grievance at the emancipation of the Negro sought to express themselves with words and deeds, even going so far occasionally as to murder a Negro who was "out of place."

(Doyle, 1937: 119)

Exactly when it was that a Black person was "out of place" was left to the discretion of any white person.

As a result of this blatant economic, political and social domination of Black people by white people, the power dynamics between the races seriously impeded open discourse in the interviews. John Blassingame in his article "Using the Testimony of Ex-Slaves: Approaches and Problems" asserts that many of the white WPA interviewers were ignorant in the ways of collecting oral histories, completely exercised white privilege in their interactions with the ex-slaves and were often blatantly condescending toward them (Davis and Gates, 1985: 84–5). White interviewers referred to the ex-slave women and men as "Aunty," "Uncle," or "Mammy," thereby perpetuating plantation dynamics. The ex-slaves, in turn, referred to their white interviewers as "Master," "Mistress," or even "lil Missy," all of them titles inextricably tied to the institution of slavery. Even worse, white interviewers openly referred to the old Black people as "darkies" or even "niggers" during the interviewing process and in their writings. Mrs William F. Holmes of Mississippi wrote of one of her interviewees, "Adam Singleton is so black, he shines; all his teeth are gone. He looks more like an ape than any darky I've visited yet" (Rawick, 1977b: 2120).

Some of the white interviewers led the interviews with loaded questions or openly accused the ex-slaves of being uncooperative or outright liars (Davis and Gates, 1985: 85).

Many of the questions centered on how the old people felt that they had been treated by white people during slavery. This created an extraordinarily delicate situation for the interviewees because that question was so closely related to and still reflected the oppressive nature of contemporary socioracial conditions. John Dollard, in his book *Caste and Class in a Southern Town* (1937), asserts:

Caste has replaced slavery as a means of maintaining the essence of the old status order of the South. . . . It defines a superior and inferior group and regulates the behavior of the members of each group. . . . American caste is pinned not to cultural but to biological features – to color, features, hair, form, and the like. . . . The upper caste would be more secure if the inferior caste . . . were geographically immobile and extremely limited in social participation.

(Dollard, 1937: 62–3)

In essence, there remained a system of subjugation of Black people that retained the civil, economic and political domination that had been inherent in the slave system.

The problem was further compounded by the fact that a number of the interviewers were descendants of slaveholders. Sometimes, as in the case of Harriet Sanders of Mississippi, the subject may have worked for the interviewer herself. Sanders, in the middle of the interview, asked the interviewer, "Miss Marcella don't you remember when I washed for you?" So, it was extremely difficult for the ex-slaves to answer questions such as "Was your master kind to you?" or "Which do you prefer, slavery or freedom?"

Not surprisingly many of the ex-slaves said that their masters had been kind and that they preferred slavery to freedom. Some even said that freedom was bad for the race as a whole. It would have been extremely unwise to indict any white people, in any manner, in front of other white people by attesting that slavery had been harsh and white people had been cruel. Nonetheless, Ishrael Massie of Virginia told a Black interviewer, "Lord chile, if ya start me I kin tell ya a mess 'bout reb [rebel] times, but I ain't tellin white folks nuthin' 'cause I'm skeered to make enemies" (Barden *et al.*, 1976: xlii). An ex-slave woman, Jennie Patterson, also asserted:

> Some of us had ole mean an' wicked marsters and mistresses dat would beat 'em unmerciful. I don' tole you I was feared to tell all I done seen in my lifetime, an' I ain' tellin' white folks but so much even now in dis new day an' time.
>
> (Barden *et al.*, 1976: xlii)

Moreover there were at least four other factors that caused the ex-slaves to respond to those questions as they did. One has to do with the idea of the personal reserve. White people controlled almost every outward aspect of Black life. Black people were able to protect the inner self by putting up a façade and showing white people only what they wanted to see and hear (Doyle, 1937: 12). In this way they could better avoid offending white sensibilities. If the ex-slaves could stay one-dimensional in the minds of the white interviewers, then they had less chance of being accused of "forgetting their place" by displaying characteristics that would imply that they felt themselves fully human and equal to white people in any way.

Therefore when asked about masters or whether they preferred freedom to slavery, many ex-slaves said they simply could not remember much about slavery at all. One very common ploy was to answer the question "Was your master kind?" by saying "My master was kind but the overseer [often 'buckra,' a poor white man] was cruel," or "My master was good, we was always well cared for, fed well and never whipped — but the negroes on the next farm over caught hell" (Barden *et al.*, 1976:

139). George P. Rawick, editor of *The American Slave: A Composite Autobiography*, agrees:

> It is hard to escape the conclusion, when one works with the narratives for a long while, that this is a formula old black people use in trying to tell about horrors and brutality they had seen and experienced without offending anyone or sounding as if they were "complaining." . . . Dozens and dozens of narratives – after insisting that, of course, masters and mistresses were good people who did not use the whip go on to describe *with gory and vivid detail whippings on "other" Plantations.*
>
> (Rawick, 1977a: xliii–xlviii; emphases added)

Indeed this ploy was also evident when the ex-slaves would begin an interview by praising the kindness of their master or mistress but end the same interview by light-heartedly relaying a horrible tale of mistreatment. Fanny Berry of Virginia talked of how her mistress was a kind, Christian woman who never harmed anyone but then went on to recount how the mistress had tortured Berry's own brother:

> My missus use to 'muse her company sometimes . . . she would take my little brother and let de dog bite his bare toes . . . dis would hurt my brother awful an he would cry out loud, too, an when he would cry out loud de company would laugh an' have a good time over it.
>
> (Barden *et al.*, 1976: 45)

This dynamic is also evident in a narrative given by Joe Bouy to a white woman interviewer. Bouy recounts:

> Ah seen a man hung onct [once] . . . De white folks takin' him off an ah put de rope roun his neck. Ole Mars Bouy took de rope an' flung it roun ma' haid after dey had hung de niggah, Ah waz plumb scairet den, sho nuf. But he waz only playin'.
>
> (Rawick, 1977a: 182)

In other words, Bouy meant to convey that his master had meant no real harm by threatening him with lynching.

Second, the idea of a Black double-consciousness must be examined. In his *Souls of Black Folk* W. E. B. DuBois asserts:

> It is a peculiar sensation this double-consciousness, this sense of always looking at one's self through the eyes of others, of measuring one's soul by the tape of a world that looks on in amused contempt and pity. One ever feels his twoness – an American, a negro.
>
> (W. E. B. DuBois, 1961: 16)

In essence Black people are possessed of two consciousnesses, two gazes, one Black and one white, and are then capable of seeing themselves and judging themselves as white people would. Inherent in DuBois's theory of double-consciousness are the ideas of internalized self-hatred and self-degradation. Thus, it is entirely possible that a few Black people did truly feel that Black people were not worthy of freedom, that they needed to be taken care of and needed to be made to work. It is true that some Black people felt that adapting the white man's ways and attitudes would be best for the race (Rawick, 1977b: 1919).

Third, it must be remembered that 1937 was a Depression year. Black people were in even worse economic shape than white people. Many of the elderly ex-bondspeople were dependent on meager government pensions in order to survive and were under the illusion that the WPA workers could affect that. Some WPA interviewers did nothing to correct that notion (Davis and Gates, 1985: 86). Others, like Esther de Sola from Mississippi, exploited the physical needs of the former bond-women and men. De Sola stated in her personal notes on her interview with Lucy Thurston that perhaps the gifts she gave the old woman had affected the interviews. "I think it was the dress which first won me my enviable spot in the heart of Lucy. Or it might have been the cookies, or the jar of preserves or the red straw hat" (Rawick, 1977b: 2115). At the end of de Sola's second interview with Lucy, Lucy asked, "What you gwine bring yo' po' ole Lucy nex' time you comes visitin' lil Missy? I needs some shoes powerful bad" (Rawick, 1977b: 2117).

Honest communication in the interviews was further complicated by the white interviewers' ignorance of African-American culture, its language and dynamics. White interviewers tended either to be completely disdainful of the former slaves and their culture or to romanticize slave culture pitifully. Either way their African-American subjects were dehumanized. Esther de Sola committed this to WPA Records about former bondswoman Lucy Thurston:

> these old darkies look past the inquiring visitors' eyes, back into those luxurious pre-war days and tell tales of the abundance, the high living, the excitement and fast pace of the courtly and chivalrous men and gracious women of the slaveholding South.
>
> (Rawick, 1977b: 2140)

The Black woman in this interview became objectified, voiceless and consequently invisible. The white woman interviewer did not see her as a human being. Consequently, it was impossible for the interviewer to understand the concept of an African-American culture, language and heritage equally important as her own.

Nowhere was this ignorance more pronounced than in the WPA treatment of the Negro dialect or that which can be called the Black English vernacular. The WPA interviewers were given a "standard dialect" form to use. The form's purpose was to provide uniformity in the interviews when they were written down. For instance, the WPA federal office did not want to see the word "and" in some places and the word "an'" in other places meaning the same thing. This form was based on the assumption that all southern African-Americans, regardless of region or background, spoke or sounded the same. This, in effect, weakened the real Black voice in the interviews because regardless of how differently the ex-slaves spoke from one another, the WPA interviewers were encouraged to record it all the same. The Black voice in the interviews was further weakened in the interviewing process itself. Many times the interviewer asked questions and wrote the answers down in the sketchiest detail, then, later, filled in the interview using the "acceptable dialect forms." In fact, there are many examples of Black people who spoke perfect Standard White English having dialect attributed to them (Davis and Gates, 1985: 88).

The standard dialect forms led to those kinds of incidents, but it is important to note that white interviewers recorded dialect when they heard Standard White English because they needed to think of Black people only as "aunties," "uncles" and "mammies." The psychological pain of racism is great to both races (though infinitely more so for Black people). Michelle Cliff in her article "Object into Subject" states:

> Through objectification – the process by which people are dehumanized, made ghostlike, given the status of the other – an image created by the oppressor replaces the actual being. . . . It is objectification that gives the impression of sanity to the process of oppression.
>
> (Robinson, 1988: 141)

In other words it would be recognizably insane to oppress Blacks who were people but not Blacks who were "niggers," "darkies," or "mammies."

That white people had little understanding of or appreciation for the culture only compounded the powerlessness of Black people in the interviews. For, ultimately, if the slave women and men did reveal something to the white interviewer, they could only hope that it would not be distorted or reinterpreted. White interviewers and/or their editors did tamper with and reshape information given in the interviews. Some interviews had slight changes and still others were almost complete fabrication (Davis and Gates, 1985: 84–5).

In 1937, white men still held political, economic and sexual dominance over African-American women and men (Jones, 1985: 150). Consequently, it was rare that Black women and men spoke openly in interviews with white men because they sat at the crux of the major ways that white men asserted dominance – over Black people, over women and over poor people (Doyle, 1937: 118). Black women and men were effectively disenfranchised by Jim Crow and had little or no political strength outside of the African-American community. Black women represented 97 per cent of all women in domestic service. Black people, men and women, comprised 80 per cent of farm laborers within the southern peonage system, and were victimized by violence, sexual and otherwise, attendant to those positions (Dollard, 1937: 95; Davis and Gates, 1985: 85). Subsequently in 1937, Blacks were still heavily dependent upon white men for economic survival.

Moreover, both Black women and men were sexually oppressed by white men. White men sought to exploit Black women either through outright rape, as Black women had no legal recourse against white rapists, or de facto rape, by taking advantage of their economic situations. The opportunity for sexual exploitation was great. Black women were doubly victimized; first, by the unwanted sexual attentions of white men and then by the resultant sexual jealousies of Black men. Black men were victimized by their powerlessness to "protect" their mates, mothers and sisters from these abuses. Consequently, white men were able to adversely affect the most intimate familial relationships in the Black community. Furthermore, the terrorism of lynching was carried out against the entire Black community; men, women and children were murdered. Even though lynching was a manifestation of political and economic repression, sexual oppression was also one of its primary objectives. Not only was it used to reinforce the notion that Black men could be murdered for even looking at white women; but it also reinforced the powerlessness of the Black community to stop the abuses on its own female members or to stop the brutally sexualized ritual of the lynchings themselves.

Consequently, it is not surprising that interviews taken by white men read like the following excerpt taken by Ed Hopkins.

> Harold Blemett was butlet [*sic*] in the handsome and spacious home of his master, Maj. Thomas Blewett. He was . . . capable but pompous and conceited as a negro politician, which made him unpopular with the White people who suffered through that Tragic Era. Blewett accepted the political changes after 1875 and behaved himself.
>
> (Rawick, 1977a: 151)

This narrative taken down in the WPA History of Pike County, Mississippi, is even more revealing. A white male reporter interviewed another white man about slavery.

> Harriet Beecher Stowe and other northern writers have given to the world the darkest picture of an institution for which the

63

Southern people were not responsible, but had brought to them by
the slave speculators of the New England states.

(Rawick, 1977a: 105)

Obviously because of the chauvinism and paternalism of these white
male interviewers, there is not one word from Black people themselves
about their experiences in bondage.

In addition there are other relationship dynamics that need to be
examined if one is to better read the interviews of the ex-slaves.
Differences in gender, class and educational levels between the interviewer and subject, in both interracial and same-race interviews, bear the
need for closer examination.

In "Using the Testimony of Ex-Slaves," John Blassingame asserts that
in spite of race relations, white women were bound to get more honest
communications from the ex-slave women and men than white men, and
that fortunately a majority of ex-slaves in most states were interviewed
by white women rather than white men (Davis and Gates, 1985: 84–5). It
is difficult to know why interviews taken by white women were more
revealing as there was no specific or ascertainable female style of the
white women interviewers. Some of the old people may have simply felt
bolder to say what they felt to these women because of their advanced
ages. In addition, since many white women were given to romanticizing
in rendering the narratives, they more than likely presented themselves
in a more genteel ladylike manner to the old people. White women may
even have been less likely to harshly counter or correct the old women
and men than white men. They likely treated the interviewees with more
compassion than white male interviewers. Indeed, white women interviewers may have identified, in part, with the oppression of African-
Americans because of the pervasive gender oppression in their own
lives. It is doubtful that white women were consciously aware of how
gender oppression circumscribed their lives and that they would have
articulated their experiences in terms of gender oppression. However,
the principle of their exclusion from white male spheres was real.
Further, these white women interviewers were relatively educated
women who may have been more critical of rigid gender roles. On this
basis they may have identified with Black people.

Though white women participated in more revealing interviews than
white men, any interviewing style or method that could be attributed to
gender was still circumscribed by race. Black and white women shared
commonalities as women, but racial politics hampered open communication. This is best exemplified by comparing how Black women said
that they felt about their mistresses when talking to a white woman
interviewer and how they described slave mistress relationships in the
Fisk ex-slave interviews taken by Ophelia Settle Egypt, a Black woman

64

sociologist from Fisk University. In the WPA interviews ex-bondswoman Mary Anderson told Pat Matthews, a white woman, that "Missus would not speak short to a slave . . . both Marster and Missus taught slaves to be obedient in a nice quiet way" (Yetman, 1970: 16). Other Black women told white women interviewers that their mistresses, too, had been kind. Others were evasive and said that they could not really remember.

But an ex-slave in the Fisk interviews gave a different account of her relationship with her mistress. She recalled how the white woman had beaten her mercilessly "till the blood run down." She continued, "I can't remember now like I can back yonder; but I can remember that as plain as day. . . . You know that old woman was mean." This particular woman expressed anti-white sentiment and anger to Mrs Egypt that she would not have to a white woman. Further, the Black woman felt that there was no way to forgive the white woman for how she had been treated (Rawick, 1974: 277).

In addition, it is apparent that white women interviewers asked the ex-slave women and men many questions that were of a sexual nature such as "Were there sex relations between slaves and whites?" or "Were there any half-white children on your plantation?" These questions were problematic for the ex-slaves to answer for many reasons; the most obvious being, as mentioned earlier, that Black people were still terrorized by the lynchings of Black men for the alleged rape of white women at the same time that Black women were still shamelessly raped and sexually exploited by white men (Jones, 1985: 149–50, 157). Moreover, white women interviewers, indeed, southern white women in general, had obvious preconceived notions about Black female sexuality that would not have allowed Black women to tell the truth about the nature of sex between Black women and white men. Deborah Gray White in her book *Ar'n't I a Woman: Female Slaves in the Plantation South* asserts that the conventional wisdom among southern whites during slavery was that Black women were naturally promiscuous. White quotes Mary Boydkin Chestnutt, the wife of a slaveholder, echoing a common sentiment regarding Black women. Chestnutt affirmed, "Who thinks any worse of a Negro or mulatto woman for being a thing we can't name" (White, 1985: 40). The apparent promiscuity of Black women was further seemingly evidenced by the birth of half-Black or "mulatto" babies. By 1937 the conventional wisdom of white people in the South regarding the sexuality of Black women had changed little (Dollard, 1937: 137, 161). So then, when asked about interracial sex or relationships by white women, Black women were evasive. When ex-slave Annie Wallace was asked by a white woman interviewer, who had noted that Annie was obviously only half-Black, who her father was, Annie replied that she had had no father to speak of. Annie's son, who sat in on the interview, later informed the interviewer that Annie's father had been white but that Annie was ashamed to say so. Instead, Annie claimed that her features were the result of Indian blood (Barden *et al.*, 1976: 293). In contrast another former slave woman told Black interviewers Emily Wilson and Claude W. Anderson:

> My mother was a slave and my father – well, the fact is so evident you can' [cannot] dodge it. It's their [white people's] stamp and not ours; therefore I don't blush when I tell you this part of the story.
>
> (Barden *et al.*, 1976: 255)

In addition, according to Deborah Gray White, white women were sexually jealous of Black women. White women expressed anger over their powerlessness to stop sexual relationships between Black women and white men. For many, the double standard was too much to bear. They both reviled and envied what they took to be sexual freedom for Black women. Consequently, some white women committed monstrous acts on their female servants. One old woman told Mrs Egypt from Fisk University:

> When his [the master's] wife would get mad she would beat her [the master's Black mistress] as long as she wanted to, and she used to lead her around by her ears, and would put hot tongs on her ears and tell her that these were her earrings.
>
> (Rawick, 1974: 134)

Thus, even though, as Blassingame contends, white women tended to get more reliable accounts than white men from the ex-slaves, the uneven power dynamic of the interview kept white women from hearing the truth about mistress/female servant relations in the way that Black interviewers did.

In fact, ex-slave women and men talked more openly to Black interviewers in general. In interviews taken by Black interviewers there were more details about hard labor; poor food and housing; cruel treatment, mutilation and even murder at the hands of whites; miscegenation and methods of resistance and survival in spite of such overwhelming odds (Davis and Gates, 1985: 86). Thus the Fisk interviews and the WPA interviews taken by Black people stand in sharp contrast to those taken by white interviewers. The ex-slaves were plainly more open to Black interviewers.

One major way that this is evident is that there is much less "dialect" recorded in the interviews. Black people were acutely aware that when speaking to white people, one might be accused of being an "uppity nigger" or "forgetting one's place" or "trying to sound white" if one used Standard White English too well. J. L. Dillard in his book *Black English* asserts that "It should always be kept in mind that the speaker of 'perfectly' Standard English might have been a bidialectal, who kept one side of his language behavior from white observers" (Dillard, 1972: 205). Dillard defines a bidialectal as a person fluent in both Standard White English and Black English. It was clear when the ex-slave women and men did not feel the need to hide behind the dialect in the interviews.

Further the Fisk interviews and WPA interviews taken by Black people tend to be truer to the essence of Black English, making it possible for the life, voice and clarity of the speaker to come through, especially as Black English is defined by June Jordan in *On Call: Political Essays*. According to Jordan, the most important tenet of Black English is that "every sentence assumes the living and active participation of at least two human beings, the listener and the speaker" (Jordan, 1985: 129). For example, one former bondsman related in his Fisk interview:

> Now it is a remarkable thing *to tell you*, some people can't see into it, but I am going *to tell you*, you can believe it if you want to – some colored people at that wouldn't be whipped by their master.
>
> (Rawick, 1974: 44; emphases added)

In their interviews with other Black people, the ex-slaves directly addressed and involved the interviewers in ways that they had not done with the white WPA interviewers. This call and response pattern is distinctly African-American. The ex-slave women and men playfully chided the younger Black interviewers about how well they had it compared to slavery days, as did one Mr Huddleston: "I remember they used to whip us; what you all need now" (Rawick, 1974: 31). Mrs Sutton, who was present at the same interview as Mr Huddleston, was anything but evasive when asked how she felt about freedom. "I can go when I please and come back when I please . . . I am a free rooster. I got nobody to tell me nothing." This last seems to prove another of Jordan's tenets of Black English, "A primary consequence of the person-centered values of Black English is the delivery of voice" (Jordan, 1985: 129).

Further, the willingness to talk, indeed the need to tell, is much more readily apparent in the Fisk narratives. Many ex-slave women and men echoed the sentiments of the woman who told Mrs Egypt, "I can just keep on talking now if you is got time to listen; yes I can just keep going" (Rawick, 1974: 153).

Even with this apparent enthusiasm of the ex-slaves to talk to other Blacks, there are other dynamics that must be addressed. For instance, gender differences affected participants in even same-race interviews. Even when both interviewer and subject were Black there were certain sexual subjects that were not readily discussed when the interviewer was male and the ex-slave female. Miscegenation was generally talked about openly in all-Black interviews, either as a stamp of white sexual oppression or surprisingly to show that many whites openly held Black lovers as their relative equals. But there is little between Black men and women in the WPA interviews on topics such as miscarriage (unless it was caused by violence to the woman), abortion, contraception, few details of sex relations of slaves, menstruation and childbirth methods. Black men and women generally did not openly discuss sexuality any more than their white counterparts. In fact, many women who were interviewed related that their own mothers had never discussed sexual matters with them at all. Many were unprepared for their first menstrual periods or first sexual experiences (Rawick, 1974: 137). It seems unlikely that in a culture which was so conservative about sexual matters, women would feel comfortable addressing sexual matters with men.

Darlene Clark Hine, in her article "Rape and the Inner Lives of Black Women in the Middle West: Preliminary Thoughts on the Culture of Dissemblance," suggests that Black women have created a culture of dissemblance. Hine asserts:

> By dissemblance I mean the behavior and attitudes of black women that created the appearance of openness and disclosure but actually shielded the truth of their inner lives and selves from their oppressors . . . white men, white women and to a lesser extent black men.
>
> (DuBois and Ruiz, 1990: 292)

I would amend Hine's provocative statement in two ways. First, this culture of dissemblance is a dynamic that is interactive with, not separate from, the personal reserve. Whereas the personal reserve involves the protection of the self, the inner self, the culture of dissemblance involves the protection of the inner selves of the group. The term "culture" implies shared values and some sharing of the personal with other Black women within the group. Hence, each Black woman within this group protects herself and her sisters against her oppressors. Second, the women within this culture of dissemblance held their inner lives sacred not only from their oppressors but from anyone outside of the group, even Black children, who were obviously not oppressors of Black women. It was not uncommon for young Black girls to be accused of acting "womanish" if they were too inquisitive about certain matters. Many mothers felt that it was enough to warn daughters to reject the sexual advances of men. Therefore it follows that many young girls were unprepared for menstruation and did not know where babies came from. One elderly Black woman told Mrs Egypt, "No, they didn't tell you a thing; I was a great big girl, 12 or 13 years old . . . we'd be going round to the parsley bed looking for babies and looking in hollow logs" (Rawick, 1974: 10).

Further, according to Evelyn Brooks Higginbotham in "Beyond the Sound of Silence: Afro-American Women in History," gender relations was one of the most important variables in determining class differences, specifically the "better class of Negroes" in African-American culture. Higginbotham affirms that this "better class" of Black people considered themselves to be "hard working, religious, clean and so far as sex was concerned, respectful of the dominant society's manners and morals" (Higginbotham, 1989: 58).

In fact, the ex-slave women and men tended to be most open with Black women interviewers. This is especially evident in light of the fact that generally Black women held no real "power over" ex-slave women and men in the way that white men and women did over Black people and Black men did over Black women. For example, in the Fisk narratives one Black woman told Mrs Egypt of a Black man who had been lynched for carrying on an affair with a white woman who had been more than willing (a thing she would never have told a white man or woman). Then the woman advised, "Dear, don't you never let no White man mess with you. I don't want to see my color mess with them" (Rawick, 1974: 71). The subject not only felt free to assert anti-white sentiment, but she also addressed the problem of sexual exploitation of Black women by white men, thus connecting the sexual oppression of Black women and Black men vis-à-vis the subject of lynching.

Another ex-slave woman told Mrs Egypt that her daughter had died at school of a "heavy hemorrhage" which could have been either a miscarriage or self-induced abortion (Rawick, 1974: 27). Another woman told her that some of the Black women on her plantation thought it an honor to "have the master" (Rawick, 1974: 209). Black women openly discussed sexual attacks and exploitation by white men. Ex-slave woman Fannie Berry related the story of another woman, Sukie, to one of the very few Black female WPA interviewers, Susie R. C. Byrd.

> Sukie was her name . . . but ole marsa was always tryin' to make Sukie his gal. . . . She tole him no. Den he grabbed her an' pull it [her dress] down off'n her shoulders. When he done dat, he fo'got 'bout whuppin her, I guess 'cause he grab hold of her an' try to pull her down on de flo'. Den dat black gal got mad. She took an' punch ole Marsa an' made him break loose an' den she gave him a shove an' push his hindparts down in de hot pot o' soap. . . . He got up holdin' his hindparts an' ran from de kitchen, not darin' to yell, cause he didn't want Miss Sarah Ann to know 'bout it.
>
> (Barden et al., 1976: 48)

But, one of the most astonishing examples was when an ex-slave woman told Mrs Egypt intimate details of her first menstrual period. "When that happened mother didn't tell us. I didn't know what had happened to me. I went running to the branch and washed myself" (Barden et al., 1976: 137).

Even though the ex-slave women and men felt comfortable enough with Mrs Egypt to relate these intimate experiences, there is evidence in the interviews that they did feel that she differed from them in terms of class and the amount of education that she had attained. One woman told Mrs Egypt:

> Here set your tail on that; set your rump on that [indicating a chair]. You are used to running around with rich folks in the parlors and things. I haven't any parlor, this is my parlor, my wash room and cook room and everything, my primp room . . . It ain't much.

(Rawick, 1974: 245)

Many educated Blacks did feel that they were in that "better class of Negroes" and felt it their duty to "uplift" the masses through education and assimilationist attitudes. Many Black educational leaders, the most notable of whom was Booker T. Washington, felt that the old ways, specifically slave folkways, had to be dropped if the race was ever to truly advance. They felt that the old slave culture and subsequent African-American culture were indeed inferior to the dominant white culture. In fact, the sociological team that sent Mrs Egypt out from Fisk to interview the former bondswomen and men defined the slavery era as "an exploitative system, in which a relatively small number of individuals equipped with superior technology and capital, directed and controlled the energies of a numerically superior but culturally inferior population" (Rawick, 1974: i). Even Higginbotham contends that African-American leaders felt that "gaining respect, even justice, from White America required changes in religious beliefs, speech patterns and also in gender roles and relations" (Higginbotham, 1989: 56).

In sum, the possession of money was not the only real determinant in constructing class. Rather, middle-class ideals regarding sex and hard work were important. In addition, skin color and vocation were important. This is not to say that all fair-skinned Black people were middle class; but, rather that special privileges were afforded them, in terms of acquiring education and training, by the white community. Many times fairer-skinned Blacks were the acknowledged relatives of prominent white families and were subsequently given middle-class social consideration by both white people and the African-American community. The African-American community was vastly affected by this preferential treatment of the lighter-skinned members of the group and had consequently developed its own values regarding color among its members (Dollard, 1937: 69).

Second, certain vocations marked class. There were a few university-educated doctors and lawyers (predominantly fair-skinned people); but, teachers and ministers predominated as leaders of the Black middle class. Hence, the educated Blacks who worked with the WPA, and Mrs

Egypt, an educator, received respect and admiration from their interviewees.

It was ironic that educated Black people were trying to collect these interviews about the lives and culture of the ex-slaves at the same time that they were propounding that the Black masses let go of those cultural folkways. Some of the ex-slave women and men felt resentment at the devaluation and delegitimation of their culture and heritage. Therefore in the Fisk narratives many of those who had been enslaved did talk about "the good old days"; but, in terms of the Black community itself, its close-knittedness, its survival in spite of incredible odds. One old man expressed his dismay and ambivalence over the whole affair to Mrs Egypt when he said:

> Yes, I was a slave and knows plenty about it but I don't care to talk about it . . . a Negro believes what he [the white man] says because he is White and has straight hair and blue eyes . . . there is always somebody on the outside that knows more about it than I do, and I was right in it . . . I think it is against the race to tell how the White folks done us in slavery. I don't want to do anything to tear down. I want to build up.

> (Rawick, 1974: 141)

This particular man did go on to give Mrs Egypt an eight-page interview. Nevertheless, he was obviously angry that the younger, more educated Blacks were willing to embrace the dominant culture's ideas on slave culture and its importance. Even so, he still felt that uplift for the race was important.

This idea of assimilation to dominant cultural norms is also a factor in explaining why the Fisk narratives read so differently from the WPA interviews. Though the syntax of the interviews reads more like Black English as it is actually spoken, there is no real "Negro dialect" in the collection. This is odd for, in fact, some southern Blacks did speak in what was called Negro dialect. The idea of bidialectism aside, the lack of dialect could be attributed to the fact that only one person, Mrs Egypt, recorded these interviews. Her voice as co-author of these interviews comes through just as clearly as those of White co-authors did. Second, the Fisk interviews had no "acceptable" list of Negro dialect. Consequently, Mrs Egypt was not influenced or prejudiced by it as the white WPA workers were. Third, given the uplift ideals of the Black intellectuals at Fisk University, they had a vested interest in having interviews that were not replete with what white people considered "darky dialect." Given the times this was, in a way, understandable. The dialect seemed to be a conveyance for sustaining myths about substandard Black intellect (Davis and Gates, 1985: 60). The lack of "Negro dialect" in the Fisk interviews may have been a reaction against that sort of stereotyping and objectification of Black people. Black English was commonly misunderstood as a deficient form of Standard White English rather than a separate and distinct language with a value system all its own. Last, the ex-slave women and men themselves, many of whom were probably to some extent bidialectals, were careful to display a more acceptable speech pattern because they were speaking to more educated Black people. Whatever the reason was, not every person interviewed by Mrs Egypt spoke Standard English in the way that it is presented in the Fisk narratives. Value judgements on "Negro dialect" from the dominant culture made more educated Black people ashamed of their Black sisters and brothers who spoke that way. That the Fisk interviews were cleaned up of "Negro dialect" is made more apparent by comparing two interviews taken by Claude W. Anderson, a Black male WPA worker. Anderson interviewed a woman called Armaci Adams who began by telling him, "My name is Armaci Adams. I was bawn in Gates County, North Carolina, but I ain' stayed down dere long" (Barden *et al.*, 1976: 1). Anderson interviewed another woman, Hannah Bailey, who spoke better Standard White English than Armaci Adams. Bailey began her interview, "I was born right here in 1850. . . . My mother? Why, yes she was a slave" (Barden *et al.*, 1976: 18). The interviews by Claude Anderson show both a respectful treatment of Black English (unlike his white WPA counterparts or the Black Fisk intellectuals) and a faithful recording of Standard White English when the ex-slaves spoke it. A thorough reading of the Fisk and WPA interviews reveals that there was no African-American cultural monolith. Black and slave culture had as many varieties in language, attitudes and tradition as did the dominant culture.

Finally and most importantly, the interviews reveal the importance of understanding who the interviewers/co-authors of oral histories are and how they affect what the subjects/co-authors are free to say. In the case of the WPA interviews, the ex-slaves felt free to reveal little if anything real to their interviewers for very concrete reasons. Their lives were still substantially controlled socially, economically and sexually by white men. Black women's discourse in interviews with white women was less than open because even though they had common ground as women, white women still exercised white privilege, which often included economic privilege, over them. In addition, even though white women may have gotten more truthful information from the aged Blacks, their romanticizations of the narratives caused them to misunderstand or misinterpret vital information. Black women spoke more openly to Black men than they did with either white men or women, but conservative gender relations and assimilation to dominant cultural norms, especially those regarding sex promoted by ideals of racial uplift, made the discussion of certain subjects unacceptable. Black women interviewers, both from Fisk and the Work Progress Administration, seemed to have participated in the most open communications with former bondswomen because they had common ground as both women and Black people. Moreover, Black women interviewers had no real means of asserting "dominance over" the lives of the women who had survived enslavement.

By examining the interviews with both authors, the interviewer and the former bondswoman or man, in mind, and what the dynamics of their relationships were, it becomes possible to find in the interviews the true voices of those who experienced bondage, first hand.

NOTES

1 "African-American" is the term that I prefer to use because it relays more fully the heritage and subsequent identity of those African descendants on the North American continent who created, from sustained African cultural memory and forced participation in European-American culture, a distinct African-American culture. However, in the interest of space, I will use the term "Black" to refer to African-Americans.

2 In the original drafts of this paper, I resisted using the terms "slave" or "ex-slave" because they did not properly convey the totality of the experience of those who had endured enslavement. "Slaves" was not the sum total of who they were; rather, they were human beings with emotions, psyches, intellects, whose condition was enslavement. Therefore I prefer to use the term "former bondswomen and men." However, in the interest of space I will use the terms "slaves" and "ex-slaves."

BIBLIOGRAPHY

Barden, T., Perdue, C. and Phillips, R. (1976) *Weevils in the Wheat: Interviews with Virginia Ex-Slaves*, Charlottesville, VA: University Press of Virginia.

Davis, C. and Gates, H. (1985) *The Slave's Narrative*, New York: Oxford University Press.

Dillard, J. L. (1972) *Black English: Its History and Usage in the United States*, New York: Random House.

Dollard, J. (1937) *Caste and Class in a Southern Town*, New York: Doubleday Anchor Books.

Doyle, B. (1937) *The Etiquette of Race Relations in the South: A Study in Social Control*, New York: Schocken Books.

DuBois, E. C. and Ruiz, V. L. (1990) *Unequal Sisters: A Multicultural Reader in U.S. Women's History*, London: Routledge.

DuBois, W. E. B. (1961) *The Souls of Black Folk*, Greenwich, CT: Fawcett Publications.

Higginbotham, E. B. (1989) "Beyond the Sound of Silence: Afro-American Women in History," *Gender and History* 1 (Spring): 50–67.

Jones, J. (1985) *Labor of Love, Labor of Sorrow: Black Women, Work and the Family from Slavery to the Present*, New York: Vintage Books.

Jordan, J. (1985) *On Call: Political Essays*, Boston, Mass.: South End Press.

Rawick, G. P. (ed.) (1974) *The American Slave: Unwritten History of Slavery* (Fisk University, Volume 18), Westport, CT: Greenwood Press.

—— (1977a) *The American Slave: A Composite Autobiography* (*Mississippi Narratives Part 1*, Volume 6), Westport, CT: Greenwood Press.

—— (1977b) *The American Slave: A Composite Autobiography* (*Mississippi Narratives Part 5*, Volume 10), Westport, CT: Greenwood Press.

Robinson, H. (1988) *Visibly Female. Feminism and Art: An Anthology*, New York: Universe Books.

White, D. G. (1985) *Ar'n't I a Woman: Female Slaves in the Plantation South*, New York: W. W. Norton.

Yetman, N. (1970) *Voices from Slavery*, New York: Holt, Rinehart & Winston.

Part II

ON THEORY AND ACTION

5

A BLACK FEMINIST PERSPECTIVE ON TRANSFORMING THE ACADEMY

The case of Spelman College

Beverly Guy-Sheftall

Spelman College, founded in 1881 in the basement of Atlanta, Georgia's Friendship Baptist Church, is the oldest and best-known college for Black women in the world.[1] Because of its historic commitment to the education of women, especially Black women, Spelman has been over the past decade and a half in the forefront of curriculum development in Women's Studies on historically Black college campuses in the USA.[2] Some of the most significant reforms in American higher education over the past three decades have come as a result of the Black Studies and Women's Studies movements. Less well known but also important has been the development within the past decade of a new field of study – Black Women's Studies – which emerged in part because of the failure of Black and Women's Studies to address adequately the unique experiences of Black women in the USA and throughout the world. In the first publication on this newly emerging discipline called Black Women's Studies, the editors, all three of whom were Black Studies scholars, attempted to define the new concept, trace its development and provide a rationale for its existence:

> Women's studies courses . . . focused almost exclusively upon the lives of white women. Black studies, which was much too often male-dominated, also ignored Black women. . . . Because of white women's racism and Black men's sexism, there was no room in either area for a serious consideration of the lives of Black women. And even when they have considered Black women, white women usually have not had the capacity to analyze racial politics and Black culture, and Black men have remained blind or resistant to the implications of sexual politics in Black women's lives.[3]

Nearly five years later, Professor Andrée Nicola McLaughlin (with Don Quinn Kelley) offered a fairly precise, more global, more holistic definition of the new interdisciplinary field of Black Women's Studies or Africana Women's Studies which had evolved after a decade and a half or so of fairly specific "Milestones in research and development":

1. An interdisciplinary field of theoretical and practical studies in race, gender and socioeconomic class from the perspective of women of African descent, and including teaching, research, advocacy and informal education in feminist theory and world cultures, women's history, studies in sexuality and public policy, social change and social movements, and the philosophy and methodologies of science. 2. Studies in the empowerment of women of African descent and/or Asian/Pacific descent, their histories and cultures, focused on issues of human freedom, self-awareness and positive self-concept, cultural identity, community development and self-determination for racially/nationally oppressed peoples worldwide. 3. A political and intellectual imperative stemming from the expansion and combining of the disciplines of Black/ Africana and Women's Studies.[4]

In 1981, exactly one hundred years after Spelman's founding, the Women's Research and Resources Center, the first of its kind on a Black college campus, was established with a small grant from the Charles Stewart Mott Foundation. A major component of the program was the development of an interdisciplinary women's studies minor with a special focus on women of African descent. Since its inception, the center has had three major goals: curriculum development in women's studies with a particular focus on the intersection of race, class and gender, and cross-cultural perspectives on the female experience; research on Black women; and community outreach, especially to Black women locally and regionally. During its early years, the center broadened its program to include an international component which focuses on Third World women, with special attention to women of African descent. In this regard, Spelman sponsored a delegation of five women, including the center director, to attend the UN Decade Conference in Nairobi.[5]

Though Spelman's involvement in women's studies is relatively recent, the college's involvement in sponsoring seminars and conferences on issues relevant to Black women is considerably older. Even as early as 1944, for example, Spelman was the site of a "Conference on Current Problems and Programs in the Higher Education of Negro Women" during which representatives of several Black colleges focused on directions for the post-war education of Black women. While a number of "women's studies" courses have been developed as electives at Spelman since 1969, they remained tangential, for the most part, to the curriculum until the implementation of a Ford Foundation-funded curriculum development project (1983) in Black Women's Studies which "main-streamed" women's studies into required core curriculum courses at the college. A chronology of the development of separate Women's Studies courses at Spelman follows: Psychology of the Sexes (1969); Psychology of Women (1970–1); Women in Africa (1972–3), taught for one year by a guest professor, then discontinued; Images of Women in Literature (1973–4), and Images of Women in the Media (1976–7) which I designed; Human Sexuality (1974–5); and Women, Values and the Law (1977–8). Since 1979 the following courses have been taught by various faculty in separate departments: Women of the Bible; Sociology of Women; Woman as Writer; Studies of Women in Theatre and Drama; Women in Management of Organizations; Black Women: Developing Public Leadership Skills; Women in America; Communication and Gender; Women, Literature and Identity; Psycho-Social and Historical Analysis of Black Women in the Twentieth Century; Women in the Economy; Race, Class and Gender in South America; Feminist Theory; and The Social Thought of African American Women.

In 1982 Spelman was chosen as the major participating institution in a two-year Black Women's Studies Faculty and Curriculum Project at the Wellesley College Center for Research on Women, funded by the Fund for the Improvement of Postsecondary Education (FIPSE). As co-sponsor of the project, the center hosted two workshops for faculty working at historically Black colleges. The center also worked with Atlanta University, the graduate institution in the Atlanta University Center, on a faculty development project in Africana Women's Studies which later evolved into a master's and doctoral program.[6]

In 1983 the center became involved in a major curriculum development project designed to incorporate Black Women's Studies into the curricula at Spelman and four participating institutions in the Atlanta area – Agnes Scott, Clark, Kennesaw and Morehouse Colleges. Funded by the Ford Foundation, this project addressed the need for a gender- and race-balanced core curriculum that is sensitive to the unique experiences of Black women. At Spelman, ten core courses and/or introductory courses in various disciplines were targeted for revision. These included Freshman English, World Literature, World Civilization, Introduction to Sociology, World Religions, and Introduction to Psychology. The center also played the major leadership role in the establishment of an interdisciplinary Women's Studies minor program at Spelman; it is unique among Women's Studies programs not only because it focuses on women of color but also because it analyzes women's experiences from a cross-cultural perspective. In June 1987, Spelman College hosted the tenth anniversary annual conference of the National Women's Studies Association (NWSA) whose theme was

"Weaving Women's Colors: A Decade of Empowerment."

In 1989, two years after her arrival, Spelman's first Black woman president, Johnnetta B. Cole, appointed a Black Women's Studies task force to consider two major questions: Should Black Women's Studies form a major and should we separately develop African-American Studies and Women's Studies? This initiative was in keeping with her initial statement to the Spelman family following her appointment as the seventh President of Spelman College in 1987:

> I envision Spelman College in the coming decade as a renowned center for scholarship on Black women. Scholars, teachers, artists, policy analysts, and community leaders will turn to Spelman for comprehensive information on the rich and diverse history, struggles, conditions and accomplishments of Black women. Expanding on the work of the Women's Research and Resource Center . . . Spelman will blossom as an intellectual center on Black women's studies.

After a year of deliberations, the task force recommended that Spelman establish two new interdisciplinary programs: Black Women's Studies or Comparative Women's Studies (the issue was unresolved) and African Diasporic Studies. All of these activities have given national visibility to Spelman College as an institution committed to Women's Studies. In the interim, during a college-wide core curriculum revision process, a requirement of Women's Studies or Afro-American Studies was added to the Spelman core for all students. President Cole's efforts also resulted in the college's Board of Trustees naming in January 1992 Beverly Guy-Sheftall the first incumbent of the Anna Julia Cooper Endowed Professorship in Women's Studies. The professorship was made possible through a 1988 challenge grant from the Charles Stewart Mott Foundation and was matched by Camille and Bill Cosby.

The remainder of this essay will focus on the development of Spelman's involvement in Women's Studies since my return to the college in 1971 after having completed a master's degree in English at Atlanta University (my theses was on Faulkner's treatment of women in his major novels) and having taught for two years at Alabama State University, a large public Black institution in the Deep South.

When I returned to Spelman to teach freshman English in the fall of 1971 (after having graduated in 1966), I came with no particular vision about the kind of Black women's college I wanted Spelman to become nor was I particularly aware of the extent of my commitment to feminism or Black Women's Studies (a non-existent concept at that time).[7] I do recall after teaching a couple of years being frustrated about my Black female students' lack of familiarity with Black women's literature, a frustration which was shared by my colleague and friend Roseann Bell, who was also teaching English. We decided rather abruptly during 1974 that we would assemble a collection of readings which would include positive literary images of Black women and would make them available to our students who we felt were in desperate need of literary role models and stories about themselves. This was before writers such as Toni Morrison, Paule Marshall and Alice Walker, to name a few, were being consumed by large numbers of college students. After a cursory review of the literature, which revealed very little, we decided to undertake a more ambitious project which was the compilation of an anthology which would include critical essays on Black women writers, interviews with Black women writers, and literary selections, mainly short fiction and poetry, which included positive/complex images of black women. After leaving Spelman College and going to Cornell University, Bell encouraged Bettye Parker to join the editorial group. Following five years of hard work, *Sturdy Black Bridges: Visions of Black Women in Literature* was published by Doubleday in 1979. This was the first anthology of Black women's literature published in the USA. By this time, the women's movement was in full swing and I had begun to immerse myself in feminist theory, women's history and Black Women's Studies, though I would not have used this term at that point. Since 1976 I had also enrolled in the doctoral program in American Studies at Emory University and was on leave from Spelman pursuing Women's Studies formally and reading everything I could in order to understand what it meant to be female, especially a Black female, in this place and throughout the world. Occasionally, I would stop and try to understand why I had become so addicted to feminist material and I began to reflect on my own experience and discovered that I was probably a good case study for the development of a Black feminist academic.

First of all, I grew up in a female-centered (not matriarchal) household and was raised by a mother who had left her husband's house and moved to her parents' home with three daughters when I was in the eighth grade. Uppermost in my memory is her insistence that we develop the kind of emotional and financial independence which would enable us to survive without men if our marriages did not work. As important was her belief that studying was more important than doing household chores, so that I became a bookworm with limited domestic skills. The extent to which my mother (who died of breast cancer eleven years ago) was more interested in our intellectual development than our preparation for wifehood was apparent by her regularly excusing us from household duties if we were doing school work and her encouraging me to bypass home economics as a ninth grader and take typing instead. When I graduated from high school at the age of 15 (she had allowed me to start the first grade early and to complete the second and third grades in one year), she insisted that I leave home and attend

81

Spelman because of its solid academic reputation and because she was convinced that the protective environment which a women's college provided would be the most suitable place for my emotional and intellectual development.

Though I needed a job upon graduation four years later, which probably would have been teaching English in the public school system, she insisted that I take advantage of a fifth year, a study program newly instituted at Wellesley College, because it would get me out of the segregated South and would "expand my horizons." I am convinced that without the kind of persistent encouragement and support from a mother who had graduated from college (I was to discover her all "A"s college transcript among other memorabilia tucked neatly away in her dresser drawer after the funeral) and pursued a career, but who had not had the opportunity to realize her own dream of becoming a certified public accountant, I would not have found myself back at Spelman in the early 1970s doing the kind of work that was to become an obsession.

My life was also altered in significant ways because of two more trips to New England during the next five years and the impact of both personal and institutional models. While on leave from Spelman at Emory in 1976, a colleague (Judy Gebre-Hiwet) and I from the English department traveled to the Boston area to examine several Women's Studies programs which were in an embryonic stage at this point. This trip turned out to have been a major turning point in my own professional development. It is important to point out that the women with whom we met were for the most part African-American. Among this group was Barbara Smith (co-editor of *All the Women are White All the Blacks are Men, But Some of Us are Brave*) who was teaching literature at Simmons College. She shared with us her course syllabi as well as Alice Walker's course syllabus on "Black Women Writers." I believe Walker had designed and taught at Wellesley College the first course with this particular focus. In our reconstruction of the history of curriculum transformation in the academy, we must include the pioneering work and vision of Alice Walker who initiated a course which has become a staple within Women's Studies and many English departments. Unlike many Black women academics, I had my first experience of Women's Studies advocates with African-American women so that I never associated the development of Women's Studies with white women only.

A second trip to New England in the fall of 1981 turned out to have been the second most important professional decision I was to make. When the center opened I decided that it was important for me to meet another Black woman who was directing an important minority women's project at a major research center for women, so I returned to Wellesley College, after having spent a year there in 1967, to meet and confer with Patricia Bell-Scott who was the director of a large grant funded by the

Women's Educational Equity Act (WEEA) at the Center for Research on Women. Pat and I later became close friends and have worked together, always harmoniously, on several projects within the past few years. This included our co-directorship of a National Endowment for the Humanities (NEH) seminar for college teachers at Spelman College in 1985 on "Images of Black Women in Literature: A Life Cycle Approach." It occurs to me that my work at Spelman might not have taken the direction it did were it not for my association with Pat who provided constant guidance, as was the case with my mother, even though we remained miles apart. My subsequent associations with the women's caucus of the Modern Language Association where I came in contact with other African-American women (among them Nellie McKay, now professor of African-American Studies at the University of Wisconsin-Madison) underscored my perceptions that the evolution of Women's Studies was intimately connected to the pioneering work of Black women.

When I returned to Spelman in 1981, with all but the dissertation completed (which focused on attitudes toward Black women at the turn of the century), I was firmly convinced, as were a few others on campus, that the college needed a women's center and a Women's Studies program which would be geared to the special educational needs of Black women since the programs which I had seen were white and middle-class in focus. I had also become immersed in the Spelman archives as I prepared to write the college's centennial history during which I became even more convinced of the appropriateness of a focus on Black Women's Studies or Comparative Women's Studies at this very special place for Black women. Though Spelman had been offering a few Women's Studies courses since the early 1970s, there was no campus-wide program with an explicitly Black feminist perspective which would address such sensitive issues as rape, male/female relationships, incest, violence against women, or abortion, to name only a few topics, nor was there broad support for the development of Women's Studies. Unfortunately, the prevailing sentiment on campus seemed to be that since we were a women's college, it was not necessary to establish explicitly women-centered programs. Initially, President Donald Stewart was not convinced of the necessity or feasibility of such new initiatives. He agreed to the development of a proposal to the Mott Foundation for the establishment of a women's center on campus after, and I believe because, he was informed that women faculty at another Atlanta University Center institution were contemplating the development of a women's center which would also be seeking funding in the national arena. Under the Mott Foundation's historically Black colleges initiative, we submitted a proposal for the establishment of the Spelman College Women's Center which was funded in 1981. As the center evolved over the years, it became more cross-cultural and global in its perspective and began to address such issues as women under apartheid.

When I reflect upon the relative ease with which the center has been able to carry out its mission of addressing Black feminist issues on the campus and making the Spelman curriculum more sensitive to Women's Studies, it occurs to me that since I happened to have been a Spelman alumna and had been teaching at the college for ten years before getting involved in an open way with "women's issues," I was perceived to be "safe." I was also astute enough at the beginning to avoid the term "feminist" which is frequently perceived, unfortunately, to be a dirty word in the Black community, even among academics. Causes for hostility to feminism within communities of color, especially during the 1970s and 1980s, are complex. The most frequently stated reasons are that feminism is a white female issue, anti-male, associated with lesbianism, and divisive because it detracts from the more urgent issue of racism. Feminism is perceived to be alien to African-Americans because we have also been generally unaware of the persistent feminist tradition in African-American intellectual history.[8] I also remained sensitive to the conservative/traditional setting in which I was operating while at the same time working very hard to address explicitly feminist issues within the Spelman environment in ways which were appropriate for a women's center director.

I suppose I am happiest about the center's considerable progress with the community service component which is evidenced by an increase in the number of women within the local community, throughout the nation and from abroad who participate in workshops, seminars and conferences sponsored or co-sponsored by the center. These activities offer a diverse group of women intellectual stimulation, support, fellowship and the opportunity to discuss topics of interest to women. Of special interest in our community outreach activities was the enrichment program for Third World women sponsored by the center (and funded by President Stewart) in collaboration with the Continuing Education Division of the college. This program which involved women from Africa, Asia, India and the West Indies, was the first of its kind designed by the college specifically for Third World women, most of whom were non-professionals. The women were enrolled in two courses (Introduction to the Computer and Introduction to Child and Adolescent Psychology) which were taught by members of the Spelman faculty. To accommodate the women who were mothers of small children, the college provided free-of-charge child care. Through social activities and informal discussions, the women shared experiences across cultural lines and developed a strong sense of cohesiveness as a group from the Third World. This activity, which culminated in a graduation exercise for the women, won the center and the college many friends among the Third

World community in Atlanta.

Because of the center's involvement in national networking among women and women's centers, Spelman began to emerge as a site for national conferences that address critical issues facing women in general and Black women in particular. For example, the center was instrumental in bringing to the campus several major conferences which received nationwide participation. The first conference, held in October 1982 and sponsored by the center, examined Black Women and Public Policy Issues in the Eighties. The second, held in June 1983 under the auspices of the National Black Women's Health Network, was the first national Black Women's Health Conference. It attracted more than 1,500 participants and was a historic and unforgettable occasion.

It was fitting that a forum for the discussion of Black women's health issues take place at Spelman since the training of health care professionals had been a critical component of the early curriculum of the college. Spelman's nurse training department, which began in 1886, was the first of its kind available to Black women in this country. The 1983 National Black Women's Health Project (NBWHP) conference was the most successful community outreach effort in which the college had been involved over its 103-year history. However, it was a bitter-sweet experience. The serious physical and mental health problems which too many Black women suffer were painful to hear about. Yet, the intensity of the commitment on the part of hundreds of women to improve the health status of Black women was heartwarming indeed! I was reminded again at the end of it all that Spelman is really a very special place for Black women. For three days it was a perfect haven and provided a brief interlude from the continuing struggle to reclaim good health for Black women. I was thrilled that my work at the center had brought me in close contact with women like Byllye Avery, founding director, who had conceived the entire project. A year following the NBWHP Conference, the center co-sponsored a national conference on "Southern Granny Midwives" with the University of Medicine and Dentistry of New Jersey and Bryant College. This unique conference attracted midwives, scholars, teachers, print and photo-journalists, archivists, and women from the Atlanta community.

Over the past several years, several significant activities and projects have demonstrated the center's and the college's commitment to research on Black women, a new priority for Spelman. Among them was a photo-documentary exhibition, "Black Women As Healers: A Noble Tradition" (also an exhibit catalogue), which was a major attraction at the Black Women's Health Conference in 1983 and curated by Jacqueline Jones Royster, director of the Comprehensive Writing Center and former research associate of the center. It is housed permanently in the center meeting/reading room. Equally impressive was the selection of the center, in 1983, for membership in the National Council of Research on Women (NCROW) and my appointment as vice-chair of the Board of the Council. Only two of the council's thirty-seven centers are directed by Black women, and Spelman has the distinction of being the only historically Black college represented at the council.

The fact that the center is asked to participate in research projects of national significance is further indication of the attention it receives as a research center. We also involved ourselves with a collaborative project with the Center for Research on Women at Memphis State University and the Duke University/University of North Carolina Women's Studies Research Center in the production of a working paper series on "Southern Women: The Intersection of Race, Class and Gender." During 1985–6, I was the recipient of a distinguished professor's chair by Delta Sigma Theta Sorority and engaged in a collaborative project with Sage Women's Educational Press, Inc. on Black mother/daughter relationships. The center was also responsible for convening the Forum on Research on Black Women, an informal group of Black women researchers, most of whom were affiliated with women's centers in various parts of the country. We met at the center for a two-year period in order to share information about our research and to develop plans for promoting both Black Women's Studies and research on Black women.

In April 1983, the center director and Patricia Bell-Scott embarked upon a collaborative project, the founding of *SAGE: A Scholarly Journal on Black Women*, which became the center's major research project. Published biannually, *SAGE* (which the center hosts) is an international forum for the discussion of critical issues affecting women of African descent throughout the world. The premier issue on Black Women's Education appeared in May, 1984; thirteen issues have been published to date. The founding of *SAGE* was a milestone in promoting research on Black women and a major step toward developing the research component of the center. A unique aspect of the journal, the only one of its kind in the world, is its global and cross-cultural perspective on Black womanhood – a perspective which includes material on African, South American and Caribbean women. A major project of *SAGE* was the preparation of a manuscript on Black mothers and daughters, published by Beacon Press as an anthology entitled *Double Stitch: Black Women Write About Mothers and Daughters* (1991); this book evolved from two special issues on mothers and daughters published by *SAGE* in 1984 and 1986.

In May, 1990, the center hosted an invitational conference on the state of the art in Black Women's Studies which was the final activity of the second-year Ford Foundation curriculum development project (extended to a third year).[9] This conference was also in many ways a celebration of nearly a decade of the existence of the Women's Center, of eight years of *SAGE*, and of Spelman and the kind of institution it is in the process of becoming. In my opening remarks, I reminded the gathering that the establishment of an explicitly feminist presence on the campus had not been easy and that in many ways I thought we had just begun. I also indicated that an important mission of the center, which had often been misunderstood, was helping to redirect and shape the national dialogue about the meaning of Women's Studies and feminism as well as Black Women's Studies and Black feminism. In other words, what we had been attempting to do would, I hope, help to redefine both Black Studies and Women's Studies as well as provide leadership in the development of Black Women's Studies. The purpose of the conference was to assemble a diverse group of colleagues who came from varying disciplinary perspectives, different institutional contexts and different ideological points of view but who were committed to the development of Black and Women's Studies and were not hostile to feminism. We were interested too in having this conversation with women of different races and from different parts of the globe. We were also as committed to including men, especially Black men, but not just any Black men! Our criterion for selection was fairly narrow – we wanted Black men who actually had taught courses focusing on Black women; who demonstrated commitment to and knowledge about the subject-matter in ways that were obvious – through publications and planning of conferences, for example. We also wanted to reconnect with some of our faculty colleagues who had participated in the Ford project over the past six years and we especially wanted to engage in dialogue with Black women who had written about and taught in the areas of Black Studies and/or Women's Studies but who had a particular focus in their work on Black women. The conference would not attempt to define Black Women's Studies in any definitive manner; it did not pretend to have assembled only the "experts" in the field. Our only ground rules were that we listen to each other; and that we proceed with a great deal of caring and sensitivity to each other because we were, each one of us, engaged in a risky but critically important undertaking. I ended by reminding us that perhaps one of the least understood phenomena might be the complexity and diversity of what it has meant and continues to mean to be Black and female both here and throughout the world.

As I reflect on the evolution of my alma mater and the impact of the center on its continued development, I remember having left Spelman in 1966 with no understanding of patriarchy or colonialism or apartheid. I did not know the conditions under which the majority of the world's women lived. I did not know what female circumcision, footbinding, purdah, or suttee were, though I did know about the horrors of the Middle Passage, lynching and the Holocaust. Though I knew the particular burden of Black women as a result of my own family history and what I had observed growing up in Memphis, Tennessee, before integration, I did not fully understand the concept of "double jeopardy" as it related to women of color, and I was ill-equipped to handle a class analysis of the plight of Black women. I did not know many of our important Black foremothers – Frances E. W. Harper, Anna Julia Cooper, Selena Sloan Butler (a Spelman alumna), Josephine St Pierre Ruffin, or even Zora Neale Hurston (an unfortunate circumstance which Alice Walker, a fellow student, also bemoans). I had not read Sojourner Truth's now famous "Ain't I A Woman" speech or William E. B. DuBois's moving account of the tragedy of Black womanhood in "The Damnation of Women" from *Darkwater* (1920), though I had read his more familiar *The Souls of Black Folk* (1903). I was unaware of the Black feminist tradition in the intellectual history of African-Americans which had been bequeathed to us by Sojourner Truth, Frederick Douglass, William E. B. Du Bois and Mary Church Terrell, to name only a few.

It is imperative that our Black female students (and our Black male students for that matter) not leave Spelman's gates at the end of four years with the gaps in their knowledge with which I left twenty-five years ago, and I am convinced that the presence of Women's Studies courses and the new core requirement (one course in either Afro-American or Women's Studies) for all students will ensure that this will not be the case. As director of a women's center at a historically Black college, I am as concerned about our students' commitment to improving the lives of women, especially Black women, no matter where they live in the world. They must be concerned about adolescent mothers with inadequate pre-natal care and limited resources; they must be concerned about rural women in Kenya and elsewhere who walk miles every day in search of firewood in order to feed their families; they must be concerned about women in South Africa who are virtually imprisoned in "homelands" far away from their husbands who must seek work in urban areas. If all of this is accomplished, and more, Spelman will have become the kind of Black women's college that all of us can revere. It will have surpassed the vision of its founders. The center remains committed and vigilant in its support of the college as it carries out its very special mission of educating Black women who will make this planet a better place for women and men to live.

My mother would have certainly been very proud of her daughter and the center. I am pleased that at least some of my dreams have been fulfilled.

NOTES

1 For historical information on Spelman College, see Florence Matilda Read, *The Story of Spelman College* (Princeton, NJ: Princeton University Press, 1961); Beverly Guy-Sheftall (with Jo Moore Stewart), *Spelman: A Centennial*

Celebration (Charlotte, NC: Delmar, 1981); Beverly Guy-Sheftall, "Black Women and Higher Education: Spelman and Bennett Colleges Revisited" (*Journal of Negro Education* 51 (1982): 275–87); and Beverly Guy-Sheftall, *Daughters of Sorrow: Attitudes Toward Black Women, 1880–1920* (Brooklyn, NY: Carlson, 1990).

2 An earlier version of this paper, "Women's Studies at Spelman College: Reminiscences from the Director," appeared in *Women's Studies International Forum* 9 (2) (1986): 151–5.

3 Hull *et al.*, 1982: xx–xxi.

4 McLaughlin and Kelley, 1989: 44–6.

5 See Guy-Sheftall, 1986a: 597–9, for my comments on our experiences at the conference.

6 See the three-volume *Africana Women's Studies Series*, published by the Africana Women's Center, Atlanta University, Atlanta, GA, 1985, which includes course syllabi and bibliographies.

7 See *All the Women are White, All the Blacks are Men, But Some of Us are Brave,* the first major text on Black Women's Studies; see also Beverly Guy-Sheftall and Patricia Bell-Scott, 1989; a special issue of *SAGE: A Scholarly Journal on Black Women* focusing on Black Women's Studies, VI (Summer 1989), which includes selected proceedings from the 1988 Inaugural Symposium of President Johnnetta B. Cole on "The Empowerment of Black Women"; and Yolanda T. Moses, "Black Women in Academe: Issues and Strategies," Project on the Status and Education of Women, Association of American Colleges, August 1989, 1–24.

8 See Beverly Guy-Sheftall, 1986b: 54–7, for a discussion of Black feminism from a historical perspective within the African-American community.

9 See Bell-Scott, Guy-Sheftall and Jones Royster, 1990, for a detailed discussion of the conference.

BIBLIOGRAPHY

Africana Women's Center (1985) *Africana Women's Studies Series*, Volumes 1–3, Atlanta, GA: Africana Women's Center.

Bell-Scott, Patricia, Guy-Sheftall, Beverly and Royster, Jacqueline Jones (1991) "The Promise and Challenge of Black Women's Studies: A Report from the Spelman Conference, May 25–26, 1990," *NWSA Journal* III (Spring): 281–8.

Guy-Sheftall, Beverly (1986a) "Reflections on Forum '85 in Nairobi, Kenya: Voices from the International Women's Studies Community," *Signs: Journal of Women in Culture and Society* (March): 587–99.

—— (1986b) "Remembering Sojourner Truth: On Black Feminism," *Catalyst* 1 (Fall): 54–7.

—— and Bell-Scott, Patricia (1989) "Black Women's Studies: A View From the Margin," in C. Pearson, J. S. Touchton and D. C. Shavlik (eds) *Educating the Majority: Women Challenge Tradition in Higher Education*, New York: Macmillan.

Hull, Gloria T., Bell-Scott, Patricia and Smith, Barbara (eds) (1982) *All the Women are White, All the Blacks are Men, But Some of Us are Brave*, Old Westbury, NY: Feminist Press.

McLaughlin, Andrée Nicola and Kelley, Don Quinn (1989) "Black Women's Studies in America," in Helen Tierney (ed.) *Encyclopedia of Women's Studies: Views from the Sciences*, Westport, CT: Greenwood Press.

6

WOMEN AND COLLECTIVE ACTION
Female models in transition

Filomina Chioma Steady

I wish to pay tribute to the memory of my mentor, Professor Edwin Ardener of Oxford University. The inspiration for this chapter comes in part from his essay entitled "Belief and the Problem of Women."[1]

In this chapter I examine in cross-cultural perspective the female problematic by recognizing the importance of female models or paradigms as transformational models. I begin by discussing the negative consequences of rendering female models invisible or marginal in methodological as well as in sociocultural terms: I then examine situations in which female models have served as transformational models. Finally I argue that female models are in danger of losing this transformational quality by becoming fragmented and assuming certain characteristics detrimental to some women.

THE FEMALE PROBLEMATIC: INTRODUCTION

The significance of women's collective action in its various manifestations can be examined within the context of three interrelated parameters. First, elements of female culture which define women's space are essential in developing feminist consciousness that is an awareness and determination to eliminate gender-based discrimination and exploitation. Second, this consciousness is a necessary prerequisite for promoting feminist ideologies as well as for transforming society. Third, in multi-ethnic and class societies female models for societal change should have at their core the articulated aspirations and agendas of women from the economically and socially oppressed groups of society.

The terms "female models," "women's space," "female culture" and "feminist ideology" will be used interchangeably to denote areas of social and symbolic action that provide general paradigms for living which are essentially but arguably female. These areas include beliefs, values, norms and linguistic expressions which illustrate the complex nature of female creativity and action, and are derived primarily from roles and expectations characteristic of socially constructed female spheres of activity. It is now generally accepted that these could include designs for living that have the following general paradigmatic characteristics. First: promotes egalitarian and cooperative values rather than hierarchical and authoritarian ones. Second: views bureaucratic rationality, meritocracy and academic objectivity as exclusionary devices to ensure male privilege and dominance. Third: prefers peace to war, and opposes the ideology of domination. Fourth: promotes nurturing and the preservation of life. Fifth: opposes and strives to eliminate global economic and political processes detrimental to women. Finally: values impulsive and experiential reasoning. With regard to the last characteristic the following datum from my fieldwork studies on women's collective action is instructive. During a period of political unrest in Freetown, Sierra Leone in the 1970s the Secretary-General of the Women's Congress (a grassroots organization within the All People's Congress – the dominant political party) made the following statement at a general meeting:

> If women were in power there would be no political unrest and instability. Women act on impulse and would have put an end to all this unrest at one go. Women have tougher minds.[2]

Being impulsive and strong may appear contradictory from an androcentric and indeed from a Eurocentric perspective, which in rendering female models invisible have weakened and devalued them. However, in this African context it provided a base for female mobilization and solidarity. During the last twenty years women have made significant changes in almost every sphere of life in every major region of the world through collective action. Nonetheless, within a social context the majority of women are still generally recognized as the main agents of reproduction of the labor force as well as secondary persons.

FEMALE MODELS ECLIPSED

Aspects of female culture can become marginalized, devalued, usurped and made invisible. The process of rendering "female culture" invisible can occur through changes in the mode of production whereby ideologies regulating the sexual division of labor and access to resources result in the relative disadvantage of women. Additionally, as Ardener and others have pointed out, women can become marginalized through the inadequacies of paradigms utilized by researchers. Until fairly recently androcentric models dominated anthropological practice and discourse for well over half a century.

Writing in the early 1970s, Ardener noted the discrepancy between what is observed in anthropology and what is reported. The problematic, according to Ardener, is as follows: Since male models are the recognized models of articulation in society and since the majority of anthropologists have been male, female models became subsumed and women became lay figures in men's drama.[3] According to Ardener, "the arena of public discourse tended to be characteristically male-dominated and the appropriate language registers often seemed to have been encoded by males. Women may be at a disadvantage when wishing to express matters of concern to them." Unless women's views are presented in a form acceptable to men and to women brought up in the male idiom, they will not be given a proper hearing. The problem then is that women are deprived of the facility to raise to a conscious level their unconscious thoughts. "Those who were not in a male world position were, as it were, muted. . . . A group is muted simply because it does not form part of the dominant communicative system of society – expressed as it must be through the dominant ideology, and that mode of production, if you wish, which is articulated with it."[4] Ardener suggests that women's ideas or models of the world around them might, nevertheless, find a way of expression in forms other than direct expository speech, possibly through symbolism, art, myth, ritual, special speech registers, etc.

The revisionist thrust of a number of studies by female anthropologists in the last two decades has served to rectify problems of women's invisibility. Collier, in a study of women in politics, for instance, shows how women are social actors and political animals whose choices affect the options open to politically active and articulate men in a number of societies.[5] Several studies of spirit possession in Africa have made women's rituals visible by showing that, contrary to the view put forward by some male anthropologists that spirit-possession cults are attempts to exercise male prerogatives, women were expressing through these rituals their fulfillment of the feminine role just as men did in their own rituals.[6]

In this sense we can regard as expressions of a female world-view not only the Bakweri mermaid rituals which Ardener describes but also several secret society rituals of the Sande society in West Africa. We may also regard old wives' tales and sorority rituals, etc., in Europe and in the USA as representative of deeper structures with meanings still to be deciphered through careful research. In my field research on the Sande female secret society, for instance, it was clear that some traditional female collective sanctions were far more effective in controlling male aggression than the modern law enforcement institutions by the patriarchal colonial system. This was possible because the traditional system stressed male/female complementarity. Many women complained to me that the control of domestic violence through traditional forms of women's collective action, which in the rural areas involved tying the culprit's hands and feet and letting him roll down a rocky hill, was no longer possible in the urban areas. Rather, in extreme cases women migrants in the city had to resort to the impersonal, ineffective and patriarchally oriented system of law enforcement.[7]

Sande/Bondo is probably the most widespread of women's "associations" in Sierra Leone. Like its male counterpart, the Poro, it embodies a repertoire of indigenous knowledge, beliefs, ethics, arts and crafts that have ensured the social, cultural and biological survival of generations. Its ritual is a necessary precondition for social transformation from childhood to womanhood and marriage. Marriage, a supremely important institution, is an inevitable stage in the life-cycle, guaranteeing regeneration and continuity of the group. Although in theory Sande membership is not compulsory it is, like marriage, desirable and inevitable. It is promoted as an ideal and sustained by strong social pressures. As a result, it has continued in full force in spite of countervening forces from the colonial encounter, from Christian and Islamic influences, from social change and from urbanization. The interaction with the supernatural is a necessary component of the transformation of status from childhood to adulthood. Sande also facilitates the revelation of the special "secret" knowledge about the society and about the virtues of womanhood that ensure fertility. The cultural management of fertility, pregnancy and childbirth is the most important function of the Sande, and the leader of the Sande is usually also a midwife. Sande therefore sustains the most vital elements of culture that are decidedly female.

Both Sande and Poro emphasize men's and women's spheres of activity and impose sanctions to ensure that these spheres are maintained with a certain degree of autonomy. Since some of these sanctions regulate behavior between the sexes Sande has functioned as an association which protects and defends women's rights. For example, Sande leaders can impose sanctions on men who disrespect or mistreat women. As a corollary, Poro leaders can also impose sanctions against women. An institutional stabilizing mechanism is thus maintained in male/female relationships while protecting the autonomy of each of their spheres of activity.

Significant, and of even greater historical and contemporary relevance, is the fact that these elements of female collective consciousness are not restricted to the female domain, and have the potential for mobilization and sociocultural transformation. One example of this potential can be drawn from Africa and another from the USA. The 1929 Igbo's War in Nigeria, condescendingly referred to in British historiography as "the Aba Riots," was an act of war against the taxation of women by the colonial government. This was a revolt against what has been described as "the violation of women's cultural space."[8] Women felt that their identity had been challenged. Through colonialism the British introduced a new system of production which involved large-scale cash crop production, processing and distribution. This altered the traditional system of subsistence agriculture which gave women certain distinct advantages in their roles as agents of biological, social, cultural and economic reproduction. As Ifeka-Moller argues, taxation of women reminded women that the new circumstances gave them an identity which placed them in the male system, depriving them of some female advantage while putting them at a disadvantage compared to men.[9] Female militancy in this regard led to a change in the British colonial taxation policy.

Another example of female collective action against male intrusion into women's space for purposes of male economic exploitation comes from the women's health care movement of the USA. Feminists argue that prior to the early part of the twentieth century American women's reproductive functions – menarche, pregnancy and menopause – were an integral part of a female culture which provided sympathetic personal support and guidance to women. All of these life-cycle events are important rites of passage for females, with significant and positive consequences for their sense of self and feminine identity. The medicalization of these crucial biological events has resulted in women's greater dependence on the health system presided over by men.[10] It has been argued further that although the twentieth century saw the disintegration and erosion of female culture by declining birth rates, increases in geographical mobility and the superficial entry of women into male culture, the demise of female culture began earlier, during the early 1800s in the USA, as males assumed obstetrical and gynecological tasks.[11] The women's health care movement can therefore be seen as a cultural revolt.

Applying feminist consciousness against cultural, methodological and socioeconomic marginalization was only a partial manifestation of the transformational nature of female models. The political dimension is even more significant. According to Ardener, "dominance occurs when one structure blocks the power of actualization of the other, so that it has no freedom of action. . . . The articulation of world structure does not only rest in their production base but at all levels of communication. . . . [A] structure is also a kind of language of many semi-logical elements which specify all action by its power of definition."[12]

FEMALE MODELS TRANSFORMED

I will attempt, at this juncture, to examine briefly the transformational aspects of women's collective action in light of these theoretical postulations. The modern women's movement seeks to overthrow the dominant structure of patriarchy by establishing and promoting the actualization of female models, not only obliquely through symbolic and ritualistic expressions but also directly through articulated speech and collective action. These actions and pronouncements have rendered women more visible and effective to the extent that female models have become a publicly recognized part of the ideological landscape. In fact, there is a sense in which one can speak of new feminist counter-culture in the areas of feminist publishing, creative expressions, festivals, rallies, lifestyles, etc.

Historical and economic forces have been instrumental in challenging the dominant structure and forcing change and recognition of alternative structures. Historically, feminist activism has produced female models which became effective and integral ingredients for social change in many regions of the world. In almost all of these instances feminist activism was linked to nationalist struggles.

One of the strategies used in many non-western countries to overthrow dominant structures was to promote the revival of a golden age of women. The importance of women and female cultures was emphasized by evoking past civilizations in which women held high status. Consequently, along with programs against imperialist and feudalist ideologies, one important ingredient of nationalist strategies of cultural revival was a call for reclaiming the lost freedoms and status from which women had been stripped. Numerous examples of the evocation of the golden age of women can be drawn from countries in many regions of the world such as Turkey, Iran, Japan, Egypt and India.[13] Feminism, as an ideology of women's collective action, has been expressed and executed more consistently when the goal embraces not only equality with men but also sociocultural transformation. In this regard feminism has two long-term goals which still have to be fulfilled:[14]

1 freedom from oppression ivolving not only equity, but also the right of women to freedom of choice and the power to control their own lives within and outside the home
2 the removal of all forms of inequality and oppression through the creation of a more just social and economic order, nationally and internationally. This means the involvement of women in national liberation struggles, in plans for national development, and in local and global strategies for change.

At a 1985 conference on "A Decade of Women's Collective Action" by the International Women's Anthropological Conference, it was found that in all regions of the world there is evidence of a history of women's collective action. In almost all instances these actions included struggles for women's issues, campaigns against cultural practices injurious to women and broader movements for societal change. Whenever women's movements emerged they did so in the wider context of social and political movements.[15]

Although feminist activities in Third World countries have been largely invisible in history, issues of women's rights and education were debated in China as early as the eighteenth century, and movements for women's social emancipation were prevalent in early-nineteenth-century India. In fact, studies show that in many countries of Asia feminist struggles have been in existence for well over a century. For the most part these struggles were linked to larger issues and responded to both internal and external pressures. As Jayawardena points out, "It is in the context of the resistance to imperialism and various forms of domination on the one hand, and to feudal monarchies, exploitative local rulers and patriarchal and religious structures on the other, that we should consider the democratic movement for women's rights and the feminist struggles that emerged in Asia."[16]

Despite women's participation in nationalist and class struggles and later in militant collective organizing, this did not necessarily change the gender imbalances in the domestic sphere. A study of poor women's groups in rural India has shown that from 1973 to 1975 women were raising the issue of wife battery and took direct action. They marched to the liquor stores and destroyed the liquor containers which were often perceived as the immediate cause of wife beating. Other issues taken up by these women included struggles against rape and sexual harassment by the rich farmers, forest officials and landlord-goons.[17] Nonetheless, these actions did not in any way militate against women's participation in the larger struggles involving general class actions and participation in larger political movements.

The transformational nature of feminist models holds true also for the West. The feminist movement had its roots in and impetus from larger historical and social movements. Historically it was the defeat of Nazism and fascism which gave rise to the feminist movement as we know it today. Women's movements and organizations in Europe played significant social roles which included relieving poverty and destitution in the nineteenth century. In Europe and the USA women's groups were active in the anti-slavery movement. The civil rights movement in the 1960s, the anti-Vietnam protests, student revolutionary activities in the US and Europe and the reinforcement of radical protest and militant uprisings in the West during this period, all had a galvanizing effect which ushered in the modern women's movement. The women's movement is therefore anchored in traditions involving much wider social change.[18]

Examples from Latin America show similar trends. According to the Latin American and Caribbean Women's Collective the women's movement should go beyond feminist issues. Solutions based on "sisterhood" invite us to enter into an imaginary paradise, and thus conceal the problem of class struggle and women's role within it. In the final analysis, the essential point is to define the relation between the women's movement and the revolutionary political movements.[19]

With regard to the Black woman, it has been pointed out in the book *The Black Woman Cross-Culturally* that for the majority of Black women liberation from sexual oppression has always been fused with liberation from other forms of oppression such as slavery, imperialism, colonialism, neocolonialism, poverty, racism and apartheid.[20]

In Africa, indigenous women's societies promoting women's rights have existed since precolonial times, and African feminism integrates indigenous patterns of feminist activism with other struggles in human rather than narrow sexist terms.[21] In a study of female militancy Ekejiuba pointed out that "in Nigeria, the traditional image of women as *working mothers*, was related to a number of factors, and namely their assumed access to the means of production, especially land, strong kinship and neighborhood support for their self-development and for raising children; strong tradition of female power and participation in all domains of life – economic, political, ritual and associational." She points out further that women were expected to order their own space, their own affairs, and protect their own interests as women. "However, although women were often galvanized into militant action to protect and enhance a space that assumed their security and status, their consciousness as women included civic concerns and a feeling of responsibility for social issues and progress."[22]

In my study of political mobilization and activism among grass-roots women in Freetown, one constant theme stressed by the Women's Congress was the fact that women's participation in government was not just a matter of necessity but a natural right.

> Women are the rightful owners of the country. We give birth to men so in a way we own them. If women stand united only good can come out of it. Sierra Leone belongs to us. . . . Women should participate in all facets of the administration, in committees, on boards as directors, in Parliament, and in the government. Many issues of the country concern women and children, so we should be consulted and we should make decisions.[23]

In other instances in contemporary Africa, women have taken collective action in response to various economic and political crises. In Uganda, for example, the general political and economic crises have not only forced women to rediscover traditional means of organizing to solve practical problems of labor, health and access to resources, but also to raise political issues concerning peace and national security.[24]

97

FEMALE MODELS FRAGMENTED

This link between women's all-inclusive participation in nationalist struggles and in political, social, cultural and economic development has been shown clearly in every aspect of feminism in the Third World. Implicit in this is the conviction that feminism has a dual mandate, to eliminate gender-based discrimination and oppression and to transform all spheres of society. As the former president of Tanzania, Julius Nyerere, puts it in stressing the importance of women's active and beneficial participation in national development: "A person cannot walk very far or very fast on one leg; how can we expect half the people to develop a nation."[25]

The foregoing has sought to demonstrate that female models, when publicly activated in the context of collective action, can function as transformational models. What we need to examine now are the internal contradictions of this model as expressed in fragmented feminist consciousness which is best illustrated in feminist developments in multi-ethnic, class-based societies.

In the West, five main stages have been generally recognized as characterizing the women's movement:

1 the period of consciousness raising, mobilization and advocacy
2 militancy and radicalization leading to direct action
3 consolidation, institution building, and counter-culture
4 fragmentation and diversification; marginalization of some groups of women
5 repression, male backlash, resistance and apathy.

The present stage of the women's movement in multi-ethnic, class-based, industrialized societies can be seen as roughly equivalent to the fourth stage, with emerging aspects of the fifth stage. It is becoming increasingly clear that women do not belong to a universal category and that the significance of being female varies with technology, setting, class, context, task, rank, race, age, profession, kinship, wealth and economics.[26] Minority women, scholars, politicians, activists as well as working-class women generally are marginalized by the women's movement. This sense of alienation has been well articulated in several international and national fora, and was a main focus of attention by several eminent speakers during the 1987 National Women's Studies Association Conference in Atlanta. It was pointed out that many of the gains of the women's movement have been made by women who belonged to certain privileged ethnic and socioeconomic groups.

What we are witnessing then is the emergence of an articulated female model which, within a female context, is itself a dominant model. For the most part it is being articulated and actualized primarily by women who have access to the instruments of communication, to information and, directly or indirectly, to the means of production, control and domination. As Cotera points out:

> So far the cry for coalition building is all on the minority side, and basically the problem is whereas women think coalitions with the women's movement are necessary, the women's movement knows they are not. Whereas minority women need to coalesce with the women's movement, or feel that they need to, the leadership of the women's movement knows it need not coalesce with anyone.[27]

Even when viewed in historical terms the marginalization of minorities and working-class women from the women's movement has been amply documented. As Cotera further points out:

> The greatest victory for the women's movement was no victory for minority women. The suffrage amendment did not enfranchise Chicanas, and Black women. . . . Minority women, whether Black, Native American, Asian-American, Chicanas, or even White ethnic women, are ambivalent about the promise of the present re-emergence of the women's movement. . . . Their ambivalence and apprehension are based on negative experiences suffered in contact with the movement of the last 10 years. . . . What is sad is that most minority and working-class women do need the movement.[28]

In studying the various manifestations of collective action by women cross-culturally, it becomes necessary then to adopt a conceptual framework which recognizes women both as a gendered group, with roles and expectations which are different from men's, and women as representatives of other groups which share interests on the basis of class, ethnic, religious and national affiliations. On one level, forms of social organization and their related symbolic systems define femaleness and maleness; establish and maintain separate spheres for men and women, and outline the nature of their power or lack thereof, within a given social context. At another level, priorities and agendas are defined on the basis of one's socioeconomic and ethnic position. In this regard it can be assumed that the more removed a group is from access to the dominant model or articulation and "the means of production that is articulated with it," the greater the likelihood for female collective action to be concentrated on struggles for the elimination of poverty and economic oppression, i.e. the basic elements of gender oppression.

Without the full involvement of the most disadvantaged women, the fifth stage of the women's movement, characterized by repression, male backlash, apathy, etc., will likely become fully implemented. It is not only men who will be instrumental in bringing about the fifth stage. If the women's movement replicates the dominant model it will result in the perpetuation rather than the elimination of patriarchy. The importance of participation by working-class, minority, oppressed and powerless women in the women's movement, for fundamental sociocultural transformations at this historical juncture of the movement's development, is critical. To paraphrase Ardener, structures of domination are also structures of articulation. So long as some women continue to remain outside the structures of articulation, the objectives of the women's movement to promote gender equity and to end gender-based discrimination, etc., will be only partially achieved.

In concluding I would like to reiterate that dominant models, whether fully or partly controlled by men or women, are likely to be inherently limited, since they represent concentration of power which will invariably prevent the development of the full potential and creative abilities of the majority of women. The prospect for major societal change will be much greater when women do not simply copy the dominant model, but develop solid analytical approaches that would ensure changes in decision-making and power relations, not only between men and women but also among women.

REFERENCES

1 Ardener, Edwin W., "Belief and the Problem of Women" (in J. La Fontaine [ed.] *The Interpretation of Ritual*, London: Tavistock Publications, 1972).
2 Steady, Filomina Chioma, *Female Power in African Politics* (Munger Africana Library Notes, Pasadena, CA: California Institute of Technology, 1975).
3 Ardener, op. cit., 2.
4 Ardener, Edwin W., "The Problem of Women Revisited" (in Shirley Ardener [ed.] *Perceiving Women*, New York: Wiley, 1975), 22.
5 Collier, Jane, "Women in Politics" (in Michele Zimbalist Rosaldo and Louise Lamphere [eds] *Women, Culture and Society*, Stanford, CA: Stanford University Press, 1974).
6 Constantinides, Pamela, "Women's Spirit Possession and Urban Adaptation in the Muslim Northern Sudan" (in P. Caplan and J. Bujra [eds] *Women United, Women Divided*, London: Tavistock Publications, 1978).
7 Steady, Filomina Chioma, "The Structure and Function of Women's Associations in an African City: A Study of the Associative Process Among Women in Freetown" (unpublished doctoral dissertation, Oxford University, 1973).
8 Ifeka-Moller, Caroline, "Female Militancy and Colonial Revolt: The Women's War of 1929, Eastern Nigeria," in Shirley Ardener (1975), op. cit. Also discussed by Shirley Ardener in the Introduction to the anthology.
9 ibid.
10 Ruzek, Sheryl, *The Women's Health Movement: Feminist Alternatives to Medical Control* (New York: Praeger, 1978).
11 ibid., 19.
12 Ardener, Edwin W. (1975), op. cit., 25.
13 Other examples have been documented widely in historical sources and recently discussed in Kumari Jayawardena. *Feminism and Nationalism in the Third World* (The Hague: Institute of Social Research, 1982) and can no

doubt be found in Africa and Latin America.

14 Exemplified in a seminar on feminist ideology held in Bangkok in 1979.

15 Reddock, Rhoda, "Overview: Constructing a Cross-Cultural Comparative framework" (*I. W. A. C. Bulletin* [1985]), 4.

16 Jayawardena, op. cit.

17 Gothaskar, Sujata, "Women's Collective Actions: An Experience in Rural India" (*I. W. A. C. Bulletin* [1985]), 4.

18 ibid.

19 Latin American and Caribbean Women's Collective, *Slaves of Slaves* (Westport, CT: Third Press, 1980).

20 Steady, Filomina Chioma, "The Black Woman Cross-Culturally: An Overview" (in Filomina Chioma Steady [ed.] *The Black Woman Cross-Culturally*, Cambridge, Mass. Schenkman, 1981).

21 ibid.

22 Ekejiuba, Felicia, "Nine Decades of Female Militancy in Nigeria" (*I. W. A. C. Bulletin* 1 [1985]), 10–11.

23 Steady, Filomina Chioma, *Female Power in African Politics: The National Congress of Sierra Leone* (Munger Africana Library Monograph, Pasadena, CA: California Institute of Technology, 1975).

24 Aworrie, Mary, "Women's Collective Actions in Uganda" (*I. W. A. C. Bulletin* 1 [1985]), 14.

25 Nyerere, Julius, speech at the preparatory regional meetings for the Nairobi World Conference on the United Nations Decade for Women, Arusha, Tanzania, 1985.

26 Wallman, S., "Difference, Differentiation, Discrimination" (*New Community* 5 [1 & 2] [1976]), 12. For African women in Africa and the Diaspora, see Filomina Chioma Steady, "African Feminism: A World-Wide Perspective" (in R. Terborg-Penn *et al.* [eds] *Women in Africa and the African Diaspora*, Washington, DC: Howard University Press, 1987).

27 Cotera, Marta, "Feminism: The Chicana and Anglo Versions" (in Margarita Melville [ed.] *Twice a Minority*, St Louis, MO: Mosby, 1980), 231.

28 ibid.

7

AFRICAN WOMEN, CULTURE AND ANOTHER DEVELOPMENT

'Molara Ogundipe-Leslie

Just as men have a right to food, they also have a social right to speak, to know, to understand the meaning of their work, to take part in public affairs and to defend their beliefs.

The rights to education, to expression, to information and to the management of production are all rights which articulate the same need of socialization.

It is therefore a perversion to imagine that the discussion on development can be limited to what is called the satisfaction of basic material needs. When peasants or workers are excluded from all responsibilities in the production system, when scientific research is subjected to profit, when education patterns are imposed that make school children or students strangers to their own culture and mere instruments to the production process, when protest is reduced to silence by force and political prisoners are tortured, can it be thought that these practices do not hinder the goals of development and that they do not inflict an injury on society?

(*What Now*:[1] 27)

The idea of "development" has been much-touted in the last two decades, universally considered necessary by the industrialized countries who have pushed the idea on to Third World countries who may or may not know what "development" means, why it is necessary and what it may cost in material or social terms. It was in fact an ideology, and very often the official ideology in countries with very different social and economic forms of organization and with different political color. Distilling the main features of development in an essay on "The Cultural Dimension of Development," J. C. Sanchez Arnau says ideology was

1) based on a mechanistic and linear conception of history which assumes that every society must go through the same stages of "development" until it reaches the stage in which the economic

102

apparatus continually ensures to the population an income level similar to that of those countries at present considered as "developed";

2) based on an ethnocentric approach which assumes that the basic goal of any society is to achieve the same values characterizing the "so-called developed" societies: spirit of enterprise, the profit-motive, competition, material security, and especially endeavors to achieve the possession of certain goods and services typical of highly industrialized societies. Therefore, those countries or societies which have not already achieved these goals or which do not share them, are not considered "different" but instead "primitive," "traditional," "under-developed" or in the best cases, "developing" countries or societies;

3) "development" is also based on an essentially economic approach, since it considers that the adequate management of the instruments of economic policy is in itself sufficient to maintain any country on the road to achieving these goals, and ultimately reaching them. Thus it globally ignores what we call her "culture," i.e. the collection of values, aspirations, beliefs, patterns of behavior and inter-personal relations, established or predominating, within a given social group or society. . . .

Development has thus essentially become a mechanism to transfer culture from industrialized to Third World countries, from the "center" to the "periphery," playing a similar role as previously played by the ideology of "progress" in the nineteenth century in Latin America and the Middle East or by colonization in Africa. In this way, societies, bereft of adequate economic means, have adopted or try to adopt a life-style only accessible to limited numbers of their population, mortgaging their economic future and losing their cultural inheritance.

(Arnau, 1981: 3–4, 5)

"Development" can not only be criticized for its features stated above, its "cultural" imperialism and ethnocentricism, but also for ignoring the social cost of its effect of upheaval on individual and collective lives and its interruption of – or interference with – the internal and natural dynamics of evolution in the societies into which it has been introduced.

Supposedly, it is in reaction to the failure of the practice of "development" thus far, that the concept of "Another Development" has been introduced. The 1975 Dag Hammarskjold report *What Now* which encapsulates and inculcates the concept of "Another Development" is a brave and admirable document which would be even more useful if it could attain the cooperation and "good faith" of the industrialized countries to achieve its stated objectives. One of the best notions in *What*

103

Now is the recognition of the need to "decolonize" the UN as a prerequisite to any affirmative action. Not only "decolonize" the UN but also and necessarily trim its unwieldy, expensive and resultantly inefficient administrative structure. In addition, *What Now* positively calls for an approach to development which recognizes cultural specificities in societies and demands an endogenous and "participatory" approach. In sum, "Another Development" claims to be "totally man-centered." It is need-oriented being geared to the satisfaction of man's needs, both material and non-material; endogenous – stemming from the heart of each society, which defines in sovereignty its values and the vision of its future; self-reliant – relying on the strength and resources of the society which pursues it, rooted at the local level in the practice of each community; ecologically sound – utilizing rationally available resources in a harmonious relation with the environment; based on structural transformations – originating in the realization of the conditions for self-management and participation in decision-making by all (Sterky, 1978: 1, 4–5).

These are large claims and large hopes. How does woman fit into these schemes and conceptions; and how does the African woman in particular? The first criticism that can be made of *What Now* is the language of its expression which is "totally man-centered." The initial quote at the top of this essay also illustrates the point. English-speaking feminists have pointed out and reiterated the need to "humanize" the very language of discourse, to "de-masculinize" it and find androgynous and generic terms to discuss what concerns and affects both men and women in society. This question of a "man-oriented" language is not so trivial when we consider how scholars in the social sciences of history, sociology, anthropology, law, etc., have regularly and frequently excluded women totally from their studies; and how "development" agents have also neglected women in the effectuating of their so-called "development" schemes.

Secondly, in *What Now*, there seems to be a primordial concern with ecology and eco-systems. The problems of ecology and what happens to eco-systems are not a priority in Third World countries; neither should they be named before the very serious problems of socioeconomics are mentioned; in particular, the problems of colonialism and neo-colonialism in their multifaceted forms.

Thirdly the argument about OPEC and Indochina can evoke a cynical attitude in the Third World reader. *What Now* argues that two elements give a political dimension to the hope for change: first, the power of OPEC countries to extort economic demands and affect economic policy; second, the example given to the whole world by Indochina that peasants with a will for independence, could organize and free themselves from "the most formidable military and technological power that the world has known" (ibid.: 5–6). Thus, the interest in "development" is not just humanistic but based on naked self-interest and the fear of a stranglehold on the West by previously powerless and scorned Third World nations. Third World radicals would argue that Third World nations should, in fact, sharpen such tools for levering the "international economic order"; they should use this potential for power which is based on a structure of dependence of the West on the Third World (Wilmot, 1976: 119–20). Wilmot argues cogently in this chapter how, in fact, the real causes of the economic crisis in the West predate the formation of OPEC in 1960, and the steep rises in the price of oil since the end of 1973. He argues that the real causes of the crisis are to be found in the structures of the western economies, primarily that of the USA, and in the economic and political decisions taken by governments in the West.

Despite *What Now*'s view of OPEC as significant because it represents a historic reversal, as historic as Vasco da Gama's arrival on the coast of West Africa which opens the period of the conquest of Africa, the document *What Now* does rightly situate the sources of the crisis of development. The crisis does lie in the poverty of the masses of the Third World, as well as that of others, whose needs, even the most basic – food, habitat, health and education – are not met. And this situation cannot be properly understood, much less transformed, unless it is seen as a whole. In the final analysis, the crises are the result of a system of exploitation which profits a power structure based largely in the industrialized world, although not without annexes in the Third World; ruling "elites" of most countries are both accomplices and rivals at the same time (*What Now*: 5). The drama of a Third World elite group exploiting its own country and competing nastily with its industrialized economic partners and "collaborators in oppression" can be exemplified by Nigeria, in particular, among other neo-colonial countries. Informative studies of the Nigerian example have been made (Williams, 1976; Turner, 1978; Usman, 1982).

Now the condition of the African woman is situated within this global socioeconomic reality. Her condition is one of living in neo-colonial or colonized countries such as South Africa and enduring the repercussions of such reality. Before an analysis is made of her condition, a definition of culture for this paper will be made. Culture will be seen in its broad, comprehensive and total meaning; not as a conglomeration of superficial aspects of life such as dance, dress, hairstyles and naked women. Culture is defined here as the total product of a people's "being" and "consciousness" which emerges from their grappling with nature and living with other humans in a collective group. Thus "their culture is itself a product and a reflection of the history built on the two relations with nature and with other men" (Ngugi wa Thiongo, 1981: 2). Culture for the present writer is the total self-expression of a people in the two relations basic to human existence in society: the relations between generic man and nature and the relations between person and person in that society. (It can be seen how this writer is trying to avoid masculine references, a very difficult feat in English!)

The very effort of defining culture is itself fraught with problems. In an effort to give a materialistic definition above – a definition usually accepted in western Marxist thought – one is pulled up short by the awareness that other cultures reject the notion; that is, the notion that the human relation to nature is one aimed at mastering, controlling, or exploiting her. *What Now* itself bemoans this exploitative attitude which now threatens eco-systems with the exhaustion of non-renewable sources. A Cherokee Indian has written about the Amerindian relation to nature which is one of harmony and the submergence of the human self to other things:

> All our lives are directed towards "tuning in" to the rest of nature. There are ceremonies for all sorts of phenomena. . . . What we are really doing is trying to get ourselves into certain rhythms of certain moods. When I dance "the Wolf Dance," I am able to put myself in a completely different place than where I normally am. I see myself and the world through different eyes for a moment, and I partake in someone else's (the wolf's) rhythm and power. But it is reciprocal. I also give my rhythm to those animals or events. In other words, I tune in.
>
> (Durham, 1981: 15–16)

Mr Durham is of the Wolf clan. There is no word for a "clan" in Cherokee; he says he is, more correctly, simply a wolf himself and the Cherokees believe that the animals are the elder of human beings. Thus human beings have to learn from animals as they have to learn from nature in general. Oriental commentators have also written widely on their view of life which is essentially different from that of the post-Renaissance West. The Asiatics see all human behavior as geared not toward the exploitation of nature and the acquisition of material goods but toward "the search for truth, as a means of self-realization and self-control, not as a means of bringing anything under domination, including nature" (Konthari, 1981: 81). Africans can be said to live in harmony with nature, to use the material world for the satisfaction of basic human, emotional and psychological needs. Such basically divergent cultural views and objectives should be very relevant to the theoreticians of *What Now* in their implementation of one of their objectives which is the satisfaction of basic human needs identified as food, health, shelter and education. But most Africans would tend to ask, then what? "We get all these fine things, yes, but to what objective?" It would be to use these things to attain their basic emotional needs in the social realm.

These are very deep cultural differences between Europe and Africa regarding the how and why of life.

Considering the wide scope of the definition of culture here, obviously this chapter cannot intend to deal with all its aspects. The chapter will confine itself to the super-structural aspects of culture – non-material products. It will consider the products of consciousness such as ideas, institutions, social patterns and the arts, and even here, it can only glance at these issues.

THE WOMAN'S CONDITION IN AFRICA: THE SIX MOUNTAINS ON HER

A brief glance at women all over the world today shows that they are oppressed. Such a glance suggests that "educational attainments," "participation rates," "occupational structure," private and public laws, family planning systems, technological advance and above all sociocultural attitudes are all weighted against them.

Across distance and boundaries in history and society, women have been placed on pedestals as goddesses, but imprisoned within domestic injustice (custom has been nothing but a tyrant hidden in every home). They have been romanticized in literature and lyrics, but commercialized in life (Ahooja-Patel, 1977: 83). They have been owned, used and worked as horses, even today.

But what is the specific condition of the women in Africa? This is a wide subject which needs ongoing research. It is now well known that Third World women adopt different postures. This is how AAWORD/AFARD[2] was born. This chapter will initiate a discussion with a take-off from a statement of Mao Tse-tung. Mao is quoted as saying that a Chinese man had three mountains on his back: the first was the oppression from outside, because China was colonized; the second was the feudal oppression of two thousand years of authoritarianism; and the third was his backwardness; but a woman had four mountains – the fourth being man (Ahooja-Patel, 1977: 85). One might say that the African woman has six mountains on her back: one is oppression from outside (colonialism and neo-colonialism?); the second is from traditional structures, feudal, slave-based, communal, etc.; the third is her backwardness (neo-colonialism?); the fourth is man; the fifth is her color, her race; and the sixth is herself. We shall attempt to discuss these in their cultural significance.

1 Oppression from outside: foreign intrusions

The African woman lives in or comes from a continent that has been subjected to nearly five hundred years of assault, battery and mastery of various kinds. These historical experiences have taken their toll and left their mark. These experiences can be dated from the historical arrival of Vasco da Gama in the 1400s, beginning with the mercantile trade with Europe which soon broadened into the trade in slaves only, followed by "the integration of Africa" into the "full capitalist system," in the nineteenth century (to borrow phrases from Samir Amin's periodicization in "Underdevelopment and Dependence in Black Africa: Origins and Contemporary Forms"). Then followed the period of political or structural integration within capitalism which was colonization. The economic and political integration of Africa into capitalism has been studied by several brilliant scholars, so the details need not delay us here (George Padmore, Kwame Nkrumah, Samir Amin and Walter Rodney, for instance). We may, however, look at the cultural outcome of these historical experiences.

The introduction of new economic activities such as slavery, the slave trade and the growing of national sole "cash crops" as opposed to food crops must have thrown the total pattern of production in African societies into severe crisis. The resultant social upheaval must have affected the position and roles of women within the production processes and the relations of production. More research needs to be done into the role of woman in precapitalist economic formations in Africa — her role in production and her relation to the economic surplus of those economic formations. The woman's social and economic place in the colonial period is more accessible to knowledge since the period is nearer; still, studies need to be done to reveal the actual nature of the woman's predicament then and to collate such information for availability. Both men and women, with the intrusion of the West, were pushed into dependent economies resulting in the pauperization and the "proletarianization" of the whole continent. Whole societies became geared to the upholding of foreign metropolitan economies, committed to the expatriation of their own surplus to the countries of the colonizing powers. Women in the labor process became the "proletariat" of the proletariats, becoming more subordinated in the new socioeconomic schemes, and often losing their old and meaningful roles within the older production processes.

Women became more marginalized in the production process as the "cash crop" became the "main crop," leading to new economic arrangements between men and women and new attitudes of male social and economic superiority. These economic changes in Africa following the intrusion of the West were inextricably linked to political changes in society, which again affected cultural attitudes toward women. The creation of a new class of subordinates — missionaries, clerks, police and soldiers — changed social aspirations in society. The traditional political structures were either completely abandoned or so distorted as to sweep away any female participation in the handling of local power and administration. The British simply swept aside previous female political structures in society, replacing them with completely male structures and positions. Modern societies have now inherited these male-dominated structures and with them the hardened attitudes of male superiority and female exclusion from public affairs which the colonial systems introduced. The colonial systems negatively encouraged or brought to the fore the traditional ideologies of patriarchy or male superiority which existed in African societies originally, anyway. The cultural outcome of these political transformations in Africa is manifold. Women are "naturally" excluded from public affairs; they are viewed as unable to hold positions of responsibility, rule men or even be visible when serious matters of state and society are being discussed. Women are viewed to need tutelage before they can be politically active; politics is considered the absolute realm of men; women are not considered fit for political positions in modern African nation-states, though their enthusiasm and campaign work are exploited by their various political parties (Ogundipe-Leslie, 1982: 17–19).

Thus colonialism has brought out the basic sexist tendencies in pre-capitalist Africa. It has calcified existing ones and they are creating conflicts since men are not yet able to adapt to them, nor are they rid of old attitudes and expectations. The effect of colonization on the total continent has myriad forms, not the least being the feelings of inferiority and dependency which have been created in both men and women. Famous studies have been done on the psychology of the oppressed and its characteristic dependency complex (Frantz Fanon, Albert Memmi, etc.). Fanon described psychological oppression as the worst form of oppression. Its continuing impact on the psyche of African men and women is sadly very significant. The feelings of inferiority affect the economic and political behavior of Africans, denuding them of creativity, self-reliance, or productivity. There is no desire or confidence to be productive or creative; rather the ruling elites only consume and spread their values to the rest of their societies. The dominant ideas of a society are the ideas of its ruling class. The ruling elites feel totally dependent on industrialized countries in material, intellectual and emotional terms. They can do nothing but imitate Europe even in ideas, generating none themselves but simply applying to their own societies ideas and practices which were not conceived for their societies. Within this cultural universe of Third World dependency, the woman is the dependant of the dependant, being pulled along in the whirligig of neo-colonial meaningless behavior. Like her male counterparts, she imitates everything European and despises her traditional culture and race while she fails to understand her own true needs.

Colonization has also affected the legal structures of African societies, introducing into them nineteenth-century European ideas of patriarchy. Women lost inherited special rights and became more subordinated. Similarly, Islam disrupted traditional societies politically and legally, creating new oppressed and subjugated statuses and roles for women. Consequently, women have contemporary legal battles to fight for their rights, in particular within family law – marriage, divorce, the sharing of property within marriage, inheritance, the possession of their own bodies and children, among other issues. In the religious cultures of societies, colonization introduced Christianity which destroyed the old religions or subverted them as Islam also did. Women sometimes lost their important and high positions in the old religions with the introduction of new patriarchal religious values. Christianity is itself a very male-dominated religion. So male-dominated is it now that women have to fight for leadership roles within Christianity, while the very idea of female leadership in Islam is inconceivable.

In the artistic cultures of African societies, western intrusion destroyed the forms of creativity and indeed the very urge to create in those forms. Women had been active in the precolonial artistic world: in rituals, music, dance, visual and plastic arts. More research needs to be done into this area to identify the nature and social significance of women's role in the field of arts. Many of these arts were destroyed with colonization, Christianity and Islam; followed by the creation of economic and emotional voids leading to an increasing population of unemployed women. Unemployment leads to other social problems such as prostitution, vagrancy, mass proletarianization, lack of self-respect and self-worth among other problems.

It is clear that foreign intrusions into Africa have had wide-ranging and cataclysmic effects on her societies and cultures. It is advisable that fuller research be done into specific aspects of the colonial impact on women, in particular in the field of culture. Foreign historical intrusions have certainly created cultural changes in the social realm affecting the self-definition of woman, the relationships of individuals to each other, the notions of female inferiority, etc. Colonization and westernization with their attendant capitalism have introduced capitalist values of greed, acquisitiveness, autonomy and individualism which have affected human relationships just as the synchronous introduction of wage labor has undermined precapitalist structures of human relations. The capitalist system of production itself draws women out of the home into low-wage slavery encouraging the subordination of women, financial disabilities and low female self-esteem.

Whatever studies we make of women in Africa, we should be aware of the need to "periodize" African history adequately. It is also necessary to recognize various social and historical categories which would affect our analysis of woman's position in Africa. We need to see problems in their class perspectives in present-day and past economic formations. In present-day Africa, we should bear in mind that problems differ from society to society, depending on their specific relation to capital and neo-colonialism. Thus woman's problems in Nigeria, a neo-colonial country, differ from those in South Africa, still a colonized country. The newly liberated areas of Africa such as Angola, Mozambique and Zimbabwe have their own unique problems. The revolutionary societies in their own place have again unique problems of "realizing" the social revolution after the armed struggle as in Guinea Bissau where women claim they are fighting two colonialisms; the second being men (Urdang, 1975). Another variable in our cultural studies should be religion – the various cultural effects of Islam, Christianity and the traditional religion on woman's position in Africa.

Obviously, this chapter cannot encompass this massive work which needs to be farmed out to researchers. But under whatever scheme the research takes place, I would like to suggest a methodology that proceeds from the material bases of the societies to the superstructural, so as to yield information about the social and living reality of the societies wherein the women are situated. It is apropos to quote a historian in Nigeria regarding the kind of reconstruction and study of African societies needed. An organizational principle of the study of Africa may well focus on

> the production process itself and in this case a categorization such as pre-capitalist may be more in keeping with the actual material environment [vis-à-vis the pre-mercantile Africa: M. O.-L.] The focus on the environment, in a sense that goes beyond routine ecological description, may well focus on the productive capacity of the areas in question and would make more possible the analysis of superstructural forms and institutions such as the State. It would also encourage a focus on issues that are crucial and would divert attention from peripheral issues to matters of importance. A focus on the productive forces at any specific period would in fact discourage static analysis and a situation where explanations tend to be frivolous and superficial. There is need for focus on production relations as manifested in forms of authority, the distribution of rights over labor power, the technical organization of labor and work relationship and all are to be seen as integrally related to the amount of cultivable land available [or other forces of production: M. O.-L.], the type of tools to which there is access, the means of subsistence and more generally the application and availability of labor. No indepth analysis of superstructural forms such as the state and political institutions [or the role and position of and attitudes to women: M. O.-L.] is possible unless in the context of

the latter. Any meaningful reconstruction of the past should take full cognizance of the inter-relationship between the "economic structure" as a whole and the "superstructural" reflexes.

(Emeagwali, 1982)

2 The heritage of tradition: the second mountain

This second mountain on the African woman's back is built of structures and attitudes inherited from indigenous history and sociological realities. African women are weighed down by superstructural forms deriving from the precolonial past. In most African societies, whether patrilineal or matrilineal, gender hierarchy or male supremacy or sex asymmetry (or whatever term we choose to use) was known and taken for granted. Even in matrilineal societies, women were still subordinated to men, considered as second in place to men; the only difference being that inheritance and authority passed through the women to the male of the line. Men are still dominant in private and public life. The ideology that men are naturally superior to women in essence and in all areas, affects the modern-day organization of societal structures. The ideology prolongs the attitudes of negative discrimination against women.

In traditional society, there was the division of labor based on sex with an attendant contempt for women's work. Men would not serve food at the revolutionary meetings in Guinea Bissau so Cabral had to dignify this "women's work" by appointing women in charge of food as members of revolutionary councils (Urdang, 1981: 251). Such an attitude is certainly a carry-over from the past. Not only was "women's work" condemned by men, it was often poorly regarded when not totally unpaid. In modern neo-colonial Africa, therefore, men tend to take lightly the labor or work of their female counterparts in the business and educational professions, considering women's jobs as "hobbies" and wondering what women do which makes them so tired at the end of the day. Proletarian and peasant women are known to work all day long and longer than men. Such attitudes toward women's work lead to discriminatory behavior in employment practices. In addition, women are considered the best hands for the most menial of jobs so that they are employed to do the most back-racking agricultural labor and other servile jobs in factories and urban life. There is a tendency in Nigeria today to use women in the building trade jobs, to carry cement and water, and to do other taxing jobs, for which they are paid less than men who often are not hewers and carriers but occupy better-paid managerial and skilled positions on the construction sites (Zack-Williams, 1982).

From the traditional past also come notions of the physical control of woman's body and its products. Under this issue come purdah, genital mutilation, the lack of control over her body's biology or its products such as children which are viewed to belong to the man of the family. She is but a beast that produces the man's children on his behalf. These aspects of the oppression of women in Africa are very important to African women though they tend not to wish to emphasize the quest for sexual freedom and promiscuity which preoccupy the Western feminist. Nonetheless, the African male fears the attainment of equal sexual freedom for women. Some men also argue that genital mutilation was not wicked or sadistic in intent since it was societal or parental effort to do the best they thought fit for their daughters. Nonetheless, backward (in the sense of unscientific), painful and undemocratic practices should be stopped. A child's body should not be mutilated without her consent.

Attitudinal forms, too many to enumerate, have certainly been inherited from the traditional past. These attitudes derive from the socio-economic formations in existence at the time and have lasted into the modern period in the fields of law, politics, religion, education, philosophy of life, etc. Serious work has to be done to educate whole populations out of these attitudes and notions. Outmoded structures such as the legal (as in marriage) and the political also need to be eradicated.

3 The other mountains

The backwardness of the African woman is the third mountain on her back; men, the fourth; race, the fifth; and herself, the sixth. We can comment only briefly on these aspects of female culture in Africa. Her backwardness is a product of colonization and neo-colonialism, comprising poverty, ignorance and the lack of a scientific attitude to experience and nature. Her race is important since the international economic order is divided along race and class lines, with the industrialized countries, the "North" of the North–South dialogue, notably white or approved white, like the Japanese. In the whole of the world, race is an important variable of imperialism and neo-colonialism. Race affects the economics and politics of North–South interaction. Within Africa herself, race problems are basic to any understanding of the societies of eastern and southern Africa. Therefore special problems exist there, as in education where a special effort has to be made to fight racist ideology, as with the Black Consciousness Movement of Steve Biko or the various and special educational programmes in Mozambique, Zimbabwe and other newly liberated areas (Van de Merwe *et al.*, 1968; Ngugi wa Thiongo, 1981; Development Dialogue, 1978: 2).

Woman has to throw off the fifth mountain on her back which is man, steeped in his centuries-old attitude of patriarchy which he does not wish to abandon because male domination is advantageous to him. Not even the most politically progressive men are completely free from patriarchal attitudes and feelings of male superiority. Thus it is up to women to combat their social disabilities; to fight for their own fundamental and democratic rights, without waiting for the happy day when men will willingly share power and privilege with them – a day that will never come. The liberation of women in society is not simply about sexual freedom for women as most men tend to think and fear, but about the large problem of the redistribution of privilege, power and property between the rich and the poor, encompassing the smaller problem of the redistribution of power, property and privilege between men and women.

The sixth mountain on woman's back – herself – is the most important. Women are shackled by their own negative self-image, by centuries of the interiorization of the ideologies of patriarchy and gender hierarchy. Their own reactions to objective problems therefore are often self-defeating and self-crippling. Woman reacts with fear, dependency complexes and attitudes to please and cajole where more self-assertive actions are needed. It is clear that programs are needed to educate women about their positions, the true causes of their plight, and possible modalities for effecting change. Both men and women need "conscientization" and this is an area where the UN and other bodies can be very useful – in the provision and funding of schemes to raise the consciousness of whole populations.

WHAT IS TO BE DONE?

What Now obviously feels that the satisfaction of basic needs identified as food, habitat, health education, is a basic prerequisite for women. The achievement of these objectives is rightly seen as dependent on basic structural transformations of societies. These transformations can only be achieved by the endogenous struggles of the people of the various and specific societies. There is not much the UN can do about this political requirement. The question not clearly asked in *What Now* and other theoretizations on changes in the Third World is what kind of political organization will best achieve the most satisfactory social existence? *What Now* seems to envision some grand ideal where the industrialized countries are forced to "abandon" or "refurbish" or "reconstruct"(?) capitalism and imperialism! Industrialized countries are to be subsumed into some all-encompassing world government which is powered by the belief that we must all work together, share and share alike, or we sink. Well! Most Third World countries are convinced that socialism is the only key to a juster society; that under the political regime, the "woman question" will be given adequate and specific attention as it has been in most socialist countries though the questions have not been solved in these countries. But state recognition of the problem of women is already a step in the right direction.

There are those who feel that the solution of the oppression of women in society revolves around two issues: education and the provision of employment for women. It is felt that employment guarantees the economic independence which leads to other forms of social and spiritual independence. Ahooja-Patel has suggested discrimination in favor of women in national and international policies, while new national policies of equal opportunity are provided. Discrimination in favor of women can be defended on the grounds that women have an unequal start in society in all areas of work and life. In addition, they are discriminated against and are at a disadvantage in all societies throughout the world – only their problems take different manifestations. The idea of discrimination in favor needs serious discussion since the blanket law of no discrimination on the grounds of sex can back-fire against women as in the famous Bakke case in the USA, regarding affirmative action for Blacks. In fact, men now use the slogan of "no discrimination" to discriminate against women, to ignore their problems where such legislation exists. It is, however, known to all that there can be a wide divergence between law in the books and social practices. In all societies, industrialized and Third World ones, women are excluded from public affairs despite incidental and cosmetic cases like Mrs Thatcher, Mrs Golda Meir, Mrs Bandaranaike, Mrs Jean Kirkpatrick or the few ministers of state, permanent secretaries and other government functionaries in African countries. And often discrimination does not always spring from legislation but from practices originating in the psychological and cultural environment (Ahooja-Patel, 1977).

So what is to be done about African women, culture and another development? Some suggestions and comments will be made:

1 First the basic social and cultural needs must be met in the concerned societies. Most development theories recognize this, but the question is how?
2 *What Now* identifies the eradication of poverty as a prerequisite. But the eradication of poverty is not only dependent on the increase both in food production in the Third World at local, national and regional levels and in the purchasing power of these countries (*What Now*: 16). The continuing poverty, the underdeveloping of Third World countries, is more basically tied to the sharp economic practices of the industrialized countries and their Third World collaborators in the ruling classes.
3 Thus, *What Now*'s recommendation of the transformation of social, economic and political structures (p. 15) is a basic requirement. This

transformation, however, can be achieved only by the populations of the countries concerned.

4 Meanwhile, to attain the basic needs of women, there must be a battle against poverty and exploitation of women in society. Women must be able to control and benefit from the products of their labor, which need to be more valued and compensated.

5 Thus, there needs to be a re-education on sex roles in whole nations. External and internal policies, schemes and projects could be set up to achieve such massive raising of consciousness.

6 On this issue, the improvement of public information already cited as an important objective in *Another Development* will be very useful (*What Now*: 17). The use of media – radio, television, printed matter – will be effective and this is where foreign bodies and funds can be of great use. Educational policies in nations also have to be geared toward this cultural need: to change oppressive and discriminatory attitudes toward women. Education must be seen as a force to liberate and inculcate positive values, particularly regarding women.

7 Finally women in the arts in Africa need encouragement and financial assistance. Women artists are relatively few in African societies and successful ones are even fewer and farther between. In the modern artistic expressions such as the novel, the film, written poetry, secular theater and painting, women artists are still fewer. Not only do educational possibilities militate against women, but women are often hard put to find capital to back their own projects or to develop themselves. This is another area in which "Another Development" agencies can be useful – setting up a foundation specifically for the training and assistance of women artists, and for the support of research into the issues concerning African women and culture.

NOTES

This paper previously appeared in *Journal of African Marxism* (1984) and in *Presence Africaine* 141 (1987).

1 The 1975 Dag Hammarskjold Report, *What Now*: 27.
2 Association of African Women for Research and Development/Association des femmes Afriques pour Recherche et Développement.

BIBLIOGRAPHY

Ahooja-Patel, Krishna (1977) "Another Development for Women," in Marc Nerfin (ed.) *Another Development: Approaches and Strategies*, Uppsala: Dag Hammarskjold Foundation: 66–89.

Amin Samir (1981) "Underdevelopment and Dependence in Black Africa: Origins and Contemporary Forms," in Cohen and Daniel (1981): 28–44.

Arnau, Juan Carlos Sanchez, "The Cultural Dimension of Development,"

Development Seeds of Change (Culture, the Forgotten Dimension) 3/4: 34–5.

Cohen, D. L. and Daniel, J. (eds) (1981) *Political Economy of Africa: Selected Readings*, London/New York: Longman.

Development Dialogue (1978: 2), special issue on *Another Development and Education*.

Durham, Jimmie (1981) "Eloheh or the Council of the Universe," *Development* 3/4.

Emeagwali, Gloria Thomas (1982) "Political Institutions in Pre-Nineteenth Century Nigeria: Some Observations on the Groundwork of Nigerian History," paper presented at the Annual Congress of the Historical Society of Nigeria, Port Harcourt, Nigeria, April 13–17.

Konthari, Rajni (1981) "The Cultural Roots of Another Development," *Development* 3/4.

Ngugi wa Thiongo (1981) "Education for a National Culture," paper presented at the seminar on Education in Zimbabwe – Past, Present and Future, held at the University of Zimbabwe, August 27–September 7.

Ogundipe, Chief (Mrs) G. T. (1977) "The Ordination of Women," Methodist Church of Nigeria, Literature Bureau.

Ogundipe-Leslie, Molara (1982) "Women in Nigeria," paper presented at the national seminar on Women in Nigeria, Department of Sociology, Ahmadu Bello University, Zaria, May 27–8.

Rodney, Walter (1972) *How Europe Underdeveloped Africa*, London: Bogle L'Ouverture Publications.

Sterky, Goran (1978) "Towards Another Development in Health," in Introductory Remarks, Development Dialogue (1978: 1): 4–5.

Turner, Terisa (1981) "Commercial Capitalism in Nigeria: the Pattern of Competition," in Cohen and Daniel (1981): 155–63.

Urdang, Stephanie (1981) "Fighting Two Colonialisms: The Women's Struggle in Guinea-Bissau," in Cohen and Daniel (1981): 213–20.

Usman, Y. Bala (1982) "Behind the Smokescreen: The Real Causes of the Current Economic Crisis" [in Nigeria], public lecture by Y. B. Usman, Secretary to the Government of Kaduna State, organized by the Kaduna State Council of the Nigerian Labor Congress, Kaduna, April 30. To be found in *Who is Responsible?: The Nigerian Workers and the Current Economic Crisis: May Day Speeches and Statements*, Kaduna, Nigeria: the PRP National Research Directorate, 1982.

Van der Merwe, H. W. *et al.* (1968) *African Perspectives on South Africa*, London: Rex Collings. See sections on dignity, and on consciousness and education.

Williams, Gavin (1976) *Nigeria, Economy and Society*, London: Rex Collings.

Wilmot, Patrick F. (1979) *In Search of Nationhood: The Theory and Practice of Nationalism in Africa*, Lagos/Ibadan: Lantern Books.

Zack-Williams, A. B. (1982) "Female Labor and Exploitation with African Social Formations: Some Theoretical Issues. (2) Women in Construction in Jos," papers presented at the national seminar on Women in Nigeria, Department of Sociology, Ahmadu Bello University, Zaria, May 27–8.

8

DISORDER IN THE HOUSE
The new world order and the
socioeconomic status of women

Patricia J. Williams

It is a depressing time for race and gender relations in the USA. By most measures, the years of the Reagan–Bush presidencies have seen ever-increasing divisions between Blacks and whites; sexual harassment and rape statistics have risen more or less steadily; and bias crimes of all sorts have soared. At the same time, it is discouraging to note that there has been a downturn in the numbers of discrimination and civil rights cases successfully litigated.

Part of this has to do with an ever more conservative judiciary, the coded nature of some forms of discrimination, and the withdrawal of federal funds from inner cities and all manner of public works. In addition, discrimination has assumed sophisticated new forms and uniforms that our labor and civil rights laws have greater difficulty recognizing. Another reality, of course, is a sociopolitical climate in which both formal and informal burdens of proof make it harder and harder to have anything recognized as discrimination.

But I think the most important reason, and the focus of this chapter, has to do with the realities of a world in which national boundaries figure less in our fortune than do the configurations of multinational corporations. Local disputes about discrimination in the workplace cannot be conceived of as simply local any more: labor problems and civil rights violations are not just matters of our laws – not in a world of free trade zones, of manufacturing islands whose operations can shift almost overnight from North Carolina to Mexico, or to Thailand, Los Angeles, or the Philippines.[1] To make constructive proposals about remediation, therefore, I think we have to look at discrimination not simply as a deviation from law in the USA; rather we must see it as part of a larger, international norm, and as consistent with a worldwide corporate culture that transcends national boundaries.

The exploitative situations of which I am thinking are particularly visible in the garment and electronics industry. In the so-called maquiladora system, "American factories and assembly plants . . . import almost all raw materials and export almost all products virtually exempt from tariffs and other trade restrictions."[2] The jerry-built factories within these free trade zones have the ability to pack up and disappear overnight if conditions are not ideally constraining of the threat of strike or other labor unrest. Women bear the brunt of this sort of exploitation: employers overwhelmingly favor female employees who are between the ages of 16 and 25 (because they are more malleable and passive); who are single (because they have no immediate responsibilities other than sending money back to a village located elsewhere, rather than having family at their side); and who have no more than a sixth grade education (so that they can read instructions, but not read too much).[3]

These kinds of concentrated inequities are paralleled in many places around the world. In the USA a society of extraordinarily rich diversity and cultural potential, 95 per cent of all corporate executives are still white and male, a figure that has not changed since 1979, when it fell from somewhere close to 100 per cent.[4] In Europe, particularly eastern Europe, the lifting of oppressive Stalinist policies has also been accompanied by an end to many economic and social programs which had been premissed on the implementation of some ideal of egalitarianism; and the granting of new political and civil rights has signaled the resurgence of powerfully conservative nationalist, sexist, anti-Semitic and ethnocentric discourses.

Against this backdrop, I find the extent to which Europeans consider and battle among themselves as "minorities" extremely interesting. Untangling the ways in which our varied fortunes and misfortunes mesh in the world requires lots of patient attention. It is easy to allow the relative freedoms found by some European immigrants in the "new world" of the USA to obscure the fact of massive ongoing discrimination, in the "old world," against women, Jews, gays and certain ethnic groups. And it is easy to overgeneralize from the privileges of the USA's great wealth, by making money or its lack the explanation for all oppressions. In doing so, however, one underestimates the extent to which markets themselves may be deeply distorted by racial and gender prejudice; one loses sight of the fact that some "successfully assimilated" ethnics in the USA have become so only by paying the high cost of burying for ever languages, customs and cultures. In short, one risks making invisible even the most explicitly biased, irrational and cruel forms of exploitation by denying the commonalities of a hand-me-down heritage of devalued humanity, even as our specific experiences with that devaluation may differ widely with time and place. The ability to see, and to fully understand, the desperate socioeconomic circumstances of women of color is, therefore, intricately linked with these evolving histories and the analytical conundrums that they present for us all.

These conversations made me think of a trip I took in February, 1990, with about ten people generally associated with Critical Legal Studies. Our Samsonite luggage packed full of trail mix and Talking Heads tapes, we took off for Czechoslovakia and Poland for a conference on rights theory. One of the things I found most interesting, among the many complicated patterns emerging there, was a series of legal attempts to include historically oppressed ethnic minorities. We had an opportunity to look at the then-current draft of the Czech-Slovak constitution (conveniently translated into English, we were informed, by the federalist society which had sponsored a string of constitutional advisors). It made provision for the cultural development and political participation of named minorities, including Germans, Hungarians and Romany nationals. Another section, however, provided that there be no preferences or allowances based on considerations having to do with race, ethnicity, or religion. I asked a highly placed government lawyer how they reconciled a "neutrality" clause with allowances for named minorities – particularly in the case of Romany peoples (or gypsies), the pursuit of whose nomadic culture has placed them in some tension with more static industrial cultures invested in notions of private property. His answer was that there was no paradox: that the Romanies were *un*cultured, so that the wording did not refer to the development of Romany culture but instead provided the leverage for "civilizing" and "lifting up" of Romanies to the general level of Czech and Slovak culture.

Furthermore, there has been in Czechoslovakia, East Germany and elsewhere, an attempt to push working women back into the home to raise children, thus releasing jobs for men in the coming unemployment expected in the advent of a free market. In particular, the teaching profession has been singled out, the "overfeminization" of universities being cited, by several government officials with whom we met, as the single biggest problem with Czechoslovakian education. Powerfully placed politicians told us jokes about women, the following one in particular said to be quite popular in Prague at that time: three women stand at the gates of Charles University – one is ugly, one is stupid, and the third is also a teacher.

In Poland, the embrace of freedom of expression has resulted in such odd trade-offs as: the open practice of Catholicism enabling a spirited movement to repeal laws permitting abortion;[5] and pornographic images becoming symbolic of the new order, their own form of religious icon.[6] The complicated iconography of *Penthouse* centerfolds was everywhere we went, in a war of imagistic oppression and proclaimed liberation.[7] Pinups were everywhere on buses, in the telegraph office, in department stores, on walls filled with political graffiti, in the monastery where our conference was held, Jesus dying on the cross hung above every doorway. Perhaps most peculiar of all was the bookstore we walked by, an ordinary bookstore, like B. Dalton's or Waldenbooks, full of computer manuals and recent fiction and textbooks and how-to-fix-your-car. There in the window sharing center stage, were two spot-lighted pictures. One was of the Polish Pope, a good, kindly and sancti-fied man, leaning on his Holy Shepherd's staff, his eyes cast upward to heaven. The other was of the February 1990 *Playboy* centerfold, who wore her hair streaming on the waves of some gentle wind and a demure though extremely long string of pearls. Her bunny ears were flopped forward in a shy downward cast, as were her eyes; a perfect madonna-of-the-first-amendment.

Furthermore, I was astonished by how often I heard the term "social parasite" when we were in Poland. It came up as a reason both why communism had failed and why capitalism or the free market is so desirable. Each on his own, working hard, and reaping the fruits of his labor, aligned with the "normal" world, unconstrained by the parasitic "elements" who will fall by the wayside and finally learn the bitter-sweet lesson of fending for themselves.

I was very worried by this rhetoric of social parasitism, this hold-over vocabulary from the old-world order of the Nazi lexicon; I remain worried. It sounded – it is – profoundly fascistic, and racist. Here's what I read between the lines: an unquestioning nationalism in which sym-bology Russian domination equals parasitism, but in which, given the rush to embrace American-style capitalism, all shortcomings are dis-missed as being caused by or limited to said parasitic elements, to wit, "Stalinist peasants," Romany nationals, African-Americans, or other "others." (On several occasions, people actually announced that in their opinion the only reason problems like homelessness and unemployment existed in the USA was because of African-Americans.)

At the same time, there was, in eastern Europe, a ubiquitous sense of embarrassment. As we exuberant Americans came marching into the Polish winter, with our Pepsi Cola and our nasal sprays, our Batman ballpoint pens and our running shoes, we had every reason to be embarrassed; and yet it was they who were. People apologized con-stantly for their standard of living, for the condition of their houses, for not having answering machines, for not living lives like they imagined ours to be. They seemed intensely self-conscious, even ashamed, of a life-style which, though considerably simpler than the American, is a perfectly hospitable one, and considerably above the global norm. As we were shown around Cracow, our hosts proudly pointed out ancient and historic buildings that had been sold to West German and Canadian hotel chains. I felt as though I were bearing witness to the so-called sale of Manhattan Island, accomplished in some updated sense – this nation of sensible subsistence farmers rushing to trade their lives and land and life-styles for the baubles of McDonald's burgers.

I worry as well that there is a quality to the massive "influx of capital" to eastern Europe that feels like a throwing-of-dollar-bills-at-the-problem. I don't mean that the money isn't needed or deeply appreciated by the recipient countries. Rather, I am referring to the spirit in which it is given by the donor countries. It felt imperialistic and condescending in the same way, if not to the same degree, as the West's financial condescension in other parts of the world, particularly the Third World. Yet at the same time what I was able to see during my trip to Poland and Czechoslovakia, more than I had been able to see in other parts of the world, was the extent to which this condescension operates as a complicated form of seduction. On the airplane to Warsaw, for example, I heard three young Polish-Americans with strong Chicago accents talking about how great it was that all their friends and relatives were finally beginning to see the light and embrace the free market. There was a profound scorn in their voices, having nothing to do with ideological discontent with communism, at least as they expressed it. Rather, it was scorn for Poland and its standard of living. It was competitive scorn, like relatives who have done well and are determined to rub it in. It was like some complicated sibling rivalry.

It reminded me of a friend I once had, a classmate from my college, whom I invited to my parents' home, in Roxbury, Massachusetts, for dinner. Afterwards, she came away, saying over and over, "Oh I'm so sorry, I didn't know. . . ." – as though my material circumstances were not only less than hers, but were so bad that I needed to be *consoled* about them. And I confess that, in the smarting wake of her comment, I was tempted to a certain shame about myself and my home; her careless, simple disrespect so profoundly devalued me that I was tempted to reassess everything that was solid, sustaining and comforting in my life as something to be "overcome."

Similarly, this western flashing-of-cash and its ability to generate massive realignments troubles me less because it is ideological than because to an increasing extent it is accompanied by a deep discourtesy, a seductive humiliation that teaches a self-worthiness premised on material possession.

In summary, the comprehensive consideration of the socioeconomic condition of women, and specifically women of color, requires our explicit care in accommodating and, yes, adjusting our own lives for the potential of a truly multicultural world. It means making room, not only in our words and in our constitutions but also in our actions, for the varied life-styles of women, of people of color, and of nomads, subsistence farmers and native peoples here and abroad – even, or maybe most particularly, those life-styles deemed incompatible with the ideologies of immediacy and capital expansion. I fear, if we do not stop and take serious and substantive account of those who have been dispossessed by the single-minded encroachments of high-tech industrialization, that this international realignment – this "New World Order," as some have called it – will presage something very grim and intolerant indeed.

It is my hope that the instability of this complicated historical moment will not eclipse entirely the willingness to consider the consequences of limiting our vision always by the bottom dollar, whether as lawyers, judges, or human beings. The extent to which a relentlessly narrow study of private cost pitted against individual benefit has replaced the larger, murkier, but infinitely more rewarding analysis of what it takes to ensure peaceful human coexistence is the most important dilemma of our time.

REFERENCES

1 Free trade zones are created by international agreements dedicated to unrestrained business interest – i.e. cheap production costs. Their most disturbing feature, in general, is the suspension of labor laws, environmental protection regulations, etc. Their existence has resulted, for example, in "[f]urniture-making plants and metal-plating shops that fled environmental restrictions in California now flourish[ing] in Tijuana, Mexico, producing toxic wastes from their use of solvents." R. Suro, "Border Boom's Dirty Residue Imperils U.S Mexico Trade," *The New York Times*, March 31, 1991: A1 at A16, col. 3.

2 ibid.

3 I am indebted for these insights to my student Letitia Comacho, whose fine paper and research sparked my own interest in this subject.

4 Mann, "The Shatterproof Ceiling," *Washington Post*, August 17, 1990: D3, col. 5.

5 "Late last spring, the Ministry of Health imposed new rules restricting access to legal abortions. The regulations, which were passed with no parliamentary debate and little notice in the media, require women to get permission for an abortion from three doctors. Any who find fault with their patients' reasons for wanting an abortion can refuse to sign the 'contract.' If one does, women must see a state-sanctioned psychologist. Most often, these, like the Church, try to persuade them to give up their babies to overcrowded orphanages, run by nuns. . . . The most serious threat to abortion rights, however, has arisen in Parliament. Last summer, Senator Walerian Piotrowski proposed a bill that would outlaw abortion, saying it would help Poland lead the way to a more moral Europe." G. Glaser, "New Poland, Same Old Story," *Village Voice*, April 2, 1991: 19.

6 "Poland is at a turning point, and we are turning to the right and into the dark," says Hanna Jankowska, a Warsaw feminist. "We are trading a red regime for one that wears black robes. Things are moving in the direction of an absolute clerical state, like Khomeini's Iran. And naturally, women are left behind." ibid.

7 "Poles want to believe that they have a free, modern society," says Hanna Jankowska. "The truth is that unfortunately we are a Third World Country, especially when it comes to women. But we have the Catholic Church and the legacy of Communism, both of which foster passivity, to contend with." ibid.: 21, col. 5.

Part III

ON CONTROLLING
OUR BODIES

9

SURVIVING RAPE
A morning/mourning ritual

Andrea Benton Rushing

For Frank who asked how I endured it, and Audre who asked me
to write about it, and those whose love leads me

I am writing because rape is . . . I am writing to understand. I am
writing so I won't be afraid. I am writing so I won't start crying
again. . . . I am writing to allow myself to feel the anger. I am
writing to keep from running toward it or away from it or into
anybody's arms. I am writing to find solutions and pass them on. I
am writing to find a language and pass it on.

I am writing, writing, writing, for my life.

(Pearl Cleage, *Mad at Miles*, p. 5)

"DON'T MOVE!" yanks my eyes open. Night light's off. Can't see. Not
in-the-swimming-pool-without-my-glasses can't see. REALLY can't see.
Need to get up and find out what's wrong, but something's pressing me
down. "DON'T MAKE A SOUND OR I'LL HAVE TO HURT YOU!"
The barked command's garbled. Have to come out of this nightmare. A
man's on top of me. One of his hands pinned both of mine above my
head. His breath's warm on my face, but his jacket's cold when he pulls
my robe and nightgown up, my underpants down. Short, flabby penis.
He is telling me how much I want him, how much he satisfies me. Maybe
I can go back to sleep or pass out until it's over. . . . Suppose he can't get
inside my vulva or ejaculate. If I make him angry, he'll cut, shoot,
strangle me. Did he kill the kitten? Where are Osula and Ann?

It's been 21,900 hours, 912 days, 130 Saturday nights, 30 months, 3
years since October 16, 1988 when I was stunned awake, straddled by a
man I did not know. First I think I'm nightmaring. . . . Then try to sink
back under sleep's blanket and weave whatever is going on into a dream
the way I do when I have to urinate or am hungry and don't want to
leave the bed's womb. Then I try to pass out. Can't because I don't know
what he'll do, because I am adrenalined, 360 degrees opposite of

relaxed. Besides, he wants me to be conscious of his omnipotence and my humiliating powerlessness. It's almost blackstrap-molasses dark. And horribly quiet.

Saying the story, I usually claim, "All I asked God for was my life. God gave me that and so much more." But there were no words in my mind when I was being raped. I chose life and did what I thought would keep me in the land of the living. My body responds to his in a vicious parody of intimacy while my brain whirls to read his mind so I can save my life by satisfying him. The sustaining, salvific prayers came from friends and ancestors on the other side of the membrane that separates the living from the dead. While I moan and whimper, some choir is singing, "I don't know where, but I know that you do. I can't see how, but I know you'll get through. God, please touch somebody right now, right now."

Will he slash my face when he's through? All he asks for is money. Not a demand. A casual request as if I'm "his woman," and he's going to run an errand. Same man who has walked through the walls of my apartment to rape me, waits, almost patiently, while I fumble through two purses for my wallet *and* he lets me take the bills out. Doesn't count the seventy dollars I hand over or mention my credit cards. He leaves the room, speaking over his shoulder, "Stay there, I'll be back," as if he were my honey getting up to fix us drinks or snacks or turn our favorite music on, as if every cell in my body wasn't trying to eject him from my life.

If you'd told me way back then that I'd still be recovering from rape now, I wouldn't have laughed in your face, but I wouldn't have believed you either. I'd faced traumas before – tenure review, major surgery, heartshattering divorce – stumbled through some and transcended others, so I expect rape to slip from me like a boiled beet's rough skin.

Since I'm living in an upscale Euro-American neighborhood, the police are as surprised – though for different reasons – as I am that the rapist was AfAm and question how I can be sure if I couldn't see him. They also wonder if I associate a smell with him. I don't, which rules out a smoker, loud cologne, and alcohol on his breath. No beard, sideburns, or goatee – though he may have a mustache. This "brother" doesn't have "good" hair, isn't balding, doesn't sport a juicy jheri-curl. He's wearing a clammy imitation leather jacket and heavyish gloves, which should have impeded unzipping his fly more than I remember them doing. He wasn't heavy on top of my 110 pounds. I don't remember feeling the scratch of his pubic hair. Does he, I wonder then and for months afterward, keep his raping ensemble in the trunk of a car? Who has he already raped? Who will he rape next?

In a clotted voice I don't recognize as mine, I talk to 911's drawling police officer who offers to stay on the phone until the patrol car arrives. Then my daughter and her best friend come in. Since they know me to be a night person, they're completely unsurprised to see me sitting at the kitchen counter at 3:30 a.m. "Mama's been raped," I blurt. "The police are on their way." At first Osula and Ann are kind of calm. When they become hysterical, I stop sobbing, have my daughter call her father, and have Ann call her mother. Get on the phone to assure both parents that I'm fine, hospital-bound for a routine check-up, but fine. And I believed I was!

The slim, short woman officer who entered the apartment first while the men hung back on the threshold has told me that I'll be asked to leave what I'm wearing at the hospital as evidence. While I write out my statement, I have Osula and Ann pack something for me to wear home and put the necessary items in a purse. As the scene-of-the-crime men go over the apartment dusting (as in grade B movies) for fingerprints they don't find, photographing the window the attacker came through and the pallet I was raped on, they speak in soft voices and wait for the detective to arrive. Osula and Ann are too traumatized to drive. So raped and night-blind (but trained to strong-Black-wonder-woman roles) I drive myself, following Detective Butler's tail lights, to a hospital I've never seen or even heard of before.

I decide to go into therapy or join a support group. Of the women I know who are rape victims and talk about it, twenty years after the attack the one who wasn't treated spews rage at the drop of a hat and, aside from going to work and visiting her large family, is a near-recluse; the one who joined a support group has kept her high-profile job and even traveled to China. Like her I have no intention of letting the rapist mangle my life.

Leaving home in September, I'd crowed to family and friends, "My daughter's off to college, and I can still touch my toes! I'm gon live like a graduate student!" After long years of being a single parent and professor, my Atlanta sabbatical (delayed a year so it will coincide with my daughter's first year away) opens another phase of my life. And I had such ambitious plans.

My loose connection with Spelman's English department includes teaching classes, grading papers, advising students, writing letters of recommendation, or going to meetings. Now I'll *finally* be able to write all day, and I have three projects at various stages of work-in-progress: *Birthmarks & Keloids* is my short story collection; "These Wild and Holy Women" is about spiritually powerful women characters in contemporary AfAm fiction; and "A Language of Their Own" is my book-to-be, about how Yoruba women's attire "speaks," what it signifies to other Yoruba and to outsiders who can read its syntax, grammar, vocabulary, cadences.

When I need a break from the rigors of writing, I'll go to AfAm bookstores, museums, art galleries, plays, dance concerts, film series, night spots. Back in a city after years in a New England university town,

I'll eat soul, Ethiopian, West Indian, Japanese and Thai food; instead of driving two and a half hours to get to church in Cambridge, Mass., I'll join an Atlanta Holy-Ghost-filled, political, and Afro-centric congregation; and, 48, keep an eye out for that good man who is so very hard to find, the husband for my old age.

Since I'm feeling fine (not a single bruise, broken fingernail, or out-of-place earring), it's a hassle to be in the dry cold of Clayton Hospital's air-conditioned examining rooms waiting the hours it takes doctors to finish treating Saturday night knife slashes and bullet gashes before one can get to me. The crisis counsellor says I seem like a woman accustomed to being in control and, since rape rendered me powerless, I may have a more difficult recovery than a more passive woman.

The next time the counsellor checks up on me, I ask what stages I can expect to go through and what I should do to recover from rape quickly and completely. Suck my teeth and groan to hear, "Each victim has to find her own way. It's hard to predict. Women mourn and mend differently." WAIT! STOP! HALT! Every six minutes some girl or woman in the USA is raped. Some recovered victim must have chronicled her journey, published her 12-step program, copywritten a recipe I can improve on. Though I scour, I never find a thing. Three years later all I can offer the next rape victim is two poems by twice-raped (!!) June Jordan. Audre Lorde's *Cancer Journals* have saved minds and lives, but there's no equivalent to guide a rape survivor. And there's no Bessie Smith, Ida Cox, Dinah Washington, Nina Simone, Koko Taylor, Sweet Honey in the Rock sound that testifies about and transcends rape's agonies.

> Way down younder by myself,
> and I couldn't hear nobody pray.

In movie and television versions of rape, *the* problems are that people think you seduced the man, police are sexistly hostile, hospital staff is icily callous, but my ordeal wasn't going that way at all. In my apartment, the Georgia police officers who look and sound like red-necks treat me with a courtesy nothing in my childhood summers in segregated Jacksonville, Florida or Dothan, Alabama prepared me for. I'm questioned gently. Did I recognize the rapist? A boyfriend? Someone who'd stalked me? Was he a college student my daughter and her friend knew? Did we have oral sex? Anal sex? Did he bite me? They accept my word that I've never seen the man before and don't even ask if I tried to fight him off. At the hospital, the in-take clerk, crisis counsellor, lab technician, nurse, doctor, billing clerk are all considerably consoling. At the time I didn't notice, but a week later their behavior upsets me. There is, I tell sympathizers, no plan to end rape. People are just refining their treatment of the inevitable.

When the crisis counsellor leaves, I scan the hospital's "Recovering from Rape" brochure:

REMEMBER. . . . You did nothing to provoke the attack. You are not at fault. You are the victim of a violent crime. Men do not rape because of sexual desire; they rape to humiliate, control, and degrade. Rape is a violent assault on the body and leaves emotional scars which can take weeks, months, or years to resolve. Each person is unique and must work through this emotional trauma in their own individual way. There is no "right" or "wrong" way to deal with this stressful time.

The counsellor describes the hospital's exam and treatment: If there's a chance that I might be pregnant, I'll get the morning-after pill; had the rapist bitten me, I'd get a tetanus shot – BITTEN ME; blood will be drawn to see if I've gotten a sexually transmitted disease, but, while waiting for the results, I'm to take antibiotics just in case. . . . The doctor – a nurse by his side – turns off the light so his ultraviolet lamp can look for traces of the rapist's semen between my legs. The second strange man in this long evening standing over my body, focused on my vulva. I've neither seen nor heard about this phase of rape's aftermath. As my nails claw the crisis counsellor's palm, I'm glad she alerted me and glad I said yes to her hand-holding offer. Hairs are pulled, one by one, from my head and vulva for DNA testing. After the lab technician takes my blood and gives me a band-aid with Daffy Duck decorations, I collapse into snuffling tears, "I was so scared and there was no one to help me."

The sun's high by the time I finally leave the hospital. So exhausted I *know* I'll go right to sleep as soon as I get home, which isn't what happens. Kay, who has met me in the emergency room with a serene smile and steadying affirmation, alternates between soothing Osula and Ann in the waiting room and chatting with me as I'm shuttled from examining room to examining room, get a douche, Xanax for my expected anxiety, and antibiotic in case I have a sexually transmitted disease (I'm recoiling from gonorrhea and syphilis. It's weeks before herpes occurs to me. Months before AIDS seems possible). Kay assigns the girls to rid the apartment of all signs of police and rapist intrusion, but broad black scuff marks from the rapist's sneakers won't come off the white window ledge. (And, later, I refuse to have them painted over because I want to *remember* why I am suffering so.) Kay suggests a Caribbean vacation. Overhearing, Osula thinks I should spend time with family in Boston, Minneapolis, or NYC. Having just moved to Atlanta, I can't plan, much less pack for, another trip. Besides, I don't intend to let the rapist – a man whose face and name I don't know, whose unschooled and country Southern accent is all I'm sure I can recognize – make me skitter scared. As hard-headed as always, I pooh-pooh advice about getting a second-floor apartment, dog or gun; and I resist all suggestions to go back to safe white Amherst. Not only don't I leave apartment 2401, I even sleep (sedated, the pallet moved from its rape location, and a woman friend spending the night in the living room) in the bedroom I was raped in. Four days later, I rent furniture for my garden apartment.

Throughout the sunny Sunday hours after the hospital, I notify family and friends that I've been raped, assuring them that my body is fine and that I'm exhilarated to be alive. I ask proven intercessors to help me glorify a wonderful God and, since "the prayers of the saints availeth much," to storm heaven on my behalf. That Sunday, and ever after, my candid talk about being raped surprises because people are accustomed to rape victims' shame and reticence. "But," I say over and over, "I am the victim, not the criminal."

Rape has its own shadings and nuances. Comparatively speaking, I haven't suffered all that much. I wasn't a virgin, incestuously raped, gang-raped, penetrated with a Coke bottle or a pool table's cue stick. Yes, I felt like the man had a weapon. No I didn't see a razor, knife, or gun. He didn't make me get up and have a drink with him, defecate or urinate on me. And my daughter and her friend left before he arrived and came home after he left. Being raped in the bed at 3:00 a.m., in an apartment I'd only lived in for a month, before I'd had time to get an Atlanta social life, by a man I didn't know, got me much more sympathy than being raped by a date or husband would have.

My core is cracked when the rapist is a man my politics have taught me to call brother. Gone are slavery, Reconstruction and lynch law days when we fear white men's rape violence. Now we learn to cringe from men who look like our fathers, uncles, nephews, godsons. I have worked so hard to keep my ties to the AfAm working class I came out of: driven two and a half hours across Massachusetts for braid styles and church; maintained my ability to talk trash, dance into the wee hours, and cook our soul food; boasted " I love a cut and shoot bar." Now the class chasm has opened and I, of all people, feel muscles from my shoulders to my toes cramp in the presence of dark men whose body language, attire, or accent echo the rapist's. Ashamed of my fear, I hate the rapist for changing me.

Swaddled in shock's soft cloak, blessedly naive about the invisible wounds rape has scalded me with, I expect to take a week or two, *even* a month to recover. *Then*, I'll finish the tedium of settling into my Atlanta life and hunker down to the writing life I've longed for for years. If I'd known, or even suspected, the hells that lurked on the other side of shock, I would have tried to overdose, instead of just asking counsellors and psychiatrists how likely it was for rape victims to commit suicide, instead of pleading to be hospitalized until "all this" was over; instead of telling two different, but equally startled, psychiatrists, eighteen months and 700 miles apart, to "shoot me and put me out of my misery."

A single hour in my life pulverized all my long-laid plans.
I couldn't have lived with that knowledge.
I'd have fallen off life's ledge.
Or jumped.

A week after the rape, a friend and I aerobic walk in autumn's crisp sunshine. She hesitates as we start past the housing complex the police have traced the rapist's sneakered footprints to. Still-I-rise Black-woman, I assure her that I'm just fine – and get excruciatingly crippling muscle spasms in my back almost immediately. Later that first anniver-sary evening, out of Xanax, unable to get D., the masseuse Kay has found for me – or E., the rape counsellor D. has referred to me – on the phone, I rely (as I've done innumerable uneventful times in the past) on the hot water bottle to loosen pain's vise. When I wake up, a patch of skin is sticking on the rubber, and I have second degree burns. On the way home from burn treatment a few days later, suffering from the loss of peripheral vision that – I later learn – often affects trauma victims, I have a car accident.

BUT I PRESS ON . . .

I give the "Writing Myself Alive" talk I've promised Spelman College, not merely so students can see and hear a woman scholar, not even so I can, for the first time in over fifteen years of college teaching, have a class that's both all female and all of African descent. It's my coming out. After years of being mother, scholar and professor, I've declared myself a writer. Daughter I call my Sun-and-moon-and-stars is a college stu-dent. I've managed to single-parent her and achieve the security of PhD, tenure and full professorship, and sustained a dismaying array of physi-cal ailments. Now it's time to live *my* life, and I'm becoming less a consumer (and decoder) of other's works and more a creator of my own. "If nothing else I ever write gets published, I'll write on because I now know that my body/mind/spirit will break if I don't."

Though I arrive late, contact lenses smeared, fingernail-polish chipped, and in the disoriented state my sister calls "back-side-to," I manage to be on a Spelman College inaugural symposium panel on Black Women and the Intellectual/Literary Tradition the weekend Johnnetta Cole is installed, the first Africana woman ever, as president of the college. It seems like *everyone* is on campus: Beverly Guy-Sheftall and Paula Giddings, Niara Sudarkasa and Joyce Ladner, Toni Cade Bambara and Gwendolyn Brooks, Pearl Cleage and Mari Evans, Louise Meriwether and Sonia Sanchez, Byllye Avery and Pearl Primus. After a vegetarian dinner full of the kind of cultural and political talk I so miss in Amherst and came to Atlanta for, with a group of sisters I haven't seen in years, haven't ever seen all together, my energy is suddenly sucked away, and I stagger out of Sisters' chapel and slow-drive home long before the Max Roach/Maxine Roach octet has played a single note.

The morning after that heady day, too exhausted to imagine brushing my teeth much less driving from suburban College Park to Atlanta's Civic Center and sitting up through the inauguration, I begin to realize that my recovery from rape isn't going to be like gum surgery, knee surgery, or (natural childbirth) having my daughter. More like coming back from a hysterectomy – stomach muscles cut – when I'd already been weakened by years of the heavy bleeding that stains clothes, makes you carry extra tampons and pads everywhere, and has you fainting in public.

Since I'd felt so good and been so clear-headed and capable in the immediate aftermath of being raped – no signs of the physical exhaustion, disorientation, anxiety, or amnesia that, later, become my almost constant companions – I was as unprepared as everyone else when shock's soft shawl slipped from my shoulders. I thought what went wrong with rape victims was they denied being raped, but I hadn't. I'd called the police, pressed charges, been hospital-examined, begun twice-a-week rape crisis counselling, even seen the pastoral counsellor at Morehouse Medical School to talk about the politics of being raped by a "brother" and helped by Euro-Americans. In spite of my intentions and efforts, I didn't become my old self again in the weeks and then months I'd set aside for rape recovery. As the hours, days, weeks, months, years marched away from the October rape day, I came to see that I would never be my old self again. "The only thing about me that's the same," I tell those who compliment how strong my voice sounds and how well I look, "is my fingerprints." "You get better," Evelyn-the-counsellor tells me, "and, because you feel *more*, feel worse."

From a December '88 journal entry . . .

> 8:45 a.m. . . . So it was dreadful to feel my body getting tenser and tenser as I became more and more awake. Tense about what time it was. Tense about when the alarm clock would go off. Tense about what I'd eat. Tense about calling the phone company. Tense about calling Dr D. for a Xanax refill. Tense about the car's possible problems. So I decided to give in and take an anti-anxiety pill, but then I couldn't find my pocketbook. Couldn't even find my glasses so I could look for the pocketbook. And all the while the kitten kept sneezing. I moaned for her to stop. And the sound of me mewling reminded me of the whimpering noises I made while I was being raped.

By January, still in twice-weekly rape crisis counselling, I finally dare to open a few windows in the apartment for the first time since I was raped, but being one of 3,000 people evacuated from an extremely bourgeois (the pastor drives a Jaguar) church near the beginning of a Sunday service has frightened me unbearably. As I watch police dogs bomb-sniff, it feels like no place is safe. I can be hurt by someone I don't know at home in bed and in church which is, as I've said for years, where I'd rather be than any other place. At my request, E. calls a psychiatrist for me. The AfAm doctor diagnoses post-traumatic stress disorder, which I thought you had to go to Vietnam to get. He prescribes Xanax for my anxiety and is surprised that I'd expected to be fully recovered from rape by now. It will, he dismays me by saying, require a year for short-term recovery and five years – FIVE! – for as close to full recovery as one gets.

By March, despite the successes I call myself having – riding MARTA public transportation and mounting a photography exhibit at Spelman – Dr P. stuns me by diagnosing clinical depression. (Only hearing him read textbook definition and having him say that my progress so far reflects my disciplined will power, persuades me.) Rape lugs me around. No sign of light at the end of the tunnel.

Rape makes me doze off at night propped up on pillows so I'll be prepared not so much "if" as "when" the rapist comes back. Lights on all over the apartment. I, nervous as my kitten, jump when she gets in or out of bed with me, and wake up almost every night at the 3:00 a.m. rape time. Raped in almost total darkness, I don't sleep soundly until dawn. And I wake up, as though demon-ridden, with crusty saliva lines around my mouth.

Before I was raped, I'd prided myself on waking up an alert that didn't need the caffeine props of coffee and tea. Afterwards, it's a daily struggle to come into consciousness and realize AGAIN that I didn't nightmare being raped. Now, as it did when I was actually being raped, my mind scrabbles for a safe place and, finding none, tries to shut off, but the strategy is no more effective than it was that gruesome night. No idea how I'll get out of bed, much less take the ten steps from the bedroom I was raped in to the bathroom I've become afraid to shower in. Grope for eyeglasses. Turn off the bedside lamp rape has made a night-time necessity. Step over the telephone wire the newly installed burglar alarm is hooked up to. Peer blinking as I did the rape night, into the living room. Tense, heart racing, afraid.

In the western Massachusetts university town I'm on sabbatical from, my days start (weather permitting) with a mile-long up and down hill walk while the Connecticut Valley's air is dewy and still. Atlanta is much warmer than Amherst, so I'd looked forward to being outside much more and alternating bicycle rides with long walks. But family, friends and police think the rapist stalked me, waited until I was alone and defenseless before he came through a living room window, so I'm much too frightened to leave the house and risk being raped again. Besides, though it takes me years to know this, my body's no longer mine. The rapist controls it. Moving feels like Herculean work and distracts my mind from being rape-alert.

"Did you stop and pray this morning?" a song from childhood Florida summer wonders, "as you started on your way? Did you ask God to guide you, walk beside you all the way? Did you stop and pray this morning? Did you kneel just one moment and say, 'Give me comfort for my soul on this old, rugged road?' Did you just remember to pray?" My mind's too centrifugal for prayer. Can neither sing the songs of Zion myself nor decide whether James Cleveland's gospel growl, Aretha Franklin's sanctified melisma, or Marion William's octave-defying witness will encourage my heart, regulate my mind, relax my forehead's accordion pleats. Exhausted from my marrow on out, I'd die if I had to will air into my lungs or work to make my blood flow. Difficult to believe I can choose an ensemble, do laundry, grocery shop, or collect the mail. Impossible to see myself doing anything I came to Atlanta to do. Foolhardy to claim one day at a time. Half-hour by half-hour is all I dare.

But I *can* make a pot of tea and focusing on that task magnetizes my mind's scattered steel filings on a north–south axis. Drop Lemon Verbena or Mellow Mint tea bags into a small pot, sweeten with an exotic honey or plain white sugar, place the pot, a tall clear glass, yogurt, a spoon and a cloth napkin on a thick wooden tray and, emboldened by my success, turn off the lights that have protected me all night and open the blinds that face the thicket behind the apartment and the grass police found the rapist's footprint path on. Then nestle back under the covers. Inhaling the tea's steam relaxes me. First ("So glad I got my religion in time!"), I read *Forward Day by Day*'s meditations; half-dozen prayers from the Book of Common Prayer, and the psalm, Old Testament reading, gospel and epistle for the day. Next, notes about my health: medicine, pains and aches, mood swings, menu, exercise. Then, as an outward and visible sign that, though horribly helpless while I was raped, I can control some things, as evidence that although I have no idea when-where-why the rapist chose me, I can figure some things out, I work a *New York Times* crossword puzzle. Finally, still desperate for motives and solutions, I read a chapter or two in a mystery.

Pre-rape, I escaped into British mysteries, and my favorites all featured men who – no matter how they differed from each other – lived in worlds as far from mine as Tolkien's Middle Earth, C. S. Lewis's Narnia, or Alice's Wonderland. Rolling manicured lawns, visiting cards; butlers, valets, chaufferus, cooks and housekeepers; port, fine sherry, and dressing for dinner; Eton–Oxford–Cambridge; tea, scones and fairy cakes; witty conversations; country villages and estates; bumblingly well-intentioned vicars and earnest innkeepers; cashmere, titles, charming eccentrics. . . . Women are never raped, police don't carry guns, crimes occur off-stage, and there is a logical explanation for every crime.

Raped, I'm a character in a cruder mystery. (File #88747812.) Detective C. L. Butler is in charge of the case. Now stories about British sleuths make my eyes slide off the page. "No, no, no," the gospel song insists, "They couldn't do. They didn't have the power that you needed to bring you through . . ."

Then my best friend sends me books about two new-style US women detectives, Sue Grafton's California-based Kinsey Milhone and Sara Paretsky's V. I. Warshawski. Week after week I gulp, as if drowningly desperate for air, their plain-spoken stories about acid-tongued, fast-thinking, single and self-employed women who not only dare to live alone, but scoff, sneer, seethe when men try to put them in their "weaker sex" place. Parched and starved, I read and reread Sue Grafton's alphabet adventures, but Sara Paretsky's books become my favourites because her Chicago-based private investigator is even more bodacious and sassy than my pre-rape self. And, in stark contrast to television and movie renditions of women as powerless victims of men, she both withstands and metes out physical violence in every single book. Murder mysteries restore order to worlds thrown out of balance. . . . The police may never find the "brother" who raped me, and I may never get to read him the seven-foot scroll detailing *all* I've suffered since he slithered into my life.

The morning ritual comforts me. If I don't do another purposeful thing all day, I *have* accomplished something. An hour and a half after my first sip of tea, I am focused enough to turn on radio jazz and churn out the six typewritten journal pages I require of myself daily. On days when I can't do the ritual or fall asleep as soon as I've done it, I know I am, once again, nailed to the dank floor of the abyss.

By the time my lease runs out at the end of June, Atlanta's warm enough for sweet and eat-them-in-the-bathtub-juicy peaches. I'm re-mastering grocery shopping and the basics of cooking. Fear has subsided enough for me to sleep with fewer lights on and ride MARTA in relative calm. Still automatically check the physique, skin color and hair-do of all the AfAm men I see to be sure they aren't the rapist returned. Carry the phone the burglar alarm's hooked up to from room to room, spend hours watching CBS soap operas and reruns of *Murder, She Wrote* and (twice a day) *Miami Vice*. No longer expect my '78 Toyota to collapse around me the way my life has, leaving me clutching the steering wheel on Atlanta's maze of highways. But . . . my sabbatical has shape-shifted into sick leave, and I've filed Social Security and TIAA/CREF claims for total disability since I'm too frightened in groups of people, too easily exhausted and too amnesiac to teach.

Summer '89, back in the college town I fled to Atlanta to escape, I can't recall what's in the drawers, closets and cabinets of a house I've lived in for a decade and am astonished at how little I remember about campus buildings, college routines, colleagues' faces, names, disciplines. When the old farmhouse makes its floor-settling night noises, I panic alert. It feels like I've sunk back to the beginning of rape recovery when, the first Saturday night I spend alone a thousand miles away from the rape site, I put knives, scissors, letter openers, potato peelers and pantyhose away with the same compulsion and dismay that drove me in Atlanta. I am back in the high-walled chasm, buried alive beneath a man in a stocking cap mask, bleeding from internal wounds people can't see when they insist on how good I look and sound.

When fast-track people in Amherst ask about my time away, they expect to hear about my photography, book proposals, chapters written, contracts signed. During my nine-month Atlanta stay, I haven't written one line or edited a single page of "A Language of Their Own," "These Wild and Holy Women," or *Birthmarks & Keloids*. Reeling toward healing, I have neither organized the negatives, photographs and slides of my Nigeria research nor mastered the word processor. My Atlanta "accomplishments" are not screaming when a man next to me in church stood close enough to hold one side of the hymnal we were singing out of and sitting between the two AfAm men AAA sent to tow my car to a Toyota dealership. My writing consists of a few personal letters, two letters of recommendation composed at a hobbled snail's pace, disability claims and my journal. Each time I'm asked how Atlanta was, the scab's scraped from my scar.

ATLANTA IS WHERE RAPE TORTURED ME
WHERE I ALMOST DIED FROM AN INVISIBLE WOUND.

Too sick to teach Fall semester, I plan to spend it in St Croix, healing in the sea and sun, but, for the first time in eighty-two years, St Croix is undone by a hurricane. My *second* away-from-Amherst plan in two years pulverized, sealing me in the tomb Amherst feels like – with no resurrection in sight. I'm Brer Rabbit. And Amherst is my tarbaby.

Winter-bare trees. Short days. Low, leaden skies. Cold. Boots, mittens, scarves, thermal underwear, snow shovels and tires, anti-freeze, rock salt. I cling, as though they could save me – to the covers when the alarm goes off. Regress back to daily naps and coloring books. Exhausted no matter how much I sleep. Even the tiniest task monumental. A kind of suicidal I talk myself out of over and over only by realizing that my Sun-and-moon-and-stars would be undone. For the first time since my ugly-duckling high school days, I cry in outbursts that last an hour and try to see the banked emotions through the prisms Dame Julian of Norwich and Rebecca Jackson (of Philadelphia) did.

My Amherst psychiatrist decides Tofranil isn't affecting my depression, prescribes Prozac and makes seemingly Simon Legree rules: Do not sleep in the clothes you wore all day and wear them again the next day; leave the house, even if it's only to get the mail, every day; go, since you have friends, family and church there, to Boston as often as your scant store of energy will allow; write. When asked, my Atlanta psychiatrist said that though raped at home I'd rather be there than anywhere else because home was where I had most control and that, as a person who "lived in my mind," getting my memory back was complicated by how many things I know. "Most people only have one language to get back. You have English, French, Spanish, and smatterings of Yoruba." My Amherst psychiatrist depicts clinical depression as a cunning illness: If you've prided yourself on the regularity of your schedule, it keeps you from going to sleep at night and getting up in the morning; if you're a sensual person, desire is expunged; if you're an intellectual, depression breaks your mind.

My morning ritual is my life-jacket. Downstairs to bigger teapot, a wider range of teas and the inventiveness to combine Mellow Mint and Tropical Escape. Sliced raw ginger and – the ingredients vary daily – pounded cloves. As the weather chills, yogurt's replaced by pears, and tangerines, warmed apple cider with ginger and vinegar or warm milk with a combination of Ovaltine and Postum alternate with tea. Winter's grip tightens, and fruit gives way to seven grain, challah and anadama bread. Using the same thick circular wooden tray I had in Atlanta, I carry a cloth napkin in a wooden ring and a tall clear glass for my elixir upstairs for myself the way I'd do for an invalid friend or a luscious man. Then burrow back in bed for the morning "work" I did in Atlanta, with additions.

Leaving Georgia has meant giving up the arc of gracious women I relied on, and I miss them so. Over and over I find myself longing for the web of loving women who surrounded Audre Lorde's mastectomy recovery. Once again, as they were in my friendless adolescence, books become my best friends, and their sister-care feeds me. Before I begin each one, I just *know* reading it will gnarl me with envy and make me even more ashamed of allowing rape to derange me so completely. But I am always wrong. Quilts in *Stitching Memories*. Poetry by Lucille Clifton, and Rita Dove, *Lionheart Gal*'s collection of feisty and backative Jamaican women's testimonies . . . Toni Morrison's heart-stopping *Beloved*. Alice Walker's *Living by the Word*. Toni Cade Bambara's *Salt Eaters*. . . . These women's stories aren't mine so I know there is still space for my frayed pieces of the patchwork quilt, and their sturdy and magical creations brave me to try. Some raped woman needs my witness. Not emotions recollected in elegant tranquility when I am *finally* out of the tunnel it takes all my faith to believe even exists. She needs to taste my terror, hear my gasps for life, watch me inch through brambles of despair, reaching for life and sanity with bleeding stigmata all over me.

The story of the people and the spirits, the story of earth, is the story of what moves, what moves on, what patterns, what dances, what sings, what balances, so life can be felt and known. The story of life is the story of moving. Of moving on.

Your place in the great circling spiral is to help in that story, in that work. To pass on to those who can understand what you have learned, what you know.

It is for this reason you have endured. . . .

. . . Pass it on. . . . That is the story of life. . . . Grow, move, give, move.

(Paula Gunn Allen, *The Woman Who Owned the Shadows*, p. 210)

10

AFRICAN-AMERICAN WOMEN AND ABORTION: 1800–1970

Loretta J. Ross

Homage I pay
to the mothers who
became mothers
before their time.
& the mothers
that became mothers
when there were no mothers
to be found.

(K. Collins, 1991: 40)

INTRODUCTION

My quest to understand the activism of African-American women seeking abortions and birth control stems from experiences shared with millions of women who want real choices as to when, and under what conditions, we will have children. Here is my definition of what it means to be "pro-life" *and* "pro-choice" – the right to have, or not to have, children and the right to raise them free from racism, sexism and poverty.

Many people mistakenly view the African-American women's struggle for abortion rights and reproductive freedom as a relatively recent phenomenon, rather than placing it in the context of our historical struggle against racism, sexism and poverty. Whether these assumptions come from population experts or the African-American community, they fail to credit us with the power to make responsible decisions for ourselves. To ask whether African-American women favor or oppose abortion is the wrong question. We obtain 24 per cent of the abortions in the United States, more than 500,000 annually (Henshaw *et al.*, 1991: 75–81). The question is not *if* we support abortion, but *how*, and when, and why.

African-American women have a long history in the struggle for reproductive freedom, but racist and sexist assumptions about us, our sexuality and our fertility have disguised our contributions to the birth control and abortion movements in the United States. Distilling facts from the myths is difficult because so many accounts of African-American history are written from perspectives that fail even to acknowledge our presence in the reproductive freedom movement.

Similarly, if a decline in African-American birth rates occurs, the population experts usually ascribe it to poverty, coercive family planning, or other external factors, ignoring the possibility that we Black women were in any way responsible for the change.

The absence of discussion about abortion rights activism by African-American women in most feminist literature is also disappointing, reflecting a commonly held view that African-American women either are too politically naive or have an underdeveloped consciousness on issues of gender equality and abortion rights.

While volumes could be written on this topic, this chapter merely aspires to be one step in the process of recording our "herstory." It remains for others to cover comprehensively various aspects of abortion, such as its medical technology, and the judicial and legislative battles that determined the legality of abortion and contraception.

Instead, I have chosen to focus on the activism; the *agency* of African-American women in the struggle both to obtain abortions and to participate in the national debate. I have also chosen to tell my own story in this chapter because, in the tradition of Paula Giddings and others, I believe it is the deliberate combination of the personal and the objective that creates the authority, authenticity and uniqueness of the African-American female experience.

Recording our history of activism is important because the voices heard in support of abortion are usually white. Even with the best intentions, white women cannot speak for us. They cannot see the world through our history or represent the authority of our lives. And, while volumes could also be written about the racism and elitism historically besetting the feminist movement, white women are not the focus of this paper.

African-American women have been reluctant to analyze our history regarding abortion and to speak out collectively and publicly in support of abortion. To do so once seemed to further arguments of Black genocide, a charge that was not necessarily paranoid in view of past attacks on African-Americans. To speak out also risked replicating the narrow focus of the white abortion rights movement, by engaging in "privileged bias," of isolating abortion from other forms of control imposed on African-American women, through racism and poverty (Joseph and Lewis, 1981: 50).

If we are to connect ourselves to our foremothers who preceded us, we must transcend the tensions between these two extremes. To paraphrase bell hooks, our struggle is not so much to move from silence into speech, but to change the nature and direction of our speech, to make a speech that is heard (hooks, 1989: 6).

I chose to write on abortion because reproductive health activism has been a part of my life for more than twenty years. I have been privileged to be a part of both the Black liberation and the women's movements and to meet many other African-American women who share a commitment to improving the quality of life for African-American women by ending racism and poverty, and by advancing gender equality.

Abortion rights and reproductive freedom are not intellectual abstractions for me, but have determined many aspects of my life. By the time I was in my twenties, I had experienced many of the reproductive crises consistent with being Black, poor and female in America. At age 15 I became a teen mother because of sexual activity coupled with sexual ignorance, not an unusual combination even today. I realized for the first time the lack of options available to pregnant teens in the 1960s. Because abortion was illegal and traveling anywhere else was not possible, I had my son in a very difficult pregnancy, after staying in a home for unwed mothers.

As a college student two years later, I became pregnant again, due to contraceptive failure. I had an abortion, which fortunately was legal in Washington, DC at the time.

It is providential that I kept my child rather than giving him up for adoption, because I was permanently sterilized by the Dalkon Shield IUD at age 23. I sued A. H. Robins, the maker of the shield, and became one of the first Black women to prevail against this multinational corporation. The company was eventually bankrupted by thousands of other women who were also sterilized. Thus my reproductive career lasted a brief eight years and included a full-term pregnancy, an abortion and sterilization.

Although winning against A. H. Robins was a moral victory, it did not mitigate the burning anger I felt because my IUD was inserted years after its dangers had already been substantially documented. Why was a defective contraceptive recommended to me? Why did I nearly die from acute pelvic inflammatory disease that several doctors failed to link to the defective IUD, preferring to believe in bizarre theories of rare venereal diseases among Black women? Doctors' diagnoses of African-American women were distorted with theories of diseases brought back by soldiers returning from Vietnam. My pelvic infection from the IUD was treated as a mysterious venereal disease. I wondered who really controlled my body. It certainly didn't seem to be me.

In the process I learned that simply surviving against the odds was personally liberating. But I also learned that for African-American women to survive, we all need liberation from devices and doctors and politicians who control our bodies.

Abortion, in and of itself, does not automatically create freedom. But it does allow women to exert some control over our biology, freeing us from the inevitability of unwanted pregnancies, and is therefore indispensable to bodily and political self-determination.

There is much yet to be written about our activism. But it was not persuasive analysis, arguments, or ideology that influenced African-American women to support abortion. We did so because we *needed* to. Necessity was the midwife to our politics.

ABORTION IN THE 1800S

Prior to the Civil War, almost 20 per cent of the total US population consisted of African-American slaves. By 1900, African-Americans were 12 per cent of the total population as the forced breeding of slavery came to an end (Littlewood, 1977: 18). However, even before the Civil War, African-American women sought to control their fertility.

Controlling women's reproduction was important to maintain the race, class and gender inequality of the slave economy. Plantation owners tried to keep knowledge of birth control and abortion away from both slaves and white women to maintain the caste system of white supremacy used to justify slavery (P. Collins, 1991: 50). Black women's fertility increased the owners' labor force and property value and "slave masters wanted adolescent girls to have children, and . . . they practiced a passive, though insidious kind of breeding" (D. White, 1985: 98). Techniques included giving pregnant women lighter workloads and more rations and bonuses to increase Black women's willingness to have children. Punitive measures were also used: infertile women were treated "like barren sows and . . . passed from one unsuspecting buyer to the next" (D. White, 1985: 101).

African-Americans used birth control and abortion as a form of resistance to slavery. Abortion and infanticide were acts of desperation, motivated not by a desire to avoid the biological birth process or the burdens of parenting, but, instead, by a commitment to resist the oppressive conditions of slavery. When Black women resorted to abortion, the stories they told were not so much about the desire to be free of pregnancy, but rather about the miserable social conditions which dissuaded them from bringing new lives into the world (Fried, 1990: 17).

Abortion as a means of controlling fertility has been a part of African culture since the time when Egypt was the cradle of civilization. Abortion-inducing herbs and methods have been discovered in ancient societies in Africa, China and the Middle East (Petchesky, 1990: 28; S. Davis, 1988: 17). African queen and pharaoh Hatshepsut, who

144

reigned in Egypt between 1500 and 179 BC, invented a method of birth control (E. White, 1990: 121). Most of these skills were lost during slavery, except the knowledge retained by midwives which spanned across time. This folk knowledge blurred the distinction between birth control and abortion.

Historians declare that it is almost impossible to determine whether slave women practiced birth control and abortion. However, careful readings of slave journals and narratives reveal that some southern whites were certain that slave women knew how to avoid pregnancy as well as how to deliberately abort their pregnancies. When Daph, a woman on the Ferry Hill plantation in Virginia, miscarried twins in 1838, the overseer reported that Daph took an abortifacient to bring about the miscarriage (D. White, 1985: 84).

Suspicions about slave abortions ran high enough to spur public comment. In an 1856 essay, Dr E. M. Pendleton claimed that planters regularly complained of whole families of women who failed to have children. Pendleton believed that "blacks are possessed of a secret by which they destroy the foetus at an early age of gestation" (D. White, 1985: 85). A Tennessee physician, Dr John H. Morgan, said that he was certain that slave women were aborting either by "medicine, violent exercise, or by external and internal manipulations" (Sterling, 1984: 40).

Toward the end of the nineteenth century, "alum water" was one of many birth control measures used in southern rural communities served by midwives. Women in urban areas used petroleum jelly and quinine. Widely available and purchased very cheaply in stores, it was placed over the mouth of the uterus. Some remedies served both purposes. For example, boiling rusty nails created a douche used as either an abortifacient or a contraceptive. Some women used quinine tablets or turpentine (orally or as a douche) and laxatives. Such concoctions were reputed to bring about severe cramps and contractions which approximated giving birth. Plant compounds like pennyroyal and papaya seeds were also used (Sterling, 1984: 40).

Despite this knowledge, folk methods of birth control and abortion were usually regarded as a sin by those influenced by Christianity. For example, the secret techniques for abortion kept by a midwife named Mollie became too much for her to bear when she converted to Christianity. She begged for forgiveness for having assisted hundreds of women in obtaining birth control and abortions (D. White, 1985: 126).

Nevertheless, African-American women informally discussed abortion and birth control and passed along the knowledge (Ward, 1986: 13–14). In 1894, *The Women's Era*, an African-American women's newsletter, wrote that "not all women are intended for mothers. Some of us have not the temperament for family life" (Giddings, 1984: 108). By the

1900s, Black women were making gains in controlling their fertility. "Their grandmothers married at twelve and fifteen," W. E. B. DuBois, one of the founders of the National Association for the Advancement of Colored People (NAACP), observed in the *Souls of Black Folk*. In 1910, he found 27 per cent of African-American women still single past the age of 15. They were also having fewer children. Half of all married, educated African-American women had no children at the turn of the century. Even more revealing, one-fourth of all Black women – the majority of them rural and uneducated – had no children at all (Giddings, 1984: 137).

BIRTH CONTROL AND ABORTION: 1915–50

One perception of the birth control movement is that it was thrust upon reluctant African-Americans by a population control establishment anxious to control Black fertility. While the population establishment may have had an agenda, African-Americans had their own view of the matter. Probably the best documented source of information about the use of birth control by African-Americans was written by Jessie M. Rodrique, who asserts that "Black women were interested in controlling their fertility and the low birth rates reflect in part a conscious use of birth control. . . . Blacks were active and effective participants in the establishment of local clinics and in the birth control debate" (DuBois and Ruiz, 1990: 333). It is both wrong, and racist, to assume that African-American women had no interest in controlling the spacing of their children and were the passive victims of medical, commercial and state policies of reproductive control.

Black fertility declined toward the end of the nineteenth century, indicative of the growing social awareness among African-Americans that birth spacing was integral to economics, health, race relations and racial progress. In fact, between 1915 and 1920, Black infant mortality actually dropped from 181 per 1,000 births to 102 for states registering 2,000 or more Black births (Giddings, 1984: 149).

African-American women saw themselves not as breeders or matriarchs, but as builders and nurturers of a race, a nation. Sojourner Truth's statement, "I feel as if the power of a nation is within me!" (Bell *et al.*, 1979: 117), affirmed the role of African-American women as "seminal forces of the endurance and creativity needed by future generations of Blacks not merely to survive, but to thrive, produce, and progress" (ibid.: 117).

W. E. B. DuBois wrote in 1919 that "the future [African-American] woman . . . must have the right of motherhood at her own discretion" (DuBois and Ruiz, 1990: 336). Joining him was historian J. A. Rogers who wrote, "I give the Negro woman credit if she endeavors to be something other than a mere breeding machine. Having children is by no means the sole reason for being" (DuBois and Ruiz, 1990: 336).

The Colored Women's Club Movement, the organized voice of African-American women during the late nineteenth and early twentieth centuries, directly addressed issues of Black women's sexuality. This movement sought to "confront and redefine morality and assess its relationship to 'true womanhood'" (Giddings, 1984: 85). Stereotypes about Black women's sexuality and alleged immorality prompted many African-American women to "make the virtues as well as the wants of the colored women known to the American people . . . to put a new social value on themselves" (Lerner, 1972: 576).

The Club Movement also denounced the rampant sterilization of Black women and supported the establishment of family planning clinics in Black communities. In 1918, the Women's Political Association of Harlem announced a scheduled lecture on birth control. The National Urban League requested of the Birth Control Federation of America (the forerunner to Planned Parenthood) that a clinic be opened in the Columbus Hill section of the Bronx. Several ministers held discussions about birth control at their churches and Adam Clayton Powell, an influential Congressional leader, spoke at public meetings in support of family planning (DuBois and Ruiz, 1990: 338).

African-American organizations including the NAACP, the National Urban League and leading Black newspapers like the *Pittsburgh Courier* and the *San Francisco Spokesman* promoted family planning. The African-American newspapers of the period reported the mortality rates of women who had septic abortions and also championed the causes of Black doctors who were arrested for performing illegal abortions (DuBois and Ruiz, 1990: 335).

The *Baltimore Afro-American* wrote that pencils, nails and hat pins were instruments commonly used for self-induced abortions and that abortions among Black women were deliberate, not the result of poor health or sexually transmitted diseases. This was clearly a "means of getting rid of unwanted children" (DuBois and Ruiz, 1990: 335). Many women died as well, a fact not lost on African-American women.

EUGENICS AND GENOCIDE

It is up to science to meet the demands of humanity . . . that life shall be given . . . "frankly, gaily," or – not at all. Which shall it be?
Stella Browne, 1922
(Petchesky, 1990: 92)

Although motherhood was a highly prized social status in Africa, fears of depopulation were not a tremendous concern before American slavery. Africa's population decreased because of the slave trade, exploitative colonial labor policies and the introduction of new diseases from Europe. In the eighteenth century, 20 per cent of the world's population lived in Africa; by the year 2000, the figure is expected to be less than 13 per cent.

In the USA, as racism, lynchings and poverty took their heavy toll on African-Americans, fears of depopulation produced among them toward the end of the nineteenth century a pronatalist trend that had not previously existed. This trend also built successfully on traditional Black values that conferred adult status on women who became biological mothers, the first significant step toward womanhood (P. Collins, 1991: 134). This shift in the critical thinking of African-Americans on population and motherhood presaged an inevitable conflict between the right of women to exercise bodily self-determination and the need of the African-American community for political and economic self-determination. In both schools of thought, wombs were to be the weapon against racism and oppression.

The opposition to fertility control for African-American women in the 1920s came primarily from the Catholic Church for religious and political reasons, from white conservatives who feared the availability of birth control for white women, and from Black nationalist leaders like Marcus Garvey who believed that the continuation of the Black race demanded increasing, rather than decreasing, the African population as a defense against racial oppression.

When the movement for birth control began, its proponents like Margaret Sanger advocated giving women control over their fertility as a means of social mobility. This argument persuaded middle-class women, both Black and white, to support birth control. However, the early feminism of the movement, which prioritized women's control over their own bodies, collapsed under the weight of support offered by the growing number of people who were concerned about the rising population of African-Americans, other people of color and immigrants. Birth control advocacy quickly became a tool of racists who argued in favor of eugenics, or other population control policies, based on fears of African-Americans and others thought to be "undesirable" to the politically powerful. The elite sought to improve their control of society through the control of breeding (Corea, 1985: 138).

The eugenics movement, begun in the late 1800s and based on pseudo-scientific theories of race and heredity, evolved into a movement of biological determinism. To promote the reproduction of self-defined "racially superior" people, its proponents argued for both "positive" methods, such as tax incentives and education for the desirable, and "negative" methods, such as sterilization, involuntary confinement and immigration restrictions for the undesirable (Petchesky, 1990: 86). It was assumed that Black and immigrant women had a "moral obligation to restrict the size of their families." While birth control was demanded as a right for privileged women, it became a duty for the poor (Fried, 1990: 20).

A leading eugenicist proposed sterilization, based on IQ tests, of at least 10 million Americans because they were mentally or physically disabled, criminal, or simply, "feeble-minded" (Hartmann, 1987: 96). By 1932, the Eugenics Society could boast that at least twenty-seven states had passed compulsory sterilization laws and that thousands of "unfit" persons had already been surgically prevented from reproducing (A. Davis, 1983: 214). Many birth control advocates believed it was important to "prevent the American people from being replaced by alien or negro stock, whether it be by immigration or by overly high birth rates among others in this country" (Hartmann, 1987: 97).

The eugenicists' view that social intervention should be used to manipulate biological reproduction echoed other white supremacist views of the day. The Ku-Klux-Klan had an estimated 5 million members at this time, including representatives in Congress (Blee, 1991: 20). It should not be difficult to understand why birth control (and abortion) came to be regarded as genocidal by some African-Americans. This view was exacerbated by the high incidence of involuntary sterilization of African-American women.

It was not helpful that Margaret Sanger, like others who followed her, opportunistically built alliances with the oftentimes racist population control establishment, thereby advancing her cause at the expense of people of color. Sanger's campaign succeeded and benefited middle-class women because it concentrated on legal rights, medical acceptance and public policy. The result was the enactment of policies that were racist enough to be supported by the population control establishment and weak enough so that control over the technology and techniques of birth control would remain in the hands of the professional medical community. The eugenics movement was broader and encompassed far more historical trends than just the feminist movement. It was international in scope and its roots were firmly established in the colonialism of the era. Feminism played its part, both wittingly and unwittingly, in the advancement of the eugenics movment in particular, and white racism in general (Petchesky, 1990: 93).

The Birth Control Federation designed a "Negro Project" in 1939 to hire several African-American ministers to travel through the South to enlist the support of African-American doctors for birth control (Gordon, 1990: 328). The project did not necessarily want strong involvement of other portions of the African-American community, especially women, and argued that "the mass of Negroes, particularly in the South, still breed carelessly and disastrously, with the result that the

149

increase among Negroes, even more than among Whites, is from that portion of the population least intelligent and fit, and least able to rear children properly" (Gordon, 1990: 328).

Not all advocates of birth control and abortion were as insensitive as the eugenicists. The *Courier*, a Black newspaper whose editorial policy favored family planning, said in 1936 that African-Americans should oppose sterilization programs being advanced by eugenicists because the burden would "fall upon colored people and it behooves us to watch the law and stop the spread of [eugenic sterilization]" (DuBois and Ruiz, 1990: 338). A clear sense of dual or "paired" values also emerged among African-American women: to want individual control over their bodies while simultaneously resisting government and private depopulation policies that blurred the distinction between incentives and coercion (Petchesky, 1990: 130). African-American women supported birth control, but at the same time they offered a strong critique of the eugenicists.

Ironically, because of the unavailability of family planning services, sterilization through hysterectomies was frequently chosen by African-American women desperate to control their fertility. Often women pleaded for the operation, because of the absence of organized, alternative birth control services. As had been proven earlier, women adapted themselves to whatever limited choices were available to help them control their lives.

THE UNDERGROUND MOVEMENT: 1950-70

The majority of abortions provided to African-American women in the 1950s and early 1960s were provided by doctors and midwives operating illegally. For example, Dr Edgar Keemer, a Black physician in Detroit, practiced outside the law for more than thirty years until his arrest in 1956. Women also traveled to Mexico to have abortions (E. White, 1990: 121).

Middle-class women could sometimes persuade doctors to arrange for a discreet abortion or to provide a referral. Poor women either had the unplanned children or went to "the lady down the street" or the "woman downstairs" – either midwives or partially trained medical personnel. Abortions from these illegal providers were usually very expensive, and many white women came to Black neighborhoods to obtain abortions this way (Ward, 1986: 15; Baehr, 1990: 13). Fees for abortions were between $50 and $75, which was expensive considering that a pregnant woman might earn $10 a day (Ward, 1986: 15).

Long after the majority of "granny" midwives in other ethnic groups had been replaced by medically based hospital practices, there were still hundreds of Black lay midwives practicing in the deep South, with midwifery lineages extending as far back as slavery. They provided most of the abortion and contraceptive services for Black southern women (E. White, 1990: 98). If complications developed, women visited physicians who operated in the poor sections of the city. Only as a last resort did they go to hospitals, fearing the legal consequences of having obtained an illegal abortion. Thus, the rate of septic abortions reported to hospitals was very low.

Dr Dorothy Brown, the first Black female general surgeon in the United States, graduated from Meharry Medical College in 1948 and while in the Tennessee State Legislature, became in the 1950s the first state legislator in the USA to introduce a bill to legalize abortion (E. White, 1990: 47). In an interview at the 1983 founding conference of the National Black Women's Health Project, Dr Brown asserted, "We should dispense quickly the notion that abortion is genocide, because genocide in this country dates back to 1619" (Worcester and Whatley, 1988: 38).

The pseudo-science of eugenics had been largely discredited after the Second World War, when worldwide condemnation followed the Nazi extermination, not only of 6 million Jews, but of countless Germans with African, Indian, or Asian blood, as well as gypsies, gay men and lesbians, the disabled, the mentally ill. In the mid-1950s, population "time bomb" theories from demographers gave rise to a newer, more legitimate and "scientific" approach to eugenics. The proponents of time bomb theories sanctimoniously argued that they were simply saving the poor from themselves.

Brochures published by groups like the Draper Fund and the Population Council showed "hordes of black and brown faces spilling over a tiny earth" (Petchesky, 1990: 118). The fund dated from 1958, when President Eisenhower appointed General William Draper, a New York investment banker and a key figure in the post-war reconstruction of Europe, to study foreign aid. The committee eventually developed an ideological link between population growth in the Third World and the USA's ability to govern world affairs. Draper told the Senate Foreign Relations Committee in 1959 that "The population problem . . . is the greatest bar to our whole economic aid program and to the progress of the world" (Hartmann, 1987: 103). By the early 1960s, the US government began supporting population control policies overseas, and linked foreign aid with depopulation policies.

The domestic side of this world-view coincided with the growth of the civil rights movement, perhaps in response to the militancy of the movement and its potential for sweeping social change. The "political instability" of the African-American population convinced many members of the white elite and middle class that Black population growth should be curbed. White Americans feared, out of proportion to reality, that a growing welfare class of African-Americans concentrated in the inner cities would not only cause rampant crime, but exacerbate the national debt, and eventually produce a political threat from majority-Black voting blocs in urban areas (Littlewood, 1977: 8).

The new "politics of population" that emerged in the mid-1960s gave rise to family planning programs in the South that were directed at predominantly Black urban areas. Family planning was designed to reduce the number of Black births to control the ever-expanding Black population. This occurred at the same time as African-American leaders were expressing interest in "taking over" the big cities and "holding them as enclaves against increasing repression" (Littlewood, 1977: 9–10). The US Congress took note, and pressured the newly created Office of Economic Opportunity to wage its war on poverty by emphasizing family planning programs for African-Americans the year after passage of the 1965 Voting Rights Act. It is interesting to note that George Bush, a Texas Congressional representative at the time, supported family planning, even though his father once lost a Senate election in Connecticut after columnist Drew Pearson "revealed" the candidate's "involvement" with Planned Parenthood on the weekend before the ballots were cast (Littlewood, 1977: 51). This support was affirmed by Richard Nixon when he took office in 1969.

Medicaid was established in the 1960s to cover medical costs for the poor. Family planning was included only after a series of fights with Catholics and conservatives at the state level. Publicly supported birth control developed in the 1960s, aided by the mass availability of the pill and the IUD. In 1967, Congress passed the Child Health Act which specified that at least 6 per cent of all maternal-child health grants to public health agencies had to be spent on family planning. This law stated that federal funds could be used to pay for services to any woman who had in the past needed, or might in the future need, welfare. It allowed family planners to offer a wide range of maternal and child care services to poor women. Joan Smith, current head of Louisiana's state-wide family planning program, said at the time, "What caught my fancy was the idea of offering services to indigent women the same as private doctors were giving. Nobody treated poor women with dignity. We said we'd do it and we did" (Ward, 1986: 42).

Some medical experts opposed family planning for African-Americans, convinced that African-American women "wanted to be pregnant and have all those children and that even if they did not want repeated pregnancies, they could not possibly understand the principles of birth control because they were not bright enough and lacked behavioral control" (Ward, 1986: 17).

Although abortion was still illegal, some public health agencies operated an "underground railroad" of referrals for women to have illegal abortions (Ward, 1986: 58). It is estimated that from 200,000 to 1 million illegal abortions occurred annually in the late 1960s (S. Davis, 1988: 12). A major strength was the informal networks of African-American women who spread the news about the availability of services and became activists in support of birth control and better health care, and for abortion rights. Underground abortions were facilitated by church- and community-based referral services and cooperative doctors' networks that emerged in cities and states in the 1960s (Petchesky, 1990: 113).

Because of the blatant racism of the population control establishment that promoted family planning, Black nationalist campaigns against family planning re-emerged. Several birth control clinics were invaded by Black Muslims associated with the Nation of Islam, who published cartoons in *Muhammed Speaks* that depicted bottles of birth control pills marked with a skull and crossbones, or graves of unborn Black infants. The Pittsburgh branch of the NAACP declared that the local family planning clinic was an instrument of genocide. William "Bouie" Haden, leader of the militant United Movement for Progress, went one step further and threatened to firebomb the Pittsburgh clinic (Littlewood, 1977: 69).

Whitney Young, leader of the Urban League, also reversed his organization's support for family planning in 1962. Marvin Davies, head of the Florida NAACP, said, "Our women need to produce more babies, not less . . . and until we comprise 30 to 35 per cent of the population, we won't really be able to affect the power structure in this country" (Littlewood, 1977: 75). This was a major ideological shift away from the early days of the NAACP and the Urban League; both organizations had formerly supported women's rights as a means of racial progress. The NAACP of the 1920s would have been horrified to find itself in the 1960s sounding more like Marcus Garvey and less like DuBois.

The Black Power conference held in Newark in 1967, organized by Amiri Baraka, passed an anti-birth control resolution. Two years later, the May 1969 issue of *The Liberator* warned, "For us to speak in favor of birth control for Afro-Americans would be comparable to speaking in favor of genocide" (Giddings, 1984: 318).

The Black Panther Party was the only nationalist group to support free abortions and contraceptives on demand (Ward, 1986: 92), although not without considerable controversy within its ranks. "Half of the women in the party used birth control and we supported it because of our free health care program. We understood the conditions of the Black community," remembers Nkenge Toure, a former member, who also recalls that there were no formal political education discussions around the issue, but there was support from many party women.[1] Kathleen Cleaver, the wife of Eldridge Cleaver, wrote that, "In order for women to obtain liberation, the struggles [Black liberation and women's rights] are going to have be united" (Giddings, 1984: 311).

This view of women's liberation within the Black Panther Party often collided with male opposition to abortion and birth control. Some male members tried to shut down family planning clinics in New Orleans and Pittsburgh (Littlewood, 1977: 97). As Angela Davis concluded, the late 1960s and early 1970s were "a period in which one of the unfortunate hallmarks of some nationalist groups was their determination to push women into the background. The brothers opposing us leaned heavily on the male supremacist trends which were winding their way through the movement" (Giddings, 1984: 317).

White conservatives saw family planning as an assault on traditional values of motherhood, while some Black radicals saw it as a race- and class-directed eugenics program, thus the assault on birth control and abortion came from both the left and the right. That such disparate forces aligned themselves against African-American women proved that both white bigots and Black leaders could find common cause in the assertion of male authority over women's decisions regarding reproduction. Both tendencies sought to reverse a trend that saw women becoming more autonomous and presenting greater social and economic threats.

In contrast, African-American women exerted a dynamic and aggressive influence on the family planning movement. They constituted the largest single bloc of support for family planning and were so visible that politicians in some states began to see them as a potential political force (Ward, 1986: 59). They were assisted in their efforts by coalitions of Presbyterian, Episcopal, Unitarian, Baptist, Lutheran and Jewish congregations, representatives of which signed a "freedom-of-conscience" statement supporting the women in Pittsburgh and other cities.

African-American women noticed that "most of the commotion about the clinics . . . seemed to be coming from men – men who do not have to bear children" (Littlewood, 1977: 72). Even when the Black men successfully shut down clinics, as in Cleveland and Pittsburgh, women organized to reopen them because they "did not appreciate being thought of as random reproduction machines that could be put to political use" (Littlewood, 1977: 79), reported William Austin, who reviewed the dispute for a study by the Urban League. African-American women fully understood that there were no Planned Parenthood clinics in poor white neighborhoods, but they still perceived the free services to be in their own best interests (Littlewood, 1977: 79). Quoting from DuBois, they declared, "We're not interested in the quantity of our race. We're interested in the quality of it" (Ward, 1986: 93).

In Pittsburgh, about seventy women members of the National Welfare Rights Organization rebuffed attempts by African-American men to close family planning clinics. In particular, they rejected the leadership of William "Bouie" Haden who, it was discovered, was on the payroll of the Catholic Church. "Who appointed him our leader anyhow?" inquired Georgiana Henderson. "He is only one person – and a man at that. He can't speak for the women of Homewood. . . . Why should I let one loudmouth tell me about having children?" (Littlewood, 1977: 72). Other African-American women around the country declared they would not tolerate male expressions of territorial rights over women's bodies.

Shirley Chisolm, a Black Congresswoman from Brooklyn, dismissed the genocide argument when asked to discuss her views on abortion and birth control:

> To label family planning and legal abortion programs "genocide" is male rhetoric, for male ears. It falls flat to female listeners and to thoughtful male ones. Women know, and so do many men, that two or three children who are wanted, prepared for, reared amid love and stability, and educated to the limit of their ability will mean more for the future of the black and brown races from which they come than any number of neglected, hungry, ill-housed and ill-clothed youngsters.
>
> (Chisolm, 1970: 114–15)

African-American women were also profoundly committed to the clinics because they knew teen pregnancy and death from septic abortions were the leading causes of death for Black women. Before the legalization of abortion, 80 per cent of deaths caused by illegal abortions involved Black and Puerto Rican women (A. Davis, 1983: 204). In Georgia between 1965 and 1967, the Black maternal death rate due to illegal abortion was 14 times that of white women (Worcester and Whatley, 1988: 136). Based on these grim statistics, programs to curb adolescent pregnancy and obtain contraceptives gained support in the African-American community. Emphasis was also placed on establishing programs for education, like Head Start, and homes for unwed mothers. Women were not blind to the incongruity of the government plan to make contraceptives free and extremely accessible to African-American communities that lacked basic health care. They used infant and maternal mortality figures to overcome resistance to family planning. "I showed them the maternal mortality statistics for the previous five years," said one birth control advocate. "Fifty-four women lost their lives during childbirth in the District of Columbia, two of them white. So if [the family planners] were really interested in something genocidal, I'd tell all the black women to go out and get pregnant, and they'll die at the rate of 25-to-1" (Littlewood, 1977: 77).

Black women succeeded in keeping family planning clinics open, and understood the essential difference between population control and birth control in their "paired values." They organized to remove Haden as a delegate from the Homewood-Brushton Citizens Renewal Council in a demonstration of political strength that frightened both Black and white men. They also learned a valuable lesson about sexist backlash that equated Black male domination with African-American progress.

A distinct Black feminist consciousness emerged to counter the reactionary views promulgated by African-American men. In 1969, Frances Beal, then head of the Black Women's Liberation Committee of the Student Nonviolent Coordinating Committee (SNCC), wrote, "Black women have the right and the responsibility to determine when it is in *the interest of the struggle to have children or not to have them and this right must not be relinquished to any* . . . to determine when it is in *her own best interests* to have children" (Morgan, 1970: 393; original emphases).

This sentiment was echoed by Toni Cade (Bambara) in 1970 when she wrote, "I've been made aware of the national call to Sisters to abandon birth control . . . to picket family planning centers and abortion-referral groups and to raise revolutionaries. What plans do you have for the care of me and the child?" (Petchesky, 1990: 137). Black feminists argued that birth control and abortion were, in themselves, revolutionary – and that African liberation in any sense could not be won without women controlling their lives. The birth control pill, in and of itself, could not liberate African-American women, but it "gives her the time to fight for liberation in those other areas" (Petchesky, 1990: 172).

By the late 1960s, family planning became "synonymous with the civil rights of poor women to medical care" (Ward, 1986: xiii). It was regarded as a key to the prevention of disease and death, and as a public health measure to address many of society's problems. However, African-American women warily watched state legislative proposals to sterilize poor women who had too many "illegitimate" children, which fueled the genocide debate. None of the proposals succeeded, largely because of the militance of women like Fannie Lou Hamer who said that "six out of every ten Negro women were . . . sterilized for no reason at all. Often the women were not told that they had been sterilized until they were released from the hospital" (Littlewood, 1977: 80). A national fertility study conducted by Princeton University found that 20 per cent of all married African-American women had been sterilized by 1970 (Fried, 1990: 23).

To African-American women, it seemed absurd to coerce them to limit their family size through involuntary sterilization when they were willing to do so voluntarily if safe methods were accessible. This combined support for birth control and abortion and opposition to sterilization, a unique view among African-American women at the time, did much to inform both the feminist and the civil rights movement in later decades. African-American women rejected the single-issue focus of the women's movement on abortion, which excluded other issues of reproductive freedom. They also opposed the myopic focus on race of the male-dominated civil rights movement, which ignored concerns of gender equality.

CONCLUSION

Historical patterns suggest that just as Black women are vital to Black movements, Black movements are vital to the progress of feminist movements. Feminism always had the greatest currency in times of Black militancy or immediately thereafter.

(Giddings, 1984: 340)

African-American women have always been concerned about our fertility, despite the myths and assumptions of others. When birth control and abortion were available, African-American women used them. When they were not, women resorted to dangerous methods limited only by their imaginations and physiology.

It is critical that the civil rights and the feminist movements acknowledge this history. We understand that we are needed in both movements, but we refuse to be pawns in a population numbers game or tokens to colorize a white movement. As we deepen our understanding of our history, we will reconceptualize how our activism is recorded because male-dominated and/or Eurocentric views of the political process produce definitions of power, activism and resistance that fail to capture the meaning of these concepts in the lives of African-American women (Collins, 1991: 140).

The fast-paced growth and militancy of the African-American women's movement will probably produce, again, its own form of backlash from some African-American men, a reaction that I call "blacklash." As Paula Giddings has predicted, "we are entering, once more, an era of Black assertiveness, one which will trigger historical tensions over the relationship of race and sex" (Giddings, 1984: 349). These tensions, however, will not keep us from taking control over our lives. As the Black Women's Liberation Group of Mt Vernon, New York wrote in 1970, "Birth control [and abortion] is the *freedom* to *fight* genocide of black women and children" (Morgan, 1970: 393).

Winning reproductive freedom will reward African-American women with true choices in our lives. We may learn, along the journey, to trust in the words of Audre Lorde:

For Black women, learning to consciously extend ourselves to each other and to call upon each other's strengths is a life-saving strategy. In the best of circumstances surrounding our lives, it requires

157

an enormous amount of mutual, consistent support for us to be emotionally able to look straight into the face of the powers aligned against us and still do our work with joy. It takes determination and practice.

(Lorde, 1988: 123)

NOTE

1 Telephone interview by the author with Nkenge Toure, former member of the Black Panther Party, March 8, 1992, Washington, DC.

BIBLIOGRAPHY

Baehr, Ninia (1990) *Abortion Without Apology: A Radical History for the 1990s*, Boston, Mass.: South End Press.

Bell, Roseann P., Parker, Bettye J. and Guy-Sheftall, Beverly (eds) (1979) *Sturdy Black Bridges: Visions of Black Women in Literature*, New York: Anchor Books.

Blee, Kathleen (1991) *Women of the Kan: Racism and Gender in the 1920s*, Berkeley, CA: University of California Press.

Burgher, Mary (1979) "Images of Self and Race in the Autobiographies of Black Women," in Bell, Parker and Guy-Sheftall, 1979: 107–22.

Chisolm, Shirley (1970) *Unbought and Unbossed*, special limited edn, New York: Hodge Taylor Associates.

Collins, Kimberly A. (1991) *Slightly Off Center*, Atlanta, GA: Say It Loud Press.

Collins, Patricia Hill (1991) *Black Feminist Thought: Knowledge, Consciousness, and the Politics of Empowerment*, London: Routledge.

Corea, Gena (1985) *The Hidden Malpractice: How American Medicine Mistreats Women*, New York: Harper & Row.

Davis, Angela (1983) *Women, Race and Class*, New York: Vintage Books.

—— (1990) "Racism, Birth Control and Reproductive Rights," in Marlene Gerber Fried (ed.) *Abortion to Reproductive Freedom: Transforming a Movement*, Boston, Mass.: South End Press: 15–26.

Davis, Susan E. (ed.) (1988) *Women Under Attack: Victories, Backlash and the Fight for Reproductive Freedom*, Committee for Abortion Rights and Against Sterilization Abuse, Boston, Mass.: South End Press.

DuBois, Ellen Carol and Ruiz, Vicki L. (eds) (1990) *Unequal Sisters: A Multicultural Reader in U.S. Women's History*, London: Routledge.

Fried, Marlene Gerber (ed.) (1990) *Abortion to Reproductive Freedom: Transforming a Movement*, Boston, Mass.: South End Press.

Giddings, Paula (1984) *When and Where I Enter . . .: The Impact of Black Women on Race and Sex in America*, New York: William Morrow.

Gordon, Linda (1990) *Woman's Body, Woman's Right: Birth Control in America*, rev. edn, New York: Penguin.

Hartmann, Betsy (1987) *Reproductive Rights and Wrongs: The Global Politics of Population Control and Contraceptive Choice*, New York: Harper & Row.

Henshaw, Stanley K., Koonin, Lisa M. and Smith, Jack C. (1991) "Characteristics of U.S. Women Having Abortions, 1987," *Family Planning Perspectives*, Alan Guttmacher Institute, 23 (2) (March/April): 75–81.

hooks, bell (1989) *Talking Back: Thinking Feminist, Thinking Black*, Boston, Mass.: South End Press.

Joseph, Gloria I. and Lewis, Jill (1981) *Common Differences: Conflicts in Black and*

White Feminist Perspectives, Boston, Mass.: South End Press.

Lerner, Gerda (1972) *Black Women in White America*, New York: Vintage Books.

Littlewood, Thomas B. (1977) *The Politics of Population Control*, Notre Dame, IN: University of Notre Dame Press.

Lorde, Audre (1988) *A Burst of Light*, Ithaca, NY: Firebrand Books.

Morgan, Robin (ed.) (1970) *Sisterhood is Powerful*, New York: Random House.

Petchesky, Rosalind Pollack (1990) *Abortion and Woman's Choice: The State, Sexuality and Reproductive Freedom*, rev. edn, Boston, Mass.: Northeastern University Press.

Rodrigue, Jessie M. (1990) "The Black Community and the Birth Control Movement," in DuBois and Ruiz, 1990: 333–42.

Simmons, Judy D. (1990) "Abortion: A Matter of Choice," in Evelyn C. White, 1990: 120–7.

Sterling, Dorothy (ed.) (1984) *We Are Your Sisters: Black Women in the Nineteenth Century*, New York: W. W. Norton.

Ward, Martha C. (1986) *Poor Women, Powerful Men: America's Great Experiment in Family Planning*, Boulder, CO: Westview Press.

White, Deborah Gray (1985) *Ar'n't I a Woman? Female Slaves in the Plantation South*, New York: W. W. Norton.

White, Evelyn C. (ed.) (1990) *The Black Women's Health Book: Speaking for Ourselves*, Seattle, WA: Seal Press.

Worcester, Nancy and Whatley, Marianne H. (eds) (1988) *Women's Health: Readings on Social, Economic and Political Issues*, Dubuque, IA: Kendall/Hunt.

11

HIV TRANSMISSION
Men are the solution

Christine Obbo

It cannot be overemphasized that although sexuality is an important component of people's lives, everywhere it is difficult to study. This has been poignantly observed in a recent workshop on human sexuality. "Human Sexuality is simultaneously one of the most fascinating and one of the most challenging domains of inquiry. Major concerns in the lives of people revolve around their sexuality. Human sexuality is a pleasurable activity: it dominates fantasy; it both establishes common bonds and identifies gulfs between people; and it occasionally conceives new life" (Zeller, 1989: 48). [However] "The AIDS epidemic caught us ill prepared to answer basic questions about people's sexual behavior. Efforts to fill this void have not always been based on sound methodological footing. Unfortunately, we are in the uncomfortable position of having to play catch up" (Catania, 1990: 88).

This chapter examines the social organization of sex-gender networks, presents self-generated problems raised in projective essays of elite adolescents and highlights women's concerns about their vulnerability to HIV infection. Success of the AIDS control educational programs can be measured only in the changed practices that follow rather than in mere knowledge. It is important to understand and to sensitize people at all levels of society about the different types of behavior and practices that are responsible for HIV transmission. Condom use and reforms that will empower women to exercise autonomy in decisions affecting their sexuality, their health and reproduction must be promoted.

Women's empowerment depends upon economic and social leverage with regard to vital resources. Men monopolize political and economic power over women because social ideologies accord them monopoly of control over resources. The most effective way to break the vicious circle would be to change the law to ensure that women have equal rights to land and cattle while also giving them adequate access to education, health services and institutional banking.

Uganda appears to have a good track record on women in politics with twenty army officers, nine ministers and thirty-eight parliamentarians.

But this has not resulted in real changes for women. Men continue to be in ascendancy and control, conveniently reflecting status even in this age of AIDS. Men must recognize the important role they have in controlling the transmission of HIV and must take responsibility as in the past for maternal and child health.

Beliefs about and perceptions of sex and gender are presented within the economic and cultural context. Attitudes, beliefs and behavior connected to HIV are presented in relation to gender sexual beliefs, stereotypes and practices, the economic status of women and the national economic crises. The study was carried out during eight months between 1989 and 1990 in a subcounty of Rakai district of Uganda. The dominant group was Baganda and, therefore, the culture information refers to them.

PERSISTING BELIEFS AND PRACTICES

People pragmatically change their activities and behavior to accommodate new circumstances. In this, they are sanctioned to varying degrees by the symbolic systems that support the dominant ideologies. Sexual and reproductive activity and the well-being of infants seem to have been longstanding preoccupations in Buganda society. Moreover, in relation to AIDS, the dominant ideological systems pertaining to sexuality – masculinity and femininity – gave men ascendancy over women.

Orley noted in 1970 that Ganda men recognized the sexual needs of women. When he asked a sample of twenty-nine village men whether, if they themselves had to go to prison for a year, it would be right to excuse their wives for sleeping with other men, only three said it would not be right (Orley, 1970). However, the study found a belief in *amakiro*, a disease of fornication (*obulwadde bwobenzi*) akin to venereal diseases, although not considered as contagious. Apparently, *amakiro* typically afflicted women within a day or two of giving birth. Although the name was also given to illnesses occurring at the time of childbirth, *amakiro* was thought to be due to adultery "committed with many different men (five upwards) during pregnancy" (Orley, 1970: 9).

Apparently, a large number of women used medicines to prevent the disease. The disease was sometimes called *ebigere* (feet), a reference to the fact that a woman who contracted it was assumed to have walked about in other houses. If it did not prove fatal to the mother and child, the mother might go mad (puerperal psychosis) and had to be guarded against killing, and even eating, the child (Orley, 1970; Bennett, 1963; Roscoe, 1911). Orley (1970) states that madness following childbirth, puerperal psychosis, does exist as a medical condition but that the child-eating mother is a widespread fantasy.

At the beginning of the century, before the present economic gender inequalities had become established, Roscoe (1911) noted that *amakiro* affected children either of whose parents had committed adultery during pregnancy or nursing. It was thought to bring nausea and general debility until the guilt was confessed. By the 1960s and 1970s, *amakiro* seems to have been established as a woman-caused disease. This was the time when women were asserting their autonomy by migrating to the cities, by buying, leasing, or borrowing land to grow cash crops to generate separate incomes, by deserting (*kunoba*) their husbands for other men or establishing themselves as independent householders (*banakyeyembekedde*), by eloping, cohabiting and having children out of wedlock.

Commenting on the 1950s and 1960s, one male informant recently said, "My parents enjoyed a monogamous marriage. I have five siblings. A brother resembled the county clerk whom my mother became involved with during a brief separation from my father. Our only sister resembles one of our neighbors. Men here do not trust other men and they threaten revenge on wives of men who cuckold them." The twenty-nine men Orley interviewed were part of this climate that assumed that women cannot be faithful to one man. It was no secret that women were faithful to men who supported them and their children economically, respected them (by not going with other women) and satisfied them sexually.

Sexual satisfaction required that women elongate their labia minora which provided a "cozy" environment for men during intercourse and also enhanced women's orgasms. The increase in unmarried or divorced women during the 1960s has been blamed on the fact that women were abandoning the practice and were therefore becoming sexually unsatisfying to men. One focus-group of discussants asserted that the premarital education given to Ganda girls stresses that they should never deny their husbands' demands for sex, and should flatter them during lovemaking by groaning at every thrust (*kusikina*), making utterances, and thanking them for their performances afterwards. Kissekka (1973) has reported that climaxing women announce, "I have presented you with your gift" (*nkuwereezza ekirabokyo*) or "I have presented you with a pint of Kenya milk" (*nkuwerezza e painti y'amata y'e Kenya*) – imported consumer goods are prestigious and milk tea is a mark of hospitality. Women further asserted that this appreciation was given even when men left them unsatisfied. Even among the Sebei, the only society in Uganda that circumcises women by removing the skin from the tip of the clitoris to reduce promiscuity and to promote fidelity by reducing female sexual pleasure, women are expected to indicate the sexual enjoyment their husbands give them.

Ganda women said that they enjoyed vigorous sex and some women who had had sex with Hima Ankole men referred to them as impotent because they seemed to attain orgasms "prematurely in five minutes" and spent a lot of time on foreplay. Among the Hima, foreplay (*akakya-bari*) is expected of men. In some interlacustrian societies, men who skip foreplay, known as *katetero* (Luhaya) and *ruganga* (Lunyarwanda), are subjected to ridicule among the women. Some educated Ganda women report their partners practice foreplay, but in focused interviews both educated and uneducated women laughed at the idea. The educated Ganda men who were interviewed made incredulous faces.

According to Orley (1970) frequency of intercourse was considered a measure of potency, i.e. an impotent man did not obtain a second erection after an orgasm and his erection lasted five minutes or less, and a potent man lasted thirty to forty minutes. Orley, who was interested in mental illness, commented that there must have been an element of exaggeration and fantasy, but the fact remains that men were scared of becoming sexually impotent (*kufiirwa*), i.e. becoming bereaved. Among the educated, men's anxieties over impotence centered on venereal diseases (Orley, 1970).

A recent study implied that the adoption of condoms among the Baganda may not be as problematic as in other ethnic groups because women are expected to clean men's organs with water and a cloth called *enkumbi* after sex. But Rakai female informants asserted that whereas women can direct men during penetration and clean them afterwards, men are suspicious of women handling their testicles and penises. Even the cleaning is rooted in the belief that sexual fluids if not cleaned are dangerous to babies (in cases of infidelity) and can be manipulated by sorcerers to cause impotence in men or barrenness in women. During two focused interviews with two groups consisting of twenty women each, informants insisted that women would be inhibited from being assertive about condoms for fear of being accused of and divorced for adultery and sorcery. As one man put it, "If a woman has condoms, then she can see as many men as she wants. A woman who is annoyed with you can, while pretending to fit you with condoms, smear medicines to render you impotent." Some of the first men to die of AIDS in Rakai district were assumed to have been ensorcered by double-crossed lovers.

The 1950s and 1960s represented periods of expanding economic opportunities. This was evident in the increased activities in land sales, crop acreages and constructions of corrugated iron-roofed houses in the rural areas. Rural–urban migration, particularly by women and families, reflected the perceived employment and higher income potentials of urban areas. Education was increasingly seen as the passport to elite status with all the associated power, prestige and privileges. Parents sacrificed a great deal to educate their children. However, in the most important positions, men were predominant. The most common way in which wealth and prestige were redistributed to the women by men was through sexual relations. The climate of expanding opportunities had emerged within the framework of existing socioeconomic systems. This granted women access to societal resources through men, who were the real owners and controllers of property, individually or collectively.

In the mid-1960s, Christian women lobbied for laws that would protect married women and their children against unofficial "wives and children" when it came to inheritance. They wanted a legal requirement that would require the registration of all marriages and divorces (Brown, 1988). (This was eventually decreed by law in 1973.) The women were chided by a predominantly male Parliament whose members felt culpable for the grievances women were raising (Brown, 1988). Men stopped laughing one day in 1963 during a debate in Parliament on the status of women, when Mrs Florence Lubega angrily implored her colleagues to stop "fathering babies" with girls who were trainee secretaries at Nakawa because this deprived the country of their services (*Uganda Argus*, 1963). Pregnancy was an obstacle to girls' education. Once women became involved in pregnancy and marriage, their life-courses irrevocably changed. Men, on the other hand, could father, marry, and continue their education because their wives provided sustaining labor.

Throughout the 1950s, Uganda women in all provinces were discussing the hardships faced by widows and children because they lacked legal protection against dispossession (Brown, 1988) and they presented memoranda about this to the governor's wife. The changes that had required monogamous marriages, and that had promoted autonomy of the nuclear family, had not benefited wives, but mistresses. In the Ugandan capital, and to a lesser extent in other towns, mistresses became a social fixture associated with elite men. In other African cities mistresses and concubines are affectionately referred to by male speakers as "deuxième bureaux" (the second office) or *nyumba ndogo* (small house) by French and Swahili speakers, respectively.

Because women are socialized to tolerate men's sexual independence, the discussions on the subject always left the impression that women do not expect male fidelity, but resent the drain on resources and loss of face among female friends. Married women regard themselves as morally superior to women who purvey sex irrespective of whether they are "bar girls" or "kept women."

There is a variety of sex workers. Unemployed women or women in poor jobs (Mandeville, 1979) who live in overcrowded low-income areas provide "quick and cheap" sex to poor men in the area, or to businessmen, civil servants, or university students. They operate out of backstreet cheap hotel rooms that are rented by the hour and whose bedding is rarely changed. There are "good time" women who serve single men whom they meet in bars or night clubs. Some of these women work in bars, others frequent amusement places. There are women employed in the lower echelons of professions who use sex to get better jobs, increase their pay, or improve their standards of living. A few women from this category do become "stars" if they are patronized and highly paid by rich men. These successful women possess beauty, wit and manipulative skills.

Researchers have described the different way women have used sex as an alternative route to social mobility when faced with legal and social restrictions (La Fontaine, 1974: Bujra, 1975; Nelson, 1979; Obbo, 1980). However, the personal conflicts felt by the women so engaged are rarely presented; the resolution to the conflicts usually involves disguising behaviors socially regarded as disreputable.

FRIENDS AND LOVERS: SOME PATTERNS OF MATING RELATIONSHIPS

Among the Baganda, a multitude of relationships is currently covered by the category of *mukwano*, a word which literally means friendship; wooing is described as *kukwana*.

Mukwano relationships can vary. They may be between teenage school-children with the boys wooing the girls with letters, messages and sweets for a long time until they either consummate the sexual relationship or break up. Sexual relations between teachers and schoolgirls are not described as *mukwano* because there is lack of mutual consent. Some women engaged in commercial sex do become very fond of generous, good-looking or regular clients and they refer to them as *mukwano*. This designation is an important one for a man to achieve because he can visit as often as he wants, and even at times when he is unable to pay (a common occurrence these days). A woman with a lover may also receive exotic and expensive gifts, be enabled to travel to desired places, helped with getting a good job, and assisted in placing her children in good schools.

Women with multiple partners use the word *mukwano* to refer to their relationships. The word is an ambiguous one: are the men merely friends, or are they sexual partners? The women never use the word *muganzi*, which can mean "favorite person," but is used specifically of someone with whom there is sexual involvement. According to one sex worker, "Having many lovers (*baganzi*) is not respectable but one can have many friends (*mikwano*) without being labeled a certain kind of woman."

Researchers, too, have been preoccupied with respectability. Research efforts have focused on sex workers who are the obvious actors in the transmission of HIV. Stable, noncommoditized sexual relations have not been actively included in studies of HIV transmission. The present research attempts to sort out such issues, particularly men's apparent tolerance of women's sexual needs and the preoccupation with female adultery and male impotence (Orley, 1970).

Rakai district has become internationally notorious as the area most devastated by AIDS, yet, strangely enough, there are no district figures to illustrate this. There is no hospital in the district and patients are forced to attend Masaka hospitals. Consequently, some Rakai cases are included among the clinical reports for Masaka district.

The research was conducted in a subcounty of Kooki county some 20 miles west of the shores of Lake Victoria and 30 miles north of the Tanzanian border. Lake Victoria was the scene of intense smuggling under Idi Amin during the 1970s, accentuated here by the proximity of an international frontier. The main road passes from Tanzania up to Masaka via Kyotera town 10 miles inland between the research area and the lake. Evidence so far suggests that AIDS developed in the mobile population focused on the lake smuggling and the border area highway. With security forces trying to control, or benefit from, the smuggling operations, the smugglers would have had to get their goods and profits safely away from the danger area further into the interior. This is the most likely way that AIDS was spread in Rakai.

An aspect of the emerging system of social stratification is that those who live quietly in rural areas without moving far from home become distinguished from the mobile population which consists not of traders only, as commonly thought, but also of businessmen (bankers, hotels and lodge owners) and professionals employed in the civil service as magistrates, district educational officers, schoolteachers, veterinary and agricultural extension officers. These two strata of the population proved to be highly significant in the incidence of AIDS.

What follows is a brief presentation of friendship networks based on common school background and workplace or residential proximity.

ELITE MATING NETWORKS

"We are all dying" was a refrain I heard at every funeral. For a long time it seemed to me like a remark anyone surrounded by morbidity and mortality would make. It was made by urbanites and ruralities alike to refer to the AIDS epidemic. The predominant heterosexual mode of HIV transmission and the nonexistence of a cure were common knowledge. The tattered appearance of sex workers at bar lodges in Masaka and Rakai towns suggested that many men were avoiding risky behaviors. However, one day after a funeral of a bank executive, people divided into groups as they hung around. In one group there was animated discussion which seemed not to refer to the epidemic in general, but was focused upon those present. Remarks that were repeated several times included:

"AIDS is a death sentence."

"This is calamity; we are all going to perish."

"It is a pity we are all going to die."

But a remark that was made by a woman who had been silent throughout the discussion provided a significant lead in the researches. She said, "It is our mating patterns that are finishing us off."

In the following months, the people in that group were interviewed regarding the meaning of the remark. The catastrophe envisaged and feared was based on the common knowledge of the widespread endogamous mating among friends and co-workers. The interview further revealed that friendship networks which were formed on the basis of school attendance, social, ethnic and religious backgrounds, and workplace associations became the basis of social, practical and emotional support. Within these networks, some relationships occasionally became sexual. A common occurrence was the case where a member of the network would quarrel and break up with a lover or wife and turn to the friends in the network for consolation or replacement. Members of the networks were secure and familiar with each other and usually ready to do anything for each other. Most of the mating was within this context.

Each person who had been in the funeral group was interviewed through open-ended, unstructured questions about their present and past close friends. People were much more likely to tell about other people's relations than their own. The results from the initial group at the funeral revealed two networks consisting of married and unmarried members. Diagram I shows the networks.

Network X was ethnically homogeneous and consisted of people aged between 30 and 45 who had attended the same secondary school. Some of them were related to each other. There were two unmarried people and one divorce in the network, and the rest were married. "A," a department head, was a member of this network. He had died of AIDS. It seemed at first that he had had no sexual relationship with the other people in the network. But, as one woman suggested, "He died recently. We are in shock. There is reluctance to acknowledge any sexual association." The survivors worried because "E," the deputy head of the department, was rumored to be afflicted with HIV (he died of AIDS five months after the research was completed). He had been married for two years before he died, but his wife showed no signs of affliction. The women in the network expressed anxiety and the unmarried male civil servants showed hostility to any reference to AIDS.

Network Y was based on networks formed when at university and it was ethnically heterogeneous. However, the world of elites seems small indeed, and networks X and Y were connected (see the diagram)

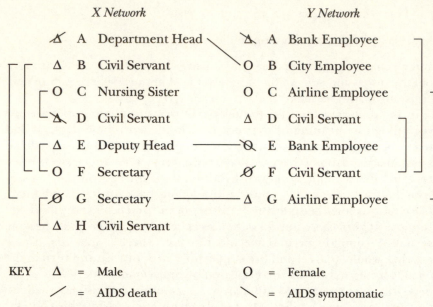

X Network			Y Network		
△	A	Department Head	△	A	Bank Employee
△	B	Civil Servant	O	B	City Employee
O	C	Nursing Sister	O	C	Airline Employee
△	D	Civil Servant	△	D	Civil Servant
△	E	Deputy Head	O	E	Bank Employee
O	F	Secretary	Ø	F	Civil Servant
Ø	G	Secretary	△	G	Airline Employee
△	H	Civil Servant			

KEY   △ = Male   O = Female

／ = AIDS death   ＼ = AIDS symptomatic

NOTE   Lines connect those sexually linked or married.

although members of each network regarded themselves as a discrete group. Network Y had had one AIDS death and two members were afflicted by the disease.

Members of the networks worried about AIDS. However, some members were sexually active inside and outside the networks. Members felt that it was safer to confine the relationships within the network, and men said that they avoided sex workers. But women said that they could not ask their male network friends to wear condoms under any circumstances. Some women, however, had experiences of contracting sexually transmitted diseases from network lovers. The *illusion* that there was no need to use condoms because the sexual relationships within the network were occasional and were with people who were known and presumed safe was being exposed by the deaths of close friends.

Most couples had faith in "zero grazing." The men increasingly stayed at home, they confided in their wives, and some even apologized to their wives for staying out late and missing family happenings. However, on the subject of condoms, the discussion centers around what men might do. For example, an official who was in charge of health education (including AIDS) in schools in 1989 had never seen condoms; when one was shown to her, she was flabbergasted. She intimated that her husband, a medical doctor, would kill her if he saw her with a condom.

There might be some exaggeration about men's supposed reactions, but the important thing is that negative reactions are anticipated.

RURAL MATING NETWORKS

Rural areas are divided into administrative units (resistance council areas) varying in size from counties through subcounties to villages. The smallest units are villages, and each has a traditional name.

After research in the field for only six months, it was impossible to see the differing patterns of deaths in the subcounty emerging. In some villages no deaths of people living locally were recorded. In other villages there were clusters of cases in some localities and of deaths in some neighborhoods. This seemed puzzling. Cases of AIDS and deaths from the disease might occur in as many as five neighboring houses; in others, every second house would be so affected.

When neighbors were asked about the patterns, men made statements like, "Women are the greatest spreaders of AIDS." The answers seemed to suggest that clandestine sexual activities were suspected. Interviews with the surviving family members and neighbors revealed close friendship between the homesteads. The couples tended to visit each other's homes for lunch or tea on Sundays. During the week, the women occasionally visited each other in the late afternoons; the men visited in the evenings while the wives prepared the evening meal. But in a neighborhood, neighbors would visit different neighbors at different times. Informants insisted that these evening visits provided ample opportunities for clandestine sexual activities. However, one rarely heard of fights because, in the words of one informant, "A cuckolded man who discovers the goings-on usually revenges by counter-cuckolding, even if it takes him a lifetime to do so." These men do not always succeed because some women either have no wish to be unfaithful to their husbands or may have wind of their husbands' carryings-on but consider that sleeping with the other women's husbands would not solve the problem. In these cases, the families usually avoid each other and hatred may develop.

There are other opportunities that allow occasional or prolonged sexual relations. For example, the practice whereby a young woman returns to her mother to spend the last weeks of her pregnancy and a period following childbirth with her was aimed at giving the woman rest from tiring chores, in order to conserve her energy for birth and also for recovery afterwards. This, however, apparently offered some men "opportunities to sneak women friends into the house when other household members were preoccupied with work." Silence was considered good manners (*buntu bulamu*) on the part of household members who saw or heard anything.

Other situations that encouraged adultery are the practice of installing women in separate homesteads by polygynous men, and the common occurrence of women deserting (*kunoba*) their husbands because of marital discord, neglect, or mistreatment. These separations were supposed to be temporary until a man came to explain himself and claim his wife. If he had beaten her, he was required to pay a fine and to promise not to repeat his actions. Both husbands and wives in this situation regard liaisons with other people as justified. Most marriages usually end in such a separation where a woman deserts her husband permanently and hides from him; there may be an attempt at reconciliation, which fails. Some marriages fail following a series of several such separations.

Informants identified these practices as contributing to the high AIDS casualty rates observed in sections of some villages. Following is a brief account of sexual networks in a village with high AIDS casualties.

The women were all full-time cultivators, and the men predominantly weekend cultivators. However, the predominant mode of employment for both men and women was full-time subsistence farming. Some men in the networks were involved in a nonagricultural occupation. In network A, one of two monogamous teachers had died. A polygynous clerk and one of his wives had died. A butcher who had been married three times had died, together with his third wife, and his surviving wife was bedridden with HIV.

It all started when the butcher's second wife deserted (*kunoba*) her husband and became the second wife of the clerk. He bought land and settled her in another county. Meanwhile, one of the teachers was having an affair with the clerk's first wife. As the clerk spent more time with his second wife, his first wife increasingly relied on the teacher to help the children with homework and book supplies. The clerk and his wife were Catholics so divorce was out of the question for her. She viewed what was going on as her cross. The teacher's wife (Maria) had, over the years, endured difficult pregnancies that had resulted in five miscarriages and three stillbirths. She had four surviving children. Like other village women, she was overworked, ate poorly and experienced frequent pregnancies. Reproductive health is a preoccupation for most village women. When Maria visited the diviner, she found out that she had been the last one to know about her husband's affairs with married and unattached women in the village during the times she was away from home in hospital. She also knew that her miscarriages were caused by the sexually transmitted infections she was always getting from her husband.

A study done in the 1960s (Arya *et al.*, 1980) supports Maria's contention. A combination of male migration from Teso district in the east to Buganda, where venereal diseases were widespread, as well as high incidences of polygyny, divorce and serial marriages in Teso, had severe consequences for women. Low fertility in Teso due to the high levels of

gonococcal infections and pelvic inflammatory diseases in women corre-
lated with the high levels of gonorrhea among the men. Maria lives in
fear of AIDS since the death of the clerk.

THE IMPORTANCE OF NETWORK RESEARCH

Sociogeographic networks have been documented by recent studies in
New York. It appears that the same networks can be used to propagate
information and to reinforce positive behavior changes (Wallace, 1991).

The information on networks presented here is limited in scope and
there is need to map out more relationships based on large samples.
However, the exercise underscores the need to be flexible enough to
follow serendipitous information as it presents itself in the field, because
it may open up issues, questions and practices that hitherto had been
overlooked. In this case, the stimulus came from informants' unsolicited
remarks and issues raised in previous studies, particularly the preoccupation with women's adultery and the popular assertion that it is women
who are the main transmitters of HIV.

The point of studying networks is to suggest the significance of
endogamous mating in some groups as revealed by high casualties from
AIDS. In order to understand the transmission of HIV in the rural and
urban areas, it is important to examine the sexual behavior of people in
all segments of the population. Elite networks are based on common
school attendance and on professional and working place associations.
The rural networks show sociogeographic networks of the rural upper
strata. The different types of sexual relationships predate AIDS, but
people at all levels of society need to be sensitized to the possible dangers
inherent in some of their sexual behaviors.

SPECULATIVE GREED, WOMEN, AND AIDS

In 1972 Asian traders and industrialists in Uganda were expelled by a
government decree, and their properties and businesses acquired and
plundered by a new class of businessmen consisting of civilians and
soldiers. This process of acquiring things (money, jobs, property) that one
had not worked for was generally known as *mafutamingi* (Swahili for "a lot
of fat") as the plunderers literally grew fat and indulged in public
conspicuous consumption behaviors. Women, wives, girlfriends, sisters,
daughters, etc., became the medium to display the new wealth.

By 1975 the Ugandan formal economy had collapsed and had been
replaced by the underground economy. Without the international business connections and know-how of international trade, people resorted
to selling smuggled coffee in return for consumer goods from neighboring countries. From the mid-1970s, women traders were prominent

participants in what became known as *magendo* trade. The name referred to the dangers involved in undertaking a smuggling journey; but when smuggling became an offence punishable by death, and still more people undertook it, the meaning of *magendo* shifted to "pilgrimage of greed." Smuggling and black-market currency exchanges took place at all points of border contact – West Nile, Bugisu and Tororo. All along Lake Victoria, fishing villages became canoe-fleeted ports by night. Coffee was smuggled to Kenya and Rwanda on long-distance ferries, but business was best across Lake Victoria into Kenya. Coffee smuggling was dangerous, but it was the best way to be paid in foreign currency. President Amin, who was airlifting coffee to the USA and the UK with the help of mercenary pilots, issued several decrees aimed at reducing coffee smuggling. An antismuggling security force operated day and night on Lake Victoria. It was legal to shoot coffee smugglers on sight. This shifted the smuggling to obscure fishing villages along the lake, and also to the trucks that operated along the Mombasa–Nairobi–Kampala–Bujumbura–Kigali highway.

"From this main artery of corruption, tentacles of the black market with its illicit deals and violent transactions penetrate into the Ugandan countryside pulling into its stream the desperate, the opportunistic, and the down-and-out" (Southall, 1980: 646–7). Trading and soldiering became so glorified that children dropped out of school to become an army of uneducated thugs living recklessly, known as *bayaye* (see Mamdani, 1983), a name which was used for unruly hooligans who terrorized people during the 1970s, by which 1989 had an added meaning: "knack of outwitting." This referred to the category of entrepreneurs who lived by speculating in the interstices of the economy by speedily obtaining driving and trade licenses, passports, import and export clearances for a fee. The late 1970s were described by informants this way: "People had money and they could exchange it into any currency. Young men dropped out of school to earn easy money. Women joined in because it was much safer for them than for men."

Men and women who were not engaged in the *magendo* trade also benefited during this time. Both anarchy and state-sponsored violence had made the villages unsafe and, instead of "spending nights hiding in banana groves with snakes and termites," people migrated to rural centers, townships and towns. Population increases at border towns, townships and fishing villages created a demand for houses and services. At truck-stops along the highways, landlords built rental rooms for merchandise, food and lodging. The main source of income for most women was selling sex. The majority of truckers in the 1970s were Somali. In 1979, one trader remarked, "One can easily tell where the trucks stop overnight by the number of Somali-looking children." But prostitution did not start with the *magendo* economy.

Conventionally, males have been encouraged to experiment in sexual matters before marriage and to experience variety in marriage partners if they can afford to do so. At the same time, female chastity is prized with emphasis upon premarital virginity and fidelity in marriage. However, virginity and fidelity cannot be adhered to in a vacuum peopled exclusively by women, and this became even more so as circumstances changed at the beginning of this century with the adoption of institutions associated with western culture.

Formal schooling meant that not all girls were marrying as virgins at a young age. Migration to work in mines, plantations and towns resulted in part-time marriages in which husbands were absent for long periods of time, while their wives stayed at home to raise the children and to maintain the farms. Since the 1950s, schoolboys or migrant laborers who made girls pregnant during vacation increasingly denied paternity because they could not afford to pay the fines demanded by the fathers or male guardians. In most cases, they either had no source of income or earned only a meager income. When men deny paternity it is the women who are stigmatized as "loose" or "bad women." Women left alone for long periods occasionally got tired of being grass widows and had liaisons with other men, the discovery of which would lead to their being divorced. Some women migrated to towns to escape the ideological double standard regarding sex, unworkable marriages and the disadvantages resulting from descent, stratification and property systems. However, economic opportunities in towns were limited, so migrant women became self-employed in service industries: beer brewing, food preparation and sex-catering for bachelor migrants. Until the early 1960s, there were only a few women in the towns. However, even when the ratio of women to men balanced out, some women were still employed in the poorly paid formal jobs, the majority were self-employed, and some resorted to prostitution for employment.

By the late 1970s, the visible actors in the urban areas were prostitutes, traders, truck drivers and soldiers. The high inflation rate created the illusion of great wealth, which everyone wanted to share. The prostitutes earned money from the traders for sexual services, the landlords earned rental money, and the services of food sellers were in great demand. The prostitutes provided sex and storage facilities for the smugglers. The soldiers extracted "road toll" (*amagendo*) cash and goods from both male and female traders; the women had to make further payments in sex.

Informants thus saw the *magendo* economy liaisons as being responsible for the spread of HIV. Residents of Kyotera and other townships where the 1979 liberation army passed insisted that the Tanzanian soldiers policed the situation so effectively that there was no looting or raping. They even rescued some women from attempted rapes. Informants insisted that it was local men who looted and raped women mainly to revenge grudges. Cases of people who have been spotted with radios, school furniture and generators stolen in 1979 are still being reported to the District Administrator. In 1989 two fathers who between them lost four daughters to AIDS planned to sue a businessman they alleged raped their daughters in 1979, but he died in July 1990.

CONDOMS AND WOMEN'S VULNERABILITY TO HIV

The preceding section highlights the interrelatedness of (1) the structural disadvantages that drove women to become sex workers before and during the speculative Ugandan economy of the 1970s and (2) the sexual vulnerability of women in hard times. These factors are important for the understanding of HIV transmission.

The majority of women's concerns over condoms focus on what men say, what men will think and what is satisfying to men. Women's wishes are usually mentioned last. Apparently even the fear of a condom's being lodged inside a woman turned out to be something no woman had herself experienced, nor had it happened to anyone the women knew; it was a story men had circulated.

Women who did not even know what condoms were, except that the name meant plastic bags (sing. *kaveera*, pl. *buveera*), expressed the following views on the subject during focused group interviews:

"Men do not want the condoms because they make sex less pleasurable."

"The village men are ignorant about them."

"The educated say they are only good with prostitutes."

"We have heard that the condom can drop off and get stuck in a woman."

"We have heard that they leak. What is the point of using them?"

"There should be something women can wear for protection; men have always brought diseases to women, but this is a killer."

"If condoms reduce the sweetness of sex, so let it be. We need to save ourselves."

"When condoms come, the problem will be for all women to have enough for each occasion."

"Men are scared to death of AIDS; they will eventually use condoms." ("When, after extinction?" one woman wanted to know.)

"As in the case of birth control pills, men will suspect women who use condoms of servicing other men."

In 1989, a case against the Family Planning Association (UFPA) was dismissed by the High Court because the litigant, on the advice of his lawyer, failed to show up on the day of the ruling. Apparently a wife had sought UFPA services while her businessman husband was in prison. Upon his release, he ordered her to stop taking the birth control pills and when she refused, he sued UFPA alleging that their sexual enjoyment had declined (*New Vision,* 1988). At issue was the suspicion that a woman who took pills must be seeing other men. This attitude has far-reaching implications for HIV transmission. Men can occasionally use condoms, but women are assumed to seek their use out of worry about "a child who doesn't look like their husband!" The young people wanted to use condoms although they had heard that they are 95 per cent unsafe (this magical figure was quoted even by youths who did not normally talk in percentages). However, the real problem that worried women and young people was that of availability and regular future supplies.

These concerns over condoms reveal that distrust is widespread. As one woman insisted, "The condoms will not work without trust between men and women." On December 2, 1988, a presidential speech directed the Ministry of Health to mount a campaign to educate people about AIDS, cautioned private doctors against spreading AIDS through negligence and warned that spreading HIV to others was like murder and would be punishable in the future. Concern was particularly expressed for the children who might become infected by adults. On December 19, 1988, the President, while attending the wedding of the Deputy Minister for Animals and Fisheries, said that marriage was one way of escaping AIDS (*Ngabo,* 1988).

Marriage has been endorsed by religious organizations as a safeguard against AIDS. The AIDS control message from the African Medical Research Foundation (AMRF), "Zero grazing," and the AIDS Control Programme (ACP) message, "Love carefully," are regarded by most people as an alternative to condoms because they endorse monogamous mating. However, women in Rakai are unhappy with this state of affairs because they suspect the HIV status of some men who married younger women. As one woman observed, "With AIDS, marriage does not constitute an absolution from past behavior, but means danger in the future." The women's assertions conflict with the belief that marriage and supposedly monogamous mating are alternative to condoms. The fact that they want men to make an effort at using condoms was highlighted by a newspaper story entitled "Muslims Warned Not to Sabotage Condoms." The article quoted the Deputy Director of the AIDS control program who spoke about ignorance of the purpose of condoms and those who cut off the tip of a sheath before using it (*Taifa Empya,* 1989).

Many preachers have condemned condoms because they promote

promiscuity. In a sermon to an elite audience in Kampala, a visiting Rakai priest reported that in one high school, a headmaster had one morning distributed condoms to students, but before the day was over, a student came back to him and said he wanted some more. "This is not our culture!" the priest insisted. "We want our child to get married." Secondly, the priest had heard that children had been spotted blowing into condoms like balloons. Thirdly, young children and farm animals were likely to swallow the condoms and die. To drive the point home, he repeated, without attribution, a newspaper report about a flood of used condoms outside amusement buildings, such as discos (*Ngabo*, 1988).

It is possible, in the urban areas where garbage collection is sporadic, that dogs and vultures scatter the garbage, exposing condoms for children to play with. However, urban goats die regularly from swallowing plastic bags; the condoms will not represent a new danger.

These warnings do not credit people with sense or care. I know from working and living with poor people in both rural and urban areas that they are fussy about body fluids – menstruation blood and semen – and that any soiled article must be disposed of carefully. The story about the headmaster, the students and the condoms, like the story of the condom getting lodged in a woman, and that of a condom being used twice, have become generic Ugandan stories to criticize condom use. They are usually told in the tone of "I was there . . . I know the person," but further focused discussions usually reveal that it is a story they heard someone repeat somewhere.

The priest's concern that condom use was a foreign influence that would stop young people from marrying was ridiculed later by the Mothers' Union members:

"We should be glad if young men are using condoms."

"It will protect the schoolgirls."

"It will protect those cohabiting without the blessing of marriage."

"It will reduce the number of terrible abortions."

"It is the mothers who suffer through these situations."

"Older men should keep their unchanging ideas and let the young change with the times. It is AIDS era."

"The future belongs to them."

"During lunch I wanted to remind him that, like condoms, drinking tea and using metal forks were not our culture."

This exchange, particularly the last remark, suggests that "not our culture" is a bogey that is invoked when people want to oppose change. In this case, women were saying that the priest as a community leader was misleading people who might be open to change.

Newspaper men presented AIDS stories in such a way as to not focus directly on men. The suggestions and implications of the stories are that women are to blame for promiscuity and the spread of HIV because they engage in international trade, carry condoms for protection, and seek sex outside polygynous marriages. One newspaper story claimed that many city women carried condoms with them, that there were parents who gave their children condoms as a protection against AIDS, and that there are even boarding-school children whose school necessities included condoms. This apparently has encouraged promiscuity among young people. The connection between women, promiscuity and AIDS was spelled out in August, 1989 at a conference organized by Muslim doctors and ACP officials. Women traders, known as Dubai women, who traveled between Uganda and the duty-free ports of the Gulf States, were blamed for the spread of AIDS. "Dubai women" is a metaphor for all successful women traders whose independence is resented by men. On the subject of polygyny, it was merely mentioned that the practice of men having many wives, so that they could not "satisfy" them, promoted promiscuity among women and was responsible for the spread of AIDS (*Taifa Empya*, 1989).

These attitudes have made women so cynical that they doubt the effectiveness of the recent laws that require a life sentence for a rape conviction, and the death penalty for having sex with a girl younger than 13 years. The women insisted that those who will be caught will be poor men who have touched the sisters and daughters of rich or powerful men. The majority of women are not protected.

The women's perspectives on these issues recorded during impromptu focused discussions in Rakai reveal anger, fear and vulnerability:

"We all live in daily fear of our new disease."

"We fear what our husbands may bring home."

"We are all going to perish through no fault of our own."

"Women are innocent. They are dying for nothing."

"I will not allow my daughter to be married without she and her boyfriend being tested first."

"AIDS has no mercy, the guilty and innocent suffer equally."

"I wish they would invent a drug women could use for protection."

"Men, now more than ever, think marriage to young women is the solution to the problem."

These quotes reflect the concerns recorded repeatedly during impromptu focused group discussions. Women expressed anxiety about the fidelity of men and wished for a drug to reduce their total dependence upon male willingness to use condoms. There was usually unanimous agreement among women that it is the local men who have transmitted HIV to their wives or girlfriends, who had not committed acts of sexual transgression. Men never denied the charge, but they would implore their wives to be understanding in this manner, "Ma'am, we are in this together, I beg you to understand and be tolerant."

In general, there is widespread insensitivity to women's concerns or sufferings. The notion that more men than women are dying from AIDS is widespread. While this is statistically true in general, in some villages more women than men have died. But even there, the ideas persist. In one subcounty where men and women have died in equal numbers, the administrator told all visitors that he had lost a quarter of the tax-payers to AIDS. On close examination, it turned out that he was referring to men only. In one village following three funerals of women on the same day, the village resistance council chairman expressed a common sentiment about women outliving men by pointing to "all the market trade taken up by women whose husbands have died of AIDS." The refrain from the assembled men was, "Good men are dying so much these days."

These biases in perception and reportage reflect the social attitudes to women as well as the economic reality. The sexual division of labor and social valuation make men's occupations visible while those of women are taken for granted and are therefore rendered invisible. Often people talked of attending the funerals of male traders, teachers, shopkeepers, farmers, etc., but women who are cultivators were generally not referred to by profession, except for a few who were teachers, nurses, traders or widows of men in the employments mentioned above.

The point is that the numbers of women dying were underreported in some villages. During an eight-month study period, seventy-three people were buried in the area: thirty-two men, twenty-seven women, and fourteen children. Fifty of the dead were repatriated from the urban areas. However, the number of afflicted women in the village at the time was ten, three times that of men. This means that attention must be paid to the periodic gender changes in the number of those dying. Women are both victims of AIDS and survivors. They seem to be blamed for surviving their husbands, who are usually older and contract HIV earlier than their wives.

CONCLUDING REMARKS: PEOPLES AND POLICIES

Uganda can boast of many firsts in connection with AIDS. An AIDS counseling group, TASO, was established by AIDS survivors in 1986. In 1987, when neighboring countries were denying the problem, Uganda established the first AIDS Control Program. In 1990, the Uganda legislature approved tougher sentences for both rape and statutory rape. There have been consistently twice as many AIDS cases among girls aged 15–19 as among boys of the same age; this reflects the tendency of older men to try to avoid AIDS by sleeping with uninfected young girls rather than the older women who they assumed were infected. The rape law makes the death sentence mandatory for those convicted of raping girls under 13, and lays down a life sentence for any rape conviction. The dynamic thirty-eight women parliamentarians and the active district women's groups are to be congratulated on their efforts to control the spread of AIDS. It is a promising beginning.

In the worst hit district of Rakai, people have accepted the scientific explanation that AIDS is caused by a virus (*akantu*, a small thing, or *akawuka*, a tiny insect). People have also accepted and acknowledged that AIDS is transmitted through sexual activities, and that condoms may make a great difference. The people are aware of how dangerous the situation is and will become, and they desperately wait for assistance from the politicians.

However, the member of Parliament for Kakuuto, the worse affected county in Rakai district, has suggested that though condoms may be appropriate for elites, the rest of the people do not know how to use and dispose of them. The real hindrance to the adoption of condoms is the elitist moralist view associating them with ignorance and promiscuity, respectively.

Nevertheless, the fact remains that new ways of doing things can be learned. Ugandans are pragmatic; they have always adopted new ideas out of necessity. On the issue of promiscuity, in Rakai there has been a reduction in the number of clients serviced by sex workers, whose shabby appearances tell all. In November, 1990, condoms received a presidential endorsement apparently as a result of glitzy, graphed, mathematical model slide-presentations by the Future Group. If condoms were not immediately adopted as intervention, economic and social catastrophe was predicted. The presidential endorsement has already led to plans to market condoms in Uganda. Protector, the commercial name chosen, is appropriate because it fits with traditional ideas about sexual health. Men need to protect their sexual partners through concern for the unborn. Maternal and child health also reflect positively on the man.

However, knowledge of the facts of HIV and AIDS, and government efforts to protect women against AIDS through legislation, are seen by women in Rakai as only the beginning. The position taken in this chapter is that knowledge and legislation, while very important, are in the long run ineffective if they do not address and confront the constraints of existing practices and attitudes.

The chapter has outlined the historical and cultural contexts of the practices and attitudes that currently hinder change. With the Structural Adjustment Programs, the climate of economic opportunities is shrinking for women even further. It is not enough to threaten men with rape legislation unless measures are taken to improve the material conditions that accord men control, power and authority over women and other subordinate household members. In the one village studied, household members observed the etiquette (based on fear) that absent wives were not to be told of the infidelities of husbands. In such a situation, women and young women are unlikely to report sex offences. With regard to the issue of men enticing girls with gifts or rides in cars or promises of jobs, the educational and employment positions will have to be improved a great deal to enable girls and later women to say "No." At the moment, men control access to wealth, prestige and power. The most effective way to break the vicious circle would be to change the law to ensure that women have equal rights to land and cattle, in addition to affording them adequate access to education, services and institutional banking.

Lastly, the data in this chapter suggest that effective control of HIV transmission depends upon men changing their attitudes toward female sexuality. Condoms have been scarce in Uganda because there is no great demand for them among men. Women think that the condoms might be their salvation from "the death sentence of AIDS." Effective AIDS education requires transformation in thinking. For example, the double standard, which is conveniently endorsed by men, enables men to have an option in the number of sexual and marriage partners they can enjoy. Women are denied such options.

The transformation will result from a critical evaluation and a re-evaluation of convenient practices in the context of survival. If women are infected, they will either die or bear AIDS-infected babies. Teenage boys in Rakai conceptualized the AIDS problem as represented by this statement from an essay: "Men infect young girls and their wives. Men must change their behaviors or else we face extinction." The fifty-eight students in the sample also wanted to undergo HIV tests and wished that condoms were available to them. The students also suggested that a peer educator approach would work for teens and adults.

The AIDS epidemic requires a drastic change of thinking that will involve awareness, assessment and action. In Rakai, people revealed awareness of the facts of the situation, they were at all times assessing the causes and they desired changes. The missing element is action to close the gap between awareness and assessment. The ground has been prepared by awareness, desperation, education and assessment. President Museveni's endorsement of condoms in November 1990 represents the first step of action.

BIBLIOGRAPHY

AIDS Control Programme (1990), Entebbe, Uganda: Ministry of Health.

Arya, O. P., Taber, S. R. and Nsanzo, H. (1980) "Gonorrhea and Female Infertility in Rural Uganda," *American Journal of Obstetrics and Gynecology* 138 (7, part 2): 929–32.

Bennett, F. J. (1963) "Custom and Child Health in Buganda vs. Concepts of Disease," *Tropical Geography and Medicine* 15: 148–53.

Brown, W. (1988) "Marriage, Divorce and Inheritance," Cambridge: African Monographs, 10.

Bujra, J. M. (1975) "Women Entrepreneurs in Early Nairobi," *Canadian Journal of African Studies* 1 (12): 213–34.

Catania, J. A. (1990) "The AIDS Epidemic: Quantitative Assessment in Human Sexuality Research," in *Human Sexuality: Research Perspectives in a World Facing AIDS*: 60–88. Background workshop papers and reports. International Development Research Centre, Ottawa, Canada. June 1989.

Kissekka, M. (1973) "On the Baganda of Central Uganda: Beliefs and Practices with Special Reference to Sexual Life, Marriage and Pregnancy, Childrearing, etc.," in A. Molnos (ed.) *Cultural Source Material for Population Planning in East Africa* Vol. 3, Nairobi: East Africa Publishing House: 148–63.

La Fontaine, J. S. (1974) "The Free Women of Kinshasa: Prostitution in a City in Zaire," in J. David (ed.) *Choice and Change: Essays in Honor of Lucy Mair*, London: Athlone Press.

Mamdani, M. (1983) *Imperialism and Fascism in Uganda*, London: Heinemann.

Mandeville, E. (1979) "Poverty Work and the Financing of Single Women in Kampala," *Africa* 49 (1): 42–58.

Nelson, C. (1979) "Dependence and Independence: Female Households in Matare Valley, Squatter Community in Nairobi, Kenya," dissertation, University of London.

New Vision (newspaper), 1988, Kampala, Uganda.

Ngabo (newspaper), September 8, 1988, Kampala, Uganda.

—— December 2, 1988, Kampala, Uganda.

—— December 19, 1988, Kampala, Uganda.

Obbo, C. and Nelson, N. (1980) *African Women: Their Struggle for Economic Independence*, London: Zed Press.

Orley, J. (1970) *Culture and Mental Illness*, Kampala: East African Publishing House.

Roscoe, J. (1911) *The Buganda*, London.

Save the Children Fund (1989) Report on orphans, Kampala, Uganda.

Southall, A. W. (1980) "Social Disorganization in Uganda: Before, During and After Amin," *Journal of Modern African Studies* 4: 627–56.

Taifa Empya (newspaper), August 1989, Kampala, Uganda.

Uganda Argus (newspaper), October 2, 1963, Kampala, Uganda.

UNICEF (1988) *Control of AIDS: Action for Survival*, Kampala, Uganda: UNICEF.

Wallace, R. (1991) "Travelling Waves of HIV Infection on a Low Dimensional 'Sociogeographic' Network," *Social Science and Medicine* (in press).

Zeller, R. A. (1989) "Qualitative Approaches to the Study of Human Sexuality," in *Human Sexuality: Research Perspectives in a World Facing AIDS*: 47–60. Background workshop papers and reports. International Development Research Centre, Ottawa, Canada. June 1989.

12

HEALTH, SOCIAL CLASS AND AFRICAN-AMERICAN WOMEN

Evelyn L. Barbee and Marilyn Little

The litany of health problems which plague African-American women at rates disproportionate to their percentage of the US population is familiar: hypertension, lupus, diabetes, maternal mortality, cervical cancer, etc. Of these problems, the success rate in terms of maintenance (in cases of chronic diseases) and cure (in cases of episodic illnesses) is affected by the constant circumscribing effect of being an African-American female in a white, patriarchal, racist society. This chapter asserts that being African-American and female constitutes a unique position in American society. The position of African-American women in American society is unique because the same ideology used during slavery to justify the roles of Black women underlies the external, controlling images of contemporary African-American women (Collins, 1990). As a result, the multiple jeopardies (King, 1988) and externally imposed images of African-American women interact in ways that serve to compromise their health status.

Consequently, the health needs of the African-American woman cannot be met by reformulation or "reform" of racist health policies or sexist health policies; rather her needs will only be addressed by looking at the point where the two sets of policies converge and form a barrier to her mental, emotional and physical well-being. Although we agree with King's (1988) conclusion that scholarly descriptions that concentrate on our multiple oppressions "have confounded our ability to discover and appreciate the ways in which African-American women are not victims," one area that has not been adequately explored, an area in which African-American women currently and historically have been victimized, is the "health care" arena.

In 1988 an estimated 30.3 million African-Americans represented more than 12 per cent of the population (US Bureau of the Census, 1989a). More than 52 per cent of these 30.3 million people were female. Within the African-American population the ratio of women to men is 110 to 100. The respective Euro-American sex ratio is 104 females for every 100 males. Although African-American males outnumber females up until the age of 20 years, after the age of 20 years the number of African-American women to men increases to the extent that the ratio at ages 65 years and over is 149:100 (US Bureau of the Census, 1989a).

In terms of family structure, 51 per cent of African-American families were married couples; 43 per cent female householders, no husband present; and 6 per cent were male householders, no wife present (US Bureau of the Census, 1989b). The respective median incomes for these households were: $27,182, $9,710 and $17,455. Among families that included children under 18 years of age, those households headed by women were four times more likely to be poor than those of two-parent families (US Bureau of the Census, 1988).

THE POSITION OF AFRICAN-AMERICAN WOMEN

Contemporary efforts to explain the position of African-American women in the USA were built upon the notion of "double jeopardy" (Beale, 1970). Beale's idea recognized that African-American women faced double discrimination because of their race and sex. Lewis's (1977) exploration of the structural position of African-American women was premised on "double jeopardy." "While inequality is *manifested* in the exclusion of a group from public life, it is actually *generated* in the group's unequal access to power and resources in a hierarchically arranged social order" (Lewis, 1977: 343). Because African-American women have membership in two subordinate groups, African-American and women, they lack access to authority and resources in society and are in structural opposition with the dominant racial/ethnic group (Euro-American) and the dominant sexual group (male) (Lewis, 1977).

In her critique of the concepts of double jeopardy and triple jeopardy (racism, sexism and classism), King (1988) noted that because each conceptualization presumes direct independent effect on status neither was able to deal with the interactive effects of sexism, racism and classism. African-American women are subjected to several, simultaneous oppressions which involve multiplicative relationships. The importance of any one factor in explaining African-American women's circumstances varies and is dependent upon the particular aspect of life under consideration and the reference group to whom African-American women are being compared (King, 1988). In regard to health, the multifaceted influences of race, gender and often social class interact in ways that render African-American women less healthy and more vulnerable to sickness than Euro-American women. Furthermore, they have to contend with their illness at the same time that they seek care from the racist, sexist and class-based system of American medicine.

While African-American women may be invisible in many spheres of life (hooks, 1981), their visibility vis-à-vis the medical establishment appears to be dependent upon procedures that need to be practiced (e.g. hysterectomies) and drugs that need to be tested (e.g. birth control). Elsewhere Barbee (1992) argued that the externally produced images of African-American women profoundly influence how medical and social professionals treat African-American women when these women are victims of violence. Here it is argued that these same images influence the kind of medical care or treatment given or not given to African-American women.

IMAGES OF AFRICAN-AMERICAN WOMEN

Because of the interactions among racism, sexism and often classism African-American women occupy a structural position in which they are viewed as subordinate to all other women and men in this society. Beliefs, myths and stereotypes about African-American women have served to intensify their status as "other." This view of the African-American woman as an object encourages the deployment of externally applied images and makes it particularly difficult to be viewed as a person, let alone an individual, by medical practitioners. As Christensen (1988: 191) noted: "No other woman has suffered physical and mental abuse, degradation, and exploitation on North American shores comparable to that experienced by the Black female."

In pointing out that race, class and gender oppression depend on powerful ideological justification for their existence, Collins (1990) identifies four externally defined, socially constructed, controlling images that are applied to African-American women. These images are mammy, the faithful, obedient domestic servant, the matriarch, the welfare mother and the Jezebel. The prevailing images of mammy, matriarch, welfare mother and Jezebel provide the ideological justification for racial oppression, gender subordination and economic exploitation (Collins, 1990). Each of these images contributes to society's and consequently medicine's view of African-American women.

The mammy image, the faithful, obedient servant, was created to justify the economic exploitation of Black women during slavery. As a social construction, its persistence is due to a need to rationalize the long-standing restriction of Black women to domestic service (Collins, 1990). In general medical workers are not receptive to questions from clients and patients. Those who subscribe to the mammy image are even less receptive to questions from African-American women. An additional danger is that those African-American women who internalize the mammy image may consciously and unconsciously sustain gender and racial exploitation in a number of ways. One of the more dangerous consequences may be a tendency to agree voluntarily to medical procedures because they believe in obeying the doctor.

Matriarchs are considered to be overly aggressive, emasculating, strong, independent, unfeminine women. The matriarch image implies the actuality of a social order in which women exercise social and political power. This image is central to the interlocking systems of race, class and gender oppression. The matriarch image allows the dominant group to blame African-American women for the success or failure of their children (Collins, 1990). An additional effect of this image is that it allows "helping" professionals to ignore African-American women when they need assistance. It is difficult to acknowledge that an African-American woman needs medical assistance when she is constantly referred to as being "strong."

Equally damaging is the welfare mother image. This is essentially an updated version of the breeder image that was created during slavery (Collins, 1990). Welfare mothers are viewed as being too lazy to work and thus are content to sit around and collect their welfare checks. This current objectification of African-American women as welfare mothers serves to label their fertility as unnecessary and dangerous. The welfare mother image provides Euro-Americans (and some African-Americans who have embraced these images without understanding their underlying ideology) with ideological justification for restricting the fertility of some African-American women because they are producing too many economically non-productive children (Davis, 1983).

The Jezebel image is one of a whore or a sexually aggressive woman (Collins, 1990). As Collins (1990) notes, the whore image is a central link in the Euro-American elite male's images of African-American women because attempts to control African-American women's sexuality lie at the heart of African-American women's oppression. Historically, the sexually promiscuous stereotype was used to contrast African-American women with the "virtuous" Euro-American woman. It also provided the rationale that justified the sexual assaults on Black women by Euro-American men (Collins, 1990; hooks, 1981). In contemporary times the Jezebel image is used as reason both for the sexual denigration of African-American women and for ignoring or minimizing such sexual abuse. The repercussions of these images on African-American women are most clearly seen in health statistics. While these "facts" are in and of themselves tragic enough, the real tragedy lies in how they have been used in an attempt to undermine the self-esteem of African-American women.

HEALTH STATISTICS AND THE RIGHT TO PRIVACY

One of the first things a poor person loses is the right to privacy. She must surrender information about her private life in exchange for a modicum of basic needs which the state grudgingly provides. The fact that the information extracted often goes beyond what is required for service is of little use to her. She is powerless and in need. *They* have the ability to determine her ineligible and consequently to affect her physical survival.

The vulnerability of the poor is ruthlessly exploited in the name of science. Countless graduate students in the health sciences have benefited from this vulnerability. Innumerable theses and dissertations have been written based on data collected from the poor. The informants were usually corralled at points of defenselessness: while waiting for WIC tickets (a nutritional supplement program for poor women and children), for emergency medical care, etc. Many of these women probably had no idea that it was unnecessary to submit to the questions. Some may have been given an option but believed compliance would improve their future service.

The data collected are never returned to the informants in a way that is useful. The original reports are written for the intellectual elite. The final dissemination of the data is through the mass media and only then if the results are newsworthy (i.e. sensational). Results are deemed newsworthy when they support the prevailing myths of our system. The master myth relevant to health is the inherent (i.e. genetic) instability of African-Americans' minds, bodies and "culture."

The right to privacy is predicated by income and mediated by race. The vast numbers of poor whites have not been an issue of interest for the intellectual elite. There has been historically a conscious choice to analyze health data by race not by income. The impact of this decision is manifested by our present inability to relieve the health problems of any Americans as we remain the only industrialized society outside of South Africa not to have a national health insurance plan (Davis, 1990). It is unquestionable that the same obstacles as in South Africa exist in the USA: the unwillingness to provide adequate health care to all regardless of color or income.

Public health statistics support the resistance to a national health insurance as they imply an inequity in health problems. When they suggest that only certain segments of the population suffer from certain diseases, and then are used to promote interventions for another segment of the population, health statistics are used as instruments of oppression. For example, although health statistics clearly indicate that coronary heart disease (CHD) is and has been a very serious problem for African-American women, public intervention programs imply that it is primarily a problem for Euro-American males. African-American women's death rate from CHD exceeds that of Euro-American women (Myers, 1986). Although there are different types of heart disease, the different types share common risk factors. For African-American women these risk factors include cigarette smoking, hypertension, obesity and diabetes. The social and structural risk factors include higher life stresses (Harburg *et al.*, 1973), truncated medical care access and lower-quality care (Yellin *et al.*, 1983).

A comparison of other CHD impact variables attributable to smoking (deaths, related lost years of life, cases, related hospital days, related days of restricted activity and related medical expenditures) between African-American and Euro-American women concluded that there were no "racial" differences (Kumanyika and Savage, 1986: 243). However, these comparisons did not take into account the fact that a large number of African-American women are heads of households and often responsible for young children. The sociocultural impact of CHD on African-American women is much greater for them and their families than it is for Euro-American women.

The prevalence of hypertension in African-American women increases with age and is 1.7 to 3 times higher in African-American women than Euro-American women in every age group (Kumanyika and Savage, 1986). In addition to being a risk factor for heart disease and heart failure, hypertension leads to pathological changes which can cause kidney disease or stroke. Demographically the highest levels of blood pressure for African-American women are in the South and the West. A major structural risk factor for hypertension is stress. Urban women's blood pressures are lower than those of rural women (Kumanyika and Savage, 1986). The aetiology for these demographic differences is unknown. Hypertension is often associated with another health problem of African-American women, obesity.

Obesity, an excess of body fat, can range from mild (120 per cent) to severe (more than 200 per cent) of the desirable or ideal body weight (Moore, 1990). Overweight, a weight in excess of the desirable body weight (Moore, 1990), is often confused with obesity. Because the prevalence of overweight in African-American women is higher than that of comparable groups of Euro-American women (Gillum, 1987), fat is a feminist issue that affects large numbers of African-American women.

Research-identified variables that make it more difficult for African-American women to lose weight are: (1) education below college level, (2) marriage and (3) low family income (Kahn *et al.*, 1991). Narratives from African-American women reveal entirely different factors:

> I work for General Electric making batteries, and from the stuff they suit me up in, I know it's killing me. My home life is not working. My old man is an alcoholic. My kids got babies. Things are not well with me. And the one thing I know I can do when I come home is to cook me a pot of food and sit down in front of the TV

and eat it. And you can't take that away from me until you're ready
to give me something in its place.

(Avery, 1990: 7)

What confound the issue in regard to weight and African-American
women are Eurocentric notions about attractiveness, biomedical deter-
minations about health and African-American cultural ideas about
beauty. Many of the negative traits associated with obesity, lack of
control, unattractiveness and slovenliness, have long been associated
with African-Americans as a "race." On the one hand, Eurocentric ideas
about obesity tend to equate fat with unattractiveness. Consequently,
those African-American women who subscribe to Euro-American standards of beauty are placed in a double bind in which one culturally
evaluated trait (obesity) reinforces this society's negative view of their
physical appearance. On the other hand, in African-American communities, a certain level of obesity is considered attractive. Historically,
African-Americans have associated degrees of overweight with well-
being. To be thin was to be "poor." The African-American community's
preference for "healthy" women has resulted in much lower rates of
anorexia and bulimia for African-American women. However, the close
relationship between adult onset diabetes and obesity requires that
African-American women closely monitor their weight.

Diabetes is a disease that has particularly severe consequences for
African-American women. Data from the 1981 National Health
Interviews demonstrated that African-American women's diabetes rate
was 38.2 per 1,000. One of the ten leading causes of death in 1988 was
diabetes mellitus and African-American women's death rate from this
was 27.3 versus 17.6 for Euro-American women (National Center for
Health Statistics, 1990). An additional problem for African-American
women is that the associations among obesity, diabetes and hypertension
increase the risk for heart disease.

Comparison health statistics between African-American and Euro-
American women that illustrate less, little or no difference in incidence
between them for a specific disease sometimes serve to mask the enor-
mity of certain problems for African-American women. Breast cancer
statistics are a case in point. For years the focus on the lower incidence of
breast cancer in African-American versus Euro-American women effectively served to mask the fact that African-American women have a
higher death rate from breast cancer than Euro-American women.
Although the breast cancer rate for African-American women is less
than that for Euro-American women, their mortality rate for this disease
exceeds that of any other group of women (National Center for Health
Statistics, 1990). Some of the reasons given for this disparity in mortality
rates are socioeconomic status (SES), later stage at diagnosis, delay in

detection and treatment, treatment differences and biological/constitutional factors (Report of the Secretary's Task Force, 1986). Since biological/constitutional factors are neither defined nor discussed in the report, they can be dismissed as factors. SES, later stage at diagnosis, and delay in treatment are related to problems of access. Poverty is a major factor in both later diagnosis and delay in treatment. The poor have not benefited from the various advances in cancer prevention, detection and treatment (American Cancer Society, 1990). However, poverty is not the only factor. McWhorter and Mayer (1987) found that when age, stage of cancer and histology were adjusted, African-American women received less aggressive surgical treatment, were less likely to be treated surgically and were more likely to be treated nonsurgically than Euro-American women.

HUMAN IMMUNODEFICIENCY VIRUS (HIV)/ AUTOIMMUNODEFICIENCY DISEASE (AIDS)

AIDS is a national problem that is wreaking devastation in the African-American community. It is one of the ten leading causes of death for the African-American population (National Center for Health Statistics, 1990). African-Americans accounted for 25 per cent of the AIDS deaths in 1988 (National Center for Health Statistics, 1990). HIV affects African-American women in a number of ways. First, African-American women and their children are part of the fastest-growing population of AIDS victims. Second, if diagnosed with AIDS, in addition to being concerned about herself, the woman has to be concerned with the effect of her death on her children. Third, the case definition of AIDS is based upon a male profile. As a result the profile does not take into account gynecological manifestations of HIV. As Anastos and Marte note: "If women's disease manifests with the same infections as it does in men, it may be recognized and reported as AIDS; if the infections, still HIV related, are different, the women are not considered to have AIDS" (1989: 6). Since eligibility for Social Security Supplemental (SSI) is based upon a diagnosis of AIDS, many women with AIDS are deemed ineligible for SSI benefits. Fourth, if a woman is pregnant and HIV positive, she is concerned with transmitting the disease to her newborn. Fifth, if she is diagnosed as HIV positive, her chances of contracting AIDS are higher and she will die sooner than her Euro-American sister. This disparity is usually accounted for by the mode of transmission. Many African-American women are exposed to HIV through intravenous drug use. As a result, the virus reaches their bloodstream much faster than it does when the virus is transmitted through sexual contact. Sixth, if someone in a woman's family, i.e. her child or partner, contracts the disease, in all likelihood she will be responsible for taking care of them.

MENTAL HEALTH

In 1979, African-American women reported a lower level of well-being than African-American males, white females and white males (Institute for Urban Affairs and Research, 1981). One third of the women surveyed reported a level of distress comparable with that of an independent sample of mental health patients (Institute for Urban Affairs and Research, 1981). Although the research on depression in African-American women reports high rates of depressive symptomatology and depression (Carrington, 1980; Dressler, 1987; Dressler and Badger, 1985; Gary *et al.*, 1985), African-American women are less likely to be medically diagnosed as depressive than Euro-American females (Smith, 1981).

Among African-Americans the highest rates of depression occur in women under 45 years of age; the lowest rates are in African-Americans aged 45 years and older. At all ages and income levels, women's depressive symptomatology is greater than men's (Gary *et al.*, 1985). Factors that increase the risk of depression in younger African-American women are: being poor, being between 18 and 45 years of age, being unemployed, high school education or less, the presence of minor children in the household, and being divorced or separated (Brown, 1990).

There is some evidence that suggests that support networks as traditionally viewed are not as useful to African-American women when they are depressed. In an examination of the relationships among economic stressors, extended kin support, active coping and depressive symptoms in a sample of 285 African-American households in a southern community, Dressler (1987) found a positive relationship between extended kin support and depressive symptoms. Women who reported higher active coping strategies reported fewer depressive symptoms. In addition to the previously discussed medical conditions two other conditions that disproportionally affect the health of African-American women are reproductive rights and violence.

REPRODUCTIVE RIGHTS VERSUS REPRODUCTIVE FREEDOM

We take issue with the notion of reproductive rights, particularly as it concerns African-American women. The national debate on reproductive rights is one that almost totally eclipses the interest and needs of African-American women. The debate, from its intellectual framework to its proposed goals, does not address the serious health problems of marginalized groups. The philosophical boundaries of the debate are seriously compromised. To talk in terms of "reproductive rights" is an intellectual abdication to a legal system primarily concerned with property rights *not* human rights. The phrase is an oxymoron. Human reproduction is not a right; it is a biological possibility. The two major opponents in the debate have chosen or accepted the media terms of "pro choice" and "right to life." The right to life seems to presume the "right" begins with conception, is most vibrant during gestation and ends at birth. The success of neither of the two will significantly improve the plight of Black females who have historically suffered disproportionally from the institutionalized attack on the Black family and "Third World" rates of infant mortality.

Tervalon (1988) notes that there are three interconnected aspects of reproductive rights: access to abortion, infant mortality and forced sterilization. Rather than talking about reproductive rights, it would be more accurate to speak of reproductive freedom. Reproductive freedom is defined here as unrestrained access to the medical knowledge (information) available in one's society that is necessary for the optimum maintenance of one's reproductive health. In addition to the aspects referred to by Tervalon, reproductive freedom would include safe, effective, affordable forms of birth control, family planning, sexual education, freedom from forced sterilization (Ditzion and Golden, 1984), the right of consenting adults to conduct their sex lives as they chose, reduction in African-American infant and maternal mortality rates, and affordable access to diagnosis and treatment of sexually transmitted diseases (STDs).

The lack of reproductive freedom has resulted in disastrous consequences for African-American women. These consequences include being three times more likely than Euro-American women to die of causes associated with pregnancy, childbirth and the puerperium (the period during and immediately after childbirth), an infant mortality rate of 17.6 (National Center for Health Statistics, 1990) and sterilization. Sterilization of African-American women encompasses a broad range of issues: (1) the right of African-American women to give informed consent to surgical procedures; (2) the racism that underlies the actions of physicians and surgeons who treat African-American women; and (3) the need for African-American women to be informed about a broad range of gynecological problems which may lead to hysterectomies or other sterilizing procedures (Black Women's Community Development Foundation, 1974). Data on sterilization in the USA demonstrate that a higher percentage of African-American women are sterilized and that the rate of sterilization of African-American women is increasing (Mosher and Pratt, 1990). The respective figures for African-American and Euro-American women's sterilization in 1982 and 1988 were 38.1 per cent versus 26.1 per cent and 30 per cent versus 22.1 per cent (Mosher and Pratt, 1990).

This high rate of sterilization underscores African-American women's lack of basic human rights. It sends a clear message about the links between African-American women's sexuality, fertility and roles within the political economy (Collins, 1990). Under slavery Black women were reproducers of human capital; slave women who reproduced often were rewarded (Giddings, 1984). Over time, changes in the political economy have transformed African-American women's fertility from a necessity for an economy in need of cheap labor to a costly threat to political and economic stability (Collins, 1990). As a result, the fertility of African-American women, particularly those who carry the image of welfare mothers, must be controlled. Additional issues of sterilization include: the relationship of African-American women to the pro- and anti-abortion movements, the role that African-American women should play in policy-making around these issues, the genocide issue, and the effort of African-American women to balance their right not to have unwanted children with their fears of genocidal national and international policies (Black Women's Community Development Foundation, 1974).

The year 1990 was to have been the target date for the completion of the "second public health revolution" (US Department of Health, Education and Welfare, 1979: vii). Goals were set to improve the health conditions of all ages of the US populace. A primary goal was to reduce the national infant mortality rate to 9 deaths per 1,000 live births. The ability of the USA as a nation to execute a second revolution was in doubt from the beginning. Joseph A, Califano in the foreward of the report which listed the goals wrote: "What is in doubt is whether we have the personal discipline and political will to solve these problems" (US Department of Health, Education and Welfare, 1979: viii). Some communities in the USA have reached the goal of "9 by 90." Other communities, poor, marginalized and dark in hue, have infant mortality rates exceeding 30 per 1,000. When the debate over reproductive rights is over, the debate that begins at the birth of each African-American child will still rage: can s/he survive? Will this child be allowed to thrive?

VIOLENCE

Although violence in African-American communities is disproportional in its effects upon women, the continued focus has been on the African-American male homicide rate. This exclusive focus on males serves to mask the violence to which African-American women are constantly exposed. For African-American women crime statistics are also health statistics. Homicide is one of the ten leading causes of death for African-American women. The reported rape rate for African-American women is almost three times that of Euro-American women (US Department of

Justice, 1991). Once raped, African-American women have a harder time getting police and medical professionals to believe them.

In popular African-American magazines rape, a crime of violence usually perpetrated against women, is explained by African-American male authorities as being caused by male frustration. Although one would like to believe that African-American male physicians might bring more sensitivity and awareness to the problems of African-American women, often male physicians are unwilling or unable to recognize either their own sexism or their own inability to understand that sexual violence transcends race. Thus in an article about rape in *Ebony* magazine, Alvin Poussaint, an African-American male psychiatrist, concluded that the high rate of rape of African-American women was due to the "feelings of rejection" of African-American males and to their need to bolster their self-esteem (Norment, 1991: 96).

Poussaint's apologist stance comes dangerously close to the rationale used historically by Euro-American males to justify their sexual abuse of African-American women. He joins the long line of African-American males who do not believe that Black males should be held responsible for their violence against African-American women (Lorde, 1990). Most rapes are planned (Amir, 1971) which suggests premeditation and hence responsibility. African-American male psychiatrists are not the only ones to beg the issue on the subject of rape in African-American communities. Ironically, Davis (1983) in an entire chapter on rape, in a book about women, while appropriately criticizing Euro-American women's treatises about the African-American male rapist, ignores the high rape rate of African-American women in African-American communities.

In addition to the high rape rate, there is also a high prevalence of sexual abuse. According to the empirical literature, African-American women are more frequently victims of sexual abuse than Euro-American women (Katz and Mazur, 1979). Furthermore, African-American women are at risk of rape and child sexual abuse across all age groups (Amir, 1971; Peters, 1976; Kercher and McShane, 1984). Wyatt (1985) found that African-American pre-teens were most likely to experience abuse in their homes from male nuclear or extended family members. African-American women reported more incidence of sexual abuse involving stepfathers, mothers' boyfriends, foster fathers, male cousins and other relatives than did Euro-American women (Wyatt, 1985).

Although battering is a strong concern of African-American women, Coley and Beckett (1988) in a twenty-year (1967–87) review of the empirical literature in counseling, psychology, social work and sociology, found only two sources on battering and African-American women. In addition to being physically battered, African-American women are also psychologically battered through music. The lyrics in some rap songs or hip hop music are especially violent toward and degrading of women. In an interesting combination of blaming the victim, transforming violence to sexism and holding women accountable for male behavior, a hip hop expert writes:

> As I once told a sister, hip hop lyrics are, among other things, what a lot of Black men say about Black women when Black women aren't around. In this sense the music is no more or less sexist than your fathers, brothers, husbands, friends and lovers and in many cases more upfront. As an unerringly precise reflection of the community, hip hop's sexist thinking will change when the community changes. Because women are the ones best able to define sexism, they will have to challenge the music – tell it how to change and make it change – if change is to come.
>
> (Allen, 1989: 117)

If males are creating and perpetuating violent, sexist lyrics, why is it women's responsibility to change them? Another question is why would African-American women take part in such music? African-American women who participate in and create women-abusing rap lyrics, have essentially embraced the external controlling images and are participating in their own oppression.

HOSPITALS ARE DANGEROUS

In addition to having to deal with the danger in the communities, African-American women are exposed to added dangers when they seek medical care. The vulnerability of African-American women is only too apparent. Dr Norma Goodwin (1990: 12) in her analysis of why African-Americans die six to seven years earlier than their white counterparts listed two factors central to the dilemma of black females: "the lack of culturally sensitive health information" and "decreased access to high quality care." These factors are excruciatingly sensitive to the economic status of the individual. The African-American woman all too often finds herself on Medicaid (health insurance for the poor) not Medicare (health insurance for the elderly). The reluctance of private physicians to accept Medicaid is not even apologetic. Even so, those individuals are better off than the estimated 35 million Americans without any form of health insurance (Edelman, 1987: x).

The absence of a national health insurance means that many African-American women receive their basic health care from public health clinics and county hospitals. The other historical source of health care is the university research hospital. Most of the major university hospitals in the country are located in economically distressed areas. For centuries marginalized groups have served the medical establishment as disease models, guinea pigs and cadavers. The ever present vulnerability of

African-American women was brought back to our memories with the exposé of medical research at Cook County Hospital in Chicago in 1988. More than 200 pregnant women were given a drug, Dilantin, without their knowledge. Fortunately, to date, the drug, used normally to treat epilepsy, has not caused damage to the resulting offspring or their mothers. The fact that such blatant abuses of human rights can occur in a publicly monitored setting only indicates the probability of what is occurring in private practices. According to the Public Citizen Health Research Group, the trend is for clinical trials to be conducted in doctors' offices (1990b: 1). That African-American women will continue to be guinea pigs sacrificed to the US medical establishment is a foregone conclusion. In 1989, the Food and Drug Administration found that there were irregularities in the informed consent forms in 75 per cent of the investigations of drug trials conducted in doctors' offices, outpatient clinics and hospitals (Public Citizen Health Research Group, 1990b: 1). Those same factors elucidated by Goodwin suggest who is mostly likely to participate in experimental drug trials.

SUMMARY

Lewis suggested in 1977 that the structural position of African-American women would cause them to become more responsive to feminist issues. One area in which Lewis's prophecy has materialized is in the area of African-American women's health. One of the first conferences exclusively devoted to African-American women's health was sponsored by the Black Women's Community Development Foundation. As B. Smith pointed out: "The health of Black women is a subject of major importance for those of us who are committed to learning, teaching, and writing about our sisters" (1982: 103).

Although there is a greater awareness of African-American women's health problems, the massive budget cuts for social and health programs under the Reagan–Bush administrations have only served to undermine the progress of and place pressure on local African-American women health initiatives. At the state level, redefinition of the eligibility requirements for Medicaid have reduced or eliminated medical coverage for large numbers of African-American women and their children. At a time when we should be concentrating on thriving, we are still concerned with survival. However, as Collins (1990: 92) noted: "Resisting by doing something that 'is not expected' could not have occurred without Black women's long-standing rejection of mammies, matriarchs, and other controlling images." The development of the National Black Women's Health Project and the organization of the First National Conference on Black women's health exemplifies doing the "unexpected." The Black Women's Health Project's first conference on Black women's health received an overwhelming response. In addition the Black Women's Health Project has developed regional networks that provide an environment that encourages African-American women to define and respond to their own health problems.

At the First National Conference on Black Women's Health Issues Christmas, an African-American woman physician made the following points about African American women's health: (1) we must not accept the blame for our condition; (2) we must be responsible for ourselves and at the same time hold the medical community and community agencies accountable, and (3) we must demand affordable, accessible, responsive facilities and medical providers (Butler, 1984). The life we want is one in which basic health care is assured. African-American women need and have a right to health. The state must try to provide safe living and workplace conditions, a safe environment, primary health care and adequate nutrition throughout life to its citizens. These rights which the state could guarantee are not on the table for debate.

BIBLIOGRAPHY

Allen, H. (1989) "Rap Is Our Music!" *Essence* 20 (12): 78–80, 114, 117, 119.

American Cancer Society (1990) *Cancer and the Poor: A Report to the Nation*, Atlanta, GA: American Cancer Society.

Amir, M. (1971) *Patterns of Forcible Rape*, Chicago: University of Chicago Press.

Anastos, K. and Marte, K. (1989) "Women – The Missing Persons in the AIDS Epidemic," *Health/PAC Bulletin* 19 (4): 6–11.

Avery, B. Y. (1990) "Breathing Life into Ourselves: The Evolution of the Black Women's Health Project," in E. White (ed.) *The Black Women's Health Book: Speaking for Ourselves*, Seattle: Seal Press: 4–10.

Barbee, E. L. (1992) "Ethnicity and Woman Abuse in the United States," in C. Sampselle (ed.) *Violence Against Women: Nursing research, practice and education issues*, Washington, DC: Hemisphere: 153–66.

Beale, F. (1970) "Double Jeopardy: To Be Black and Female," in T. Cade (ed.) *The Black Female*, New York: New American Library: 90–100.

Black Women's Community Development Foundation (1974) *Miniconsultation on the Mental and Physical Health Problems of Black Women*, Washington, DC: Black Women's Community Development Foundation.

Brown, D. R. (1990) "Depression Among Blacks," in D. S. Ruiz (ed.) *Handbook of Mental Health and Mental Disorder Among Black Americans*, New York: Greenwood Press: 71–93.

Butler, E. (1984) "The First National Conference on Black Women's Health Issues," in N. Worcester and M. H. Whatley (eds) *Women's Health: Readings in Social, Economic & Political Issues*, Dubuque, IA: Kendall/Hunt: 37–42.

Carrington, C. H. (1980) "Depression in Black Women: A Theoretical Appraisal," in L. F. Rodgers-Rose (ed.) *The Black Woman*, Beverly Hills, CA: Sage: 265–71.

Christensen, C. P. (1988) "Issues in Sex Therapy with Ethnic and Racial Minority Women," *Women & Therapy* 7: 187–205.

Coley, S. M. and Beckett, J. O. (1988) "Black Battered Women: A Review of the Literature," *Journal of Counselling and Development* 66: 266–70.

Collins, P. H. (1990) *Black Feminist Thought: Knowledge, Consciousness, and the Politics of Empowerment*, Boston, Mass.: Unwin Hyman.

Davis, A. Y. (1983) *Women, Race and Class*, New York: Vintage Books.

Ditzion, J. and Golden, J. (1984) "Introduction," in Boston Women's Health Book Collective, *The New Our Bodies Ourselves*, New York: Simon & Schuster: 201–2.

Dressler, W. W. (1987) "The Stress Process in a Southern Black Community: Implications for Prevention Research," *Human Organization* 46: 211–20.

Dressler, W. W. and Badger, L. W. (1985) "Epidemiology of Depressive Symptoms in Black Communities," *Journal of Nervous and Mental Disease* 173: 212–20.

Edelman, M. W. (1987) *Families in Peril*, Cambridge, Mass.: Harvard University Press.

Gary, L. E., Brown, D. R., Milburn, N. G., Thomas, V. G. and Lockley, D. S. (1985) *Pathways: A Study of Black Informal Support Networks*, Washington, DC: Institute for Urban Affairs and Research, Howard University.

Giddings, P. (1984) *When and Where I Enter . . .: The Impact of Black Women on Race and Sex in America*, Toronto: Bantam Books.

Gillum, R. F. (1987) "Overweight and Obesity in Black Women: A Review of Published Data from the National Center for Health Statistics," *Journal of the National Medical Association* 79: 865–71.

Goodwin, N. J. (1990) "Health and the African-American Community," *Crisis* 97 (8): 12 and 50.

Harburg, E., Erfurt, J. C., Chape, L. S., Hauestein, L. S., Schull, W. J. and Schork, M. A. (1973) "Socioecological Stress Areas and Black-White Blood Pressure: Detroit," *Journal of Chronic Diseases* 26: 595–611.

hooks, bell (1981) *Ain't I a Woman: Black Women and Feminism*; Boston, Mass.: South End Press.

Institute for Urban Affairs and Research. (1981) Statistical Profile of the Black Female, Washington, DC: Howard University 7 (1): 1–4.

Kahn, H. S., Williamson, D. F. and Stevens, J. A. (1991) "Race and Weight Change in US Women: The Roles of Socioeconomic and Marital Status," *American Journal of Public Health* 81: 319–23.

Katz, S. and Mazur, M. (1979) *Understanding the Rape Victim: A Synthesis of Research Findings*, New York: Wiley.

Kercher, G. and McShane, M. (1984) "The Prevalence of Child Sexual Abuse Victimization in an Adult Sample of Texas Residents," *Child Abuse and Neglect* 8: 495–502.

King, D. K. (1988) "Multiple Jeopardy, Multiple Consciousness: The Context of a Black Feminist Ideology," *Signs: Journal of Women in Culture and Society* 14 (1) (August): 42–72.

Kumanyika, S. and Savage, D. D. (1986) "Ischemic Heart Disease Risk Factors in Black Americans," in Report of the Secretary's Task Force on Black & Minority Health, Vol. IV, *Cardiovascular and Cerebrovascular Disease, Part 2*, US Department of Health and Human Services, Washington, DC: US Government Printing Office: 229–90.

Lewis, D. (1977) "A Response to Inequality: Black Women, Racism and Sexism," *Signs: Journal of Women in Culture and Society* 3: 339–405.

Lorde, A. (1990) *Need: a Chorale for Black Woman Voices*, Latham, NY: Kitchen Table Press.

McAdoo, H. P. (1990) "A Portrait of African American Families in the United States," in S. E. Rix (ed.) *The American Woman, 1990–91: A status report*, New

York: W. W. Norton: 71–93.

McWhorter, W. P. and Mayer, W. J. (1987) "Black/White Differences in Type of Initial Breast Cancer Treatment and Implications for Survival," *American Journal of Public Health* 77: 1515–17.

Moore, M. C. (1990) "Nutritional Alterations," in P. G. Beare and J. L. Myers (eds) *Principles and Practices of Adult Health Nursing*, St Louis, MO: Mosby: 343–84.

Mosher, W. D. and Pratt, W. F. (1990) *Contraceptive Use in the United States, 1973–88*, Advance data from vital and health statistics; no. 182, Hyattsville, MD: National Center for Health Statistics.

Myers, H. F. (1986) "Coronary Heart Disease in Black Populations: Current Research, Treatment and Prevention Needs," in Report of the Secretary's Task Force on Black & Minority Health, Vol. IV, *Cardiovascular and Cerebrovascular Disease, Part 2*, US Department of Health and Human Services, Washington, DC: US Government Printing Office: 303–44.

National Center for Health Statistics (1990) *Advance Report of Final Mortality Statistics, 1988*, Monthly Vital Statistics report; Vol. 39, no. 7, supplement, Hyattsville, MD: Public Health Service.

Nieboer, H. J. (1971) *Slavery as an Industrial System*, 2nd edn, New York: Burt Franklin.

Norment, L. (1991) "What's Behind the Dramatic Rise in Rapes?" *Ebony* 46 (11) (September): 92, 94, 96–8.

Peters, J. J. (1976) "Children Who Are Victims of Sexual Assault and the Psychology of Offenders," *American Journal of Psychotherapy* 30: 393–421.

Public Citizen Health Research Group (1990a) *Health Letter* 6 (8).

—— (1990b) *Health Letter* 6 (11).

Report of the Secretary's Task Force on Black & Minority Health (n.d.) Vol. III, *Cancer* US Department of Health and Human Services, Washington, DC: US Government Printing Office.

Smith, B. (1982) "Black Women's Health: Notes for a Course," in G. T. Hull, P. Bell-Scott and B. Smith (eds) *All the Women are White, All the Blacks are Men, But Some of Us are Brave*, Old Westbury, NY: Feminist Press: 103–14.

Smith, E. J. (1981) "Mental Health and Service Delivery Systems for Black Women," *Journal of Black Studies* 17: 126–41.

Tervalon, M. (1988) "Black Women's Reproductive Rights," in N. Worcester and M. H. Whatley (eds) *Women's Health: Readings in Social, Economic & Political Issues*, Dubuque, IA: Kendall/Hunt: 136–7.

US Bureau of the Census Current Population Reports (1988) series P-60, no. 161, *Money, Income and Poverty Status in the United States: 1987*, Washington, DC: US Government Printing Office: August.

US Bureau of the Census Current Population Reports (1989a) series P-25, no. 1018, *Projections of the Population of the United States by Age, Sex and Race: 1988 to 2080*, Washington, DC: US Government Printing Office: January.

US Bureau of the Census Current Population Reports (1989b) series P-20, no. 433, *Marital Status and Living Arrangements: March, 1988*, Washington, DC: US Government Printing Office: January.

US Department of Justice, Office of Justice Programs, Bureau of Justice Statistics (1991) *Criminal Victimization in the United States: 1973–88 Trends*, Washington, DC: US Government Printing Office: July.

US Department of Health, Education and Welfare (1979) *Healthy People*, Washington, DC: US Government Printing Office.

Wyatt, G. E. (1985) "The Sexual Abuse of Afro-American and White Women in

Childhood," *Child Abuse and Neglect* 9: 507–19.
Yellin, E. H., Kramer, I. S. and Epstein, W. V. (1983) "Is Health Care Use Equivalent Across Social Groups? A Diagnosis-Based Study," *American Journal of Public Health* 73: 563–71.

Part IV

ON THE LANGUAGE
OF IDENTITIES

13

PERFORMANCE, TRANSCRIPTION AND THE LANGUAGES OF THE SELF

Interrogating identity as a "post-colonial" poet

Abena P. A. Busia

In the half-life, half-light of alien tongues,
In the uncanny fluency of the other's language,
We relive the past in rituals of revival,
Unravelling memories in slow time; gathering the present.

(A. P. A. Busia)

Of the various titles which lie hidden beneath the one given above, perhaps the two which need to be unearthed are one of the earliest, "Interrogating Hybridity," after "Interrogating Identity" by Homi Bhabha, a paper which I first read for a faculty seminar at UCLA in the winter of 1989 and to which this is, in part, a response, and one of the last, "Translating Identity," a title suggested to me, as fate and the condition of migratory "post-colonial" subjects would have it, by friends of Homi Bhabha's, several years later, and half a world away, in Canberra, Australia in the summer of 1991. For these words are, in part, a dance across his words. For me, his paper acts as a kind of choreographic blueprint whose steps I refuse to follow completely. Parts of his paper just plain provoked me, and yet at the same time empowered me to think critically, and think differently, about my own work as a poet. I hear his call, my response is not always the expected harmonious one, but the echo of his words remains. Thus these words are as much a dance away from as a dance toward a fellow traveler; another colonial subject – same empire, different continent; his (male) voice of theoretical critical inquiry into other people's poems makes me high step and kick into a meditation on my praxis as a (female) poet.

I do not intend to rehearse Bhabha's arguments here. What is more critical for me, at this juncture, is to indicate the subtitles by which

Bhabha divided his paper. These subtitles – "The Deep Me"; "The Written Me"; "Doubling"; "The Subaltern Subject"; "The Post-Colonial Subject"; "Between the Evil Eye and 'I'" – were all of them suggestive to me, and sent me leaping off in so many directions, like watching myself dance in a cracked or dimly polished mirror.

The indeterminate aspects of "identity" that slide between the concept of "hybridity" and the concept of "translation" suggest, though, like the refracted image in a mirror, they cannot contain, the issues at stake for those of us – migrants, exiles and other kinds of homeless – troubled by the anxiety of trying to name ourselves in different tongues and voices, and place ourselves in or out of the manifold places from which we speak. Thus for me, this paper also has its origins in a series of incidents separated by time and different locations across the North American continent. Incidents which were profoundly felt at the time, yet remained for years without articulation. The question of the language, or languages, of identity that I am articulating here is occasioned by incidents other than only the impulse to respond to the words of a fellow migrant. They take me beyond the present place, literally and figuratively, from which I speak.

The places from which I speak are manifold. In this context, I speak as a professional academic working in the USA. Yet the USA is not the place of my formal education and training. I speak also as a British subject in many senses: in the sense of that being one of my legal national identifications; and in the sense of the UK being the place of my education. Particularly relevant here is the sense of my being born literally a British colonial subject and continuously regarded as one in the post-independence years of exile in England. The UK is the place of my exile, it is not the place of my birth. I am a Ghanaian by birth.

And I speak here also as a poet, and the dual focus of my presentation here is myself in performance as a poet, and the performance, oral and written, of one poem in particular around which crystallize many of the issues in this interrogation of identity. I see myself in this instance as a representative self, in the company of fellow travelers whose actions and words on a daily basis question settled definitions of identity. I am a Ghanaian-born poet, educated in the UK, teaching in the universities of the USA. The specifics are mine, the condition is common:

> Any attempt on [our] part, to frame the problem of identity leads inevitably to being caught athwart the frame, at once inside and outside . . . performing a certain problem of identification between nations and cultures, between foreign and floating signs.

Thus for me, Homi Bhabha's location of the starting point:

> between history and literature, where the authoritative power of naming is undone by the political and poetical conditions of its

meaning; where the language of the self is disseminated in the hybrid tongues and traditions that determine the place from which one speaks – as other.

(Bhabha, n.d.: 5)

is profound on many levels; as other, we speak the self in hybrid tongues to disempower or undo the conditions of our misnaming or our unseeing.

Many of Bhabha's writings interrogate identity on a national scale; for me this strikes a constant note of dissonance. In the context of writing, identity and nationality, the language of national identity and national-ism remains destructive to the place of woman and the will of the mother. Whether we are clearing a space for the wonders of Babylon, before the Areopagus or facing Mount Kenya, we have violated our mothers' bodies or bathed in our mothers' blood to claim and proclaim those stories. In the context of colonial histories, no colonial subject, and in particular no female subject, can enter a discourse on the subject of writing, writing history, history and identity, and not be aware that the history as it is written, the narrative coherence of nations and subject peoples, has been antithetical to the subject histories of females and the female principle. Even in the contemporary context little space has been found for the articulation of the place of women in the creation of new nationalist mythologies and ideologies. We must learn the lessons of our histories, one of which is the recognition of a certain dilemma that the will to be coherent (as in the creation of nationalist myths of origin) contends against a recognition that particular acts of narrative coher-ence, obliterate.

The effect of Bhabha's words was to make me dance around and witness myself – a perplexed "post-colonial," "post-modern" female poet performing a "troubled problematic of identity" from the perspective of a subjectivity very much bound by psychological and ethical problems of a personhood committed to re-figuring speech. In "Interrogating Identity" Bhabha's paradigms, his exemplars of other voices, are also poets, and in his explication of their positioning of the colonial dilemma I recognized my familiars. Bhabha's interrogation on the mediations between self and other, other inscriptions and other tongues, begins with the words of two poems, Adil Jusswalla's "Missing Person," and Meiling Jin's "Strangers in a Hostile Landscape." Different as these two poems are, what they share is a sense of "the impossibility of claiming an origin for the Self (or Other) within a tradition of representation that conceives of identity as the satisfaction of a totalizing, plenitudinous object of vision," and thus finding different strategies of subverting that gaze whose satisfaction lies through reifying us as "other"; through the articulation of imperial disinvestment of one's language in the case of

Jusswalla and the self-disembodiment in the case of Meiling Jin. One of the dilemmas we face is that in the language of the colonial, we must negotiate visions of the self in tongues which inscribe our own invisibilities. Yet not quite.

This interrogation of the discursive and disciplinary place from which I pose these questions of identity brings into focus a number of seemingly contradictory factors involving the negotiation between self-perception and self as object of external gaze. I locate myself in Bhabha's discussion because his acknowledgement of post-modernism's movement in focusing "on shifting the frame of identity from the field of vision to the space of writing," crystallized for me autobiographical moments of self-awareness which profoundly resist this shift. For myself as colonial subject, this recognition is predicated on the consciousness of being seen as "other" within a whole nexus of factors involving imperial histories, national identities and personal autobiographies.

In April, 1983 I was asked to take part in a poetry reading at the annual African Literature Association Conference, that year held at the University of Illinois, Champaign-Urbana. It was to be my first-ever public poetry reading and I concentrated on which poems I would recite. It was not until the last minute, therefore, that I gave any serious consideration to the matter of my dress. I did not know myself well enough. It was with horror, at the last minute, that I realized I simply could not go and read my poems wearing a European cocktail dress. This conviction came upon me, and it was a deep inner refusal. The imperative of the situation made me *register* but not stop to interrogate the impulse. I went "ethnic."

I was reminded of this moment again in reading Bhabha's negotiations on Barthes' negotiations between "The Deep Me" and "The Written Me." His discussion on how the *language* of identity comes to be invested with visuality recalled to mind that still moment when, about to perform poetry, I recognized my own investment with my sense of self *as dressed*. (I recognize that as a woman I had a choice, a more accessible choice, than "ethnic" males might have felt they had in a similar situation.) Again, this was a choice on the question of gender, nationality and gendered nationality that I took completely for granted. I registered all this without either interrogating or articulating it at the time, or in fact for years later. I look upon it now as a moment when the question of the language of poetry became embodied, the language of identity had a visuality in my clothed self. At the time my immediate concern was simply to get dressed, and go.

In December, 1984, the International African Institute in New York mounted an exhibition entitled "Beauty By Design: The Aesthetics of African Adornment." In conjunction with this exhibition, the institute arranged a discussion panel on adornment in Africa today, and I spoke about dress and adaptation. My concern was as a Ghanaian woman to speak about how to dress as a Ghanaian in a European context. Some of my concerns were practical; for example, what do you do in the mid-winter snows of New York if you do not want to look trussed up like a turkey, or ruin the lines of your *ntamaa*? How to avoid wearing visible and heavy turtlenecks under cotton sleeveless blouses? On that occasion, I wore cloth to give a practical demonstration of the aesthetics of adaption which range from the obvious choice of thin woolens to the not-so-obvious selection of woolen fabrics themselves which retain as near as possible the aesthetics of the now traditionally used cotton prints. In these commonplace acts of translation what accommodation is made by us between historical notions of layering and assemblage and those which are also an indication of the aesthetics of change?

I mention this incident because it was the first time I had ever been required to make a sustained critique of my habitual practice and recognize the accommodations I make seemingly without deliberation on a daily basis. I recognize the source of my aesthetic practice in cultures "other" than the ones in which I live and work.

By the end of the following year, I had stopped ever making pro-fessional appearances outside of my home classroom wearing anything other than *ntamaa* or at least carrying a *kente* cloth.

Dress is a form of language, textuality has a bodily as well as a written surface. Yet, how much of it is internal and how much a construction of the self in the face of the external gazes? In particular, the recognition of inhabiting a social world where identity is seen as "the satisfaction of a plentitudinous object of vision." In such contexts the "I" that speaks out of these clothes is avowedly a disruptive being, an "I" that makes the challenge to the viewer "to see what is invisible"; to force the look that cannot otherwise see me to recognize my presence. Dress, thus, can have a dual focus – to make you see my African-ness, as well as to dress me as I see myself, conscious of other traditions of adornment and other indices of social being.

The manifold traditions of dress in a West African, specifically Ghanaian, context are part of my make-up. For me to wear *ntamaa* is a natural mode of dress. To assemble beads on my person is not a response merely to the chic vagaries of western taste. I wrapped my hair as a child years before the concept was popularized in the western world. Thus the assertion of identity through a mode of dress is seen as visibly antagonistic only in contexts in which (I am conscious) my appearance is seen as obvious display. My decision to make no public appearances in an academic context unless wearing *ntamaa* was made taking note of that fact. Nonetheless, this move was decided several years after that inarticu-late moment of self-awareness when my poetic self realized that cocktail dressing was a violation of my words.

So there is another translation operating here; the one that mediates between myself as "scholar" and myself as "poet." My own mediating between "deep" and "written" selves also made me realize that I have never given a poetry reading without looking obviously Ghanaian. Although I had made many professional appearances as a professor and critic, on none of these occassions had I ever felt the resistance to "European" dress that I felt when presenting myself as poet for the first time.

I am trying to isolate (or is it conflate?) several identifying gestures on the question of visibility and visual perceptions centered around my remembrance of my reluctance to dress like a colonial subject when reading poems in a once-colonial tongue. I need in this particular context to question my sense of self; there are so many half-repeated movements in this vital dance.

My professorial prose-writing self speaks in European dress, the poetry-speaking self refuses to do so – a gesture I accept without question, "unconsciously" as a "true" resistance of the real and deep me. However, this is not so simply true. The division is not so sharply drawn, the self not so neatly divided. What is at issue is not either my written (prose) or my spoken (poetic) selves. My engagement with writing is in itself a curious problematic. All my written prose words, all my published papers, are always first spoken. Beginning with the 200,000 words of the first draft of my doctoral dissertation, every word of mine that has appeared in public has had its origins in words spoken, recorded and later transcribed and edited. That long-ago young scholar in European dress was engaged, as I am still now, in oral performance.

Yet still, I am not unduly concerned, as yet, about the state of "written" unpreparedness of my texts, once spoken. I am quite happy to let anyone read whatever of my prose transcriptions and unfinished papers they want. However, as a poet I am unwilling to have my "unfinished" poems read. I am prepared to recite them in draft form and even to declare them as drafts, yet I evidence an extreme reluctance to have them *read* in draft form. I make a distinction between words heard through my voice which I can modulate, and unfinished poems read on the page. What is the difference between the voice of poetry and the voice of prose? Or, more correctly, what of "myself" is invested in this difference?

My professorial prose-writing self speaks in European dress, the poetry-speaking self refuses to do so – a gesture I accept without question, "unconsciously" as a "true" resistance of the real and deep me. Later, the prose-speaking me embraces this gesture not as resistance but as valid, and only later recognizes that it *can be seen* as aggressive. A mode not of resistance but rebellion – a rebellion which can, however, then be subverted by leaving me standing on the margins – what, after all, can one expect of a native woman? The aggression becomes deliberate and dress an index of manifold oppositional stands. But this is not the entire drama. The divisions are not so sharply drawn, we are not so neatly divided. Underneath it all remains that moment of epiphany. I can play visual games with how I am seen and dressed, but it does not denude that moment when I made identification with my words and how I saw myself. And it does not belie my constant negotiation with various selves which results in hybrid modes of dress.

In every instance, my various identifications – as scholar, as poet, as Black, as female, as African, as an exile, as an Afro-Saxon living in Afro-America – are always present. Even in my identification as Ghanaian, which I stated so boldly at the start, I am the child of a woman whose people are patrilineal who married a man whose people are matrilineal. Am I thus doubly claimed, or doubly dispossessed? None of these categories is mutually exclusive. They coexist and are the boundaries within which I must exist or which I have to cross every waking moment.

The space between the assertion of identity and its interrogation lies between my prose and my poetry, between my poetry and its performance. It also lies crucially between one poem's performance and its transcription.

Mawu/Mawo	*Mawu/Mawo*
mmmmmmmmmmm	mmmmmmmmmmm
mmm mmm mmm	mmm mmm mmm
mm mm mmmmm	mm mm mmmmm
mmm mmm a	mmm mmm a
mma mma aa	mma mma aa
maaa	maaa
mmmmmmaaaaa	mmmmmmaaaaa
maaa	maaa
maaaa	maaaa
mama mama	mama mother
ma ma	I I've
wo	given birth
ma ma wo	I, I've given birth
mama ma wo	ma, I've given birth
ma ma wo	mama, I've given birth
ma wo	given birth
mawu	mawu
mawu!	mawu!
mawu ae! ma wo	oh mawu! I've given birth
ma wo	I've given birth
ma wo	I've given birth

mmaa wo	women give birth
mmaa wo	women give birth
mmaa wo	women give birth
mama mawu	mama mawu
mama mawu	mother mawu
mama mawu	mother mawu
a wo	has given birth
a wo	given birth
mawu a wo	mawu has given birth
mawu a wo	mawu has given birth
mawu a wo *wo*	mawu has borne *you* [s]
mawu a wo *wo*	mawu has borne *you* [s]
mawu a wo mama	mawu has borne mama
mawu a wo mama	mawu has borne mama
mawu a wo mu	mawu has borne you [pl]
mawu a wo mu	mawu has borne you [pl]
mawu a wo mu ma	mawu has borne masses of you
mawu a wo mu ma	mawu has borne masses of you
mawu a wo mmaa	mawu has borne women
mawu a wo mmaa	mawu has borne women
mawu wo mmaa	mawu bears women
mawu wo mmaa	mawu bears women
mawu wo mmaa	mawu bears women
mawu wo mmaen	mawu bears nations
mmmmmmmmmmmm	mmmmmmmmmmmm
A!	A!

I didn't "write" this poem, I "heard" it, and composed it in the spring of 1987, after a conversation with my mother. It is written in Twi which is my father's language, yet it also has at its roots the name *Mawu*, the name of the goddess in my mother's tongue. Before I turn to the question of transcription and inscription raised by this work, I must explain the poem.

I was born of parents from two different ethnic groups in Ghana. My father was an Asante from the Brong-Ahafo region about 100 miles north and west of the ancient imperial city of Kumasi. My mother is a Ga, the people who are the original inhabitants of the coastal region now taken up by the cosmopolitan capital city of Accra. Amongst my mother's people, one of the names for the supreme creator, represented as female, is *Mawu*. If you take this name and say it with variations of tone and stress in Twi, my father's language, it has a variation of meanings, all centered around the idea of women giving birth. Thus, this poem arises out of the particular circumstances of my parentage. Using the nomenclature from my mother's language, it is a play on words in my father's on the idea of God and the women created in Her likeness as life-giving.

In performance there were obvious tensions to explain to an English-speaking audience; the processes of the transitions of meaning from, for example, the shift from *ma wo*, "I have given birth," to *mmaa wo*, "Women give birth." Transcription is difficult for there is aural play evident when the poem is chanted, but there is also a visual play in tension. And then, some things are lost in the translation; for example, the play on *mama*, the almost universal word for human mothers, dividing itself into *ma ma*, the "I have, I have" preceding the first *ma wo*, "I have given birth" at the opening of the poem. Following this, the *ma wo, ma wo*, "I have given birth, I have given birth" collapses into *mawu*, the first evocation of the name of the goddess. This, though, is one of the sources of tension, the question of orthography itself. But this is a tension I only became acutely aware of many years after I "wrote" the poem, when I was asked to submit it for publication.

The processes upon which the poem is built would be more obvious written in English as I had initially conceived it; *ma wu ma wu* collapsing into *mawu*. The play then would be as visual in English as it is aural in *Twi*. For the "o" in *wo* is close to the short "u" sound as written in English in the name of the goddess.

The problem of post-colonial poetic transcription for me resides right here. In the need to transcribe my own oral performance of a poem intended to be heard, I was caught "athwart the frame." In the first place, my working notes from which I performed the poem were comprehensible only to me, for my orthography is relentlessly English. My personal copy was like a musical notation to guide the inflections of my uncertain tongue to meet the demands of the poem's swift incantatory rhythms in a language which is not often the language of my thoughts and has never been the language of my inscriptions.

Also, in the case of inscribing this particular poem, the problem was particularly acute as great care must be taken in both writing and chanting this poem, for the poem in both instances easily transgresses the thin border between birth and death. Changes in intonation and vowel sounds whether oral or written, change the meaning of the work. For example, the "o" sound in the *ma wo* of "I have given birth," is a vowel close to the English "u." It must be pronounced like the "wo" at the start of "woman," and not the round "o" as in "woe" or "pony," which makes no sense, nor, far more crucial, like the "u" as found in "puny" for then the entire meaning changes from "I have given birth" to "I have died."

With one stroke, I faced the problematic of embodiment and invisibility; legitimacy and creativity are disrupted by the needs of orthography in other tongues. To give birth and to die, always united, were embodied for me at this moment of transcription, mediating between the languages of the self and my others – mother, father, colonizer – all with their legitimate and varying claims, all of them legitimated by my words and facing obliteration by my inscriptions.

In returning to Bhabha's paper a few years later, I read my work again, differently. Bhabha tells us that Jusswalla gives a meditation on the hegemonic power of the imperial "A," as opposed to the equivalent Hindi vowel, "an er . . . a cough." In response I shift from imperial "A"s to the Alpha and Omega and meditate on the negotiation between the law-giving writing Father and the creative life-giving Mother. The "u" of the name of the goddess of female creativity is part of the IOU of collective history. But this is not to set up more hegemonic oppositions; blood for law, Mother for Father, to invert the process of national histories and invoke a counter-hegemonic myth. The title of the poem both transgresses and transcends the divisions, the doubling but not quite of *Mawu/Mawo* a mediation indicating the complex of negotiations, both heard and written, invisible in performance, starkly visible in print.

This title is a divided appellation. Yet, is this the articulation of the *agonism* of difference, or is it a unified other? That structure of difference that produces a continual hybridity in post-colonial discourse is not necessarily an ontology of lack. If my poem is the embodiment of the historical specificities of doubling and death, the call and its negation, it is also the embodiment of creation and its celebration. What I initially perceived as the threat of mistranslation, the terror of obliterating birth by death, becomes rather a unity.

If I had left the poem as I had logically conceived it, it would have read correctly in English but the opposite of its intention in the inscribed Twi. Correct in the language of my thoughts but contradicted by my speech in performance. The title makes visible the dilemma; the enunciation evokes the duality, the dialectical hinge between birth and death.

The actual problematic of writing focuses on this vacillation, *Ma/wu* pronouncing birth with the sign of its own death; *Ma/wo* traces of divine finality in the spoken name of the written Lord. In the certainty of the Alpha, the "a" remains constant. The limits of my utterance embrace the evocation of birth and the sign of death, a splitting of the divine principle of creativity but bounded by common vowel and consonant sounds. We reincorporate the imperial beginnings between our common and constant consonant sounds, "m" and its inversion, "w." The imperial "a" is translated into a vehicle of transformations, the Alpha embedded in the name of the goddess. It is fortuitous that the dilemma hinges around the "o," the Omega. The "o" of Omega is an appropriate substitution, but not quite. Meanings remain vicariously addressed, and birth is the appropriate other of death. The anxiety of writing is transformed.

212

It is possible not only to write but to be an alternate text. The evidence of hybrid or translatable selves is textual and performative, not lack but plentitude. We are not caught athwart frames, we are shifting frames. The hybridities are racial/cultural as much as textual, so I create for performance a creation poem on the name of an African goddess mediating between the birth and death of Alpha and Omega to finally embrace humanity.

Would I have felt the issue of dress so keenly if I only wrote poems in Twi?

BIBLIOGRAPHY

Bhabha, Homi (n.d.) "Interrogating Identity," London: ICA Identity Documents 6.
Busia, Abena P. A. (1990) "Migrations" and "Mawu/Mawo," both from *Testimonies of Exile*, Trenton, NJ: Africa World Press.

14

LIVING THE TEXTS *OUT*

Lesbians and the uses of Black women's traditions

Cheryl Clarke

I am a mannish dyke, muffidiver, bulldagger, butch, feminist, femme, and PROUD.
> Political poster, New Brunswick, NJ, November 1991

To rethink becoming a Black lesbian writer and reader of Black women writers provokes feelings of pleasure and trepidation. To reflect on any one of the three subversive identities – lesbian, Black, poet – that fill my work and days is to reflect on the expectation I place on the writing and the writer to be useful. Black and lesbian have always been bolder identities for me, threatening always to subsume the poet. I dreamed of writing years before I was sleeping/being with women, years before I craved literacy of my blackness. Blackness – my own and others' – contextualizes the dangerous parts of myself, gives them voice and visibility. I do not give up *Black* for "African-American." I remain connected to what the term signifies for me as a participant in the late 1960s Black consciousness movement in the USA. Blackness – that reclaiming of culture, that will to revolution; embracing the remarkable and violated past, the very tenuous present, and the unpromised future as an African in diaspora, an ex-slave, lesbian, poet.

The first serious work of fiction I read by a black writer was Baldwin's *Another Country* in 1963, and it was the first novel I read that treated homosexuality, albeit male. *Another Country* made me imagine freedom from traditional monogamous heterosexuality and set me to thinking about the possibility of a "variant" life. There is nothing, however, in the novel to recommend lesbianism, only an inelegant put-down of Jane, an unkempt older white woman and lover of Vivaldo, who Rufus, the tragic Black character, says "dresses like a bulldagger" (Baldwin, 1962: 31). *Another Country* unsettled me for ever and made me see the complexity of living as a sexual person.

The dialectic of Blackness and homosexuality was too subversive in the heterosexist Black consciousness movement of the late 1960s. Eldridge Cleaver, among others, attacked Baldwin for his homosexuality in *Soul on Ice*, which became the sacred (male) text during the Black Power movement. Poets abounded then: Sonia Sanchez, Nikki Giovanni, Carolyn Rodgers, Mari Evans, LeRoi Jones, Don L. Lee, Audre Lorde, joined by the distinguished Gwendolyn Brooks. All obligatorily espoused heterosexuality – except for Lorde and Brooks. They taught me how to make use of anger and gave me a rhetoric and the beginnings of a poetics. Blackness and Black people – ancestors and contemporaries – have been a self-replenishing store of poetry and knowing.

FINDING WORDS TO LIVE BY

> I'm not one of those who believes
> That an act of valor, for a woman
> Need take place inside her.
>
> (Lindsay, 1970)

Never far away. Always within reach. The anthologies. The novels. The journals. The broadsides. The pamphlets. Toni Cade Bambara's *The Black Woman: An Anthology* (1970) was the first autonomous collection of writings with feminist leanings published by Black women or any women of color in response to the resurgence of feminism in the late 1960s. Though I was not a lesbian in 1970, I was nonetheless struck by Bambara's stunning proposal for the resolution of antagonisms between Black women and Black men in her essay "On the Issue of Roles":

> Perhaps we [black people] need to let go of manhood and femininity and concentrate on blackhood. . . . It perhaps takes less heart to pick up the gun than to face the task of creating a new identity, a new self, perhaps an *androgynous* self, via commitment to struggle.
>
> (Cade Bambara, 1970: 103; emphases added)

Though Bambara was not a lesbian either and none of the articles in her anthology dealt with lesbianism, she and the other contributors – among them Alice Walker, Sherley Anne Williams (Shirley Williams), Audre Lorde, Frances Beale, Nikki Giovanni – were clearly preoccupied, as was I, with gender role expectations and male domination in the Black community/movement. These preoccupations were a precursor and a model for many other women of color, primarily lesbians, in the USA to examine nearly a decade later the intersections of race, gender, class and (hetero)sexuality in our lives and to write about them.

Before 1973, I had no conception of Black lesbians except as exotic

215

subjects of curiosity and an adolescent memory which I was to recount in a 1983 essay, entitled "The Failure to Transform: Homophobia in the Black Community":

> I can recall being about 12 years old when I first saw a black lesbian couple. I was walking down the street with my best friend, Kathy. I saw two young women [in their early 20s] walking together in the opposite direction. One wore a doo-rag, a Banlon button-down, and high-top sneakers. The other woman wore pink brush rollers, spit curls plastered with geech, an Oxford-tailored shirt, a mohair sweater, fitted skirt with a kick pleat, black stockings, and the famous I. Miller flat, sling-back shoe, the most prestigious pair of kicks any Dee Cee black girl could own. I asked Kathy, "Who are they?" "Bulldaggers," she answered. "What's that?" I asked again. "You know, they go with each other," Kathy responded. "Why?" I continued. "Protection," Kathy said casually. "Protection?" I repeated. "Yeah, at least they won't get pregnant," Kathy explained.
>
> (Clarke, 1983b: 206)

I was studying at Rutgers University right after Stonewall[1] and saw the beginning of the gay liberation movement there, led by Black gay activist Lionel Cuffie. Cuffie's anti-sexist and anti-heterosexist politics helped me see the connections among oppressions of Black people, women, and gay men and lesbians. In 1973, at one of the early gay[2] conferences at Rutgers University – trying to resolve the confusion of a Black identity and lesbian desire – I witnessed a contingent of *out* Black lesbians from New York City. When I heard those women – one of whom had been a classmate of mine at Howard University – talk boldly about the intersections of race, class, gender and their impack on Black women who were lesbians and our accountability to be struggling against and organizing around our oppression as well as celebrating our liberation from traditional and boring gender role expectations, I was transformed and asked myself the question: *With these women out here, why am I in the closet?* I realized that the major contradictions between Blackness and lesbianism were the sexist and heterosexist postures of the Afro-American (bourgeois) community. Witnessing a political Black lesbian community in the flesh was indispensable to this reconciliation of identities/cultures and saved me from wasting years in the closet of false consciousness.

I had already realized the potency of a rebellious literature and orality and would not have been able to nourish myself on feminist and lesbian-feminist writing had I not first found my anger in the poetry of the previously named writers of the Black arts movement. Later, I would connect with my feminist roots by reading the fiction of Black women, whose texts I live and write by: *Their Eyes Were Watching God* (Hurston, 1937), *Quicksand* and *Passing* (Larsen, 1928, 1929), *The Street* (Petry,

1943), *Lady Sings the Blues* (Holiday, 1956), *The Bluest Eye* and *Sula* (Morrison, 1971, 1973), *The Third Life of Grange Copeland, In Love and Trouble* and *Meridian* (Walker, 1970, 1973, 1976), Alexis Deveaux's surreal street theatre *Spirits in the Street* (1974), *Gorilla My Love* and *The Salt Eaters* (Bambara, 1972, 1980), Paule Marshall's tragic *Brown Girl, Brownstones* (1959) and her homophobic *Chosen Place, Timeless People* (1969), and all the Ladies in Red, Blue, Green in Ntozake Shange's *For Colored Girls Who Have Considered Suicide When The Rainbow Is Enuff* (1975). I stored the language of all their relentless, outrageous, angry and protective ghosts. I learned well to be the Black woman who turned up and "with a single glance from eyes that burned away their own lashes . . . discredited your elements" (Morrison, 1981: 39).

And when I used pretenders (drugs, cigarettes, food) to distract myself, I could feel them pulling me to poetry as patient and relentless as Hannah Kemhuff in Walker's "The Revenge of Hannah Kemhuff" (1973): "I can survive as long as I need with the bitterness that has laid every day in my soul" (67). And when I questioned their faith, I heard Eva Peace in Morrison's *Sula* (1974: 69) berating her Hannah:

> [W]hat you talkin' 'bout did I love you girl
> I stayed alive for you can't you get that through
> your thick head or what is that between your ears, heifer.

In 1975, speaking at the Socialist Feminist Conference at Antioch College in Yellow Springs, Ohio, Charlotte Bunch, "still, in part, a separatist," sternly educated the 1,100 women who attended – more than half of whom were intensely anti-lesbian, 200 of whom were out dykes and the rest were closeted dykes and bisexuals – about lesbian-feminism:

> Lesbianism is more than a question of civil rights and culture. . . .
> It is an extension of the analysis of sexuality itself as an institution.
> It is a commitment to women as a political group, which is the basis
> of a political/economic strategy leading to power for women, not
> just an "alternative community."
>
> (Bunch, 1987: 175)

The Socialist Feminist Conference was a left nightmare. However, I was fortunate to have been there. I met another Black lesbian feminist, Barbara Smith, whose life and work have remained crucial to me as a lesbian writer since 1975. In addition to the fact that she was/is a strong reader of Black women's literature, Barbara Smith was central in the USA to building a Black lesbian-feminist movement as well as a radical Black feminist consciousness, all of whom have been inspired and motivated by Black women novelists, as the writers, in turn, have been inspired and motivated by the Black and women's political movements. Smith wrote her groundbreaking essay, "Toward a Black Feminist

Criticism" (1977), which appeared in the lesbian-feminist journal *Conditions: Two*.[3] Smith made four important moves in this article: challenged white feminist critics on their literary elitism and erasure of Black women writers, developed Black feminist criteria for the evaluation of works by Black women writers, called our attention to Black women writers' subjectivity, and *read* Toni Morrison's *Sula* as a lesbian novel. This caused no end of controversy among the (heterosexist) Black literati who expressed themselves vituperatively when she delivered a talk based on the article at a Black Writers' Conference at Howard in 1978. Smith also organized four Black feminist retreats between 1977 and 1980. Most of us who participated were lesbians, others were bisexual and straight, all of us were progressive and radical, middle class and college-educated. These gatherings served to break down the isolation of being Black and feminist, and gave us the courage, if not the confidence, to do our anti-sexist, anti-heterosexist and anti-racist feminist work. They helped me particularly to recognize historical Black women's leadership.

During that time Smith participated in the writing of "The Combahee River Collective Statement,"[4] which defined Black feminist politics, practice, issues and organizing, and was particularly distinguished by the concept that there is a simultaneity and no hierarchy of oppressions.

In 1979, Smith and co-editor Lorraine Bethel guest-edited *Conditions: Five*, "The Black Women's Issue." *Conditions: Five* was the first text to enunciate a pronounced Black feminist politic since Cade's *The Black Woman* (1970). However, its signal importance rests on the fact that the editors included the writings and perspectives of *out* Black lesbians. I might add, though Audre Lorde's poetry appeared in *The Black Woman*, she could not be out in that work, though she was a lesbian then; and though she had been out in her writing a number of years by 1979, *Conditions: Five* gave Audre Lorde a visible community. Bethel and Smith stated, "We placed a priority on writing concerning itself with the issues of feminism and lesbianism as they related to black women." Smith and Bethel called for all women of color to produce "autonomous publications that embody their particular identity." It was in this special issue that I came out as a writer – not as a poet, though. Two years later, I came out as a poet in an anthology simply, bluntly, beautifully titled, *Lesbian Poetry* (1981), edited by Elly Bulkin and Joan Larkin for the now defunct Persephone Press. (Bulkin also edited a companion volume, *Lesbian Fiction*, that same year for Persephone.)

Following upon the success of *Conditions: Five* in 1979 and the initiatives of diverse feminists of color in the USA, other feminist journals and presses took up Smith's and Bethel's challenge and published writings by other culturally marginalized women within the feminist community. The 1980s was a watershed of multicultural feminist publishing and all of it either self-published or published by independent feminist presses, which challenged the racism, anti-Semitism, class biases of the lesbian-feminist movement: the self-published *Top Ranking: Articles on Racism and Classism in the Lesbian Community* (Gibbs and Bennett, 1980), *This Bridge Called My Back: Writings by Radical Women of Color* (Anzaldua and Moraga, 1981); *All the Women are White, All the Blacks are Men, But Some of Us are Brave: Black Women's Studies* (Hull, Bell-Scott and Smith, 1981), *Nice Jewish Girls* (Beck, 1982), *Home Girls: A Black Feminist Anthology* (Smith, 1983); *Sinister Wisdom's A Gathering of Spirit: North American Women's Issue* (Brant, 1983); *Calyx's Bearing Witness/ Sobreviviendo: An Anthology of Writing and Art by Native American/Latina Women* (Cochran, 1984). And while these various publications published writing by all women, lesbian leadership, i.e. editors, publishers, booksellers, reviewers, across all lines of race, culture, class and education, made these publications possible, caused them to be read, have kept me going, and have made it possible for writers like myself to be useful. In 1981, I became a member of the editorial collective of *Conditions*, where my primary task was to facilitate the growth of writing by lesbians.

When asked in an interview for Gerda Lerner's *Black Women in White America: A Documentary History*, Ella Baker defined herself as a "facilitator" rather than a "leader" (Baker, 1973). She further elaborated that she saw herself as someone who made it possible for other people, who wanted to, to take leadership in their communities. Lesbian-feminists are facilitators. Our movement was buttressed by the publication of writing by women, most of whom were lesbians or women for whom relationships with women were an integral part of their lives, whose writing – in diverse forms and genres – would not have seen print were it not for our network. The network is worldwide and necessary.

Jewelle Gomez (1983) and SDiane Bogus (1990) – both Black lesbians – historicize the Black lesbian image in literature. Gomez does so from a critical perspective and Bogus attempts to be more theoretical, though is less careful about some of her facts.[5] Both agree that, in terms of the works written from the 1920s to the 1980s by white women and Black men in which there are Black lesbian characters, none is an authentic portrayal. They disagree, however, in terms of their perceptions of the authenticity of the images of Black lesbians in books by Black women writers – lesbian and straight. And they differ most decidedly in their assessments of the influence and value of Black lesbian fiction writer Ann Allen Shockley, about whom there has always been a great deal of ambivalence among feminist and lesbian readers, reviewers and critics – Black and white. Gomez, in "A Cultural Legacy Denied and Discovered: Black Lesbians in Fiction by Women," states that the main flaws of Shockley's *Loving Her* (1974) and *Say Jesus and Come To Me* (1982), both of which depict dubious images of Black lesbians, are "not dissimilar from that of her white counterparts: the inability to place a Black Lesbian in a believable cultural context in an artful way" (Gomez, 1983: 114). Gomez goes on to cite Walker's *The Color Purple* and Lorde's *Zami* as exemplary texts which do not divorce "women-loving-women" from the Black community. Bogus, in "The 'Queen B' Figure in Black Literature," explores the etymology of the term "bulldagger" (i.e. "Queen *B*") and the bulldagger's presence in a larger range of texts than Gomez, takes Gomez and other critics to task for not recognizing "the import" of *Loving Her*, "that 'first' published black lesbian portrait drawn by a black woman" (Bogus, 1990: 277), suggests that Walker would not have been able to create Shug Avery had it not been for Shockley, and does not situate *Zami* within the "Queen B" legacy.

Historically important as it is, *Loving Her*, which I read after being out for only a year, did not satisfy my need for models. Looking for lesbians in fiction and most poetry was an unsatisfying quest back in the 1970s. Judy Grahn's *Common Woman Poems* (1969), narrative poems presenting images of working-class white women among whom were lesbians, intruded upon my store of images and preserved themselves there among the Hannahs, Scylla and Selina, Ruby, Janey, Helga, the Ladies in Green, Red, Blue *et al*. I was not to encounter positive Black lesbian images until Audre Lorde's *Zami* in 1982 and Walker's *The Color Purple* in 1983. However, despite and because of Lorde's lush, evocative prose, the narrator of *Zami* was too mythic and Shug and Celie were too unselfconscious as lesbians; Barbara Smith cites this as a lack of "verisimilitude" in the novel and questions whether Celie and Shug should be identified as lesbians at all (1990: 237).

LOOKING FOR LESBIANS: FINDING ANGER . . .

Anger has been a critical trope for me, a black woman, ex-slave, poet, lesbian trafficking among enemies. During the early days of the 1980s I felt myself and other Black lesbians many times being "cancelled out" (Lorde, 1988) as feminists – our contributions and our status as women unacknowledged by other Black feminists. Frustrated by the Black Movement's treatment of Black women, the jewelry-maker and cultural worker, Ruby, in Toni Cade Bambara's *The Salt Eaters*, expresses well the anger of Black lesbians:

> I'm sick of leaflets and T-shirts and moufy causes and nothing changing. All I want is a good blowtorch and some paying customers for a change. And if one more rat-tooth muthafucka strolls into my shop asking to trade some cockeyed painting looking like a

portable toilet for one of my masterpiece bracelets, I'm gonna run amuck in the streets, I swear.

(Bambara, 1980: 201)

Following in the tradition of militancy established by the 1960s Black consciousness movement, I took my first foray into what had been the domain of Black men – the essay – and wrote the manifesto-style "Lesbianism: an Act of Resistance," which appeared in *This Bridge*. As I reread this article today, I am amazed at how much it reads like a revision of the writings of the Furies Collective.[6] However, my model for this essay is the homophobic father I wanted to "kill" – LeRoi Jones (aka Amiri Baraka). "Lesbianism: an Act of Resistance" attempted to talk about who lesbians are and the domain of our politics and struggle as well as to locate Black lesbians within that world. It is loud and uncompromising in its criticism of the homophobia/heterosexism of the Black community and ends with an incomplete critique of the silence and hostility among lesbians of color and white lesbians regarding interracial lesbian relationships. It cautions that political alliances must be made on the basis of politics "not the specious basis of skin color" (Clarke, 1981: 135).

Sometimes the murkiness of my anger caused me to slay members of my own family for the "murder" of my lesbian sisters. "The Failure to Transform: Homophobia in the Black Community" in *Home Girls* attempted to be a critique of anti-gay and anti-lesbian postures on the part of Black intellectuals. So, everybody from Baraka to bell hooks caught hell in that piece. The "Pentalog," "Conversations and Questions: Black Women on Black Women Writers" – a five-person conversation participated in by Jewelle L. Gomez, Evelynn Hammonds, Linda Powell, Bonnie Johnson and myself, which I edited for *Conditions: Nine* in 1983 – was another platform for critiquing our extended family for its heterosexism, for exploring what it means to be a Black woman writing about Black women writers, and advancing a Black lesbian aesthetics/politics. We *read* everybody in this – Black feminist critics, white feminist editors of feminist publications, Black lesbian writers, and some of our best friends. A particularly controversial concept was Linda Powell's revision of Samuel Johnson's metaphor of the "dancing dog,"[7] which she applied to the false praise by white women of the mediocre writing of Black women. After providing the parable of the "dancing dog," Powell continues:

LINDA: Now, the truth is this dog didn't do anything that remotely resembled dancing. However, it wasn't bad for a dog. So, it's been my experience that what's been operating in the women's community is that whole thing that if a black woman speaks the language and is nice around white folk, the "dancing dog" is in operation. She can speak at conferences. She can write reviews. And even if she's mediocre, it's not bad for a negro. Occasionally, they hit pay dirt. . . . They'll get something that's higher quality than much of the material they print. But it's not because they met [you], or they spoke to [you], or they knew [your] work or [your] involvement in women's issues. No, but because they saw [you] at a party, [you were] dressed nice, [you're] black, and [you] went to Sarah Lawrence.

(Clarke *et al.*, 1983: 102)

The "Pentalog" was laced with acerbic and caustic commentary. No Black feminist writer, scholar, or critic was spared our wit – not Alice Walker, not June Jordan, not Deborah McDowell, not bell hooks, not Ann Allen Shockley, not Pat Parker, not Barbara Smith, not Mary Helen Washington, *et al.* ad infinitum. As I rethink this experience, the most problematic question the "Pentalog" raises, as a piece of literature and as an historical document, is audience. How appropriate was it for us to give such public vent (and venom) to issues of conflict among Black women – lesbian-feminist to lesbian-feminist, lesbian-feminist to straight feminist – in a publication like *Conditions*, whose readership was largely white women, or so it was said. We were asked the proverbial question by both white women and other women of color: "Why did you air your dirty laundry in public?" Having seen that argument played out for more than a decade by that time, I had come to regard the question as a form of censorship. Can dirty laundry be aired any other place than outside? Really?

I do not apologize for the murders but echo the sparse words of Electra in the adaptation by Black playwright Adrienne Kennedy of Euripides' play.

I am guilty too. I burned with desperate rage against you, yet . . . I loved you . . . although I hated you.

(Kennedy, 1988: 138)

So, finally, I come to myself, my own blank page, where I had to speak the love that cannot call its name, to sing the thing not named, and give a body to that "nameless . . . shameful impulse"[8] in poetry. With all this and the memory of Baldwin's *Another Country*, I set out in 1982 to negotiate my own Black lesbian subjectivity.

Narratives: Poems in the Tradition of Black Women is my first negotiation. I went to the Afro-American narrative tradition – written and oral – for language, directness, lyricism, terseness and pathos. *Cane* and *Maud Martha* insinuated a framework for these fifteen poems – each telling a different Black woman's story. *In Love and Trouble* and *The Bluest Eye* helped me see the violations and the triumphs of the souls of Black women. *Narratives* was a way for me, as a Black lesbian poet, to enter into dialogue with all the Black writers I had been reading since I was 17.

My everyday life as a Black lesbian poet is marked by the struggle to be a sexual Black lesbian, the struggle for the language of sexuality, and the struggle not to be the "beached whale of the sexual universe" (Spillers, 1984: 74). For many years, I said, along with many lesbians, that lesbianism is a political identity – *more* than *just* a sexual identity. What is this "more than"? *In addition to* or *better*? And "not just who you sleep with"? *Not just* meaning *merely* or just *not only*? And "more than who you sleep with"? Meaning *greater* or *in addition to*? Too much minimizing and dismissing of a major component of lesbian oppression – heterosexist repression of our sexuality. After the virulent antagonisms between anti-pornography feminists and anti-censorship feminists (among whom I count myself) in the early 1980s, I used poetry to reclaim lesbian sexuality and desire – in its diverse poetic and real forms. *Living as a Lesbian*, my second book of poetry, in 1986, quarreled with this dismissal of sex and served to advance another Black lesbian aesthetic and politic. Audre Lorde gave us the first and most searing in *The Black Unicorn*.

Sarah Vaughn singing "Lullabye of Birdland" to the trumpet inter-polations of Clifford Brown (1954) was a driving counterpoint for these poems. I plainly wanted to advance Audre Lorde's thesis in her 1978 piece "Uses of the Erotic," by promoting the concept of lesbian sexuality, a poetry of itself in all its irony and paradox. Lorde's words:

> When I speak of the erotic, then, I speak of it as an assertion of the lifeforce of women; of that creative energy empowered, the knowl-edge and use of which we are now reclaiming in our language, our history, our dancing, our loving, our work, our lives. Within the celebration of the erotic in all our endeavors, my work becomes a conscious decision – a longed-for bed which I enter gratefully and from which I rise empowered.
>
> (Lorde, 1984: 55)

The lyric genre predominates here and all the Black women's vocal music I had listened to since my childhood. A disconnected morose seven-part sonnet sequence demarcates each section of this book and tracks a narrative consciousness from the deaths of Martin Luther King and Otis Redding to the return of a friend to the struggle in southern Africa. The poems of each section enunciate the themes of sex, death and loss. In addition to sonnets, there is a sestina, two villanelles, and one ballade. The poems address local, national and global issues, e.g. the assassination of Indira Gandhi, the murder of Kimako Baraka, the Miami riots of 1980. Out of forty-five poems, twenty-three address lesbianism and explicit lesbian sexuality; and five poems bear the phrase "Living as a Lesbian" in their titles to signify the lesbian subjectivity of this book. Lesbians like this book. I was trying to please lesbians.

In 1989, I returned to the tradition of narrative poetry in my last book, *Humid Pitch*. The scope of it is broader than *Narratives*. Lesbianism is in sharp relief. *Humid Pitch* attempts something heretical for a lesbian-feminist poet: male homosexuality and female bisexuality. This may account for the low number of reviews it received in the feminist presses. *Humid Pitch* unearths the untold or not told-enough tales of Black women, triumphant lesbians, ambivalent men, slave women and the children who survive childhood. Pivotal to this work is the poem "Epic of Song," a 60-page narrative poem based loosely on the legend of the relationship between Ma Rainey and Bessie Smith.[9] Also I try to tell a triumphant story, to say that a "lady" can sing the blues and live to tell about it. Black women's vocal music is vital to all Black women – poets, novelists, critics, theorists, scholars – writing about Black women. "Epic of Song" pays tribute to Black women artists, who were often autonomous and sexually independent. The book attempts to evoke the language and color of the blues, of Black women's talk, the history of R&B. Several of my readers have criticized me for returning to the safety of the narrative form after the boldness of the lyrics in *Living as a Lesbian*. I don't agree or disagree. Each book has its own risks.

In my next book, *experimental love*, I listen for and attempt to hear the quotidian world of myself, to translate my historic and current tragedy into indelible memory, and to love my failures. There is sex but a less invincible, less certain sex – a sex which gives itself sparingly.

Nothing is promised here and everything could be finally destroyed as the old woman looks out on the rubble of what was her backyard after a Smart bomb or a nuclear holocaust. Lesbians are not virtuous here. They travel with latex. The sonnets return as well as a satirical pantoum; the lesbian living underground returns aboveground. Slavery is revisited, as always. There is no relentless pulling here and no ease of discovery.

I see my lesbian poetics as a way of entering into dialogue – from the margins – with Black feminist critics, theorists and writers. My work has been to imagine an historical Black woman-to-woman eroticism and living – overt, discrete, coded, or latent as it might be. To imagine Black women's sexuality as a polymorphous erotic that does not exclude desire for men but also does not privilege it. To imagine, without apology, voluptuous Black women's sexualities. Audience is never an amorphous or theoretical concept for me. Long before I published, I was reading my poetry and witnessing the transformative power of orality. Orality helps me mediate the silence of the blank page and the relentless din of memory. The poem's power is not only the poet's working of her craft but how that working connects with people's experience of the poet saying out loud what has been distorted, suppressed, forbidden.

Audre Lorde, Judy Grahn and Pat Parker are my foresisters and made it possible for me and many other lesbian poets to do our work during the 1980s. I was among a sisterhood of lesbian poets who interpreted the love that had finally begun to shout its name and its complexity in tongues of images and viscerally, writing a new cultural history. Our words were interstitial galaxies among the stories, letters, conversations, journal entries and diverse prose forms in all the journals and anthologies mentioned previously. Joy Harjo, Chrystos, Irena Klepfisz, Sapphire, Dorothy Allison, Gloria Anzaldua, Paula Gunn Allen, Minnie Bruce Pratt, Jewelle L. Gomez, Terri L. Jewell, and others whose names and words reverberate in the memory of those welcome audiences. Finally, lesbians and lesbian community have made it possible for me to call myself a poet. While I am privileged to write openly as a lesbian and to have my work appreciated and to sleep with a woman, I am still reminded that this ain't no place to love a woman.

NOTES

1 The Stonewall Riots occurred the weekend of June 28, 1969 on Christopher Street in New York City as police stormed the Stonewall, a gay male bar, and gay men – mostly Black and Latino – fought back for three days. These riots caused gays and lesbians around the country to come out of their closets and fight against heterosexist oppression.

2 In 1973, men and women were identifying as "gay." Women reclaimed the term "lesbian" soon after as they began to leave male-dominated gay liberation organizations and establish their own lesbian-feminist or lesbian-separatist organizations and enterprises.

3 *Conditions*, founded in 1976 in Brooklyn, NY, was, along with *Sinister Wisdom*, one of the first lesbian-feminist literary journals, preceded by *Quest* and *13th Moon*. *Conditions* called itself "a magazine of writing by women, with an emphasis on writing by lesbians" and called for any "women for whom relationships with women are an integral part of their lives" to submit their writing. Elly Bulkin, Rima Shore, Irena Klepfisz and Jan Clausen were the original editorial collective. In 1981, three of the four founding editors took action to make the collective a multicultural, multiracial, multi-ethnic, and class-diverse group. Throughout its history *Conditions* maintained an all-lesbian collective. The year 1990 was the last in which it published as a journal.

4 "The Combahee River Collective Statement" was prepared by a Black feminist group in Boston of which Smith was a member, and originally appeared in *Capitalist Patriarchy: The Case for Socialist Feminism*, edited by Zillah Eisenstein (New York: Monthly Review Press, 1978). The statement was later reprinted in *Home Girls: A Black Feminist Anthology*, edited by Barʋara Smith (Latham, NY: Kitchen Table, Women of Color Press, 1983).

5 *Clara's Old Man* (1967), by Black and male chauvinist Ed Bullins, was a play *not a novel*, as Bogus says, which depicted a stereotypic Black lesbian relationship. While many feel Shockley cannot depict an authentic Black lesbian character, Shockley is a lesbian and not a "nonlesbian" as Bogus states in her article.

6 In 1971, Charlotte Bunch and Rita Mae Brown left the organized straight feminist movement and formed a separate lesbian political group called the Furies Collective. According to Bunch, "The Furies . . . committed ourselves to developing a lesbian-feminist political analysis, culture, and movement. . . . [F]ollowing the path of other oppressed groups, we concluded that we could influence it [the women's movement] best by building our own power base and politics first" (Bunch, 1987: 9).

7 See Mary Ellman, *Thinking About Women* (New York: Harvest Book, 1968), 31 for a similar discussion of (white) women writers and male critics.

8 This phrase from Nella Larsen's novel *Passing*, was used by Deborah McDowell as part of the title for her 1988 essay, "'That nameless . . . shameful impulse': Sexuality in Nella Larsen's *Quicksand* and *Passing*" (in *Studies in Black American Literature*, Vol. III, *Black Feminist Criticism and Critical Theory*, ed. Joe Weixlman and Houston Baker, Greenwood, Fla: Penkevill, 1988). Its use in my text is appropriate, for McDowell reads the phrase as a reference to Irene Redfield's suppressed homoerotic desire for Clare Kendry.

9 According to Chris Albertson in *Bessie* his 1972 biography of Bessie Smith (*c.* 1894–1937), the legend that Ma Rainey (1886–1939) and her husband kidnaped young Bessie Smith and taught her how to sing is merely a "colorful story." By 1916, when Bessie joined the Raineys, she had been on her own for several years. Though Albertson looks at both Ma's and Bessie's bisexuality and their relationships and sexual exploits with women, he cautions against believing that Ma Rainey "initiated [Bessie to embrace her own sex] . . . a theory supported by no more evidence than the improbable story of Bessie's 'kidnaping'." Chris Albertson, Bessie (New York: Stein & Day, 1972), 104, 117.

BIBLIOGRAPHY

Baker, Ella (1973) "Developing Leadership," in Gerda Lerner (ed.) *Black Women in White America: A Documentary History*, New York: Vintage Books: 345–52.
Baldwin, James (1962) *Another Country*, New York: Dial Press.
Bambara, Toni Cade (1970) "On the Issue of Roles," in *The Black Woman: An Anthology*, New York: New American Library: 101–10.
—— (1980) *The Salt Eaters*, New York: Random House.
Bogus, SDiane (1990) "The 'Queen B' Figure in Black Literature," in K. Jay and J. Glasgow (eds) *Lesbian Texts and Contexts: Radical Revisions*, New York: New York University Press: 275–90.
Bunch, Charlotte (1987) "Not For Lesbians Only," in *Passionate Politics: Essays 1968 to 1986, Feminist Theory in Action*, New York: St Martin's Press: 174–81.
Clarke, Cheryl (1983a) "Lesbianism: an Act of Resistance," in G. Anzaldua and C. Moraga (eds) *This Bridge Called My Back: Writings by Radical Women of Color*, Latham, NY: Kitchen Table, Women of Color Press: 128–37.
——, (1983b) "The Failure to Transform: Homophobia in the Black Community," in Barbara Smith (ed.) *Home Girls: A Black Feminist Anthology*, Latham, NY: Kitchen Table, Women of Color Press: 197–208.
—— *et al.* (1983) "Conversations and Questions: Black Women on Black Women Writers," *Conditions: Nine*: 88–140.
Gomez, Jewelle L. (1983) "A Cultural Legacy Denied and Discovered: Black Lesbians in Fiction by Women," in Barbara Smith (ed.) *Home Girls: A Black Feminist Anthology*, Latham, NY: Kitchen Table, Women of Color Press: 110–23.

Kennedy, Adrienne (1988) *Electra*, in *Adrienne Kennedy in One Act*, Minneapolis, MN: University of Minnesota Press.

Lindsay, Kay (1970) "Poem," in Toni Cade Bambara (ed.) *The Black Woman: An Anthology*, New York: New American Library: 17.

Lorde, Audre (1983) "Uses of the Erotic," in *Sister Outsider: Essays and Speeches*, Trumansburg, NY: Crossing Press: 53–9.

——, (1988) "To the Poet Who Happens to Be Black and the Black Poet Who Happens to Be a Woman," in *Our Dead Behind Us*, New York: W. W. Norton: 7.

Morrison, Toni (1974) *Sula*, New York: Knopf.

—— (1981) *Tarbaby*, New York: New American Library.

Smith, Barbara (1977) "Toward a Black Feminist Criticism," *Conditions: Two*: 25–44.

Smith, Barbara and Bethel, Lorraine (eds) (1979) "Introduction," *Conditions: Five*: 11–14.

Spillers, Hortense (1984) "Interstices: A Small Drama of Words," in Carol Vance (ed.) *Pleasure and Danger: Exploring Female Sexuality*, New York: Routledge & Kegan Paul.

Walker, Alice (1973) "The Revenge of Hannah Kemhuff," in *In Love and Trouble*, New York: Harvest/HBJ Book: 60–80.

15

IN SEARCH OF A DISCOURSE AND CRITIQUE/S THAT CENTER THE ART OF BLACK WOMEN ARTISTS

Freida High W. Tesfagiorgis

A CRITICAL CALL: AN INTRODUCTION

Black women artists in the USA confront the attitude and practice of negation and marginalization in conventional art history and criticism,[1] the cornerstone discourses of the dominant art world Euro-patriarchy.[2] However, beyond the hegemonic utterances of artwriting[3] and art world practice,[4] their largely dismissed voices and unexhibited works evince a pervasive presence that intimates the longevity and complexity of their lives, works and interventions within their diverse contexts.[5] The art history and criticism of African-Americanists prioritize the lives and works of African-American men while inscribing women as complements, those of Euro-American feminists center the work and issues of Euro-American women while marginalizing American women of color. Black women artists, in the last decade of the twentieth century, remain semi-muffled, semi-invisible and relatively obscure.[6]

For Black women artists the contradiction between their material culture and their configured negation, complementarity and/or marginality in discourses on art constitutes the crisis they consistently resist: one that must be vehemently confronted in the 1990s and beyond if history's given course is to be altered. A discourse that would prioritize the lives and concerns of Black women artists is urgently needed.

Without a discourse of their own, Black women artists remain fixed in the trajectory of displacement, hardly moving beyond the defensive posture of merely responding to their objectification and misrepresentation by others, the severity of this predicament is clearly evident in the agency of protest consistently registered in their voices, a sign of the need not only for a drastic change but also for a specific discourse wherein that change can be seriously initiated.

In substantiating the call for the proposed discourse, beyond reiterating the imponderables of exclusionism in dominant artwriting and art world practice, I will first identify a range of responses of Black women artists to their marginalization in art world contexts; secondly, discuss the empowering function of discourse to subjectivize the objectified, thus explicating the potential of a self-initiated discourse to transform its subjects from a state of exclusion, marginalization, fragmentation and victimization to one of empowered visibility and action;[7] thirdly, argue that an appropriate theoretical perspective is Black feminism since the latter takes into account the simultaneity-multiplicative construct of race, class, gender and sexuality fundamental to understanding the lives, thought, production and interventions of Black women artists. I will speak as a Black woman artist/scholar who is involved in the project of claiming the histories, voices, visibility and cultural production of Black artists who, like others, have participated in the shaping of the sociocultural fabric of the world. Finally, I will identify aspects of a working Black feminist critique, a tool to structure a critical history of the art of Black women artists. Ultimately, I expect to demonstrate the necessity of locating a broad terrain wherein critical lenses could be situated (but not fixed) to illuminate the lives, works and interventions of Black women artists within their multiple landscapes and, in addition, to suggest how a view through such lenses might contribute to both the recovery and reconsideration of these relatively unknown subjects.[8]

DISPERSED VOICES OF RESISTANCE AND SELF-DETERMINATION

Black women artists on both sides of the Atlantic Ocean acknowledge and respond to their historical crises of victimization, defiance and self-determination. The breadth and depth of their crises are implicated in the unifying character of dissent in their voices and actions. Though this chapter focuses on the USA, Black women artists globally are diachronically and synchronically linked through colonialism, slavery, racism and capitalism and in their various countries confront the international transgressive art network that is characterized by Eurocentrism, sexism, elitism, imperialism and capitalism.

In the USA, American artist/philosopher Adrian Piper challenges what she identifies as the "triple negation" of "Colored Women Artists" in Eurocentric discourses, a problem that she describes as discrimination against them because of their race, gender and profession (Piper, 1990b: 16). Delineating specific "strategies" that Euro-patriarchists and Euro-feminist/women employ to dismiss the work of "colored women artists," Piper observes that such art critics and art historians: (1) exoticize/objectify women of color, thus investigating the psychosociological self of the speaker rather than the presumed subject of discussion, which is rendered silent; (2) deflect away from the meaning in the art object by raising "Euroethnic homogeneity" questions of "otherness"; and (3) make generalizations about Black women artists based on "gender and race stereotypes."[9] Such approaches rather than describing, interpreting and evaluating concrete works of art or offering art-critical insight, alternatively obscure the subject, thus failing to serve properly either the work under consideration, the audience to whom the critic speaks, or the artist who is rendered unimportant by the misinterpretation or dismissal of her work.

Overlaying Piper's critique, New York painter Howardina Pindell challenges the negation and marginalization of all people of color in the dominant art world, particularly in major museums in New York and elsewhere which almost exclusively exhibit works by men of European descent (Pindell, 1989: 32–6). Pindell encourages people of color to work together to open "closed doors"; the visual arts are emphatically not a "white neighborhood" (Pindell, 1989: 36). Pindell's activism interpenetrates that of various people of color including the African-American cultural nationalist patriarchy; the different cultural groups operating from their particular ideological positions to counteract art world racism (as well as sexism in the case of feminists) (Failing, 1989: 124–31). For example, Pindell's critique overlays that of African-Americanist art historian/artist David Driskell (not regarded as a cultural nationalist) which confronts the contradictions in the actions of Eurocentrists who attack Black art exhibitions, supposedly on the basis of their objections to segregated shows and group privilege, while they simultaneously offer "group" privilege of various types to "white males," including "all white male exhibitions" (Driskell, 1987: 13–15). But though Pindell's activism, in her various contexts, coalesces with that of Driskell in opposing art world exclusionism, it also diverges from it by underscoring the specific professional problems encountered by Black women artists, thereby concurring more so with Piper's challenge of the multiple oppressions of Black women artists. The given perspectives and problems articulated by Piper, Pindell and other Black women artists demonstrate the need for a discourse wherein their work, lives and other concerns can be critically investigated.

Black women artists in other parts of the African diaspora and Africa engage in similar dialectics. In her catalogue introduction to an exhibition by Black women artists at the Institute of Contemporary Art in London in 1985 British painter Libaina Himid, for example, remarks: "We are claiming what is ours and making ourselves visible. We are eleven of the hundreds of creative Black Women in Britain today. We are here to stay" (quoted in Parker and Pollock, 1990: 67). Do not Himid's rebellious remarks resemble those of American Blacks, including males such as Driskell who adamantly reaffirm the here-to-stayness of Black artists, their works and exhibits in the face of racism and sexism? Is it not evident that Black women artists on both sides of the Atlantic utilize resistant speech indicative of a shared determincy to self-inscribe a visibility that is absent in the dominant art world? And is there any doubt that their oppression and their resistance to it are interrelated?

Moreover, in what other ways beyond speech of resistance do Black women artists register their thoughts and acts of self-determination? One answer to this latter question lies in the character of their work, particularly in their choices of form and subject-matter which often encode specific aesthetic and moral values that resist dominant modernist styles or are beyond dominant tendencies in postmodernist pluralism/s. For example, New York artists Faith Ringgold like most artists produces work with expressive content that represents her individual aesthetic taste, imagination and social interests.[10] Having departed from "conventional" European oil-on-canvas techniques since the early 1970s, before that became fashionable, Ringgold insists on redefining art by innovatively synthesizing "crafts" (sewing) and "fine arts" (painting), thus subverting the separation between so-called "low" and "high" art that is paramount in dominant discourses on art. Such a practice not only contributes to the artist's distinctive style that displays dynamic tactile qualities, but also explicitly illustrates the fundamental connection between the "low" and "high" arts in African-American traditions whether visual (spatial) or ephemeral phenomena. Ringgold's forms synthesize academic painting techniques with colorful, high-contrast, multi-rhythmic, textural materials, aesthetic qualities that are evident in folk-quilting traditions.

In recognizing the importance of both the ordinary taken-for-granted knowledge and skill developed in African-American cultural traditions, and the knowledge and skill derived from more formal academic settings, novelist and critic Alice Walker calls attention to the varied manifestations of the creative spirit as she laments the limited viewpoints employed by those in search of artists and artistic production and admonishes the searchers: "We have constantly looked high, when we should have looked high – and low" (Walker, 1983: 239). She recalled a quilt nearly a century old hanging at the Smithsonian Institution in Washington, DC that was identified as the product of "an anonymous Black woman in Alabama," "an artist who left her mark in the only materials she could afford, and in the only medium her position in society allowed her to use" (ibid.).

Art historians, historians, anthropologists and philosophers, especially African-Americanists, have recovered hundreds of vernacular forms that were utilized in everyday life, art/artifacts that are both aesthetically pleasing and functional, and that have vitally contributed to American culture since the period of forced migration and slavery. Such objects, part of a much larger corpus of art works that have developed over a 400-year period, can be seen today in places ranging from the Old Slave Mart Museum in Charleston, South Carolina (quilts, baskets, metalwork, woodcarvings, etc.) and the Boston Museum of Fine Arts (Harriet Powers's quilt) to, say, something found on your grandmother's bed or in a relative's barn in Mississippi. Because of their formal structure, media and utilitarian purpose, these works, consciously or unconsciously valued by their communities for both their intrinsic and extrinsic significance, are identified by Eurocentric scholars as crafts or "low" arts and are de-legitimated by the discipline of art history because they are outside of Eurocentric definitions of art. These very forms contribute to the "cultural memory" of African-American/American life and history discussed by such scholars as John Blassingame, Robert Thompson, Reginia Perry and John Vlach. It is apparent in such scholars' works that the crafted/vernacular forms, the so-called "low" entities of material culture, vitally inform the aesthetic tastes of many Black and other Americans today, and that there is an obvious connection between them and the so-called "high" or fine arts produced by many African-Americans whose aesthetic judgements are informed by vernacular cultural traditions inherited within families and communities, as well as by judgements introduced and reinforced in lecture halls and studios of institutions where African-Americans and others are socialized to recognize/accept/adopt European-derived canons, many of then reinforced by cultural institutions such as fine art museums or the popular media industry; the former exclude African-American art, the latter manipulate and distort African-American imagery.

That Ringgold dares, as many African-American artists do, to retain or reclaim aesthetic values of African-American traditions, knowing that such qualities will be rejected and/or marginalized by the dominant art establishment, is the most immanent indication of her self-determination. She is often discussed in terms of her feminist ideology, and her work in association with the reclamation of women's work; thus emphasis is placed on the rebellious character of artist and work alike. However, the employing of material cultural theory situate the art object and better understand its extrinsic values, particularly associated beliefs, perspectives, expressions which can offer deeper insight into the contextual significance of the work (Prown, 1982: 1–18), makes clear that Ringgold and her work are in fact rather conventional though innovative within African-American traditions. Intertextual readings of folk art, fine art, performance, dress, music, sculpture and folklore among other works reveal the continum consequent on the inextricable relationship between the "low" and "high" aspects of culture in African-American traditions,[11] a factor fundamental to Ringgold's production.

However, within the context of the dominant art world, which separates folk art from fine art, Ringgold's work is interpreted as revolutionary, rebellious, political feminist production because it defies form, meaning, technique, aesthetics and function that are encoded in European-derived canons. Formalist, iconographical and feminist interpretations limit our understanding of the complexity of Ringgold and her work. Whether she is conventional or rebellious depends on the canon utilized to make that determination. Interpretation of her work in relation to her feminist ideology needs to be expanded with greater depth to substantially consider its intertextual and contextual cultural grounding.

The Ugandan painter Therese Mosoke, one of the few known African women artists, utilizes mixed media (dye and ink on canvas) to render her own truth and imagination in subject-matter that might be perceived as catering to a tourist audience: wildlife in Kenya. Despite the controversial nature of the subject-matter, however, she nevertheless continues to paint it, in an expressive style that bears her distinct signature. Her evocative compositions stimulate emotional responses perhaps not too dissimilar from her own special feelings for the wildlife that offers her "almost an inexhaustible kind of subject matter."[12] Mosoke has achieved the status of a successful independent artist whose work is her art; i.e. she lives off her work so to speak. Given her position, however, she does confront the polemical challenge of being "true" to one's self and the consistent pressure of tourism and the limited exhibition opportunities in Kenya. Her determination to simultaneously strive for individuality and work successfully with popularized subject-matter is an indication of her independence.

Also from Africa (Nigeria), but living in London, Sokari Douglas Camp produces sculpture in metal, a material that within African conventions is restricted to the masculine sphere of production (blacksmiths, bronzecasters, etc.).[13] Camp's persistence in working with materials and subject-matter of her choice indicates her self-determination; she has placed herself in an environment where she can freely produce what she chooses without experiencing the limitations imposed on her by Kalabari or other traditions.[14] Drawing heavily on themes of masquerade and associated symbolic forms, colors, textures and sounds, Camp generally constructs spiritual and human figures and objects in welded metal, utilizing processes of accumulation (and reduction) to achieve the desired effect. These forms are often juxtaposed in display to reconstruct ritual and context. Her style is impressionistic with a characteristic interplay of dynamic mass and voids. Paramount in her structures are rhythmic geometricized and curvilinear designs that are harmoniously enhanced by luminous mono-, bi-, or polychromatic surfaces. Mirrors, feathers, paint, nails and other details contribute to the imaginative presentment of each figure, which resonates with a dynamic quality that is heightened by kinetics (movement, sounds, etc.). Camp's work, in form and subject matter, is heavily influenced by Kalabari traditions. Yet the artist, like Ringgold and Mosoke, demonstrates a distinctive personal vision that is recognizable in her individual style. Her representation of women is a particularly distinctive mark in contemporary African art, for unlike the prevailing stereotypical prototypes – ritualized puberty figure, mother, youthful beauty, etc. – Camp's impressionistic representation of the female subject effectively evokes character, power and action (see her "Woman, part of Audience Ensemble," 1986, steel and paint, 75.5″), a sign of the provocative imagination, skill, subjective knowledge and experience that give rise to the basic assumption of women's differences in personalities and roles, as well as her desire to deploy those assumptions in her dominant themes. Camp's work cannot be divorced either from her identity as a Kalabari woman or from the individual freedom with which she works as a contemporary sculptor. Her work and life stimulate both greater thought about the divergent identities of women artists of African descent – the stylistic and thematic differences in our works of art, and the complexities scholars will encounter in developing the critical art history that must synthesize conventional and new art-historical methods – and also further investigation of the appropriate histories and cultures that will allow us to get beyond the mystification surrounding the artistic products of Black women in art history and art world practice.

Ringgold, Mosoke and Camp are among the many Black women artists who produce convincing works of art with eloquence and integrity. Most of them remain unrecorded in the dominant discourses on art and largely unknown either to the professional art world or to the public audience, because of the controlling institutional biases of the art world and its canonized scholarly proclivities.

The persistence of these artists, African-American and African, is perhaps partially derived from the strength retained, reclaimed and synthesized in cultural and ideological patterns extant in their various communities, factors to which they and many other Black artists had been exposed in their material conditions prior to, and during, their academic training. Paradoxically, the determinacy implicit in such influence inheres an expressive freedom leading to the kind of imaginative and dynamic works discussed, yet it is also weighted by the canon problematic in prevailing discourses that negates the artists' importance to conventional and even postmodern art history and criticism.

Interestingly, some Black women artists observe that their "outsider" status in Eurocentric discourses, with its critical distance from the mainstream, stimulates a greater sense of independence and creative freedom. Piper finds joy and freedom in the margins, in the company of artists who are doing "much of the really advanced, exciting, [and] original work," with a clear view of "the narrow range of aesthetic options validated by the mainstream" (Piper, 1990a: 12–13). Ringgold, too, emphasizes that since she is on the outside anyway, she can do what she wants.[15] Sociologist Pat Hill Collins uses the term "outsider within" to identify this distanced marginal placement and the special viewpoint that some Black women say they acquire within the construct of Eurocentric exclusionism, and surmises that it provides "a special perspective on self, family and society" which contributes to "distinctive analyses" (Collins, 1991: 40). It is not surprising that the voices of the artist and sociologist interpenetrate in exposing the specific inclusion/exclusion dichotomy/advantage that is experienced by Black women within the contexts of systems dominated by the Euro-patriarchy.

Any interpretation of such remarks as acceptance of the given status would be naive. In any case, who is to say that a similar joy and freedom might not exist for the "outsider within" if she were positioned more centrally within the currents of the dominant art (or other) world/s with the full benefits of such placement? In the area of art in particular, Piper and Ringgold are among the most vocal American women who continue to resist established boundaries in the art world that exclude people of color, especially women. Ringgold herself has for some twenty-five years addressed the interests and problems of Black and other women (and men) in various discourses, often articulating her own personal narrative to underscore the reality of Black women's subjugated identities and experiences. She most recently commented, "Everything about my life has to do with the fact that I am a black woman. The way I work has everything to do with that, because I am struggling against being a victim which is what black women become in this society" (Flomenhaft, 1990: 14).

Sociologist Deborah King identifies the shared distinctive circumstances of Black women in general as the phenomenon of "multiple jeopardy," a quality that she describes as socially constructed by the simultaneity and multiplicative relationships among their race, gender and class, and to which she attributes a shared "multiple consciousness."[16] In support, sociologist Pat Hill Collins specifies that the commonalities among Black women are grounded in two major interlocking factors: (1) Black women's "political and economic status that provide(d) them with a distinctive set of experiences" and (2) distinctive Black feminist consciousness stimulated by the experience derived from their material realities.[17] Though their discussions refer specifically to the circumstances and awareness of Black women in the USA they are applicable to the shared realities of Black women artists globally for, regardless of where they live, Black women artists inherit a common devalued (though different) status that has major adverse economic, political and cultural implications for their lives and production.

Only the rare art historian, critic or theorist offers substantive interpretations of works and thoughts of Black women artists. Among them, art historian Leslie King-Hammond reconstructs empirical facts, the basis of art criticism,[18] art history and theory, in her quest to make justifiable aesthetic judgements of the art objects and performances of Black women artists. King-Hammond stresses production over the victimization in her analyses, concluding that in spite of their material conditions, "these artists speak eloquently of the vision and presence of a people long overdue for inclusion in the art world of this country." Based on the material evidence that I have seen in the USA, London and various countries in Africa, I must add that Black women artists (and all people of color) throughout the world are long overdue for inclusion in art history and in the systematic operations of the global art world.[19]

With a self-activated and sustained discourse characterized by the knowledge and conviction of self-determination evident in the fragmented voices of Black women artists, art historians and others, a major shift in the focus on Black women artists can be implemented. Most importantly, that shift could transform defensive discussions to more insightful interpretative exchanges that would lead to the construction of a critical art history.[20] In addition, more effective strategies for dismantling the exclusionary devices of the dominant art establishment could conceivably be constructed. Such objectives, in their entirety, could be identified as a Black feminist art project that would be both academic and political in character, its monumentality beyond my scope here. But it must begin with a distinctive discourse that would center Black women artists for such a discourse would circulate and debate facts, critiques and theories while inscribing them into history.

CLAIMIN' DISCOURSE

The act of claiming a particular discourse, in and of itself, asserts a claim for visibility and registers a theoretical position.

Discourse, literary critic Terry Eagleton informs us, constitutes "language grasped as utterance, as involving speaking and writing subjects and therefore also, at least potentially, readers or listeners" (Eagleton, 1989: 115). As intersubjective communication, discourse is language that encodes cultural conventions (Fowler, 1990: 90), a crucial point for as poet and literary critic Abena Busia explains, "Language is not 'innocent': It is ideologically and culturally bound, and it both expresses and conceals our realities. . . . Language can also shape our realities, and either enslave, by concealing what it might truly express, or liberate, by exposing what might otherwise remain concealed" (Busia, 1988: 6–7). The exclusion of Black women artists from dominant artwriting, except in voyeuristic discourses that forcibly manipulate them into passive positions of "othering" reveals just how potent and rupturing Euro-patriarchical language and power can be to their lives. For the language of art truly controls the system of art, and that very language has concealed the art and ideas of Black women artists for hundreds of years.

With a self-initiated and sustained discourse of our own, we Black women artists could begin collectively to recover our lives, which might prove to be even more nurturing than our individual self-recovery or than our exclusive bonding in other groups which maintain different priorities.[21] By speaking a shared language derived from shared knowledge/s and cultural and social experiences, Black women artists could collectively discover each other, and our collective history. The proposed discourse would process the exchange of our particular sub-jectivities and become the source of our self-knowing. Such a source could subvert the current proscriptions of our erasure, marginalization, fragmentation, "Other-ness" and isolation with the inscription of our self-defined divergent qualities of presence, centralization, wholeness, Self-ness, and empowerment with some measure of continuity.

Currently we are talking across the boundaries of geography and professional and personal commitments. But with a sustained discourse of our own, we could circumvent the continuous closures and exclusions and could also collectively decide the proper tone and focus for investi-gating what is truly important to us as artists and artists/scholars (art historians, curators, etc.) in our efforts to be properly seen, heard, effective, and actively engaged in our contexts according to our own definitions.

Literary critic Barbara Johnson reminds us that to assume the position of speaking subject "means to activate the network of discourse from where one stands" (Johnson, 1989: 43). Speech, cultural theorist bell hooks elaborates, is a "revolutionary gesture" that makes one primary in "talk, discourse, writing and action" (hooks, 1989: 12). As subjects active-ly engage speech, they acquire a performative power to take nourish-ment from multiple sources and subsequently to construct a new synthesis of knowledge (Johnson, 1989: 43). Such a synthesis for Black women artists could contribute to our empowerment at both intellectual and practical levels, and thus potentially lead to the development of an irreversible collective critical art history and activism that would not only make us visible and effective in the various institutions of the dominant art establishment, but also increase our effectiveness in our multiple communities.

How would the proposed discourse differ from the circulating knowl-edge in ongoing discourses? The answer to this question might be implicit in the current fragmented articulations of Black women artists/scholars, the most vocal thus far, who would initialize the discourse with their affective ambience of shared, though diverse, social and cultural values. As both the primary speaking subjects and the primary subjects of investigation, they would connect the knowledge that now exists in fragmented states, prioritizing, meditating and circulating it according to their judgements. Since no other identities have given priority to either Black women artists or their works, it appears natural that Black women artists/scholars would collectively initiate and lead a discourse that would continue to challenge their own adverse circumstances and even more importantly contribute to the recovery and analysis of their own production, and would welcome others to participate in its construction and expansion; I would identify such a development as a Black feminist art-historical discourse.

In her elucidation of the transformative value of speech/discourse hooks underscores the implications of a Black feminist art-historical discourse particularly for many heretofore silenced and disconnected Black women artists. She observes:

> Moving from silence into speech is for the oppressed, the colonized, the exploited, and those who stand and struggle side by side a gesture of defiance that heals, that makes new life and new growth possible. It is that act of speech, of "talking back," that is no mere gesture of empty words, that is the expression of our movement from object to subject – the liberated voice.
>
> (hooks, 1989: 9)

Speech/discourse, in this regard, is both a theoretical and social practice (Eagleton, 1990: 24). As such, observes historian E. Frances White, it intertwines ideological and material conditions that "help to organize our social existence and social reproduction through the production of signs and practices that give meaning to our lives" (E. F. White, 1990: 77). The proposed discourse for Black women artists, therefore, would not merely remove them from object to subject and from margin to center, but serve as an apparatus wherein qualified artists and scholars would interpret and evaluate the ideological and material signs relevant to their existence and their diverse forms of production and interests.

The empowering function of discourse, particularly within the hierarchy of power and knowledge, is insightfully explained by French theorist Michel Foucault who observes that those in power control "domains of knowledge," thus subjugating, disguising or disqualifying knowledges that in their judgement are "located low down on the hierarchy, beneath the required level of cognition or scientificity" (Foucault, 1980: 84). According to this theory, those who have historically controlled the domains of knowledge and power in the art world have historically circulated and legitimated their knowledge and the material objects derived from that knowledge which they identify as

238

truth and quality. Foucault exposes how the "normalization" of Euro-patriarchist knowledge has functioned simultaneously to validate Eurocentric judgements of various kinds including aesthetic while dis-qualifying those of others, and reminds us of the subjugation of knowl-edge pertaining to Black artists in general, and also of the counteraction of cultural nationalists (in particular) to that subjugation. The problem-atic of power and knowledge is clearly apparent in the juxtaposition of the language, ideologies and production of the ruling order of the art world and those of cultural nationalist ateliers, Afri-COBRA of Chicago and Weusi of New York (Gaither, 1989: 17–34), which avow the aesthe-tic values of African-American traditions. Most importantly the polemi-cal relationship between Eurocentric dominance and African-American resistance signifies the empowering function of speech/discourse in both established Eurocentric "regimes of thought" and in rupture, or what Foucault would call the "insurrection of subjugated knowledge" (Foucault, 1980: 81) of oppressed peoples, better known to us as our traditions which are by no means fixed.

In general, Foucault's analyses are especially insightful in elucidating what Black artists and cultural theorists have long articulated: that Eurocentric self-validating histories, theories, critiques, exhibitions and among other factors patronage function to (self) enthrone Eurocentric perspectives, aesthetic values and objects of European civilization that are historically derived from "the ancients"; meaning Greeks not Africans, Asians, or diverse people of color. They also help to explain how such judgements place art works by people of color low-down, or even below the "scale" of the self-validating Eurocentric hierarchy. What becomes particularly clear in the power-knowledge construct is the critical interplay of knowledge, identity, speech and power that decides the visibility and invisibility of subjects. But above all in relation to Black women artists, it underscores the need for a specific site wherein the insurrection of subjugated knowledge pertaining to Black women artists could occur and deploy qualitative interpretations of its subjects.[22]

The proposed discourse must assert language to refashion dominance in its various forms without losing sight of the critical art-historical component wherein the recovery of empirical data, the exchange of the knowledge derived from them and the construction and inscription of texts based on them must occur. Essentially, the challenge of opposition cannot overshadow the challenge of construction. Literary critic Henry Gates urges us "to address the political black signified, that is, the cultural vision and critical language that underpin the search through literature and art for a profound reordering and humanizing of every-day existence" (Gates, 1992: 82). Given such challenges, a Black feminist art-historical discourse must intervene in existing knowledge/s with new subjects, canons and methods that will provide new facts about and analyses of the lives, production and interventions of Black women artists. Ultimately it would contribute to the revision of art history and criticism, art education, museum practices and other oppressive institutionalized operatives that are fast becoming outdated with changing demographics.

As an apparatus for change, the proposed discourse would be directed by the ideological proclivities of the speaking subjects. Any attempt to centralize it in existing discourses (at this stage) would be antithetical to the goal of circulating, synthesizing and debating the knowledge of artists/scholars and others who are seriously interested in the art, lives and interventions of Black women artists since existing discourses maintain other priorities;[23] our marginality in those discourses is totally unacceptable. As the major site wherein the knowledge/s of Black women artists, artists/scholars and art historians, and others would be exchanged, the discourse would adhere to its immanent objective to circulate knowledge, language, power for its Black women subjects, thus ultimately contributing to the "new growth" of a more comprehensive art history and larger art world practice.

THEORIZING BLACK FEMINISM/S: AN ARTIST/ SCHOLAR SPEAKS

My search for a discourse and critique appropriate to understanding the thoughts, cultural production and interventions of Black women artists has led me to the domain of knowledge of Black feminist theory, criticism, history and practice, wherein I found that the historical gaps and silences of Black women were displaced by Black women's visibility in intelligible analyses and acts informed by a distinctive critical gaze/s that simultaneously consider/s race, class, gender and sexuality.[24] Black feminist theory, unlike any other, prioritizes the knowledge and interests of Black women as it makes available critical thought about their oppression, self-definition, self-determination and intervention by presenting a wide range of analyses that engage social, historical, cultural, economic, literary and psychoanalytical theory and empirical facts. Critical thought about our art engages our material conditions and cultural attitudes among other factors which are commonplace considerations in discourses on Black feminist theory, therefore sharing much common intellectual ground with the knowledge in this interdisciplinary area.

In spite of the commonalities among Black women that are grounded in shared historical conditions, the multiplicity of positions articulated in debates within Black feminist theory reveals divergent critical stances that are healthy for scholarly growth. Particularly irreconcilable at this point (perhaps for ever) are arguments pointing out problems of hetero-

240

sexism and unacknowleged imperialism based in theoretical differences among constructionists, essentialists, cultural nationalists, lesbian critiques, complementarists and so on.

The constructionist stance which rejects any notion of essentialism or innatism is clearly presented by sociologists King and Collins who emphasize the importance of socially constructed material conditions (especially African-American) as a framework for investigation. White assumes a Black feminist historical materialist perspective in her specific critique of the oppositional debates on African-American history and culture and in her anti-essentialist stance observes, "Black feminists do not have an essential, biologically-based claim on understanding black women's experience since we are divided by class, region, and sexual orientation. Even we have multiple identities that create tensions and contradictions among us. We need not all agree nor need we all speak with one voice" (E. F. White, 1990: 82). Concurring, literary theorist Hazel Carby stresses the importance of recognizing both diversity and specificity in Black feminist thought: "We must be historically specific and aware of the differently oriented social interests within one and the same sign community. In these terms, black and feminist cannot be absolute, transhistorical forms (or form) of identity" (Carby, 1987: 17). Specificity means recognizing the particular historical and social constructs that contribute to the production of the material conditions, objects and ephemeral forms of Black women and others.

Essentialism, the binary opposition of constructionism, "is most commonly understood as a belief in the real, true essence of things, the invariable and fixed properties which define the 'whatness' of a given entity" (Fuss, 1989: xi). In her germinal essay "Toward a Black Feminist Criticism" in 1977,[25] literary critic, publisher and activist Barbara Smith presented the need for a Black feminist critique that would take into account race, gender, class and sexuality, create a "climate in which Black lesbian writers [could] survive" and develop analyses appropriate to the eye of a "woman-identified-women" (Smith, 1982: 173). Smith's call asserted the importance of identity and experience as essential to the proposed critique which necessitated an interlocking political movement (Smith, 1982: 159). Her perspective was somewhat similar to the cultural/political critiques of Euro-cultural feminists who articulated an essential female experience during that period and also recalls arguments of cultural nationalists of the late 1960s (and beyond) who defined and debated its relationship to "Black art" and "Black culture." But most importantly, Smith's discussion broke the silence on heterosexism in dominant and oppositional discourses.

Though path-breaking, Smith's "blueprint" is criticized by Black feminists for various reasons. Literary critic Deborah McDowell questions whether a "lesbian aesthetic" approach might not be too reductive and whether the question of identity might impose a "separatist" problematic along with other issues (McDowell, 1980: 153–9). Hazel Carby posits critiques that overlay those of McDowell, though she also criticizes McDowell's "mystifying" methodology. In assessing both Smith's and Black feminist criticism in general, she rejects the "reliance on common, or shared, experience," and the assumption of a Black female language and African-American canonicity (Carby, 1987: 16). Alternatively, Carby's constructionist stance stresses the need for a "material account of the cultural production" of Black women in "societies that are structured in dominance by race, class and gender," and in addition, for specificity in the investigation of sexuality ideologies and other questions in Black feminist theory and criticism (Carby, 1987: 18). This cursory consideration of various viewpoints within Black feminist theory, particularly the dominant constructionist and essentialist issues, reveals overlapping and divergent positions that are critical to an understanding of the complexities of Black feminist thoughts, conditions and productions and also of the importance of working across the boundaries of disciplines in that quest. The common factors in the debates among literary theorists and sociologists are interactive with the debates among artists, art historians, curators and others who consider questions of identity, creative production, canonicity and the African-continuum among other issues. Given the groundwork that has been laid in those areas, their debate can critically inform developments in the arts.

My own position in this debate is that essentialism, constructionism and other stances warrant more careful investigation. It seems that closure on essentialism is premature at this juncture particularly since serious debates within Black feminist theory have hardly begun. As we explore issues of race, gender, class and sexuality, we must recognize that both natural and socially constructed factors are inextricably bound, and are of such complexity that the various issues within and beyond the debate of that binary opposition require greater scrutiny than time has allowed. Will constructionism remain the prevailing tenet in Black feminist theory? An increasing number of voices are emerging to contribute to this discussion.

In addition to the given dynamics in Black feminist theorizing, the problem of heterosexism and imperialism needs to be interrogated. Feminist discourse could learn much by consistently engaging lesbian critiques which are, in fact, feminist critiques. Clearly as we oppose the domination of Euro-patriarchists, Afri-patriarchists and Euro-feminists, we ironically assert domination of a different order in our heterosexist assumptions and language about which we must be more critical.

Theorist/poet Andre Lorde's adamant claim of speech and the distinctive subjects of her speech exemplifies the centrality of lesbian critiques to Black feminist theory. For example, her powerful yet simple, very personal statement made in 1977 at the Modern Language Association effectively drew attention to the alarming reality of one's mortality, and to the tragedy of the unspoken word of the living body: "My silences had not protected me. Your silence will not protect you" (Lorde, 1984: 41). Lorde's piercing words were/are especially empowering to disempowered women who were/are afraid to speak, and especially to Black women artists who are prominent among disempowered women. She continued:

> What do you need to say? What are the tyrannies you swallow day by day and attempt to make your own, until you will sicken and die of them, still in silence? Perhaps for some of you here today, I am the face of one of your fears. Because I am woman, because I am Black, because I am lesbian, because I am myself – a Black woman warrior poet doing my work – come to ask you, are you doing yours?
>
> (Lorde, 1984: 42)

Lorde's words are especially pertinent to Black women artists for they underscore the severity of our silence. In addition to interrogating the Euro-patriarchy and others about our buried histories, we must also question our own silence and fears which contribute to our own absence in artwriting and negation in this world.

Black feminist theory seeks to explain how both positive and negative factors have influenced and been influenced by the interventions of Black women in their social structures, as it challenges the hierarchies of powers within those structures. It stimulates debate about Black women's heroic acts of self-determination: abolitionism, suffrage, temperance, racial uplift, painting, teaching, among other roles that evince their existence, achievement and outright rebellion. It also stimulates thought about the longevity of our oppression through various periods of history: forced migration-enslavement, forced labor, breeding rape, self-gratifying rape, mythologized imagery, beatings, lynching and death among other types of domination, along with our resistance to them. By enlarging such issues, Black feminist theory coalesces with Black feminist history, criticism and social practice to clarify relevant ideological and political formations that are essential to the survival, challenges and future developments in Black women's lives and interventions in society.

Theories function to explain and challenge "patterns of cultural power" (Ferguson, 1990: 5). Eagleton explains that theory "on a dramatic scale happens when it is both possible and necessary for it to do so – when the traditional rationales which have silently underpinned our daily practices stand in danger of being discredited, and need either to be revised or discarded" (Eagleton, 1990: 26). Black feminist theorizing occurs because we Black women are very aware of our historical oppressive conditions, and given that awareness we find it not only both possible and necessary to be self-reflexive about them, but also both possible and necessary to change them. In articulating that awareness, in Busia's words, we recognize that we "are speaking from a state of Siege" (Busia, 1988: 2). Black feminist theorizing illuminates the diverse circumstances of that siege as it conjoins the social praxis to confront problems inherent in our material conditions and culture, and subsequently to project emancipatory thought and action on our own behalf.

Though the perspective of Black feminist theory requires knowledge of Black women's social history, its utilization as a tool of investigation does not imply acceptance of the base-superstructure model of historical determinism that is found in the social history of art. Such a model constructs art as sign or expression of determinants that occur in the economic base of society; i.e. as the "epiphenomenon of base action" (Bryson *et al.*, 1991: 67). My interest in Black women's material conditions is derived from the understanding of art as an integral component of the social structure wherein those conditions are produced. Historian/art historian Jan Vansina observes that art cannot be viewed as an object situated in a cultural milieu (Vansina, 1984: 121); rather, it has to be seen as an integral part of its social structure. Nor can I see art situated above that social structure, emerging from the dictates of economic imperatives, a view more related to Marxist analyses. In any case, the primacy of economics in such an approach is much too limited since a Black feminist stance necessarily takes into account the simultaneity/ multiplicative factor of race, gender, class and sexuality. The main point here is that Black feminist theory presupposes an historical knowledge of Black women's material conditions and culture. Given that art is material culture that is interactive with those conditions, a systematic investigation of the interrelationship between the art, artists, larger historical conditions and Black women's particular circumstances among other factors must be significantly considered in the construction of a critical art history that centers Black women artists. Art is neither a mere reflection of historical events, nor a mere instrument of ideology, though it cannot be divorced from either; most importantly, it actively contributes to the social structure wherein it is situated.

Given that the work of Black women artists (and of others as well) is interactive with the multiple factors of their existence, and therefore cannot be substantively studied in isolation from the sociological, psychological and other aspects of Black women's material realities, Black feminist theory becomes a critical tool for exploring contextual questions pertaining to their identity and production. Its critiques of patriarchy, race, gender, class, sexuality and imperialism are especially important in this regard. Overall, the conceptual focus, fact-finding and analytical methods derived from Black feminist theorizing and praxis underscore the relevance of both to formulating a critical art history of Black women's artistic production.

Given that the act of theory targets history, then joins it in the process of altering it (Eagleton, 1990: 27), theorizing for Black women inscribes its distinctive critical subjectivities. Its inscription constructs a position from which to negotiate the circulation of knowledge and actions of, by and about Black women and other subjects of interest. But it must be clear that the "joining" of the history after the "targeting" in the discipline of art history and the dominant art world would in itself remain polemical for the theorizing of Black feminism/s has never and can never simply assimilate into bodies of knowledge, nor can it at any point become fixed; it historically changes according to need. It would assert its critical difference by inserting contrasting viewpoints, reiterating the abnormalcy of the European "normalcy" in art world and other discourses. The juxtaposition of our interpretations with those of Euro-patriarchists (and others) exposes a critical difference in aesthetic values that is inextricably bound to differences in specific histories and cultures. Black feminist theorizing, in this regard, emphatically declares that historical and cultural knowledge are essential to the understanding and appreciation of the art object and other phenomena pertaining to art. It therefore stimulates thought about cultural difference/conflict as it questions the legitimacy of critical judgement that emerges from one position within cultural conflict to judge the "Other" that it has veiled, and therefore has yet to understand.

Black feminist theorizing to date has given minimal attention to art and where it has, the focus is on popular art and culture; i.e film, video and music.[26] Michele Wallace and bell hooks are the most prominent scholars, particularly in film criticism. Their theories intersect with the artwriting of historians, curators, artists and others who have given particular attention to visual and/or performing art by Black women.[27]

Given the precedent that Black feminist theorizing has established in subjectivizing the thought and challenges of Black women, and given its analytical approach, it is evident that a discourse and critique that center the art of Black women artists would benefit tremendously from its perspective/s.

A WORKING BLACK FEMINIST CRITIQUE OF THE VISUAL ARTS

The critique within the proposed Black feminist art-historical discourse would constitute a significant component of a critical art history. Because of the differences between art history and criticism, the former concerned with the reconstruction of the history of the art objects and the latter with an evaluative response to the art objects that are recovered by

245

art history, the two disciplines are recognized as separate yet interrelated (Ackerman, 1963: 162). However, art historians necessarily make critical evaluation that goes beyond basic art-historical methods, and critics significantly contribute to the development of art history; hence the boundary is sometimes problematic. Within the proposed discourse, criticism must be developed along with Black women's art history (African-American, British, Nigerian, etc.) since the latter is hardly known. Pre-eminent is the archeological recovery of buried art objects and lives, and the description and systematization of relevant empirical data both diachronically and synchronically. This project includes the discovery, description and attribution of art works to artists and their particular historical periods among other problems. The fundamental task is to locate and organize a vast body of data for study, interpretation and evaluation. Essentially, the significance of this beginning phase for Black women artists would mean the systematic recovery and historicizing of their work, little of which has been done to date. Most of what has been written lies within the history of African-American art, is secondary to male production, and for the most part is without critiques of class, gender and sexuality, though racial and aesthetic difference are traditionally considered in discussions of style, historical periods, and cultural and political movements.

Inextricably bound to the task of historicism is the formulation of analytical methods that would contribute to an understanding of the polyvalent production of Black women artists and to other scholarly/ social interests of the Black feminist imagination/s. As art historian Michael Pondro expounds, the archeological question requires us to "provide answers on diverse matters of fact, on sources, patronage, purposes, techniques, contemporaneous responses and ideals"; while the critical history itself requires us to examine questions of sustained purposes and interests that are "both [irreducible] to the conditions of their emergence as well as [inextricable] from them" (Pondro, 1989: xviii). Hence a careful balance of formal and extra-formal investigations must constitute a significant element in the proposed critique. Analyses of form, iconography and iconology, engaged in that critique, should consider integrally the simultaneity-multiplicative construct of race, class, gender and sexuality, a consideration beyond conventional criticism which is largely formalist in its focus on the intrinsic qualities of the art object, though new art history and criticism both include and move beyond formalism (Flemming, 1991: 8).

Art educator Paulette Flemming criticizes the conventional art critics who "in vernacular and academic settings arbitrate meaning, significance, and value of art forms, stabilizing meaning or offering new insight into those forms with which they are familiar and explaining and evaluating those with which they are unfamiliar" (Flemming, 1991: 9).

She calls attention to the inadequate perspectives in existing art criticism, attributing them to the lack of research and theory development in its fundamental teaching. Her critique of enthroned models of criticism in the educational system such as E. Feldman's "critical performance" (description, analysis, interpretation and evaluation) and H. S. Broudy's "aesthetic scanning" (discussions of sensory, formal, expressive, and technical qualities) and others (Flemming, 1991: 9) reveals the limitations of those approaches, as does her interrogation of criticism's claim of universality based on the belief that "the aesthetic experience, formal qualities of the art object, and pansocial human activities" are universally accessible (Flemming, 1991: 9). Flemming's rejection of the cultural elitism and legitimacy given to "certain artworlds" overlays that of Black feminist theory in general as does her reiteration of the need to recognize cultural difference and the subjective response to aesthetic experience; qualities in which art criticism must engage if it is to be pluralistically valid.

Functionalist and contextualist theories are important to the proposed Black feminist critique, though at present apt to show limitations with greater focus on extrinsic factors sometimes to the detriment of intrinsic and historical considerations. Africanists, for example, utilize functionalism and contextualism to concentrate on art and cultural phenomena, often focusing on a specific ethnic area wherein they give primary attention to ritual, audience and symbolism, and their collective significance. Historian/art historian Jan Vansina criticizes the limitation of this conventional anthropological ahistorical approach and calls for the inscription of an historical (diachronic) approach to the study of African art (Vansina, 1984).

Marxist archeological and critical scholarship, which overlaps the Africanist, is also useful to a Black feminist critique though its emphasis on the economic base of social history and its insistence on the instrumental value of art to society are somewhat problematic. The Marxist and functionalist/contextualist critiques of African art are especially relevant to those of cultural nationalists, particularly in regard to the latter's concern with the social value of Black aesthetics and the functions of art and artists in society; as the work and philosophy of the Afri-COBRA group demonstrate (Thorson, 1990: 26–31). An examination of selected social issues along with the examination of art objects contributes to understanding the dynamics of events and attitudes of historical periods in relation to the themes and styles of art objects, and the ideologies of artists. This means that investigations of art must include intrinsic and extrinsic analyses.

Feminist analyses in general are assumed to be fundamental to a Black feminist critique in that they raise questions of gender in formal, contextual, psychoanalytical or other critical approaches. Their interrogation of patriarchy, elitism and classism is especially useful; however, the assumed Europeanisms of British Marxist scholars that suppress or dismiss critical awareness of the art of people of African descent reveal their limitations.[28] Some American feminist critiques also fail on the issue of race,[29] others do ascribe to minimal inclusion with discussions of art by African-American women in the USA and/or the inclusion of essays by Black women art historians, critics, etc.[30]

What is especially important about the various voices of contextualism and functionalism is a fundamental rejection of the formalist paradigm of modernist criticism that Roger Fry, Clive Bell, Clement Greenberg and other critics dogmatically utilized, convinced that appreciation of the art object must rest on its intrinsic values, i.e. its "significant form" alone.[31] Such rejection coalesces with the conventions of such African-Americanist scholars as philosopher Alain Locke and art historians artists James Porter, David Driskell, Samella Lewis and Richard Powell, whose critical approaches synthesize formalism and contextualism from diverse perspectives to document and integrally interpret form, content, social and cultural meanings, audiences and reception among other factors.[32] African-Americanist approaches in the area of art history and criticism are most relevant to the proposed critique since their investigations engage material culture and social history that include the issue of race and more recently gender in the archeological recovery of the lives and works of Black women and men.

Contextualism and functionalism, as Africanist anthropologist Warren d'Azevedo explains, alert us to the importance of understanding both the art object's aesthetic qualities and the context in which it originates: "The significance of any object – its 'form' – can be ascertained only with reference to the esthetic values of the members of a given sociocultural system for whom it functions esthetically" (d'Azevedo, 1958: 702–14).

Black feminist art criticism must both utilize aspects of existing paradigms and introduce new ways of thinking about art as it inserts its distinctiveness in subjects and perspectives, to: (1) assert the visibility and production of Black women artists in the USA and in other areas of the African diaspora and Africa, uncovering and documenting their lives, works and interventions in society; (2) reject any question of universal truth or beauty since its basic assumption is that art is interactive with the specific cultural values of the context in which it originates and to which it contributes; (3) recognize the importance of both the African continuum and the European continuum in the development of African-American art which, in fact, is American art; (4) reject the established hierarchy of materials extant in conventional art history, and alternatively recognize the diversity in the artistic production (fine art, crafts and popular) by academic and nonacademic artists and assume that each has to be evaluated in terms of its particular form, function and value to its audience/s; (5) examine representation, particularly in regard to the history and politics of race, gender, class and sexuality; (6) speak across the boundaries of race, class, gender, sexuality, age and discipline, to be enriched by and to enrich existing knowledge; (7) remain open to utilizing aspects of conventional methods (style-iconography-iconology) and revised approaches (influenced by literary criticism, anthropology, sociology, psychology and interrelated political movements) while exploring new ways to inscribe and critique a yet to be written critical history of art of Black women artists.

Given its anticipated performative function, a Black feminist critique would resist the basic assumptions in the canons of art history that identify artists as "great"/inspired "geniuses" and their art as "masterpieces", an idea highly influenced by Florentine culture and derived from the ideals of ancient Greek models (Vasari, 1987: vii). Its interrogation of the canon would recognize that the current exclusionary art world practices are based on judgements derived from Eurocentric art-historical knowledge, particularly that developed during the Italian Renaissance with artist/art historian Giorgio Vasari's publication, *Le Vite de'più eccellenti Pittori, Scultori e Architettori Italiani* [Lives of the most excellent Painters, Sculptors and Architects]; dated 1550 and expanded 1568. Because of its official standardization of the discipline of art history, Vasari's *Lives* has been identified as "perhaps the most important book on the history of art ever written" (Osborne, 1987: 1177). Art historian Hans Belting observes that Renaissance art historiography "erected a canon of values, and in particular a standard of ideal or classic beauty," a norm of historical progress toward "a universal classicism, against which all other epochs are to be measured" (Belting, 1987: 8). In her resistant reading art historian Nannette Solomon surmises, "Vasari introduced a structure or discursive form that, in its incessant repetition, produced and perpetuated the dominance of a particular gender, class, and race as the purveyors of an art and culture" (Solomon, 1992: 223). A Black feminist critique would reject the preeminence and persistence of that influence and its adverse impact on art history texts, university curricula and museums throughout the world, and especially in art world practices that enthrone art/artifacts of European cultures while devaluing those of people of color (see Lewis, 1982: 42).

Art historian John Tagg reminds us that any adequate critique of art history must critique not only its paradigm of art, but also its "repertoire of legitimate objects with which art histories have engaged," since art history "operates with and defends a given definition of its object of knowledge, while limiting the permissible methods for constructing and establishing such knowledge" (Tagg, 1992: 42–3). African-Americanists and Euro-feminists have already legitimated their own forms in their publications, museums, galleries, exhibitions and other networks, but Black women artists have minimally benefited from these developments. Ultimately, the concept "canon" has to be challenged with the question "Whose canon?" By recognizing canonicity within constructs of its particular culture, whether Italian Renaissance or Yoruba antiquities, the critical art historian must reject universalizing tendencies, and work toward constructing analyses based on informed judgements that are validated by cultural grounding.

Material cultural theory would be particularly useful here for it raises many questions beyond conventional approaches that would allow the incorporation of vernacular forms into art history. Jules D. Prown informs us that material culture refers to manmade artifacts as well as to the study of beliefs through artifacts, of "values, ideas, attitudes, and assumptions – of a particular community or society at a given time" (Prown, 1982: 1–18). The inclusion of vernacular forms by pioneer African-American James Porter set the precedent for considering crafts with fine arts. An understanding of vernacular forms is highly significant to the development of a critical art history of African-American art for pottery, basketry, quiltmaking and others provide primary evidence of historical, material and aesthetic links to the history of African-American fine arts in the USA, and links to the past/African heritage; i.e. African art, aesthetics and cultural elements that entered the country with enslaved Africans during forced migration and slavery. Material culture as discussed by John Vlach, Robert Thompson and others offers some direction for the proposed critique; however, they fall short of gender analyses though women's material production is included. We must go beyond mere inclusion.

Given the precedent in African-American art history surveys to include both "fine art" and "folk art" and the interrelated qualities of the two, the proposed critical art history must carefully inscribe both and show how they contribute to the overall picture, but with greater depth. It would resist the problematic assumption of a hierarchy in materials, recognizing that the life and work of nineteenth-century Harriet Powers (1837–1911), an enslaved and later "freed" quilter of Athens, Georgia, are as important for investigation as those of Edmonia Lewis (c. 1845–c. 1911), a "free" woman of color who produced marble sculpture in the neo-classical tradition during the same period. Both artists significantly participated in the shaping of the history of African-American art and both interacted within their various contexts to make an imprint that merits attention. Powers is often excluded and Lewis often included in Euro-feminist and African-American art-historical scholarship, though brief discussion of quilting and other craft traditions occurs; but Powers is included and Lewis excluded in the work of material culturalists. A Black feminist critique must carefully review the data of both, and of those who produce on either side of the "fine art"/"craft" boundary, in order to reconstruct the proposed critical art history.

The craft tradition is significant material evidence of woman's personal expression, aesthetic taste, productive labor, and intervention in her given social structure. Crafted forms constitute a functional body of work that was and remains interactive with fine arts in the larger scheme of development in African-American women's art history and often signify a Black woman's difference in artistic production, raising the debate of essentialism and constructionism. Regardless of the stance there taken, a distinct expressiveness in quiltmaking forms by Black women has become well known through the scholarship of Maude Wahlman, John Vlach, Reginia Perry, Eli Leon and others. Specific identifiable qualities in quiltmaking traditions[33] and other African-American folk art forms are derived from conventional aesthetic values within the communities wherein those works are produced and whose aesthetic and moral tastes they, in turn, influence. Vernacular values are diffused with the migration of African-Americans (including fine artists), for Black women took their traditional skills with them and generally passed them on to their daughters.[34]

But simply inscribing folk, fine art and popular art by Black women artists is not enough to justify the uniqueness of a Black feminist critique. Here the multiplicative-simultaneity factor of race, gender, class and sexuality requires specific attention, in regard to Black women's work, the works of others and many critical issues.

A brief contextual consideration of nineteenth-century artists Harriet Powers and Edmonia Lewis will exemplify the potential instrumental value of a Black feminist critique in the production of a critical art history.

Lewis was northern, "free" (not enslaved), college-educated, "privileged" (access to limited economic and patriarchal power) and single (free of man and child); Powers was enslaved and later emancipated, "uneducated," without privilege (money and power), married and with children. Lewis was born possibly in New York, possibly in Greenhigh, Ohio; attended Oberlin College and later made her mark in art history, after expatriating to Rome in 1865; she is believed to have died there c. 1911. Powers, on the other hand, lived and died in Georgia. Little is known about her life or travel, except that she and her husband were landowners and that she was able to care for herself after his departure, perhaps through her farm animals and sewing abilities (Fry, 1990: 84–91). The works of both artists are preserved in major museum collections, though only two of Powers's are known; but Powers's works were powerful enough to launch her into posterity. Powers's quilts are, in fact, canonical works: they link African-American quilting traditions to African textile traditions (West and Central), though often compared specifically with the Fon appliqué of the Republic of Benin. The quilt shown (Figure 1) consists of fifteen rectangular and square motifs arranged in strip design, each framing human, animal, or astronomical silhouettes in high-contrast colors. The pictorial character that combines imagery from biblical, local history and social commentary is linked to the Fon appliqué in its structure, technique and narrative function. Its formal rhythmical style, combining both structured organization and improvisational qualities, reveals a dynamically controlled horizontal composition with limited color scheme, dominated by warm tonalities, though dramatically activated by its high-contrast design. Art historian Gladys-Marie Fry notes that Powers's "fascination with biblical animals and characters probably stemmed from hearing vivid sermons in church on Sundays" and that the core of Powers's religious imagery invoked biblical figures who "struggled successfully against overwhelming odds" (Fry, 1990: 84–5). Could this work perhaps be seen as a composition that expressed the artist's personal view of life, a view related to her desire to intervene in her contexts to present aesthetic beauty that articulated her particular sociopolitical stance? Is it possible to interpret the selection of particular empowered imagery, consonant with prevailing African-American religious-political metaphors of her period, as a practice expressive of her own individuality and shared "cultural memory" and material conditions? Representation of religious genre and historical events suggests this possibility. The Bible quilt is of special interest in this regard. How might such imagery be interpreted in light of Powers's low economic status, strong religious beliefs, and her victimization by slavery, racism and patriarchy? Such thoughts would be invoked and investigated in a Black feminist critique.

The question of subject-matter in Lewis's work is also important in addition to form and context. Hagar, for example, though different in materials and style from Powers's biblical imagery, faced tremendous odds as the Egyptian maidservant of Hebrew Sarah, wife of Abraham. Renita Weems calls attention to Hagar's symbolism; slave woman, powerless, reproductive/exploited/manipulated body, unprotected, cast out into the desert with her son/Abraham's son; a story of victimization. Yet Lewis, daughter of a Chippewa mother (who remained in her environment and maintained her life-style) and an African-American butler father, rendered Hagar in an ennobled dramatic gesture, subverting the oppressive imagery of Hagar and in a sense of oppressed people of color as did other African-American women such as educator Anna Julia Cooper (1858–1964), who "authored the first black feminist analysis of the condition of blacks and women" (Guy-Sheftall, 1990: 25). Lewis's works intervened in public spaces in exhibitions to assert the dignified representation of Black, Native American and biblical figures (Figure 2), displaying a resonance that radically expanded conventions of her neo-

Figure 1 Quilt by Harriet Powers, *c.* 1895–8; 69 × 105″, containing 15 squares; cotton, with appliquéd detail of biblical and astronomical silhouettes in high-contrast colors. Museum of Fine Arts, Boston, Mass.

classical style beyond Greek influence. Her sculpted marble forms, characteristically ennobling Black and Native American subjects in gesture and overall effect with a characteristic dramatic grandeur, were oppositional to prevailing degrading representations of Black people in the popular Euro-patriarchist media that proliferated during her period (Lemons, 1977: 102–16). They also differed from the hierarchically encoded and delimited representations of Black subjects by fine artists of European descent.[35] In referring to Hagar (1875), Lewis noted that the subject-matter was inspired by her "strong sympathy for all women who have struggled and suffered" (Hartigan, 1985: 94). The empowered presentment of the form immediately calls to mind the strong female biblical characters of African-American orators and educators who synthesized religious beliefs and political resistance. Though her work adheres to the European canon, some of her subject-matter and its iconography emerge from specific lived experience, social conditions and interpretations interactive with those experiences and conditions.

The form and meaning in the works of Powers and Lewis reveal that the artists intervened in their contexts with their own particular Black feminist or womanist voice and drew upon shared cultural and social attitudes not unrelated to their shared racial identities. Their materials are related to the class and opportunities available to each, while their aesthetic effect is related to the qualities that most appealed to their individual sensitivities. Meaning and associative values in the two works substantiate the point that "low" craft and "high" fine art traditions in the history of African-American art interpenetrate each other and are both essential to the critical art history of Black women's art.

Unlike Powers, who apparently "stayed put" as wife and mother, and unlike Black women of the intelligentsia, Cooper and Stewart, who grounded themselves in the ideals of the "Cult of True Womanhood" of the nineteenth century as they fought for the rights of Black women and men, Lewis chose to bypass such ideals and, independent of children, men and the "Cult", became a member of the "White, Marmorean Flock" of American women sculptors in Rome (Thorp, 1959), where she reportedly exhibited her "strong-mindedness" (Hartigan, 1985: 94) though tenuously regarded as an "exotic" other.

By reviewing the imprint of these important nineteenth-century figures, one can resist the canonical debate of high *v.* low art and begin to think with greater depth about the importance of fine art and craft to African-American life and history and to the construction of a critical art history that centers the lives and production of Black women artists.

The question that art historian Linda Nochlin asked in 1971, "Why Have There Been No Great Women Artists?"[36] assumes that greatness is defined by the ideology of the speaker and his/her constituency, and therefore remains problematic. A Black feminist critique would instead

Figure 2 "Hagar" by Edmonia Lewis, 1875; 52⅝ × 15¼ × 17″; marble sculpture of the biblical exiled Egyptian maidservant. Smithsonian Institution, National Museum of American Art, Washington, DC.

ask who were/are Black women artists; what styles, subject-matter and meanings did they produce in their various forms; how did their specific circumstances contribute to or restrict their production; how did those works intervene in the society of which they were a part; what was their particular reception; where, by whom and why? Questions pertaining to Black women's simultaneous production (art)/reproduction (children) roles and those addressing woman-identified-women must be integrally explored. Simultaneously it must debunk historical racialist theories that promoted "Negro" inferiority with articulations that declared the "Negro's inability to produce art though having a 'natural talent for music'" (Fredrickson, 1971: 105), theories fundamental to the current exclusionism extant in the art world today for they reinforce the stereo-typed idea that while African-Americans might appear to appreciate the visual art, they were/are "manifestly unable to produce it" (Hartigan, 1985: 73). Such myths cannot be ignored though they cannot be the focus of discussion in a Black feminist critique.

As Black women artists speak and work throughout the country today, they reveal cultural and political commonalities that are coextensive with their shared histories and material conditions, though their differences are apparent in the individuality of their personalities and vision. Their different styles, media, themes, reputations and professional roles dis-play a heterogeneous body of work that ranges from abstract formalized structures meant to invoke mere aesthetic contemplation, to evocative performance pieces which synthesize aesthetic and extra-aesthetic quali-ties that are intended to activate immediate political responses from the spectator. No monolithic quality defines their style, though there is often some reference to their identities, and beyond the work itself, a commonality in the race and gender of those identities; also class and sexuality though perhaps more variable. It is their identity, in fact, that situates them outside of dominant art history and at the periphery of the art establishment. Those locations and the artists' response to them are coextensive with their collective history, culture and ideologies that link them to each other and to other African-American women in the USA, past and present. To engage these various aspects of Black women artists' lives and works is the challenge of a Black feminist critique and the larger art-historical discourse. Until that particular discourse is constructed, Black women artists and their production will remain be-hind the veils of art history. But as we collectively activate our knowledge and power, we can inscribe new discourses on art wherein we can locate our histories and construct critiques that will appropriately inscribe our lives, production and interventions in this world.

NOTES

1 Art history is a discipline that regulates the scholarly investigation of selected works of art and the historical evidence pertaining to them. The discipline systematically focuses on the fine art and lives of men of European descent. It chronicles developments of works of art (primarily painting, sculpture and architecture) by styles and periods, giving attention to form (structure), iconography (meaning), iconology (subject-matter, meaning and cultural attitudes), biography and historical contexts among other concerns. Its conventional purpose is to provide knowledge about developments of "major works" "masterpieces" by "major figures" "geniuses" and ultimately to influence appreciation of them. Despite much debate over the past twenty years about its racial and gender biases, little has been done to alter the exclusion of people of color in the basic texts, professional journals, museum practices, etc. The art of African-Americans and various people of color (excepting forms of Africa often designated as "primitive") remain virtually excluded. The past decade, however, has seen an increasing number of exhibitions of the art of people of color, an influence perhaps of the rhetoric of multiculturalism, but group exhibitions are disproportionately male and the solo exhibition is invariably a "one man show". Criticism is integrally related to art history, though it produces evaluative responses to art objects. Such responses are grounded in the art-historical knowledge and cultural values/biases/subjectivities of the critics who are, by and large, Eurocentric in their orientation.

2 The patriarchy of men of European descent that regulates the art world operates a hierarchical system that asserts Euro-male superiority and domination over everyone else and the value of Euro-male production over that of others. In referring to the networking powers of Euro-male dominance, Elizabeth Grosz identifies three terms in particular that she says are not mutually exclusive: (1) sexism – an empirical phenomenon wherein women are treated as unequal to men; (2) patriarchy – a structure that "systematically evalutes masculinity in positive and femininity in negative terms"; (3) phallocentrism – two types, the first being modes of representation that reduce differences to a common denominator of masculinity, and the second a process of hierarchization wherein one sex is judged as better than its counterpart (Grosz, 1990: 152). See Royland and Klein, 1990: 277. The noted terms and definitions identify the character and operation of the dominant art world.

3 Artwriting is the term used by David Carrier (1991: introduction) to refer to texts by art historians and art critics.

4 The term "art world" generally refers to "universes of regularized responses" that "coalesce around the production, creation, distribution, and evalution of various" art works. See Vlach and Bronner, 1986: 1–10. The dominant art world (Euro-partriarchy) places emphasis on fine art, setting and regulating standards according to the particular interests of its controllers. Vlach and Bronner call attention to the networks of folk art and utilize the term "folk art worlds" to designate different aspects of the larger network that is yet another component of the overall multilayered system of art. The term "art worlds" is appropriate since there are others beside the dominant one; i.e. African-American, Euro-feminist, Africanist, Chicano/a, etc. Each of the structures, developed because of specific interest, reclaims and promotes the art of specific heritage/s as they interpenetrate the dominant art world, while

257

resisting devaluation and exclusion from museum and gallery spaces. I will use "art world" or "dominant art establishment" to refer to the ruling fine art world of the Euro-patriarchy.

5 See: Bontemps, 1980; Driskell, 1976; Lewis, 1990; Jones, 1990; Sims, 1990; Vlach, 1990.

6 Many Black women artists have articulated the problems that they encounter in the "art world", concurring that those problems are often related to race, gender and difference in aesthetic taste. See Piper, 1990b: 15–20.

7 Black women artists do not have to justify calling for a specific discourse wherein their own interests can become the central focus, but I expound on the hierarchical system of the dominant art world (which includes art history) in order to clarify its oppressiveness to artists of color, and to show how a Black feminist self-help discourse and subsequent continuous collective strategies could substantively empower and appropriately inscribe Black women's production and other specificities pertaining to their lives. The harshness and longevity of the political forces that Black artists and other people of color have consistently faced as they produced works of art and searched for spaces wherein to present them to the public, explains why throughout the country our works are seen primarily in the relatively few museums and galleries designated for people of color to somewhat remedy the problem of exclusion in the art world. While the latter are crucial for reaching particular communities whose visual forms have been de-legitimated by rulers of the dominant art world, there has to be a public outcry from the culturally subordinated (people of color) to confront the abuse of power, and the biased use of public money to fund exhibits near-exclusively of men and women of European descent; to elevate Euro-patriarchical values over all others. Black women are especially jeopardized by the biases against their race, gender and class.

8 I have presented various aspects of this paper at the following seminars and conferences: (1) Black Feminist Seminar, University of Wisconsin-Madison, 1990 (this paper was developed specifically for this forum); (2) Feminist Art History Conference, Barnard College, 1990; (3) College Art Association/ Women's Caucus for the Arts, Washington, DC, 1991; (4) Follow-up Black Feminist Seminar, Spelman College, Atlanta, Georgia, 1991.

9 Piper identifies specific comments made by Euro-American critics to illustrate Eurocentric biases, generalizations and impositions on African-American artists (often masked by utterances citing undefined notions of quality): Rosalind Krauss "doubts that there is any unrecognized African-American art of quality because if it doesn't bring itself to her attention, it probably doesn't exist"; Roberta Smith notes "that the real problem with the art of African-Americans is that it just isn't any good, that it would be in the mainstream galleries if it were, that she's been up to The Studio Museum in Harlem a couple of times and hasn't seen anything worthwhile, that it's all too derivative"; Hilton Kramer protests "the current interest in issues of race and gender that, he claims, leave quality by the wayside" (Piper, 1990b: 15–17). Such remarks are representative of the prevailing Eurocentric proclivities with which Black women, men and all people of color must contend; one has to question and critically interrogate uniformed/uneducated judgements by individuals who merely observe isolated objects with no historical depth. They reinforce the ongoing devaluation of Afro-American art from the beginning of an art history which is grounded in the cultural hegemony of Europeanism. The noted statements of the postmodernist era are, in fact, no

different from the negative Eurocentric critiques of modernism. We all remember Hilton Kramer from the 1960s with his hostilities toward Black art.

10 See: Flomenhaft, 1990; Wallace, 1984; Tesfagiorgis, 1987a (reproduced in Garrard and Boude, 1992).

11 See Tesfagiorgis, 1987a, for more in-depth discussion of Ringgold's work. On African-American art and culture, see Powell, 1989 and Thompson, 1983. For example, Thompson discusses the multiple meter in African-American music (derived from traditional African music) and the emphatic multistrip composition in African-American textiles (derived from textile traditions in various regions in Africa). Maultsby, 1990, extends her discussion of the interplay of aesthetics and function in African-American and African music to include the visuality of performance and calls attention to the "array of colors and fashions seen in concert halls, Black churches, and other Black performance sites" as well as the dynamics of body language and other visual qualities that she links to African traditions.

12 See Tesfagiorgis, 1989; an interview with Therese Mosoke, in Nairobi, Kenya where Mosoke lives.

13 Tesfagiorgis, 1987b: an interview with Sokari Douglas Camp, in London, UK, where Camp lives. I had the opportunity to interview Sokari Douglas Camp in her London studio where I also viewed her work and acquired minimal understanding of her conceptualizations and processes. (This research trip was funded by the University of Wisconsin Graduate School.) Later I was able to interact with her works in a formal display at her one-woman exhibition at the National Museum of African Art, Smithsonian (November 11, 1988–January 29, 1989).

14 Douglas briefly studied woodcarving with the neo-traditionalist Lamidi Fakeye, defying gender boundaries since woodcarving in Nigeria and other African countries is conventionally a male profession. She also briefly studied a powerful Kalabari priestess, Amonia Horsfall. Such opportunities were related to her Kalabari, Nigeria identity, academic training and somewhat outsider status given that she has lived in London much of her life though also in her hometown periodically.

15 In discussing the freedom that she feels by recognizing her "outsider" relationship to the dominant art world, particularly to the "tastemakers," Ringgold indicates that such a position negates their influence because "she is not a member of those groups who would profit from being on the cutting edge." "I'm not a man and I'm not white. So I can do what I want and that has been my greatest gift. It's kind of a backhanded gift, but it sets me free," she insists. See Flomenhaft, 1990: 15.

16 This concept expands sociologist Frances Beale's concept of "double jeopardy, double consciousness" that referred to the racism and sexism experienced by Black women. See King, 1988.

17 Collins, 1989. Not all Black women artists claim a Black feminist consciousness; in fact some disclaim it. The same is true of Black women in general. Other nomenclatures have been imposed to identify the assertive stance taken by Black women both to enact self-determination and to resist oppression; i.e. the term "womanist" was proposed by Alice Walker and Chikwenye Okonjo Ogunyemi, etc. "Afrofemcentrism," which I proposed as an either/or term for Black feminism, was rejected by theorist Molefi Asante (in discussions at the University of Wisconsin-Madison, December, 1991) because he viewed Afrocentrism as an ideology that encompassed the stance of men

and women; though he did note that gender differences were being discussed at Temple University where he was chair of the Department of
Afro-American Studies at the time. I will use "Black feminism", the prevailing term used to identify the currents of Black women's critical social engagement at various levels, as I continue to rethink Afrofemcentrism. However,
the various terms are not fixed, and regardless of what, if any, we settle on,
what matters is that Black women are articulating their empowerment in oral
and written form while actively asserting their thoughts and actions to
transform society.

18 For greater discussion of criticism see: Pepper, 1970; George Dickie,
Evaluating Art, Philadelphia, PA: Temple University Press, 1988; Jim
Cromen, *Criticism: History, Theory and Practice of Art Criticism in Art Education*,
Reston, VA: National Art Education Association, 1990.

19 In an exhibition catalogue, King-Hammond and Sims (1989: Introduction)
discuss the works of the thirteen exhibited multi-media artists, eleven of
them Black women and two Black men. The text's illuminating and insightful interpretations offer a minuscule view of the wealth of art by Black
women and men that remains largely hidden in the gaps of Eurocentric art
history, criticism and the larger art world.

20 Pondro, 1989. Pondro uses the term "critical art history" to signify artwriting
that includes art history and art criticism.

21 Bonding in various groups is a must for Black women artists, especially with
Africans, Native Americans, Chicano/as, Asian-Americans, Euro-feminists
and "radicals." What especially unites these various groups is their resistance
to the overt and covert racism in the art world. While intellectual exchange
across the cultures (through group discussions, exhibitions and political
strategies, etc.) is very important, it is also necessary that individuals discuss
shared problems which are particular to specific group identities. Of course
we Black women artists are greatly enriched by our culture; but that would
also be discussed in the proposed sustained discourse. Essentially as we need
to interact with various groups, we also need to interact among ourselves in
order to address our own specific shared conditions.

22 Busia discusses language as a tool of domination, particularly in relation to its
function in the European colonization of African countries. She notes that
language "can be and has been used as one of the central instruments of
Empire, as those who have been colonized know." Her assessment of language is applicable to the dynamics of domination and resistance in the art
world. See Busia, 1988: 6.

23 I have participated for many years in various professional sites where discourses are varied. Though diverse perspectives and lively debates ensued in
each site, certain ideologies prevailed that were regulated by the dominant
speaking subjects: College Arts Association (dominated by Euro-
patriarchists); National Conference of Artists (cultural nationalists/male and
female); Women's Caucus for the Arts (Euro-American feminists); Feminist
Art History Conference (Euro-American feminists); National Council of
Black Studies (African-Americanists of cultural nationalist proclivities);
African Studies Association (Euro-Africanists); Arts Council of African
Studies Association (Euro-Africanists with few African and African-
American Africanists). In the sites of each professional organization an
exciting body of knowledge circulates and I have learned from each. But
there is that glaring absence of Black women. When art historian Ann
Sutherland Harris enthusiastically proclaimed to the participants at the

Feminist Art History Conference in 1990 at Barnard College that "we had taken over art history," it was clear that the few people of color who were in that room in 1990 were as invisible to her then as they were/are in her exhibition and catalogue text (with Linda Nochlin), *Women Artists: 1550–1950* produced in 1976. While I did remind her and others that the "we" was a misnomer, the shock of that statement remains with me. Although Black women artists do, in fact, operate in various discourses, it is high time that we convened at a national level to talk academics and politics with each other.

24 See: Hull, Bell-Scott and Smith, 1982; Smith, 1983; Steady, 1981; Braxton and McLaughlin, 1990; Wall, 1989; Davies and Graves, 1986; Carby, 1987; hooks, 1981, 1984, 1990; Davis, 1981, 1989; Guy-Sheftall, 1990; Terborg-Penn, Harley and Rushing, 1989; D. G. White, 1985; Wallace, 1990.

25 This essay was first presented July 1977. Smith, 1982.

26 Michele Wallace's work is particularly insightful in this regard, especially her film criticism. Wallace makes it clear, for example, that as Black male film-makers join the workforce of Hollywood, their production also joins the existing practice of exploiting the images of Black women. The shift of authority from White to Black male producer/speaker extends the tradition of locking Black women into negative imagery that reduces them to passive, sexualized objects of various types. See Wallace, 1990.

27 Like Wallace, bell hooks is a significant cultural critic; see 1981, 1984 and especially 1990. See art historians/curators/artists: Lewis, 1984, 1990; Sims, 1990;, Jones, 1990; Wilson, 1988; Tesfagiorgis, 1990; Frieda High W. Tesfagiorgis, "Elizabeth Catlett," *Black Women in the United States: An Historical Encyclopedia*, Boston, Mass.: South End Press, 1993. Wallace and hooks are foremost among Black feminist theorists to discuss the visual arts. Their focus tends, however, to be on popular and folk art, though Wallace does include fine art. Black women art historians, curators and artists are significantly contributing to the recovery and reinscribing of the lives, works and interventions of Black women artists. Our task, however, has hardly begun.

28 See Pollock, 1988, and Wolfe, 1990.

29 Ann Sutherland Harris and Linda Nochlin (1976) definitely fail.

30 Chatwick, 1990; Garrard and Boude, 1992; Raven *et al.*, 1988.

31 Greenberg, 1965; Chipp, 1975.

32 See: Locke, 1925; Porter, 1943; Driskell, 1976; Lewis, 1990; Powell, 1989; Richard Powell, *Homecoming: The Art and Life of William H. Johnson*, Washington, DC: the National Museum of American Art, Smithsonian Institution, 1991; Robinson and Greenhouse, 1991; Wright and Reynolds, 1989; Campbell, 1985; Leon, 1987. Other catalogue texts: Studio Museum in Harlem, *Harlem Renaissance: Art of Black America*, New York: Harry N. Abrams, 1987; the Abby Aldrich Rockefeller Folk Art Center, *Joshua Johnson: Freeman and Early American Portrait Painter*, Williamsburg, MD: the Abby Aldrich Rockefeller Folk Art Center and Maryland Historical Society, 1987; Philadelphia Museum of Art, *Henry Ossawa Tanner*, New York: Rizzoli, 1991; Studio Museum in Harlem, *Memory and Metaphor: The Art of Romare Bearden, 1940–1987*, New York: Oxford University Press, 1991. Fortunately, there is an increasing interest in African-American art; the focus on male subjects and marginalization of women, however, need to be corrected.

33 Vernacular principles and such elements as color scheme (generally warm and high contrast), polyrhythms, strip design, and others have been defined and linked to specific qualities in various locations of Africa. See: Vlach,

1990; Thompson, 1983; Ferris, 1983; University Art Museum, University of Southwestern Louisiana, *Baking in the Sun: Visionary Images from the South*, Lafayette, LA, 1987; Wardlaw *et al.*, 1989; Tesfagiorgis, 1992: 28–37, 39.
34 Above texts reveal this pattern. Also see: Kunene-Pointer, 1985.
35 See Boime, 1990; Fredrickson, 1971; McElroy *et al.*, 1990.
36 This is a vital essay in feminist art history which was first published in 1971 and has been reprinted in Nochlin, 1988.

BIBLIOGRAPHY

Ackerman, J. (1963) "Western Art History," in his *Art and Archeology*, Englewood Cliffs, NJ: Prentice-Hall.
Belting, H. (1987) *End of Art History*, Chicago: University of Chicago Press.
Boime, A. (1990) *The Art of Exclusion: Representing Black in the Nineteenth Century*, Washington, DC: Smithsonian Press.
Bontemps, A. and J. (1980) *Forever Free: Art by African-American Women 1962–1980* (exhibition catalogue), Alexandria, VA: Stephenson.
Braxton, J. M. and McLaughlin, A. N. (eds) (1990) *Wild Women in the Whirlwind: Afro-American Culture and the Contemporary Literary Renaissance*, New Brunswick, NJ: Rutgers University Press.
Bryson, N., Holly, M. A. and Moxey, K. (eds) (1991) "Semiology and Visual Interpretation," in *Visual Theory: Painting & Interpretation*, New York: HarperCollins.
Busia, A. P. A. (1988) "Words Whispered over Voids: A Context for Black Women's Rebellious Voices in the Novel of the African Diaspora," *Studies in Black American Literature*, Volume III, *Black Feminist Criticism and Critical Theory*, ed. Joe Weixlman and Houston A. Baker, Jr, Greenwood, Fla: Penkevill.
Campbell, M. S. (1985) *Tradition and Conflict*, New York: Studio Museum in Harlem.
Carby, H. (1987) *Reconstructing Womanhood: The Emergence of the Afro-American Woman Novelist*, Oxford: Oxford University Press.
Carrier, D. (1991) *Principles of Art History Writing*, University Park, PA: Pennsylvania State University Press.
Chatwick, W. (1990) *Women, Art, and Society*, London: Thames & Hudson.
Chipp, H. (1975) *Theories of Modern Art: A Source Book by Artists and Critics*, Berkeley, CA: University of California Press.
Collins, P. H. (1989) "The Social Construction of Black Feminist Thought," *Signs: Journal of Women in Culture and Society* (4) (Summer): 745–73.
—— (1991) "Learning from the Outsider Within: The Sociological Significance of Black Feminist Thought," in *(En) Gendering Knowledge: Feminists in Academe*, ed. Joan E. Hartman and Ellen Messer-Davidow, Knoxville, Tenn.: University of Tennessee Press.
Davies, C. B. and Graves, A. A. (eds) (1986) *Ngambika: Studies of Women in African Literature*, Trenton, NJ: Africa World Press.
Davis, A. (1981) *Women, Race and Class*, New York: Random House.
—— (1989) *Women, Culture and Politics*, New York: Random House.
d'Azevedo, W. L. (1958) "A Structural Approach to Aesthetics: Toward a Definition of Art in Anthropology," *American Anthropologist* (5): 702–14.
Driskell, D. (1976) *Two Centuries of Black American Art* (exhibition catalogue), Los Angeles, CA: Los Angeles Country Museum.
—— (1987) "Speakeasy", *New Art Examiner* 15 (September): 13–15.

Eagleton, T. (1989) *Literary Theory: An Introduction*, Minneapolis, MN: University of Minnesota Press.

—— (1990) *The Significance of Theory*, Oxford: Basil Blackwell.

Failing, P. (1989) "Black Artists Today: A Case of Exclusion," *Art News* (March): 124–31.

Ferguson, R. (1990) "A Box of Tools: Theory and Practice", in *Discourses: Conversations in Postmodern Art and Culture*, ed. Russell Ferguson, William Olander, Marcia Tucker and Karen Fiss, Cambridge, Mass.: Massachusetts Institute of Technology.

Ferris, R. (ed.) (1983) *Afro-American Folk Art and Crafts*, Jackson, Miss.: University Press of Mississippi.

Flemming, P. (1991) "Pluralistic Approaches to Art Criticism," in *Pluralistic Approaches to Art Criticism*, ed. Doug Blandy and Kristin G. Congdon, Bowling Green, OH: Bowling Green State University Press: 60–5.

Flomenhaft, E. (1990) *Faith Ringgold: A 25 Year Survey*, Heightsend, LI: Fine Arts Museum of Long Island.

Foucault, M. (1980) *Knowledge/Power: Selected Interviews & Other Writings 1972–1977*, ed. Colin Gordon, New York: Pantheon Books.

Fowler, R. (1990) "Feminist Knowledge: Critique and Construct," in Sneja Gunew (ed.) *Feminist Knowledge: Critique and Construct*, London: Routledge: 13–35.

Fredrickson, G. M. (1971) *The Black Image in the White Mind: The Debate on Afro-American Destiny, 1817–1914*, New York: Harper & Row.

Fry, G.-M. (1990) "Harriet Powers: Portrait of an African-American Quilter," in *Stitched from the Soul: Slave Quilts from the Ante-Bellum South* (exhibition catalogue), New York: Dutton Studio Books in association with Museum of American Folk Art: 84–91.

Fuss, D. (1989) *Essentially Speaking: Feminism, Nature & Difference*, London: Routledge.

Gaither, E. (1989) "Heritage Reclaimed: An Historical Perspective and Chronology," in *Black Art: Ancestral Legacy: The African Impulse in African-American Art* (exhibition catalogue), Dallas, Tex.: Dallas Museum of Art: 11–54.

Garrard, M. D. and Boude, N. (1992) *The Expanding Discourse: Feminism and Art History*, New York: HarperCollins.

Gates, H. L., Jr (1992) *Loose Canons: Notes on the Culture Wars*, New York: Oxford University Press.

Greenberg, C. (1965) *Art and Culture: Critical Essays*, Boston, Mass.: Beacon Press.

Grosz, E. (1990) "Philosophy," in Sneja Gunew (ed.) *Feminist Knowledge: Critique and Construct*, London: Routledge: 59–120.

Guy-Sheftall, B. (1990) *Daughters of Sorrow: Attitudes Toward Black Women, 1880–1920*, Brooklyn: Carlson.

Harris, A. S. and Nochlin, L. (1976) *Women Artists: 1550–1950*, Los Angeles, CA: County Museum of Art; distrib. New York: Random House.

Hartigan, L. R. (1985) *Sharing Traditions: Five Black Artists in Nineteenth-Century America* (exhibition catalogue), Washington, DC: Smithsonian Institution Press.

hooks, b. (1981) *Ain't a Woman: Black Women and Feminism*, Boston, Mass.: South End Press.

—— (1984) *Feminist Theory: From Margin to Center*, Boston, Mass.: South End Press.

—— (1989) *Talking Back: Thinking Feminist, Thinking Black*, Boston, Mass.: South End Press.

—— (1990) *Yearning: Race, Gender, and Cultural Politics*, Boston, Mass.: South End Press.

Hull, G. T., Bell-Scott, P. and Smith, B. (eds) (1982) *All the Women are White, All the Blacks are Men, But Some of Us are Brave*, Old Westbury, NY: Feminist Press.

Johnson, B. E. (1989) *Afro-American Literary Study in the 1990s*, Chicago: University of Chicago Press.

Jones, K. (1990) "In Their Own Image," *Art Forum* 29 (November): 132–8.

King, D. (1988) "Multiple Jeopardy, Multiple Consciousness: The Context of a Black Feminist Ideology," *Signs: Journal of Women in Culture and Society* 14 (1) (August): 42–72.

King-Hammond, L. and Sims, L. S. (curators) (1989) *Art As A Verb* (exhibition catalogue, Baltimore, MD: Maryland Institute, College of Art.

Kunene-Pointer, L. (1985) "Continuities of African-American Quilting Traditions in Wisconsin" MA thesis, Department of Afro-American Studies, University of Wisconsin-Madison.

Lemons, S. (1977) "Black Stereotypes as Reflected in Popular Culture, 1880–1920," *American Quarterly* 29: 102–16.

Leon, E. (1987) *Who'd A Thought It: Improvisation in African-American Quiltmaking*, San Francisco: San Francisco Craft & Folk Art Museum.

Lewis, S. (1982) "Beyond Traditional Boundaries: Collecting for Black Art Museums," *Museum News* (3) (January/February).

—— (1984) *Elizabeth Catlett*, Claremont, CA: Handcraft Studios.

—— (ed.) (1990) *International Review of African-American Art (African-American Women Artists: Another Generation)* (2) (October).

—— (1990) *Art: African-American* reprint edn, Los Angeles, CA: Handcraft Studios.

Locke, A. (1925) "Ancestral Legacy," *The New Negro*, New York: Maxwell Macmillan: 254–67.

Lorde, A. (1984) *Sister Outsider, Essays & Speeches*, Freedom, CA: Crossing Press.

McDowall, D. (1980) "New Directions in Black Feminist Criticism," *Black Feminist Literary Forum* 14 (4) (Winter): 153–8.

McElroy, G. C. *et. al.* (1990) *Facing History: The Black Image in American Art 1710–1940*, Washington, DC: Bedford Arts.

Maultsby, P. (1990) "Africanisms in African-American Music," *Africanisms in American Culture*, ed. Joseph E. Holloway, Bloomington, IN: Indiana University Press: 185–210.

Nochlin, L. (1988 [1971]) "Why Have There Been No Great Women Artists?" in *Women, Art, and Power and Other Essays*, New York: Harper & Row: 145–78.

Osborne, H. (1987) *The Oxford Companion to Art*, Oxford: Clarendon Press.

Parker, R. and Pollock, G. (eds) (1990) "Fifteen Years of Feminist Action: From Practical Strategies to Strategic Practices," in *Framing Feminism: Art and the Women's Movement 1970–1985*, London: Pandora Press (Routledge & Kegan Paul): 3–78.

Pepper, S. C. (1970) *The Basis of Criticism in the Arts*, Cambridge, Mass.: Harvard University Press.

Perry, R. (1982) "Black American Folk Art: Origins and Early Manifestations," in *Black Folk Art in America: 1930–1980* (exhibition catalogue), Jackson, Miss.: University Press of Mississippi.

Pindell, H. (1989) "Art World Racism: A Documentation," *New Art Examiner* 16 (7) (March).

Piper, A. (1990a) "The Joy of Marginality," *Art Papers* 14 (4) (July–August): 12–13.

—— (1990b) "The Triple Negation of Colored Women," *Next Generation:*

Southern Black Aesthetics catalogue): Southeastern Center for Contemporary Art.

Pollock, G. (1988) *Vision and Difference: Feminity, Feminism and the Histories of Art*, New York: Routledge.

Pondro, M. (1989) *The Critical Historians of Art*, New Haven, CT: Yale University Press.

Porter, J. (1942) "Four Problems in the History of Negro Art," *Journal of Negro History* 27 (January)

—— (1943) *Modern Negro Art*, New York: Dryden Press.

Powell, R. J. (1989) *The Blues Aesthetic: Black Culture and Modernism* (exhibition catalogue), Washington, DC: Washington Project for the Arts.

Prown, J. D. (1982) "Mind in Matter: An Introduction to Material Culture Theory and Method," *Winterthur Portfolio* 17 (Spring): 1–18.

Raven, A., Langer, C. L. and Frueh, J. (eds) (1988) *Feminist Art Criticism: An Anthology*, Ann Arbor, Mich.: UMI Research Press.

Ringgold, F. (1984) *Faith Ringgold: Twenty Years of Painting, Sculpture and Performance (1963–1983)*, ed. Michele Wallace, New York: Studio Museum in Harlem.

—— (1990) "Interviewing Faith Ringgold/A Contemporary Heroine" (interview by curator Eleanor Flomenhaft), *Faith Ringgold: A 25 Year Survey*, Heightsend, LI: Fine Arts Museum of Long Island.

Robinson, J. T. and Greenhouse, W. (1991) *The Art of Archibald J. Motley, Jr*, Chicago: Chicago Historical Society.

Royland, R. and Klein, R. D. (1990) "Radical Feminism: Critique and Construct," in Sneja Gunew (ed.) *Feminist Knowledge: Critique and Construct*, London: Routledge: 271–300.

Sims, L. (1990) "The Mirror: The Other," *Art Forum* 28 (March): 111–15.

Smith, B. (1982) "Toward a Black Feminist Criticism," in Gloria T. Hull, Patricia Bell-Scott and Barbara Smith (eds) *All the Women are White, All the Blacks are Men, But Some of Us are Brave*, Old Westbury, NY: Feminist Press: 157–75.

—— (ed.) (1983) *Home Girls: A Black Feminist Anthology*, New York: Kitchen Table, Women of Color Press.

Solomon, N. (1992) "The Art Historical Canon: Sins of Omission," in Joan E. Hartman and Ellen Messer-Davidow (eds) *(En)Gendering Knowledge: Feminists in Academe*, Knoxville, Tenn.: University of Tennessee Press.

Steady, F. C. (ed.) (1981) *The Black Woman Cross-Culturally*, Cambridge, Mass.: Schenkman.

Tagg, J. (1992) *Grounds of Dispute: Art History, Cultural Politics and the Discursive Field*, Minneapolis, Minn.: University of Minnesota Press.

Terborg-Penn, R., Harley, S. and Rushing, A. B. (eds) (1989) *Women in Africa and the African Diaspora*, Washington, DC: Howard University Press.

Tesfagiorgis, F. H. W. (1987a) "Afrofemcentrism and its Fruition in the Art of Elizabeth Catlett and Faith Ringgold (A View of Women by Women)," *SAGE: A Scholarly Journal on Black Women* IV (1) (Spring): 25–32.

—— (1987b) "Interview with Sokari Douglas Camp" (taped field interview), August 26, London, UK.

—— (1989) "Interview with Therese Mosoke" (taped field interview), September, Nairobi, Kenya.

—— (1990) "African Artists" and "African-American Artists," *Women's Studies Encyclopedia Project: Literature, Arts and Learning* II (Fall).

—— (1992) *Black Art: Ancestral Legacy, African Arts* (catalogue review) XXV (2) (April).

Thompson, R. (1983) *Flash of the Spirit: African and Afro-American Art and Philosophy*, New York: Random House.

Thorp, M. F. (1959) "The White, Marmorean Flock," *New England Quarterly* 32 (2) (June).

Thorson, A. (1990) "AfriCobra – Then and Now: An Interview with Jeff Donaldson," *New Art Examiner* 17 (March): 26–31.

Vansina, J. (1984) *African Art and History*, New York: Longman.

Vasari, G. (1987) *Lives of the Artists*, trans. G. Bull, Vol. II, New York: Penguin.

Vlach, J. (1990) *The Afro-American Tradition in the Decorative Arts*, Athens, Ga: University of Georgia Press.

—— and Bronner, S. J. (eds) (1986) *Folk Art and Art Worlds*, Ann Arbor, Mich.: UMI Research Press.

Walker, A. (1983) *In Search of Our Mothers' Gardens*, New York: Harcourt Brace Jovanovich.

Wall, C. (ed.) (1989) *Changing Our Own Words: Essays on Criticism, Theory and Writing by Black Women*, New Brunswick, NJ: Rutgers University Press.

Wallace, M. (ed.) (1984) *Faith Ringgold: Twenty Years of Painting, Sculpture and Performance (1963–1983)*, New York: Studio Museum in Harlem.

—— (1990) *Invisibility Blues: From Pop to Theory*, London: Verso.

Wardlaw, A. *et al.* (1989) *Black Art: Ancestral Legacy: The African Impulse in African-American Art*, Dallas, Tex.: Dallas Museum of Art.

Weems, R. J. (1988) *Just A Sister Away: A Womanist Vision of Women's Relationships in the Bible*, San Diego, CA: LuraMedia.

White, D. G. (1985) *Ar'n't I a Woman? Female Slaves in the Plantation South*, New York: W. W. Norton.

White, E. F. (1990) "Africa on My Mind: Gender, Contemporary Discourse and African-American Nationalism," *Journal of Women's History* II (1) (Spring).

Wilson, J. (1988) "Art," in *Black Arts Annual 1987/88*, ed. Donald Bogle New York: Garland.

Wolfe, Janet (1990) *Feminine Sentences: Essays on Women and Culture*, Berkeley, CA: University of California Press.

Wreford, H. (1886) "A Negro Sculptress," *The Athenaeum*, no. 2001 (March 3): 177.

Wright, B. J., Reynolds, G. A. *et al.* (1989) *Against the Odds: African-American Artists and the Harmon Foundation*, Newark, NJ: Newark Museum.

16

ACKNOWLEDGING DIFFERENCES

Can women find unity through diversity?

Nellie Y. McKay

PREFACE

On October 18, 1991, I gave the keynote address at the annual meeting of the North Central Women's Studies Association. I was asked to speak on "Acknowledging Differences: Can Women Find Unity Through Diversity?"[1] That issue is neither trivial nor uncommon in feminist discourse today. After years of seeming not to understand the complaints of Black and Third World feminists, large numbers of white feminists are genuinely concerned about the meanings of sisterhood between themselves and feminists (as well as all women) of color. The invitation to address a regional Women's Studies meeting on the subject was part of an effort by those women and me seriously to explore this problem.

For some weeks before the event I pondered my subject and wrote parts of the usual "academic" response to the dilemma. As a literary critic, I drew on literary texts to illuminate my political views and to reach toward hope for a sisterhood across the barriers of race and class. Personally, I believe that, with the will to do so, women can find unity in spite of their differences. I count my genuine friends from across a wide spectrum of women and men, including white feminists: white middle-class women whom I trust in all the ways one does for all true friends of any group. These are women who understand that, in spite of our mutual affection for each other, for many years I keenly felt the absence of and longed for a Black women's community in my university; and who recognize that when one Black faculty woman, for any reason, leaves my institution, I am bereft. Nor am I the only Black feminist to have such important connections across the formidable barriers that separate groups of women from each other. Still, the larger problem: a sense of trust between the groups continues to elude us. I did not take my assignment lightly, but until it happened, I could not have imagined

267

the impact that the Anita Hill/Clarence Thomas confrontation in Washington DC on the weekend before October 18 would have on the talk I gave that evening.

A casual onlooker, unaware of my early morning habits, would have observed nothing different in my behavior last Wednesday morning (October 16) from other mornings when I go to school. At approximately 6:30 a.m. I left my house and walked to campus through the thin veil of darkness that lingers over earth, even at that hour, at this time of the year. Full daylight did not arrive until I reached my office some twenty-five minutes later. There, resting my brief case on its accustomed chair, I walked across the street to the upscale coffee shop where the student waitpeople knew, without my having to tell them, that I wanted a *caffé latte* and a plain wheat bagel "to go." Friends and colleagues know that my habit of arriving at the office at this early hour is a daily routine that is part of my religion. They know that I work in my office, and mornings are my best work times. Then too, I love the morning, to watch the sky as the sun rises, and to listen to the birds in this otherwise peaceful town before traffic gains momentum. At the end of the walk, I love the hour or so in the office when the only phone call comes from a friend whose regular "good morning" is now part of my ritual too, and before the regular work day falls into place. Those close to me also know that I begin my day writing a letter to a Black woman friend from graduate school, and that she and I have written to each other on an almost daily basis for more than sixteen years. That intimacy in "talking" to (often arguing with) my friend this way grounds me, whatever else is happening in my life.

But outward appearances of sameness in my life were deceiving on Wednesday morning, October 16, 1991. Like most other Americans, I had given every moment I could of the days immediately before, to listening to the Clarence Thomas/Anita Hill Senate proceedings in the nation's capital on the radio in my office. Between the Senate meetings, the local NPR station ran talk shows on which I heard the residents of my state, most of them not Black, express their opinions on the drama. A great deal of what I heard enraged me. From the beginning, public opinion ran substantially in Thomas's favor, and woman victim-bashing carried the days.

In the weeks before Anita Hill became a factor in this case, I had turned from initial depression at the nomination of the candidate for the Supreme Court to "burying the body." As much as I hated the idea, feeling that Clarence Thomas's nomination was an insult to all Black people and an obscenity as the person to replace Justice Marshall (whom no one can replace), I believed that George Bush's racism, and that of powerful white America, insured his confirmation. Good stoic that I am,

I told my friends: "As badly as we feel, we have to go on with our lives."

Then came Anita Hill, and like most people I know, my mood changed from absolute futility to new hope: maybe the taint of such an accusation would derail Clarence Thomas on his way to the High Court after all. I hoped – a hope tempered by enormous fears and apprehensions for what I knew then lay ahead for Anita Hill.

I thought long and carefully about the meaning of Anita Hill before she ever appeared at the Senate hearings on Friday (October 11). On the surface of the case, she had nothing to gain, even if Thomas was denied confirmation, and whether he were or not, she had everything to lose. I concluded that she was either telling the truth or she was the world's prize fool. She had to have known that she was not fighting Clarence Thomas, but rather the power of a corrupt White House leadership. Still, that was only the surface of the case. The underside was much more complicated.

However this situation resolved itself, I knew it was going to be dreadful for Clarence Thomas, for Anita Hill and for the entire Black community. My proud, conservative, now dead father would have been appalled beyond belief that a decent, educated young Black woman agreed to stand up in public and accuse Clarence Thomas of such unspeakable behavior as she made claim he had enacted. Figuratively, my father would have gone into mourning and covered his head with sackcloth and ashes at the very thought. I cannot swear that my father never harassed a woman, but I know for sure he would have probably killed or had to be restrained from killing the man, white or Black, who dared harass his daughters in like manner had he known of it. But my father would have also been ashamed of Anita Hill or his daughters if either dared to speak publicly of sexual harassment by a Black man, even if he knew the accusation were true. He would have believed that the racial damage in such an act far outweighed the gender good. But I am not my father, and many times before his death he had gone into sackcloth and mourning over actions of mine, even ones such as my participation in the March on Washington in 1963 and my 1970 decision to wear my hair in an Afro. In 1989, the year of his death, he told me he had never forgiven me for abandoning straightened hair.

Nor do I mention my father here frivolously. The pain he would have felt over Anita Hill's agreement to publicly accuse Clarence Thomas of sexual harassment is very real in the Black community, and the relationships between Black women and men, especially of middle-class Black women and men, have been honed on that pain. Like some of my friends, I pondered the wisdom of Hill's decision to testify in public, and even before she did, thoughts of the aftermath literally left me with wrenching stomach pains. In my mind, there is no question of the negative effects of this incident on the Black community – the only issue for me is the extent of the damage that it would do. And yet, if she were telling the truth, I knew that Anita Hill was doing the hard, brave, right and only moral thing under the circumstances. Wednesday morning, October 9, when I knew she would be going to Washington, I sent Anita Hill a telegram of support from Black women at my university. I worried for her. She was my sister who dared to break not only her long silence, but the conspiracy of silence Black women in this country have held for a long time to protect them from white racists and keep peace with their Black brothers. Like others who rallied around her, I wanted Hill to feel the arms of unknown sisters around her no matter what happened in Washington. This was little enough of a thing to do for her.

On Friday I listened to almost every word that Anita Hill said in the Senate hearings, subordinating my body functions to the activities on that House floor that day. On Saturday and Sunday I listened to those who supported her and those who supported Clarence Thomas. In my gut, I believed Anita Hill, and I was proud of her even as I decried the spectacle of the revelations, the rebuttals, and the ineptness of the democrats who seemed on her side. The proceedings were dreadful, and my heart sank at every new word added to the record. There were no winners here, only tattered losers strewn across hundreds of new pages of history.

Then came Tuesday and the Senate voted, and as we knew he would be before it happened, Clarence Thomas became the newest member on the Supreme Court. Barring accidents, he will be there for at least the next forty years. Thus, Wednesday morning, October 16, 1991, was different for me from all other mornings that I had walked the scant two miles between my home and my university office. I hurt for myself and those whom I knew were old enough to hurt as I did, but my sadness was even greater for 11-year-old Nicholas, the next generation person in my family, and for all the children of my friends who will be middle-aged or older before Justice Thomas resigns or dies. I have experienced and lived through other national social trauma. This was different. I thought about the three letters I received on the previous day from my daily correspondent — letters full of the motions of our lives: the joys and woes of teaching very bright Black students in an Ivy League university, her exhilaration and anxieties associated with the then still-pending final confirmation hearings on Thomas. I thought about the cancerous racism that made Clarence Thomas the Supreme Court justice who would help to destroy everything that Justice Marshall and his liberal cohorts had fought to achieve for poor and helpless Black and white people, and that never again in my lifetime would there probably be a Black spokesperson in such a high place to plead the cause for the things in which I believed. Many of my friends and I come from the generation that had unwanted babies or coathanger abortions prior to Roe *v.* Wade. Some of us became statistics – hopes for a future out of poverty and the ghetto dashed by too-early, too-often motherhood; others died or almost died. How could I not think about Clarence Thomas's vote on the Court on Roe *v.* Wade? And then, in despair, I thought of what the ugly public struggle between these two brilliant Black people meant for millions of young Black women and men, who even without this fiasco, are in crisis over who they are and what they mean to each other. And finally, I thought about what I was asked to speak about at this conference.

I had thought seriously about this conference and my role in it for a couple of weeks. During that time I had written almost two dozen pages of a talk, pages that found their way into the garbage can almost as soon as they came out of my printer. I simply could not satisfy myself on a convincing approach to the subject. Because of phone interruptions, I stayed in the office until after 10:00 p.m. on Tuesday evening, struggling without success to find a way out of my dilemma. And here I was in tranquil and beautiful Madison, walking briskly on another glorious fall morning, but hardly noticing the beauty of the day and too preoccupied to enjoy it. I was less than two days away from getting on a plane for Columbus, Ohio, with no paper to deliver. Clarence Thomas and Anita Hill; my friends' and my own concerns for the academic and personal welfares of our Black women students in particular; the late-night phone calls on Tuesday from friends in Madison and across the country in the aftermath of the confirmation ("Just tell me one thing," one friend began her conversation when I picked up the phone, "before I cut my wrists." "Don't," I said); and thoughts of my still non-existent paper for the conference all swirled like a giant storm in my mind. It was a different morning for me. But by my walk's end I also knew that each of these things that assailed me in this early hour was connected to the others – that while I was preparing to address an academic audience whose members I assumed find solutions to their academic problems in academic discourse, acknowledging differences and searching for unity amidst diversity, for women and for men, is not an academic undertaking. I could not write an "academic" paper; I needed to reach into my own subjectiveness, not for formulaic answers, but to bring real life, real hurt, real pain, real joys and achievements into the arena of this search. And at this moment, for me, the events leading up to the confirmation of Clarence Thomas as the next jurist on the Supreme Court meet those requirements. I felt that until I could find connections between the Clarence Thomas/Anita Hill confrontation, the daily plight of semi-traumatized Black women in Ivy League universities and Big Ten schools, of young Black women and men in the academy or out in the corporate sector struggling to reconcile themselves to each other, and white academic women asking me, a Black academic woman, if it is possible to find unity in white women's/Black women's diversity, I would have nothing to say. Without the insights that develop on this level, there is nothing to do either, except to throw up my hands and say, as one white male friend of mine insists, "Our civilization is in an irreversible decline."

So, with Black female faith in hope, which I think is better than my white male friend's pessimism – but then, for centuries, Black women have lived on hope, for they had nothing else – I will try to make some connections between this disparate group of my personal concerns, the question you asked me to address, and my literary background. In line with my faith in our possibilities, I observe that my colleague Linda Gordon speaks eloquently for our interconnections, pointing out that as groups and individuals, we are not bounded objects in orbit around each other, but that we create ourselves in relationships with each other. We are the outcome of the intersections of our conflicts and cooperations, and the influences we exert on each other (Gordon, 1991: 106).

Women of color, lesbians, and poor and working-class women always knew they were different from white heterosexual middle-class women, and that their differences made them socially inferior and subordinate to that group. Conversely, white heterosexual middle-class women took advantage of the privilege of their superior position to marginalize and oppress other women. Changes in these power relations began to occur in the early 1970s, as the contemporary women's liberation movement of that decade gained momentum. In their struggle against patriarchal oppression, dominant (white) women discovered their need for the support of other groups of women, but at the same time neglected to recognize how different they were from those women. Consequently, they were severely criticized by the "others" for generalizing women's experiences. "Patriarchal oppression," wrote Johnnetta Cole, an Afro-American woman, "is not limited to women of one race or of one particular ethnic group, women in one class, women of one age group or sexual preference, women who live in one part of the country, women of any one religion, or women with certain physical abilities or disabilities. Yet, while oppression of women knows no such limitations, we cannot, therefore, conclude that the oppression of all women is identical" (Cole, 1986: 1).

Forced to recognize their differences from the others, how best to recognize difference without aggravating the problem between dominant and less privileged groups of women became an important issue for white women in the movement, and a subject for Women's Studies inquiry in the academy. As we know, since that is why I am here, efforts toward reconciliation between dominant white women and Black and other women of color have yet to be achieved. The wounds inflicted by generations of privileged women on less privileged women, and the continued insensitivity of many white women today are embedded in race, and retard progress toward unity. Anxious to avoid further rifts between them, many white women still deny differences based on past experiences between themselves and others, and focus on the commonalities of gender. Johnnetta Cole offers insight into the folly of such an approach. She asks: "Are US women bound by our similarities or divided by our differences?" And responds: "Both." For, she continues, "To address our commonalities without dealing with our differences is to misunderstand and distort that which separates as well as that which binds us as women."

Speaking specifically of the experiences of Black and white women in the USA, for Black women there is a long and painful history embedded in the differences that separate them from white women. This history begins with the first African slave woman who encountered a white woman on this continent. The impact of slavery on the Black slave/white mistress relationship is by no one better portrayed in American literature than William Faulkner, who sets up these relations as dramatic confrontations. One scene between white Rosa Coldfield and Black slave woman Clytemnestra in *Absalom, Absalom!* makes that point. After her meeting with Clytie, for the rest of her life, Rosa is haunted by the memory of the Black woman (daughter of white Thomas Sutpen), who, by the touch of her (Clytie's) hand stops her (Rosa) from ascending the flight of stairs leading to the room where her (Rosa's) niece Judith mourns over the dead body of her husband-to-be and brother, Charles Bon. For Clytie's touch does much more than to prevent the older woman (Rosa) from reaching Judith without hindrance. Describing the incident many years later, Rosa's outrage at the "*black arresting and untimorous hand*" upon her "*white woman's flesh*" remains consuming. In that moment of contact, as critic Minrose Gwin writes, Rosa is shocked into recognition that Clytie and Judith are sisters. Even more importantly, she experiences the "dark terror of cross-racial relationships engendered by slavery. Clytie's touch upon her arm becomes in Rosa's memory an encounter of the flesh which, paradoxically, both intensifies and abrogates the differentiations of color" (Gwin, 1985: 3). The touch is an "electrifying moment of *interconnection* and *rejection*" (emphases added) between the women, an irresolvable tension that nevertheless binds them "finally and irrevocably, to a despairing heritage of human connection dissolved by racial antipathy" (Gwin, 1985: 4). Although Faulkner writes this of women in the South, the "often *violent* connection pitting black female will against white female racism" is a condition that penetrates all of American cultural and literary consciousness (Gwin, 1985: 4). Clytie's touch and Rosa's cry speak to the anguish of racial differences inscribed in the complexities of race, sex, rage and power in Black and white women's relationships.

Black women too have written, directly and obliquely, of their feelings on the slave experience. For contemporaneous examples we can look to the now fairly well-known slave narratives or the writings of nineteenth-century free Black women on their relationships with white women. Lesser known but as sobering a document as any of the period is Lucy Terry's eighteenth-century poem, "Bars Fight," her only extant writing. This short poem (twenty-eight lines long), the earliest known written literature by an African in this country, is a 16-year-old slave woman's eye-witness account of the 1746 Indian raid on the English village of Deerfield, Massachusetts. The first five lines of her poem record the date and the actions of sixty Indians who ambushed and massacred two white village families, the remainder of the verse identifies the victims of the struggle. Incidentally, Terry's work is the "fullest contemporary account of that bloody tragedy" (Shockley, 1989: 13). These were "valiant" men, many of whom were slain, wrote Lucy Terry: "Samuel Allen like a hero fout," but was captured and carried off to Canada. "Eleazer Hawkes was killed outright,/Before he had time to fight," and Oliver Amsden, Simeon Amsden and Adonijah Gillet, in spite of brave resistance, were also killed. One man, John Saddler, escaped. Terry tells their stories by emphasizing the dignity of the fight they put up.

Only one woman is mentioned in the poem, and unlike the men, to whom the author gives two or three lines each, the woman receives six satirical lines:

> Eunice Allen see the Indians comeing,
> And hoped to save herself by running,
> And had not her petticoats stopt her,
> The awful creatures had not cotched her,
> And tommyhawked her on the head,
> And left her on the ground for dead.

For me, the most significant aspect of this poem is not that a slave woman wrote it in 1746 (impressive as that is), but what it tells me about Lucy Terry's attitude toward white women. Terry was brought to America around 1735, aged 5 and purchased by Ebenezer Wells who took her to his home in Deerfield. In 1756 she married a Black man of means from Vermont, Abijah Prince, who bought her freedom. The Princes lived in Deerfield until 1760, where Lucy proved herself an entertaining raconteur. Young people often gathered at her house to hear her speak. In Vermont, the family lived in Guilford, a thriving village of writers and poets, where Abijah owned a hundred acres of land. Lucy, the mother of six children, made history when in 1785 she petitioned the governor's council of Vermont for protection (which she received) against threats from a neighbor, and again when she was not successful in overturning the color ban that denied her sons admission to Williams College. Still, for three hours, she spoke brilliantly before the trustees of the college, using the law and scripture as rhetorical weapons against racial discrimination. Some years later she gained national prominence by arguing her own case before the Supreme Court against a neighbor who encroached on her land. Active throughout her life, she died at age 91.

This much we know of Lucy Terry. What does her poem reveal about her relationships with white women? I believe that Terry's attitude toward Eunice Allen reflected some feelings toward them based on her enslavement. An intelligent woman who was never afraid to fight for her rights in struggles against human injustice, no doubt, she deeply resented servitude. In New England, she must have spent much of her time around women – to whom she was perhaps primarily responsible. While there is no evidence that she suffered great physical or mental abuse (after all, she did learn to read and write), her verse indicates she felt no bonds with the white women around her, no sense of obligation to sympathize with them in their adversity.[2] That Eunice Allen loses her head because of the encumbrance of her petticoats, distinctly female garments that symbolized the womanhood denied to female slaves, many of which Lucy Terry probably labored over during long hours of tedious laundry, must have struck her as an ultimate irony in Black and white women's life conditions. Later in her life, from her position as a free woman, she fought against the racial oppression of herself and her family in the courts where white men held power. Sometimes she won, and sometimes she lost. But as a slave woman in close contact with white women, she had no recourse against the injustice of her condition. Yet, she must not have felt completely like a victim. Expressing her sentiments, here she used the power of her pen to immortalize a singularly biting attack against her oppression by white female status and privilege. Not portrayed as the bitter confrontation that appears in Faulkner's novel, "Bars Fight" is hardly less meaningful in the context of slave and white women's relationships.

But what, you ask me, is the connection between Lucy Terry and Eunice Allen, Clarence Thomas and Anita Hill, Black women and men whose chances for reasonable personal relationships I believe are further endangered by the Hill/Thomas sad drama played out in front of the eyes of and in the hearing of the majority of the people of this nation, to feminist white women scholars asking a feminist Black woman scholar how to effect a better relationship between differences, diversity and unity among women? Today, almost 200 years after she wrote "Bars Fight," the experiences of Lucy Terry remain a ghost that stalks the dark corners of contemporary living. The heritage of Lucy Terry is still with us. Today, many white women, even educated well-meaning ones, are still unaware of and insensitive to some of the most significant issues that retard better relationships with Black women. The Thomas/Hill drama offers a case in point.

When the announcement of Anita Hill's accusation against Clarence Thomas, and her agreement to testify before the Senate reached the newspapers last week, white feminists were among the first to applaud the Norman, Oklahoma university professor. The white feminist community had indeed opposed Thomas's confirmation, and Anita Hill was exactly the kind of standard-bearer who seemed perfect to help their cause. Across the country, and in Washington, white women were vocal in their praise of Hill's bravery and in their commendations of the help her action would give to the cause of sexual harassment. With them, I believed then that her willingness to go public with her allegations would do more for sexual harassment than had been accomplished in twenty years of feminist agitation. As serious as this matter is, no one who has ever been involved in cases of sexual harassment, on a college campus for instance, comes away from it without knowing what an almost impossible battle it still remains. Those who wish to free the workplace or our educational institutions from this blight can use all the help they can get. Anita Hill was a brave, courageous woman who deserves our full support.

But, in my experience, as the confrontation moved toward a climax last weekend, too many white feminists seemed to have overlooked one very important aspect of the case. In a rare triumphant moment of almost universal gender awareness, these women forgot that for Black women, issues of gender are always connected to race, that the two are inseparable. Under no circumstances can Black women forget that. And although Black feminists, even radical Black feminists, have been trying to impress the significance of this truth on white feminists for more than twenty years, some still do not understand. Black women cannot choose between their commitment to feminism and the struggle with their men for racial justice. Many white feminists still do not recognize the structures that differentiate their experiences from those of Black women, structures that make the gender question, by itself, central to white women against patriarchy. This differentiation between Black and white women made Hill's allegations of Thomas's misconduct extremely complicated for Black women. Every Black feminist listening or watching the proceedings through those three dreadful days and nights, believing that Anita Hill was telling the truth, and despising Clarence Thomas for his part in the drama, was fully aware of the complications of the politics of race and gender.

Certainly Thomas's cry of rage that race was a major factor in the hearings was justified. But he was categorically wrong to suggest that the racial politics in the proceedings was a result of Anita Hill's allegations. He was also correct in naming Black male sexuality as the other part of a duo that for more than a hundred years empowered white men, in the name of protecting white women, to practice the most vicious form of violence against Black men. At the same time, I despise Clarence Thomas for using Anita Hill as the means to reach back for the blackness he spent forty-three years avoiding when he felt the nomination slipping from his grasp. In his effort to reach the Supreme Court at all costs, a despicable Thomas wilfully distorted the source of racism in the nomination and hearings, and trivialized the horror of the lynchings of thousands of Black women and men. In short, Clarence Thomas resorted to the worst display of racial politics in exchange for the power he craved. His actions comprised a bitter, almost unspeakable irony: Clarence Thomas on the stand, defending himself against sexual accusations brought against him by a Black woman, whose female forebears had protected their Black men – fathers, brothers, sons, husbands, lovers, friends – as best they could from the ropes he profaned. I suspect too, that the sizeable Black women's support for Thomas and their opposition to Hill, a support largely from women who not only have no formal identification with feminism but deny such connections vehemently even though their lives belie their words, resulted from feelings similar to those my father would have expressed. Yet, too many well-meaning white feminists did not understand or appreciate the complexities of the situation they witnessed on their television screens. These were difficult moments for millions of Black women feminists and intellectuals. And it is not surprising that this event, more than any other I can easily recall, triggers my sense of what has been until now an irreconcilable intellectual and visceral division between the majority of Black and white women.

While Black and white women have had difficult relations because of white women's racism, the complexities they experience at the conjunction of race and sex are considerably greater. The power and control that white men wielded on this site can best be observed in the history of white-on-Black rape and the violence of actual lynchings that Black men suffered on allegations of Black-on-white rape. Perhaps Alice Walker best captured the complications in women's relations over these issues in her story, "Advancing Luna – And Ida B. Wells" (Walker, 1971: 85–104).

"Advancing Luna" is the first-person account of a Black woman who finds it impossible to empathize or even sympathize with her white friend/roommate who claims, in confidence, to have been raped by a Black man. The allegation once spoken, the friends never discuss it again, but the accusation becomes a wall between them that never goes away. Eventually it destroys their friendship. The process of the disintegration of their relationship is the story told by the Black protagonist.

The protagonist reveals that before the revelation of the alleged violation, she had been genuinely fond of the other women. She believes too that her friend was raped. Conversely, even before learning of the allegations, she (the narrator) had felt only contempt for the accused. The presumed rape victim does not publicly report her victimization because the incident occurred in the South, and she knows full well the consequences to the Black community should the white authorities get wind of such a happening. Her silence, born, she believes, of her sensitivity to the racial politics of the situation, and her commitment to the goals of the civil rights movement, make her commendable. Yet, the story is about the death of a friendship between two women: the tragedy of women's cross-racial relationships at the intersection of race and sex. "Why did this happen?" a reader might ask.

The dilemma in Walker's story – the protagonist's ambivalence between race or sex loyalty – reveals the core of the race/sex problem that overshadows Black and white women's relationships. In her case, in writing the story, she eventually breaks the silence that first her friend and then she and her friend together kept over the alleged rape, to the destruction of their relationship. Although the Clarence Thomas/Anita Hill story is neither cross-racial nor one of rape, for Black feminists, the politics of raising voice or remaining silent, and reconciling the seemingly impossible race and gender connundrum relating to the alleged sexual misconduct of the Black male creates analogies between Walker's fiction and the live drama of incidents like last week's female/male encounter. Because Black male sexuality remains entwined with the politics of race and white male power, Black and white women continue to be held hostage by historical fear and the threat of white male violence against Black men.

So far, I have spent my time in observing how differences between Black and white women make it difficult for unifying relations to occur between them. Only a week ago I detected among too many white feminists an insensitivity to what I, as one Black feminist, was feeling over the Clarence Thomas/Anita Hill episode. But I did not think this insensitivity was confined only to my town or only to situations as explosive as this one. Many feminists who appeared on the national scene in support of Anita Hill also seemed oblivious to the issues that troubled some Black women.

But you came to hear me because you expect me to help you to find answers to the still very knotty problems of changing the dynamic of which I speak. To repeat what I said at the beginning of this talk, I have no formulas to make it right. Still, I am here because, in spite of my disappointment on how slowly we have progressed toward our goal, and in spite of the confirmation of Judge Thomas, and in spite of some very dark days ahead, I remain hopeful for us: white and Black women who genuinely wish to resolve the problems of mistrust between us arising from our differences.

"Differences," "diversity" and "unity" together comprise a new trio in our thinking, and in spite of all that I have said, also suggest positive interactive relations between diverse women/people. What can we do to bring this about in a time when the historical ground is littered with the skeletons of a shared history that refuse to be swept into an unmarked grave? At this time, we need to begin to think even more seriously than we have done until now of learning to respect differences and strive to celebrate those things we hold in common without denying the differences. We need to work harder to build bridges of understanding and trust between ourselves, bridges to close the gap now separating white women, particularly the privileged, from women of color (with and without privilege), so that we may set in motion the process of healing, without which our ultimate goals can never be achieved. Although I paint a rather bleak picture of where we are now, for the first time in our shared history we have real possibilities for building those bridges across the chasm of fear, anger, hate and distrust that had for centuries developed between white women and women of color. For we have reached an activist place in history, and the quest for understanding each other that motivates us is an activist political undertaking. That most white feminists no longer universalize the experiences of women and talk about differences with women of color is not an inconsequential move from where we were a decade and a half ago. White and Black women also know that they will not solve issues of understanding each other through lip-service or wish fulfillment, but only in conjunction with actions bespeaking a radical politics of change on the part of women who have traditionally enjoyed and participated in the privileges of race, class and sexual identity, and who, from their positions of privilege, have oppressed women of color. Let me hasten to add that I know that the problem is not one that was necessarily created by women, or one that they alone can be blamed for. I fully realize that many important gains over dehumanizing human behavior toward other human beings will only be achieved when powerful white men understand the meanings of their relationships to all women and people different from themselves. Still, women have major responsibilities in seeking better relationships with women across differences, including those of racial lines, and must work to that end.

My emphasis on the political nature of what women need to do to reflect the acceptance of differences and the desire to create unity among themselves and other women is especially important for my colleagues – academic women – one of the privileged groups in our society. Women in the academy have significant roles to play in helping to bring our stated goals to pass, not only inside of the safe walls of our work space, but outside of them, in the world where other life occurs. For we must stretch our minds beyond the boundaries of our offices and classrooms, beyond the next article we write for an academic journal, and beyond the covers of our next book. In the "business as usual mode" of our lives, our focuses on our articles and books and other professional activities are fine in themselves and crucial both to ensure ourselves paychecks and for our intellectual nourishment. But we have to go beyond them to take responsibility and active roles outside of them. That is, we have to ask ourselves hard questions. For instance: How does what we do seek, or is there a part of what we do, in our classrooms, in the articles we write, in the non-academic activities in which we engage, that actively seeks to break down our resistance to genuine acceptance of differences between ourselves and other women, and promote steps toward a better understanding of each other? What do our students learn from us that helps them to make their lives also count in this effort? Abstract theories and concepts of knowledge serve our professional advancement and peer respect requirements well, but need also to translate into action that advances the cause of improving our understanding of women (and men) outside of our immediate doors. Women in the academy are members of the American community and, as leaders in that community, should act as moral agents for change. We must seek to transform our "differences into more rational, power-conscious, and subversive" steps toward positive social change. The social transformation to which we aspire unites differences and diversity without erasing the specificities of the histories and cultures that give each group of American citizens its own identity. Coming to terms with some differences will always present great difficulties for us, difficulties that may appear almost insurmountable at times. Yet, we must face them honestly. We cannot afford to let them overcome us if we expect to find unity in our diversity. And again, as Linda Gordon advises, we must go further than the difficulties and attempt to locate the ties that, we hope, unite us. For, as Cherrie Moraga notes: "it is [in] looking to the nightmare that the dream is found. There the survivor emerges to insist on a future, a vision . . . born out of what is female" (Moraga, 1991: 27). We need a women's movement with the stated goal of acknowledging differences and finding unity in diversity. Then we will be a movement of survivors, a movement with a future unfettered by the problems that still besiege us. I close with words of wisdom from Bonnie Thornton Dill, another Black woman who has spent her entire career in struggle with these issues inside the women's movement and in the academy:

> When we have reached the point where the differences between us *enrich* our political and social action rather than divide it, we will have gone beyond the personal and will, in fact, be "political enough."
>
> (Dill, 1983: 186)

I pray for that day for all of us.

POSTSCRIPT

June, 1992

Many months have gone by and much has happened since the evening that I gave this talk to a Women's Studies group in Ohio. Clarence Thomas now sits on the Supreme Court, and his performance there already confirms what some of us thought he would be like. A changed Anita Hill is back in her classroom but now also speaks publicly, not of her experiences with the Senate Committee but on sexual harassment and the law. In that capacity, her ordeal led her to join the collective struggle against male oppression of women. A large number of other women and men, across race and political opinions, have also spoken and written about the events surrounding Anita Hill and Clarence Thomas on that fateful October weekend: journalists and academics, in newspapers, magazines and books. Few (if any) Americans have not been profoundly touched by that event, and vital memories linger on.

The hearings were awful and the direct outcome disappointed and saddened many, with Black women feeling the most pained. But they have gone on with their lives, and many are gratified that the event has not retired into oblivion. Perhaps the most immediately positive outcome was the spontaneous mobilization of Black feminists into a new political organization: "African-American Women in Defense of Ourselves." The group advertised its intentions in the *New York Times* and in several Black newspapers across the country in November 1991, with funds that came from 1,603 outraged Black women whose signatures were attached, and from white feminists and Black men of conscience. Although the latter were told that they could not add their names to the statement, they rose to the support of their Black sisters.[3] This is indeed the most hopeful sign we have of an effort to save the lives of Black women and perhaps bridge the gulf of differences and diversity between women and men of all colors and origins. *Never Again* will African-American women in the USA permit one of their group to stand alone as the Anita Hills of this country have stood on the auction block of racism and sexism for generations, and just maybe now the voices of white women and Black men will join the loud chorus of *Never Again! Never Again!*

NOTES

1 A shorter version of the autobiographical section of this chapter appears as "Anita Hill and Clarence Thomas: Personal Reflections on Social Equality and the Rights of Women" (publication date not known) in *SAGE: A Scholarly Journal on Black Women* Vol. VII, no. 2 (Fall 1990).

2 I am reminded of the southern black mammie characters in much of white and Black literature, the women who are always there for white (and Black) people, especially women, with sympathy and help in times of trouble.

Terry's poem makes an excellent foil to a character like Aunt Hagar, the grandmother, in Langston Hughes's novel *Not Without Laughter*. Hughes writes of her, in a scene following a tornado, "He [her grandson] heard a [white] girl screaming . . . up there . . . and he knew that Aunt Hagar was putting cold cloths on her head, or rubbing her hands, or driving folks out of the room . . . [a]ll the neighborhood, white or colored, called [her] when something happened" (Hughes, 1930: 9).

3 I especially acknowledge the efforts of Professor Tom Holt, historian, the University of Chicago, who, immediately after the Hill/Thomas hearings publicly called on 100 Black men to show their support for Black women by donating funds to help to defray at least one half of the cost of the newspaper advertising for "African-American Women in Defense of Ourselves."

BIBLIOGRAPHY

Cole, Johnnetta B. (ed.) (1986) *All American Women: Lines that Divide, Ties that Bind*, New York: Free Press.

Dill, Bonnie Thornton (1983) "'On the Hem of Life': Race, Class, and the Prospects of Sisterhood," in Amy Swerdlow and Hannah Lessinglaw (eds) *Class, Race and Sex*, Boston, Mass.: G. K. Hall.

Gordon, Linda (1991) "On Difference," *Genders*, no. 10 (Spring): 106.

Gwin, Minrose C. (1985) *Black and White Women of the Old South: The Peculiar Sisterhood in American Literature*, Knoxville, TN: University of Tennessee Press.

Hughes, Langston (1930) *Not Without Laughter*, New York: Knopf.

Moraga, Cherrie (1991) "La Guera," in Margaret L. Andersen and Patricia Hill Collins (eds) *Race, Class, and Gender: An Anthology*, Belmont, CA: Wadsworth.

Shockley, Ann Allen (1989) *Afro-American Women Writers 1746–1933: An Anthology and Critical Guide*, New York: New American Library. Originally printed in George Sheldon (1895–6) *History of Deerfield*, Vol. II, Deerfield, Mass.: 899.

Walker, Alice (1971) *You Can't Keep a Good Woman Down*, New York: Harcourt Brace Jovanovich.

AFTER/WORDS

". . . and this is what we've decided to tell you after everything we've shared . . ."

Abena P. A. Busia

SETTING THE SCENE

It is important to understand the context and the scene of the origins of these remarks. They are reflections on words spoken at the end of three days of intensive discussion during which we, a community of Black women, have been meeting in seclusion discussing ourselves, our lives and our work in an academic context as single women, working mothers, scholars, artists and activists. We have claimed this space, a seminar room at the University of Wisconsin at Madison, as our own. We have claimed it as our own spiritually. We have also claimed it as our own aesthetically, thanks in most part to Freida High W. Tesfagiorgis.

The day we arrived we found that Freida had brought in her own art work – that which she had created as well as that which she owned – to decorate the space. Thus the room was draped with African prints and batiks on the walls and table, African sculptures standing about and as a centerpiece, Freida's own art work "Witch Wench" (Figure 3).This work was later to be a central part of her own presentation on creating a critical language for African and African-American women as artists. This art work, by one of us, is a dramatization of our anguish and our triumph; a reminder of our history, and our strength in survival.

Our discussions have been far-ranging, and have so far been private. We have been seated around a large seminar table sharing our lives, sharing our ideas, discussing each other's work without intervention, agreeing with each other, arguing with each other, listening to each other.

Over the days we had none of us left that room, except to eat, and even that always together. We held our discussions there, we had our coffee breaks there, and broke up only in the evenings for dinner and sleep. In this space then, we have had only one "external" obligation, to fulfill the request by the university that we at least share, with anyone

283

Figure 3 "Witch Wench" by Freida High W. Tesfagiorgis, 1989; 38″ × 24″; acrylic/mixed media. Artist's collection.

who chose to come, the purpose and subject of our deliberations, a request which we readily acceded to when initially asked, but which had taken on a quite different dynamic by the time when, at the end of those days, we had to fling open our doors and try to find a way of sharing our experiences with people who were at that point really strangers, even if we knew them. The intensity and the high intellectual engagement that we had committed to each other over the preceding days had created an intimacy we did not want broken.

The room was arranged so that those entering had rows of chairs at the end of our table at which they could all sit. The first thing that happened was that one of the visitors, without asking and without being asked, came and sat at the table. Almost as a woman, with a range of passion ranging from incredulity to outrage, we asked her to leave that space and sit with everyone else. She did not seem to understand. We could not understand why she did not see her behaviour as inappropriately intrusive.

So into this room full of African, Afro-Caribbean and Afro-American women scholars, activists and artists comes an assembly of men and women, Anglo-American, Afro-American and Ethnic-American, graduate students and other professors to listen to what we had to say.

The public event proved remarkable in a number of ways. In the first place it was on campus at three o'clock on the Saturday before final exams; not exactly a propitious moment for a public debate. Much to our surprise the room was packed, with a whole range of people; some curious about what we had been doing, some very worried about what we might have been doing, some truly supportive. We decided Stanlie should give an introduction, explaining why she had had the idea for the meeting, and why she had selected all of us to be there. Then the group chose me to share comments about what we had discussed after our meeting started. They trusted me to say whatever I chose without prior discussion. I spoke from notes. This postlude is not simply a reconstruction from those notes, but a reflection around those notes and the circumstances under which we met then, and subsequently.

BEDROCK CONCERNS

Stanlie explained (as she has in her introduction) that as a group of scholars we felt the need to meet to discuss what it meant to be Black feminists in the academic context. We had gathered as a community to discuss our commonality as Black women, academics, activists and artists. Yet to do this we also had to discuss our differences, across continents and nations, across states, academies and disciplines. We needed to ask ourselves what it meant to be African-American as opposed to African; what it meant to be Africans in the USA as opposed to Africans at home; what it meant to be African-Americans who had been in Africa and for whom Africa was the field of study. What had been our various experiences?

Given our background from different continents and nations, from different classes and social backgrounds, what did we have to share with each other? Is being "Black" and "female," whatever they mean, sufficient? We met here together because we met each other first in other places and feel ourselves to be somehow a community within communities of other people constituting themselves in different ways. We meet, some of us in African Studies or Literature Associations, Social Science Associations, Legal and Medical Associations, and so on. We have different forms of identity. Each of us has different particulars which have led us on different paths. Nonetheless, those various particulars also led us together to this room. What have those different paths been and what has their bearing been on the way in which we identify ourselves in this room? How had we learned to negotiate these paths in the past and in the present, what lessons can we share with each other to find a language to articulate all of these negotiations?

We shared that as women in the academy we recognize the need for strategies to articulate all of these multiple identities. Whether or not we called them "Theory," we are trying to theorize these negotiations of our existence and stake a claim for their existence in the marketplace of ideas in which we work.

What has been the role of the nation-states from which each of us comes? Are we migrants, political exiles, economic exiles? In this context what has been the impact and role of our educational backgrounds? How have we been shaped by the educational policies of those places from which we come? In the case of Africa and the Caribbean this raised the whole question of the influence and impact of colonial education. For example, those of us from Africa are still negotiating between native forms of education, native educational and leadership roles, and the potentially disruptive or subversive factors of western schooling. In the case of the USA, we questioned educational policies within the USA as they have affected Black people. What difference does it make to come from *de jure* segregated southern as opposed to *de facto* segregated northern backgrounds?

How did we get through school? When did we go through school? When did our parents go through school? How did our parents get through school? And what of physical, psychological, or intellectual nurturing? Who were our mentors? Who helped us learn to negotiate all of these factors? How does a practicing Black feminist negotiate the history of her own education; negotiate the histories of its theories and praxis, especially in the face of the reality that at times that praxis has been one of the practice of violence against her – physical, psychological, or intellectual. This needs to be taken into account whether that violence is through words or through visual media. What did our schoolmates think of us, and how did they see us? What were held up to us as the standards of excellence, beauty, achievement? And how did we – do we – deal with the contradictions that of necessity faced us? How do we deal with the contradictions of all these educational statuses?

What has our profession as teachers meant to us? How do we interact amongst each other as professional academics, as teachers, with our students? In what ways do all of these practical issues inform the ways in which we talk about ourselves, our lives, our work? How do we negotiate theory and practice or theories and practices in our daily academic lives?

To give an example that for all women is highly charged and deeply personal as well as a very public issue, how do we negotiate the contradictions of US social and British imperial history as regards the historical oppression of women, especially as they pertain to issues of sexuality and gender relations? These were the questions which motivated our deliberations.

ON SILENCES

This question of gender relations as they cut across race was for us one of the most profound exchanges that we shared. Missing from this final collection is the paper that Nellie McKay had originally shared with the group which has been replaced in print by her reflections on the Clarence Thomas/Anita Hill debate and debacle. It is important to set the time frame of our meetings; our first one preceded the Thomas/Hill hearings by over a year; our second took place right in the middle of the Senate judiciary hearings.

Nellie McKay at that first meeting had given her presentation on "Advancing Luna – And Ida B. Wells," Alice Walker's civil rights short story centered around the confessional narrative of a young Black writer dealing with the progress and disintegration of her friendship with a rich young white woman she had befriended in the civil rights era who, years later, as a gesture of intimate friendship, confessed to having been raped by a Black male "freedom rides" co-worker. She claims not to have "cried rape" at the time because she knew, given the time, place, and sociohistorical context of interracial "rape," what the consequences of such an outcry would be. She unburdens herself to speak years later, thinking that such intimacy would cement the relationship. The intimacy split the friendship.

Several months later the Clarence Thomas/Anita Hill hearings that took place on Capitol Hill seemed to us a befitting coda to the issues raised for us by that story, and we made the collective editorial decision to permit Nellie McKay to send as a substitute the one article for the other. It was not an arbitrary gesture, for this issue of race, sexuality and gender relations haunted us in very intense discussions, at both meetings. When I was giving my remarks to the assembled audience at the first meeting, we carried fresh in our minds the details of a discussion which we knew we did not wish to share.

What it is important to note, however, is that we were asked to. Somebody in the audience asked us specifically, "Did you discuss issues of sexuality?" to which Beverly Guy-Sheftall replied, "*Yes we did*," in a way which made it clear that the conversation would end right there.

Looking back on that moment what strikes me is that the question should be raised at all. That it would occur to a white female graduate student that this was an appropriate question to ask a group of Black women professors in an *open* public forum is in itself telling. Telling also was our silence – our collective silence – on the content of our discussion. Not that we did not want to share the fact that sexuality was an important issue, but that that discussion in itself had been the most painful one that we amongst ourselves had shared. It had been a discussion the details of which, at *that* moment, we did not choose to air or share with *that* public. But what was it we were keeping silent about?

The context of the discussion of the Alice Walker story was agreed upon by all of us. The fact that what we were dealing with was the consequences of what Ida B. Wells had pointed out at the turn of the century; the sense that Black women cannot be raped. This was both a legal reality, as well as, more importantly, a firmly held social reality; Black women were held to lack the necessary prerequisites of moral womanhood that would make the crime of rape against them conceivable in any social sense.

But for us what we also had to deal with was the fictional Black heroine faced with the secret knowledge of rape of her white friend by a Black man; that is to say, the exigencies of having to choose between being a *woman* and being *Black* when the society continues to articulate these as oppositional stances, "all the women are white and all the Blacks are men." What do those of us who are "brave" do? The answers to that were as different for us sitting in that room as our theoretical, personal and intellectual backgrounds.

The discussion amongst us brought home to us the extent to which on this issue we remain divided, even as Black women; issues of ideological race cloud issues of gender for us also. As a result of the discussion on "Advancing Luna", Beverly Guy-Sheftall was courageous enough to share her experience of a relationship parallel but by no means identical to the situation in the story. In her case the man was also Black, a black South African. That is, that iconographic "politically correct" figure of the courageous Black male liberator of the 1980s (who replaces the Afro-American radical man of the 1960s) to whom we all owe our allegiance and support in the struggle against apartheid. Beverly shared her experience of her relationship with this man, which became a relationship that turned to violence, dangerous violence, both physical and psychological, against her.

What was hard for her was discussing how difficult it was first to get anyone to believe her, and second, when it became clear that she was being victimized, dealing with the horror that almost unanimously the assumption was that somehow it was *she*, and not the violent man, who should be held accountable for the deterioration of the relationship. Even her closest friends resented the fact that when she felt her life to be threatened after he had set her car on fire, she had called the police.

To make that matter worse, when retelling the story in the room that had for us become almost a sacred space, she had to relive, even amongst a community of supposedly sympathetic Black women, the terror of that rejection of her version of the story, and thus, of her. It was difficult for us, as a group, to go through the experience of the division that Beverly's story caused. Some of us understood immediately the implications of her situation and why she had spoken. Others took her through the "third degree," and were relentless in their interrogation until one of them stopped in mid-sentence when she finally heard herself asking, "Well how many times and how badly did he beat you?"

By the time she heard herself ask this, a question which evoked for every woman in that room the image of hostile, usually male authority figures challenging *any* woman claiming to be the victim of assault and battery or rape, we were all too emotionally drained to make the excruciating choice between recognizing the betrayal of a sister that even *thinking* that question represented, and the collective growth and transformation that *stopping* asking in mid-sentence illuminated.

ON CLAIMING SPEECH

So we confessed only to our agreement on the context of the discussion of Alice Walker's story. In public we spoke out about how the story opened up for us a discussion on the ways in which the history of oppressive attitudes has its continuing consequences. For example, despite the fact that it has never been in dispute that that young woman was found comatose and abused in a trash bag with excrement on her face, the generally held assumption is that Tawana Brawley cannot be believed and that therefore nothing serious happened to her, and whatever it was that did happen she must have been complicit. The resulting problematic interaction of race, gender and legal theory that such cases bring out has continuing consequences in our daily lives. Around the time of our second meeting in Atlanta Anita Hill was making all these intersections only too painfully clear once more.

In Madison Patricia Williams brought out, for instance, that for race, gender and legal practice such attitudes lead to such "facts" as that Black women do not exist as a theoretical category in legal classification. To give a simple example: anyone attempting to do research on women and race law cannot call up a library search on "Black women." They would have to request "women and the law" and get everything on gender law and then go case by case to see which applied to Black women, or "Blacks and the law," get everything on race law, and go case by case to see which applied to women. Or to give another example: to this day Black women have not won a *class action* suit based on issues of race *and* gender. The way the law reads is that either it is a civil rights issue, and if Black men in the same context are not being discriminated against it is not a civil rights issue and the case gets thrown out, or it is a gender issue and if white women in the same context are not being discriminated against it's not a gender issue and the case gets thrown out. The simultaneity of these two categories is not a "reality" for any but those of us who live it, on a continuous and daily basis.

The discussion on "Advancing Luna" helped us focus on this dynamic of language. One of the issues brought home to us was the different ways in which our various disciplines have faced the challenges of opening up spaces for the recognition of the many, dynamic articulations of Black women's lives. The social scientists among us made it clear that they felt that those of us in the humanities were in this respect at an advantage, had made greater strides toward a clearing of such spaces.

What they singled out most was that gesture undertaken in the story, and by Beverly, of being able to claim the testimonial form, that form which claims our praxis as exemplars of our own theoretical discourses. To claim the personal, the testimonial "I" violates all the rules of dispassionate objectivity under which we had all been trained. The social scientists felt that there had been some improvement – usually by breaking out of the constructed male-centered male pathological orientations of their disciplines that made black women invisible. The medical theorists and practitioners amongst us are engaged in finding out ways of judging and fighting against notions of objectivity which have in fact theorized and structured oppression of Black women built into their "logical objective" frameworks.

Even those of us in the humanities felt that we faced another kind of danger, the imperialism of being subsumed under the voices of those Black male academic impresarios to whom the prestige presses constantly seem to accord authority over the lives and works of Black women. The fashion of male feminism or critical cross-dressing which seems to take precedence over Black women's voices is simply another battle in the long war of attrition around public refusal to acknowledge that Black women and not white women or Black men can in fact be the authorities on our lives.

More importantly therefore, we concerned ourselves with our own abilities to shift those paradigms, to claim our own words, not in terms of a constantly oppositional "other" but in terms of our own sense of authority, continuity and community. The issue for us is not of being always *against* "whiteness" or *against* "maleness" but in claiming out of our blackness and femaleness that continuing strength which had sustained us and which will continue to sustain us. At the same time we are not interested in finding a mega-theory to create *the* story of *the* Black woman, so much as to sustain ourselves and give voice to our many different voices and to articulate our many different practices.

So perhaps finally one of the most painful and yet liberating moments for us as a group came at the end of the public discussion when the most profound question came not from other faculty or graduate students but from the sole representative of the next generation of black women, Stanlie James's daughter Reagan who, in response to Patricia William's comment about the invisibility of Black women in certain discourses, asked, "Who says we don't exist, and how is it people can't see that we are making ourselves visible?"

CODA: ATLANTA

In many respects Atlanta was both a continuation and a radical change. It was a radical change because rather than having to claim our own space, Spelman College was by definition "our" space. We were the guests of Dr Johnnetta Cole, and Beverly Guy-Sheftall and the Women's Studies Center. We were a Black women's collective discussing Black feminist issues at a traditionally Black women's college, with a Black woman president.

Our tradition of celebrating our own creativity which had started at Madison continued here also. As has been said, Freida had decorated the room and shared her art work with us in Madison. In Atlanta the seminar room at Spelman was decorated with art work by Black women, in particular the wonderful poster of the "Sunday School Picnic" by Faith Ringgold. Also in Madison we had attended a reception hosted for us by Chancellor Donna Shalala in her residence. On that occasion we were privileged to hear one of our members, 'Molara Ogundipe-Leslie, read her poetry. Similarly, at Spelman, I was asked to give a poetry reading our first evening, at a reception celebrating the published works of all those of us present. Our continuing objective was to celebrate every aspect of our creativity.

Our objective was also to celebrate our activities in communities outside the classroom. To give an opportunity, as one example, for Evelyn

Barbee to speak of her work with women in the community on health issues; to celebrate the fact that at that second meeting in Atlanta our friend and colleague Patricia Williams was late arriving because she came to us straight from testifying against the seating of Clarence Thomas on behalf of the Center for Constitutional Rights. These aspects of our lives were emphasized in Atlanta by the unexpected presence amongst us of Susan Taylor of *Essence* magazine. Susan Taylor was in Atlanta to hold a fund-raising for "Aid to Imprisoned Mothers," an organization established and run by a Black woman lawyer named Sandra Barnhill, for the purpose of giving counseling and legal assistance to imprisoned mothers and their families. Susan Taylor had been due to leave but stayed to share with us in our conversations, responding to the papers that she heard that morning. Through this connection I was put in touch with Sandra Barnhill who as a result came to New York to speak at a forum I helped organize through the Riverside Church Prison Ministries, of which I am a member, on the specific problem of women in prison. This gesture emphasized one of the aspects we wanted to underscore about the ways in which all our lives, and all aspects of our lives, are interconnected.

In Atlanta we met specifically as an editorial committee of the whole. And throughout the entire process of this book once we had decided that we wanted to publish our works, we did work as a collective. Stanlie James and I undertook the work of negotiating a contract, and organizing the collecting and editing of papers, but we did not work in isolation. We worked together as a team; most of the papers were available in their second drafts at the Atlanta meeting, where we designated someone specifically not in the writer's field to read and comment on each paper, and the papers and responses were shared and collectively discussed. We were deliberately interdisciplinary in our reading process. Even those few of us not physically present in Atlanta had their papers distributed for comment so that there could be communal exchange of ideas and input. We discussed collectively together in the room and later with individuals everything from what the title of the work should be to the way the papers were grouped together. What mattered to us was the way in which the process worked. Those were the things that we celebrated as a group in those days we shared inside rooms behind locked doors. We have unlocked those doors to bring you this, our gift offering.

INDEX

293